MOVIE CENSORSHIP AND AMERIC

MOVIE CENSORSHIP AND AMERICAN CULTURE

Edited by Francis G. Couvares

Smithsonian Institution Press

Washington and London

Grateful acknowledgment is made to Johns Hopkins University Press for permission to reprint, in slightly modified form, the following essays from *American Quarterly* 44, no. 4 (Dec. 1992): Daniel Czitrom, "The Politics of Performance: Theater Licensing and the Origins of Movie Censorship in New York"; Richard Maltby, "'To Prevent the Prevalent Type of Book': Censorship and Adaptation in Hollywood, 1924–1934"; Francis G. Couvares, "Hollywood, Main Street, and the Church: Trying to Censor the Movies before the Production Code"; and Ruth Vasey, "Foreign Parts: Hollywood's Global Distribution and the Representation of ethnicity." Thanks also to John Libbey & Company for permission to reprint a revised version of Charles Musser's essay, "Passions and the Passion Play: Theater, Film, and Religion in America, 1880–1900," from *Film History* 5 (Dec. 1993): 419–56.

Library of Congress Cataloging-in-Publication Data
Movie censorship and American culture / edited by Francis G. Couvares
     p.   cm.
  Includes bibliographical references and index.
  ISBN 1-56098-668-9 (cloth : alk. paper) — ISBN 1-56098-669-7 (paper : alk. paper)
  1. Motion pictures—Censorship—United States. 2. Motion pictures—Moral and ethical aspects. I. Couvares, Francis G., 1948–
PN1995.62.M68   1996
363.3'1—dc20   95-41185

British Library Cataloguing-in-Publication Data is available

Manufactured in the United States of America
03 02 01 00 99   5 4 3 2

∞ The paper used in this publication meets the minimum requirements of the American National Standard for Information Sciences—Permanence of Papers for Printed Library Materials Z39.48-1984.

On the cover: Demonstrators protest *The Year of the Dragon* in 1985. Photo by Kevin Cohen, courtesy *New York Post.*

THIS REPRINT EDITION HAS BEEN PRODUCED USING ON-DEMAND PRINTING TECHNOLOGY, WHICH ENABLES PUBLISHERS TO ISSUE SMALL QUANTITIES OF BOOKS ON AN AS-NEEDED BASIS.

TO GEORGE AND MARGARET

Contents

CONTENTS

Acknowledgments

The idea for this volume originated with Mark Hirsch of the Smithsonian Institution Press. He encouraged me to take on the task of compiling and editing the essays, and he offered enthusiastic and skillful editorial support throughout the process. The germ of the idea, however, had sprouted a few years earlier. In 1990 I delivered a paper at the meeting of the British Association of American Studies, held at the University of Exeter; Richard Maltby and Ruth Vasey also delivered papers there. Later that year I chaired a panel for the American Studies Association meeting in New Orleans in which Richard and Ruth delivered papers and I offered commentary. Gary Kulik, then editor of the *American Quarterly,* asked us to submit our essays for publication and subsequently asked me to coedit the issue on movie censorship that would appear in December 1992. I thank Gary for his encouragement and continuing support over the years.

I wish also to thank Deans Ronald Rosbottom and Lisa Raskin of Amherst College, who supplied crucial grants that allowed me to bring the manuscript to completion. Mara Benjamin proved herself to be a research assistant extraordinaire: smart, energetic, a fine prose stylist, and, not incidentally, possessed of a healthy sense of humor (which we both needed). Rhea Cabin continued to demonstrate in her services to this project why she is the best secretary and departmental assistant in the world. Thanks also are due to Janet Lorenz of the Margaret Herrick Library, Academy of Motion Picture Arts and Sciences, who proved invaluable in locating illustrations; and to Sam Gill, master of the archives at the academy, who has made it possible in a thousand ways for scholars such as those represented in this volume to do their work. Special thanks to Daniel Czitrom for critically evaluating a draft of my introduction, and for much else; and to John Kneebone, Kathryn H. Fuller, and Andrea Friedman.

Finally, I express my gratitude to all the contributors to this volume. Their work has reminded me why, as subjects of study, movies are so fascinating and censorship is so important.

Introduction

FRANCIS G. COUVARES

The image—or what is represented on it—may rouse our shame, hostility, or fury; but it would certainly not cause us to wreak violence upon it; and we certainly would not break it. Or would we? No one can answer the question with complete confidence. For whatever reasons—whether directly related to the image or not . . . —we recognize the potential for such a lapse in ourselves. . . . [A]lthough for the most part we absolutely prefer to isolate such deeds, to put them well beyond the psychological pale, still we recognize the dim stirrings of antipathy or involvement that outleaps control in the iconoclast.

> David Freedberg, *The Power of Images: Studies in the History and Theory of Response*

Each side [in the censorship debate of the 1930s] believed in the power of the movies.

> Ruth A. Inglis, *Freedom of the Movies: A Report on Self-Regulation from the Commission on Freedom of the Press*

In *Highbrow/Lowbrow*, Lawrence Levine records "a wonderful instance of how nineteenth-century American audiences tended to see drama as both reality and representation simultaneously." During a performance of *Othello* in Albany, New York, "a canal boatman screamed at Iago . . . , 'You damned-lying scoundrel, I would like to get a hold of you after the show and wring your infernal neck.'"[1] In thinking about the history of efforts to censor the movies in the twentieth century, it is worth taking note of this "lapse" for several reasons.

The first reason is that the boatman's outburst was not an isolated event but a moment in the long history of *Kulturkampf,* or culture war, within which the struggle to control the movies is but one part. Movies arrived in the United States in 1896 with a great splash and within a decade had become the most popular form of amusement among lower-class (and growing numbers of other) Americans. Not long thereafter, in 1907, the city of Chicago enacted the first movie censorship law in America. From early warnings that silent melodramas and comedies threatened the capitalist order, the purity of the Anglo-Saxon race, or the progress of womanhood, to contemporary claims that *The Last Temptation of Christ* is anti-Christian or that *Basic Instinct* is antihomosexual, would-be censors have always assumed the capacity of movies to arouse passionate feelings in audiences. This is, of course, precisely what they have always been meant to do. From the start, moguls and moralists alike recognized that the moving picture deserved its adjective in a double sense: it seemed to mimic the real world of people and things in motion, and it moved viewers to states of feeling that could be difficult to control and difficult to resist.

Nevertheless, fear of volatile or vulnerable audiences was not born with the cinema. Since the commercialization of leisure in the late eighteenth century, and certainly since the emergence of the dime novel, the penny press, and the popular theater in the nineteenth century, censors have urged the suppression of "cheap amusements" precisely because they arouse strong desires and strong antipathies in an untrustworthy public.[2] In our day, battles continue to rage over the representation of sex, violence, crime, ethnicity, and other controversial subjects in a variety of media. The movies, then, arrived on the scene of an on-going social and cultural drama; they helped to reshape the story, but they neither solely authored the script nor devised the setting. One purpose of the present collection of essays, therefore, is to correct a tendency toward a Hollywood-centered interpretation of movie censorship.

There is another reason to consider Levine's anecdote. It reminds us that, as individuals and as members of groups, spectators draw on a range of real-life experiences in making sense and use of the moving images that have become a regular part of their leisure. Some versions of film theory assert that the very technical practices and narrative conventions of the movies—already established before World War I—obviated most possibilities of active and critical viewership (and, perhaps, of active and critical citizenship) by "constructing" viewers as consumers, more broadly as subjects of advanced capitalism, and, indeed, as men and women.[3] The essays in this volume, however, suggest otherwise. The very intensity and variety of responses to movies suggest that the

2

Dream Machine was not quite a Hegemony Machine. Although undeniably powerful, neither Hollywood nor the other culture industries controlled the contexts within which their products were consumed. They therefore fully controlled neither the meaning nor the effect of that consumption.

Advocates of censorship insisted that movies directly affected behavior, usually for ill. Whatever evidence existed (or exists) for such claims, the Vulnerable Viewer was a necessary construct in the mental universe of the censor.[4] Sometimes imagined as foreign, sometimes as female, and almost always as young, the Vulnerable Viewer needed protection and protectors. Although vicious and distasteful content could readily be found in the cinema—witness the racism of *The Birth of a Nation* (1915) or the sometimes jocular, sometimes grim contempt for women in genres as different as Keystone comedies and *film noir*—the safety promised by the censors was not forthcoming because, as in all protection rackets, there was more in it for the protector than for those allegedly being protected. Newspaper editors looking for circulation, preachers looking for true believers, sociologists and psychologists looking for grants, and congressional witch-hunters looking for subversives, among others, quickly realized that going after the "intimate strangers"[5] on the screen was an almost certain way of generating intense interest or a passionate following. It was to advance a variety of agendas—for example, to score symbolic points against ethnic antagonists, to shore up the authority of religious institutions and leaders, to score political points with constituents worried about crime, to reassure middle-class parents that children passing out of their orbit of control would not be corrupted by alien values, to buttress claims about the capacity of social science to diagnose and cure social ills—that advocates of censorship sought to turn Hollywood dreams into nightmares.

Censorship battles reveal the bonds and cleavages in society by mobilizing people's emotions and sometimes their political energies in defense of values and commitments and in opposition to adversaries perceived to be dangerous and alien. In the language of contemporary cultural criticism, it can be said that censorship battles help mark out the terrain of conflict over discursive practices in a culture. The more one looks at debates over discrete representations of sexuality or ethnicity or other controversial subjects in Hollywood, the more it becomes clear that the aim of both advocates and opponents of censorship is directed at bigger cultural and political game. Whatever their outcome, those contests reveal what is at stake whenever people at a given time in a given social setting negotiate the boundaries of what may be said and heard, or shown and seen.

Censorship battles also reveal that, as Stuart Hall would have it, "hegemonizing is hard work," perhaps even a losing proposition.[6] Economic and

3

cultural elites could not agree on what to do about Hollywood: some promoted the close regulation of movies by custodians of conservative morality; others promoted the free market of ideas and amusements; still others looked to education and "cultural adjustment" to bring movies and morals into closer alignment. Although their responses are harder to trace, ordinary viewers, despite "consumerist" habits, challenged the moral legitimacy of the entertainment industry, sometimes associating their challenge with broader critiques (not all of them "progressive") of American social, economic, and political institutions. Other viewers associated a defense of Hollywood with commitments to civil liberty and personal freedom. Still others, no doubt, found themselves perfectly capable of ignoring the allure of the screen. For many Americans, nevertheless, embracing or contesting the Dream Machine became a way of defining individual or group identity. Despite evidence that Hollywood helped to revise fashion and slang, reshape dating habits, and even reinforce racial stereotypes, there is little evidence that it colonized the "mass mind."[7] Hollywood's influence has always been contingent on broader and deeper forces within a complex society, and, therefore, telling its story requires a history that goes beyond both celebration and demonization.

The urge to celebrate the progress of what seemed a magical and democratic medium arose quite early in the history of the motion picture.[8] So did the urge to record its baleful effects on society and culture, not to mention on the minds and hearts of viewers.[9] Professional historians, on the other hand, paid little attention to movies or to other forms of popular culture until recently. For a long time, the "official" history of movie censorship assumed the shape of an appropriately melodramatic story. As narrated by Will Hays, the Republican politico who became "Czar" of the industry trade association; Raymond Moley, the New Deal braintruster who became a lobbyist and publicist for the Hays Office; and Martin Quigley, the devout Catholic layman and editor of the *Motion Picture Herald,* who cowrote the Production Code in 1930, the onset of rigorous self-regulation in 1934 was a tale of "responsible" businessmen holding off the dogs both of "indecency" in the movies and of "zealotry" on the part of the promoters of censorship. Called to conscience by the Catholic Church and its Legion of Decency, Hollywood heroically assumed the burden of cultural authority, empowering the Hays Office to impose "moral standards" on the studios.[10] What is wrong with this story lies not so much in what it tells as in what it leaves out. It leaves out both the internal history of discursive and institutional practices in the movie industry and the external history of the society and culture within which that industry evolved. It is precisely those stories that historians have begun to tell in the last two decades.

4

With the notable exception of Lewis Jacobs's *The Rise of the American Film* (1939), scholarly inattention to movie history remained undisturbed until the 1970s. Then, a generation of scholars influenced by European historians of popular culture and *mentalité*[11] turned to the movies (and other "mass" media) to explore the character and development of modern American culture. The progenitor of most of this recent historical work is Robert Sklar's *Movie-Made America* (1975), which, along with Garth Jowett's *Film: The Democratic Art,* published for the American Film Institute a year later, put movie history on the map. Relying on careful research and skillful narrative, and employing a broad theoretical framework, both historians went a long way toward achieving what Sklar defined as his major task: "to elucidate the nature of cultural power in the modern United States, and more important, its connections with economic, social and political power."[12]

In two central chapters of his book, in particular, Sklar explained the rise of industry self-censorship in the 1930s in terms more nuanced and broad-ranging than had any other commentator up to that time. In his account, self-censorship was not simply the grudging response of immigrant entrepreneurs to hostile demands for conformity by conservative, old-line Americans. It was part of a much broader cultural warfare—a series of "struggles over power and purpose in American society"[13]—that preceded and transcended the movie business. Though part of a broader struggle, nevertheless, the Hollywood battlefront was particularly vigorous and consequential. On the movie screens, in the movie houses, within the movie studios, and within the regulatory mechanisms of local censorship and industry self-censorship, the *Kulturkampf* came to be waged with dramatic—and sometimes comic—intensity. In that drama, Sklar made it clear, the Hollywood moguls were not cast as heroic defenders of civil liberty, nor were their adversaries cast as cartoon bluenoses: the story was rather one of uneasy, at times bitter, at other times remarkably genial negotiation over the disposition of cultural space. The movie moguls—oligopoly capitalists who presented themselves to the world as immigrant success stories—were intent on grasping both money and respectability. Conversely, most of the clergymen, reformers, and politicians who took aim at Hollywood were intent not on wrecking the Dream Machine but on coming to terms with the most popular medium of communication and persuasion in their world and thereby securing their own cultural authority and political power.

Like Sklar, each of the authors in this volume finds significant connection between the evolution of censorship and self-censorship in Hollywood and a range of other twentieth-century American social processes: first, the consolidation of the culture industries and the spread of consumer markets; second, the expanded range and continuing limits of government regulation of those industries and markets; third, the evolution and political ramifications of interethnic conflict on the local, national, and even international level; and fourth, the transformation of gender relations and the roles of women in American society.

In pursuing these themes, the essays in this volume have further profited from recent developments in cultural studies and social history. Poststructuralist theory—especially "reader response" theory—has freed film scholars to move beyond the study of *auteurs* and beyond either formalist analyses or narrow production histories of individual films.[14] "The new social history" has spawned a series of detailed studies of the several contexts within which movies were made, seen, and fought over and has led film historians to explore long-ignored or newly available archival sources. The very large National Board of Review collection in the New York Public Library has provided a gold mine of information about the evolution of the early movie industry, its audiences, and critics. Even more important has been the opening of the records of the Production Code Administration in the mid 1980s, which gave film historians a chance to investigate the day-to-day operations of the Hollywood regulatory apparatus. The case files of individual films, containing internal memoranda of the Hays Office, communications with studios, and considerable correspondence with individuals and organizations concerned with movie morality, contain copious evidence of those negotiations over the boundaries of acceptable representation that are at the heart of all recent studies of censorship.[15] At the same time, historians began scouring the records of state and local censorship boards and religious and other interest groups, turning up large quantities of evidence of grass-roots censorship efforts. This onrush of new data stimulated and was itself in part a response to the growing sophistication of cultural theory and history.

Marybeth Hamilton, whose essay in this volume recounts the saga of Mae West and the censors, uses a variety of these sources and approaches to reinforce the argument made by Sklar that the Hays Office "cut the movies off from many of the most important moral and social themes of the contemporary world," even as it enabled Hollywood to launch a "golden age" of screwball comedies, westerns, detective thrillers, and musicals. Her Mae West patrols the frontiers of sexuality and race relations until driven to ground by the forces of respectability and their culture police in the Production Code Administration. But Richard Maltby's account of Hollywood's adaptation of literary sources calls into question both Sklar's and Hamilton's formulation here: those "important moral and social themes" were, in his view, never truly "available" to Hollywood. In Maltby's reading, neither the producers, nor the Hays Office regulators, nor the critics, nor, to be sure, the public ever expected Hollywood to depart from its "assigned location in American cultural topography," that of the provider of an easily "consumable commodity." Hollywood delivered predictable doses of modest pleasure to an undifferentiated market while reaffirming the centrality of consumerism to the American psychic and political economy.

As the above indicates, the historians whose work is sampled in this volume do not agree on all matters, large or small. Nevertheless, most agree that the often convoluted debates over whether and how a particular film should be censored offer a sensitive measure of both cultural conflict and cultural "recuperation." As my essay and those of Daniel Czitrom and Charles Musser argue, the threat of "cosmopolitan" culture loomed large in the early reaction to movies and to other urban commercial amusements from the mid-nineteenth to the mid-twentieth century. That threat appeared to elite and not-so-elite Americans to be serious enough to require the elaboration of careful strategies of defense and containment. Each engagement on the skirmish line of this culture war threw off sparks which, though flickering and indirect, cast some light upon the central concerns of a hierarchical, yet diverse and tumultuous industrial society. Moreover, Ruth Vasey's exploration of foreign responses to American movies suggests that the power of motion picture images to entice and unsettle viewers and cultural custodians alike extended well beyond the society in which those images were produced. From the simple ethnic insult, to the violation of traditional sexual codes, to the more elusive but insidious suggestion of the relativity of values and behaviors, American movies seemed to spread an alien, imperial culture (even as they retained much of the allure of the exotic) to people of other cultures.

All of the authors in this collection, whatever their other views, read individual movies as both bearers of the marks of cultural conflict and reshapers of continuing conflicts. Musser tracks the odd logic whereby the movie screen was allowed—as the stage was not—to portray the passion tale for devout Christians. He shows, nonetheless, that the gate of acceptability provided by Christian opinion was narrow indeed, hedged between a quite secular faith in American technological progress and a dread of many of the consequences of that progress for traditional belief. Alison Parker shows how the Woman's Christian Temperance Union, reeling from the failures and eventual repeal of Prohibition, saw in "mothering the movies" an alternative way to tame an immoral society. Neither simple bluenoses, as they were sometimes stereotyped, nor the heroic child-savers they imagined themselves to be, the WCTU

FRANCIS G. COUVARES

crusaders reflected both the subordination of women and their recent political empowerment in early twentieth-century America. Charlene Regester uncovers the long-buried tale of Oscar Micheaux and the censors. She shows that, while white filmmakers encountered sometimes maddening, sometimes ludicrous opposition from censors and interest groups, the black artist-entrepreneur Micheaux faced additional and far more powerful obstacles. His major themes —the horrors of white supremacy and the complicated divisions within the African American community—evoked, on the one hand, the racial fears of whites and, on the other hand, the outrage of fellow-blacks who resented one of their own airing their community's dirty laundry in public. Charles Lyons makes it clear in his survey of recent protests against movies that, especially in regard to the cinematic treatment of sex and ethnicity, the sources of outrage, the tactics of mobilization, and even the language of protest have not changed very much over the century. Protests from the right against "sacrilegious" movies and from the left against cinematic stereotypes of women, gays, and racial minorities recapitulate to a surprising degree the battles of the first half of the century recounted in other essays. He also suggests that, however similar the tactics and strategies of different protestors, in the end the right wields greater power within the American political and cultural arena and has therefore been more successful in turning censorious intent into censorship result.

Taken as a whole, the work of these historians demonstrates the *cultural,* as opposed to the narrowly economic, logic of consolidation of the industries of amusement in the modern United States. Hollywood and its sibling industries consolidated not only in response to economic imperatives but also in response to demands from elites and organized interests for centralized supervision of an increasingly heterogeneous culture. As Parker, Lyons, Garth Jowett, and I show in different ways, and as Vasey makes even clearer on an international scale, a continuing tension existed between the economic imperatives of the industry and the insistence by a variety of groups "out there" in the world that movies affirm their cultural values, or at least not assault them. That tension led Hollywood to search for an elusive consensus that would allow it to wear the mantle of cultural affirmation without being strangled by it. At every turn the only really passionate loyalty of the moguls was to making money, their only real enemy "controversy" in any guise. The essays in this volume reveal the active complicity in censorship of elements of the industry intent on avoiding controversy—from the exhibitors who helped form the National Board of Censorship in New York in 1909, to the studio bosses and Wall Street financiers who authorized the Catholic solution in 1934 and the anticommunist solution in 1947.[16] Finally, as Jowett suggests, Hollywood only swung into ac-

8

tion against censorship after the federal courts had ordered it to break up its oligopoly structure, thereby requiring the film industry to find ways to secure audiences other than by manufacturing and distributing "consensus."

In tracing the decline of Hollywood's golden age under the multiple assaults of antitrust action and anticommunist investigations (not to mention the economic competition of television), both Jowett and Stephen Vaughn make clear the limits of Hollywood's power. A thicket of contending forces threatened the security of the Hollywood oligopoly—and its self-censorship apparatus—well before the Supreme Court struck the first blow against state censorship in 1952 and thereby pulled the rug out from under the Production Code. Moreover, as Vaughn's essay suggests, even though overtly political themes had always played a fairly small part in Hollywood movies and movie censorship, the political implications of a medium regularly said to shape the myths and dreams and feelings of millions were never very far from the surface. When the national mobilization accompanying World War II and the anticommunist passions of the cold war forced Hollywood to promote patriotism and open itself to the search for subversives, those latent fears of the Dream Machine emerged with a vengeance. The melodrama played out under the lights of the congressional hearings was only a more lurid version of the censorship wars that had marked the psychic landscape of Hollywood for years.

Ranging broadly over the century and using a variety of sources and methods, the essays in this collection, individually and taken together, tell a tale with more than one trajectory and with no simple moral. The struggles they recount over the representation of sex, crime, religion, race and ethnicity, and other "controversial" matters on the movie screen were fought among fluid and diverse coalitions that employed a variety of political devices to gain advantage. Much was at stake—enormous sums of money, social status and prestige, cultural authority, institutional power, and, yes, even principles of artistic integrity and free expression. In regard to the last, in particular, it is worth drawing explicit connection between the Hollywood censorship wars of an earlier day and the culture wars of our own. To do so will require a brief exploration of the term *censorship* and its uses in debates over freedom of expression.

In this introduction and in the essays below, the word *censorship* is employed in a variety of ways. No consistent definition has been offered for the simple reason that, in both past and present, *censorship* has been used to refer to related but quite different practices: governmental prior restraint on expression; criminal prosecution and punishment for obscenity; administrative regulation of expressive content by either independent parties or producers themselves; the intentions, activities, and effects of individuals and groups who exert pressure on producers to alter their products or on distributors to cease marketing them; conscious and unconscious editorial evasions and silences practiced by writers, directors, and other personnel involved in the production of cultural commodities. However, it is worth briefly outlining the two most important ways of defining and using the term *censorship* and exploring what is at stake in each. In the process it should become apparent that matters beyond the archive, the library, and the scholar's study gave impetus to this work, as surely as did those developments in social history and cultural theory discussed above.

First, the classical liberal definition of censorship has the virtue of clarity but the vice of narrowness. In its listing for the word "censor," immediately after referring to the ancient Roman usage, the *Oxford English Dictionary* captures this first meaning well: "An official in some countries whose duty it is to inspect all books, journals, dramatic pieces, etc., before publication, to secure that they shall contain nothing immoral, heretical, or offensive to the government." As used, for example, in debates over the constitutionality of laws restricting free expression, censorship means prior restraint on such expression mandated by law and imposed by police, judicial, or administrative power. All other restraints on free expression—from after-the-fact obscenity and libel prosecutions, to self-regulation by trade associations or informal oversight groups, to boycotts or protests that exert pressure on producers, to conformity (conscious or unconscious) to conventions of taste or "quality"—fall outside the terrain of censorship. Even though some of these latter restraints may exercise an undesirable degree of control over expression, the classic liberal argument insists that, without the legitimacy and force given them by state sanction, such pressures are more or less self-correcting or, at least, partly balanced by countervailing voices. Prior censorship, on the other hand, removes voices from the debate and gives dominant interests a sovereignty over legitimate expression that cumulatively narrows the possibilities of thought and action in the future, thereby subverting the possibilities of both self-government and personal freedom.[17]

There is still much to be said for the classic liberal formulation, despite both radical and conservative critiques of it in recent years. But, especially in their postmodernist guise, recent critics have mounted a massive assault on the entire Enlightenment project that undergirded the liberal formulation. In the process, censorship has come to be reconceived not as one or more discrete acts of repressive control over free expression, but as a "normal" and "constitutive" part, indeed, a very condition, of free expression.[18] As the *OED* reveals in a second definition of the word "censor"—"One who judges or criticizes. . . . One who censures or blames; an adverse critic; one given to fault-finding"—the line between censorship and criticism is not so easy to draw. Regulating the boundaries and terms of expression is, in the postmodernist view, what every community must do in order that speech (or any other assertion of meaning) be both comprehensible and compatible with that community's fundamental interests. The question, then, becomes not *whether* but *which* censorship: that of the court or the church? that of the bourgeoisie or the proletariat? that of the left or of the right? that of the oligopolized marketplace or of democratic movements for racial and sexual equality? Rather than defining freedom negatively as individual liberty from external control, postmodernists see freedom as the power to affirm one definition of reality—and the interests it thereby legitimizes—as against another.

Thus, according to Stanley Fish, in contemporary democratic societies, expression that undermines the very possibility of democratic community, for example, "hate speech" or "hard-core" pornography, cannot be permitted. The claim that "free-speech principles" protect racist and sexist speech is merely "a bad argument . . . [masking] motives that would not withstand close scrutiny."[19] Those motives, it seems, include an unspoken desire to retain patriarchal or white-supremacist advantages, or, at least, an unwillingness to inconvenience oneself in order to safeguard women and nonwhites from the injuries inflicted by hostile expressive acts. I am inclined to reject not only the essentially ad hominem nature of this last argument, but also Fish's conflation of critical, moral, and political arguments for the redefinition of censorship. For cultural historians, conceiving censorship as one tactic in a spectrum of arguments and campaigns for the regulation of representation contributes to a more nuanced history of the interaction of group conflict, corporate and state power, and cultural authority in the modern world. When it comes to contemporary legal and governmental restraint on or punishment of expression, however, neither Fish, nor Catharine MacKinnon, nor other advocates of suppression make a strong case for abandoning the protection that expressive conduct has enjoyed in liberal societies, especially in the United States. Neither takes very seriously the idea of "moral independence" as a value; and neither pays attention to the vital interconnections between the struggles of civil libertarians and those of labor organizers, women's liberationists, and civil rights activists over the course of American history.[20]

Neither this introduction nor the essays that follow can resolve these questions or track all of their implications. But they do offer some historical perspective on them. They show what has changed and what has remained the same in the perennial debates over free speech and censorship. Representations of sex, ethnicity, and violent crime have been, from the start of the movie era up to the present, the principal targets of outrage. In the past as in the present, coalitions promoting and opposing censorship have been surprisingly diverse, yoking together arguments and political forces that seem both "progressive" and "reactionary." The contradictions contained in these coalitions reflect the contradictory nature of "mass culture." Given the reach of the corporation and the marketplace in the twentieth century, the urge to protect persons from the harms that may be inflicted on them by commercial interests is a leading impulse of "progressive" politics, including that of feminists and advocates of racial and ethnic equality. On the other hand, the protection of potential victims, especially women and children—and perhaps the nation itself—has been the objective of patriarchal, nativist, anticommunist, and other repressive movements. Likewise, given the enormous growth of state power in the last century, a variety of movements and interests—labor organizers, suffragists and birth control promoters, artists and writers, as well as movie moguls, tobacco advertisers, and pornographers—have employed civil libertarian arguments to ward off government violation of their rights or protest government failure to protect their rights. Within this expanded context, calls for and against censorship come to be seen as parts of a complex and continuing social drama in which the parties in conflict engage, albeit in different ways, fundamental questions about how to live in a modern, industrial capitalist, democratic, and plural society.

As two decades of work on the history of popular culture has amply demonstrated, the spread of new forms of leisure and amusement, as well as the "social purity movements"[21] and other campaigns aimed at controlling them, are not peripheral or second-order events that play upon the surface of more fundamental economic or political developments. Determining what is legitimate to say and hear and see—whether in church, at the fair, in the press, on the street corner, in the union hall, or in the movie theater—is a central activity of all societies and social groups. And tracking such battles over legitimacy has become a central activity of historians. Indeed, such battles increasingly present openings through which the historian may travel into the recesses of social life, marking along the way the cultural and political practices that are nowhere else so accessible to observation. The tendency of human beings to respond vigorously to representations of their lives and of their world, however refracted by art, offers an opportunity to historical and cultural studies that is now being exploited by the scholars who have contributed to this volume, and by many others.

Finally, the contributors to this volume invite readers to approach these essays as citizens as well as scholars. As Americans today debate the value and the potential harm of angry rap lyrics, titillating rock videos, stark photographic treatments of nudity and sexuality, violent television shows, politically charged comic books and performance art, and on-line electronic "smut," it may be useful to recall the history of movie censorship chronicled in these pages. The first great medium of mass culture set the pattern for much that has followed in the culture wars of the twentieth century. Possessing the power to engage intensely the emotions of viewers from all classes and segments of society, the moving picture earned the attention of millions of viewers and legions of critics and scholars. Whether it is the democratic art or the manipulator of the masses; whether it records our dreams and nightmares or fashions them; whether our responsiveness to it indicates our vulnerability to influence or our power of imaginative engagement; whether the politics of censorship is about the protection of the vulnerable or the suppression of the imaginative—these remain questions that continue to shape our world and that the history narrated in these essays may help us address, if not answer.

NOTES

1. Lawrence W. Levine, *Highbrow/Lowbrow: The Emergence of Cultural Hierarchy in America* (Cambridge, Mass., 1988), 30.

2. See Neil McKendrick, John Brewer, and J. H. Plumb, *The Birth of a Consumer Society: The Commercialization of Eighteenth-Century England* (Bloomington, Ind., 1982); Michael Denning, *Mechanic Accents: Dime Novels and Working-Class Culture in America* (New York, 1987); and Kathy Peiss, *Cheap Amusements: Working Women and Leisure in Turn-of-the-Century New York* (Philadelphia, 1986).

3. See, for example, Laura Mulvey, "Visual Pleasure and Narrative Cinema," *Screen* 16 (autumn 1975): 6–18. Alternatives to such an approach can be found in Tania Modleski, ed., *Studies in Entertainment: Critical Approaches to Mass Culture* (Bloomington, Ind., 1986), especially in essays by Modleski, Dana Polan, and Andreas Huyssen. See also Miriam Hansen, *Babel and Babylon: Spectatorship in American Silent Film* (Cambridge, Mass., 1991); Lea Jacobs, *The Wages of Sin: Censorship and the Fallen Woman Film, 1928–1942* (Madison, Wis., 1991); Gaylyn Studlar, "Discourses of Gender and Ethnicity: The Construction and De(con)struction of Rudolph Valentino as Other," *Film Criticism* 13 (1989), and "The Perils of Pleasure? Fan Magazine Discourse as Women's Commodified Culture in the 1920s," *Wide Angle* 13 (1991); and Mary Beth Haralovich, "The Proletarian Woman's Film of the 1930s: Contending with Censorship and Entertainment," *Screen* 31 (1990): 172–87.

4. See, in Walter Kendrick, *The Secret Museum: Pornography in Modern Culture* (New York, 1987), a discussion of the "Young Person" as a figure in the rhetorical land-

scape of antipornography crusaders. My Vulnerable Viewer is direct kin to the Young Reader.

5. This evocative term is the title of Richard Schickel's *Intimate Strangers: The Culture of Celebrity* (New York, 1985).

6. See Stuart Hall, "Notes on Deconstructing 'The Popular,'" in Raphael Samuel, ed., *People's History and Socialist Theory* (London, 1973), 227–40, and "Cultural Studies: Two Paradigms," in Richard Collins, James Curran, Nicholas Garman, Paddy Scannell, Philip Schlesinger, and Colin Sparks, *Media, Culture and Society: A Critical Reader* (London, 1986), 33–48. See also what might be called the "common sense" reading of hegemony theory by social historians of popular culture: John Clarke, "Pessimism versus Populism: The Problematic Politics of Popular Culture," in Richard Butsch, ed., *For Fun and Profit: The Transformation of Leisure into Consumption* (Philadelphia, 1990), 28–46; and Ronald Edsforth, "Popular Culture and Politics in Modern America: An Introduction," in Ronald Edsforth and Larry Bennett, eds., *Popular Culture and Political Change in Modern America* (Albany, 1991), 11–15. For the most open-ended of the many interpreters of hegemony theory and the "cultural studies" approach, see John Fiske, *Reading the Popular* (Boston, 1989).

7. On social science debates over the "mass mind," see Daniel J. Czitrom, *Media and the American Mind: From Morse to McLuhan* (Chapel Hill, 1982).

8. Terry Ramsaye, *A Million and One Nights: A History of the Motion Picture* (New York, 1926).

9. See Lamar T. Beman, *Selected Articles on Censorship of the Theater and Moving Pictures,* the Handbook Series, series 3, vol. 6 (New York, 1931).

10. See Raymond Moley, *The Hays Office* (Indianapolis, 1929); Martin Quigley, *Decency in Motion Pictures* (New York, 1937); and Will H. Hays, *See and Hear* (1929). See also Louis Nizer, *New Courts of Industry: Self-Regulation under the Motion Picture Code* (New York, 1935).

11. See Natalie Zemon Davis, *Society and Culture in Early Modern France* (Stanford, 1975); Peter Burke, *Popular Culture in Early Modern Europe* (New York, 1978); and Robert Darnton, *The Kiss of Lamourette: Reflections in Cultural History* (New York, 1990), especially 253–92.

12. Robert Sklar, *Movie-Made America: A Cultural History of American Movies* (New York, 1975), vi; Lewis Jacobs, *The Rise of American Film: A Critical History* (New York, 1939); and Garth Jowett, *Film: The Democratic Art* (Boston, 1976). Also contributing to the scholarly legitimacy of movie history is Lary May, *Screening out the Past: The Birth of Mass Culture and the Motion Picture Industry* (New York, 1980), which notably interweaves the history of movies with that of the decline of Victorian culture and the rise of the "Consumer Ideal."

13. Sklar, *Movie-Made America,* 161.

14. See Robert Sklar, "Oh! Althusser!: Historiography and the Rise of Cinema Studies," *Radical History Review* 41 (1988): 10–35, reprinted in Sklar and Charles Musser, eds., *Resisting Images: Essays on Cinema and History* (Philadelphia, 1990), 12–35. See also John E. O'Connor, ed., *Image as Artifact: The Historical Analysis of Film and Television* (Malabar, Fla., 1990), especially the essays by Robert Sklar and Janet Staiger.

15. The first book-length study of censorship to make full use of the Production

Code Administration files, along with archival records of the Catholic Church and other organizations, is Gregory D. Black, *Hollywood Censored: Morality Codes, Catholics, and the Movies* (New York, 1994).

16. See Stephen Vaughn, "Financiers, Movie Producers, and the Church: Economic Origins of the Production Code," in Bruce A. Austin, ed., *Current Research in Film: Audiences, Economics, and Law*, vol. 4 (Norwood, N.J., 1988): 201–17.

17. See Harry Kalven, Jr., *A Worthy Tradition: Freedom of Speech in America* (New York, 1988).

18. See Sue Curry Jansen, *Censorship: The Knot that Binds Power and Knowledge* (New York, 1988).

19. Stanley Fish, "There's No Such Thing as Free Speech and It's a Good Thing, Too," in Paul Berman, ed., *Debating P.C.: The Controversy over Political Correctness on College Campuses* (New York, 1992), 244.

20. Andrea Dworkin and Catharine A. MacKinnon, *Pornography and Civil Rights: A New Day for Women's Equality* (1988); Catharine A. Mackinnon, *Feminism Unmodified: Discourses on Life and Law* (Cambridge, Mass., 1987), 163–97. On the limits of this view, see Varda Burstyn, ed., *Women against Censorship* (Vancouver, 1985); Ronald Dworkin, *A Matter of Principle* (Cambridge, Mass., 1985), 335–72; Dworkin, "Liberty and Pornography," *New York Review of Books,* August 15, 1991, 12–16; and Dworkin, "The Coming Battle over Free Speech," ibid., June 11, 1992, 55–64. On the connection between civil liberties and rights struggles, see Samuel Walker, *In Defense of American Liberties: A History of the ACLU* (New York 1990); and Thomas Haskell, "The Curious Persistence of Rights Talk in the 'Age of Interpretation,'" *Journal of American History* 74 (December 1987): 984–1012, along with other essays in this "Special Issue on the Constitution and American Life." Austin Sarat and Thomas R. Kearns, eds., *The Fate of the Law* (Ann Arbor, 1991), offers a series of thoughtful essays from a variety of postmodernist perspectives on these and related issues. See also Mari J. Matsuda, Charles R. Lawrence III, Richard Delgado, and Kimberle Williams Crenshaw, eds., *Words that Wound: Critical Race Theory, Assaultive Speech and the First Amendment* (Boulder, Colo., 1993), and a sharp riposte from Henry Louis Gates, Jr., "Let Them Talk," *New Republic,* September 20 and 27, 1993, 37–49. See my effort to give historical grounds for skepticism about newfangled forms of speech suppression: "The Good Censor: Race, Sex, and Censorship in the Early Cinema," *Yale Journal of Criticism* 7 (fall 1994): 233–51.

21. See Margaret Hunt, "The De-eroticization of Women's Liberation: Social Purity Movements and the Revolutionary Feminism of Sheila Jeffries," *Feminist Review* 34 (spring 1990): 23–46. Another interesting, if very different, meditation on the meanings and uses of censorship in modern European history is Natalie Zemon Davis, "Rabelais among the Censors (1940s, 1540s)," *Representations* 32 (fall 1990): 1–32.

The Politics of Performance

Theater Licensing and the Origins of Movie Censorship in New York

DANIEL CZITROM

The movies were born in the city. While historians of early film have begun to pay more attention to special issues such as technology, patent wars, industrial practice, and the movies' aesthetic debt to earlier forms of cultural expression, there has been little analysis of the specifically urban world that made motion pictures the most popular form of commercial entertainment by World War I. The political, legal, and economic wrangles surrounding the nascent movie business in New York City established the template for the ownership and control of the mature industry, as well as the basic pattern for film censorship. In the first center of movie production and exhibition during the early part of the century, the especially knotty issues involving the licensing and censoring of movies—who could show them and what they could show—were fiercely contested. These battles over the regulation of representation need to be understood against the historical backdrop of urban cultural politics.

Movies reinforced and reconfigured a set of controversies that, since the mid-nineteenth century, had been fought out largely over the licensing and regulation of theatrical space. These issues included the alleged dangers commercial entertainments posed to children, disputes over Sunday blue laws, the licensing authority of the police department, and the connections between plebeian culture and the underworld. The process that determined which entertainments were licensed and which were licentious had always been fundamentally political and volatile. The continual controversies over commercial enterprises loosely described as "theatrical" involved complicated relations among entrepreneurs, the licensing authority of the state, the police power, and neighborhood audiences.

By 1908 the movie business faced a crisis of exhibition: the older traditions of theater licensing proved inadequate for regulating the emergent new medium. Progressive reformers, movie exhibitors, and movie producers sought to split movies off from such live urban entertainments as vaudeville, burlesque, and concert saloons. Progressive social service agencies and activists embraced movies as an alternative to older entertainment traditions closely allied with machine politics and the urban vice economy. Movie entrepreneurs cultivated the new alliance with reformers as a way to shed the stigma of the street, attract a middle-class patronage, and increase their profits. For their part, reformers saw that alliance as a way to achieve what John Collier, the general secretary of the National Board of Censorship, called "the redemption of leisure." New York's movie wars—fought over theaters and screens, in the courts and the streets—illuminate a crucial transformation: the supplanting of locally based, municipally licensed cheap theater by the nationally organized, industrial oligopoly that came to dominate our popular culture.

The whole question of what, precisely, constituted a "theatrical performance" had remained ambiguous ever since the New York state legislature passed the first comprehensive licensing act in 1839. That act, a response to intense lobbying by the Society for the Reformation of Juvenile Delinquents (SRJD), had rested on the strongly held belief in a direct, causal relationship between the theater and delinquent or criminal behavior. It required any "theater, circus, or building, garden or grounds, for exhibiting theatrical or equestrian performances" in New York City to obtain a license from the mayor, with all collected fees to be forwarded to the SRJD. The law also set a penalty of $500 for every violation, and it authorized the society, as an agent of the state, to sue and collect on those penalties. During the Civil War the city experienced a boom in "concert saloons," and the explosive issue of separating prostitution and alcohol from entertainment spaces led the legislature in 1862 to pass a new act to "Regulate Places of Public Amusement." Its key features banned alcoholic beverages on the premises of performance and made illegal the employment of females to wait on spectators.[1]

Over the next four decades, two kinds of regulation coexisted in the highly profitable yet unstable world of New York popular amusements. One was an internal supervision within the entertainment business itself, led by the trade press and certain entrepreneurs who sought to expand their audience by distancing their attractions from associations with alcohol and prostitution. The most influential figure in this process was Tony Pastor, often called the father of American vaudeville. While Pastor gained his first notoriety during the concert-saloon boom of the early 1860s, he soon moved to create a "high class variety" by freeing the entertainment from its earlier associations. By 1881 he had become the leading variety-theater manager in the city and moved into his Fourteenth Street Theater, on the ground floor of the new Tammany Hall. Pastor embodied the urge toward respectability and wider commercial success, and his theater is rightly viewed as the prototype for the mainstream vaudeville that dominated the American popular stage from the 1880s until the rise of radio. He regulated his theater with an eye toward increasing profit, making special efforts to attract a female clientele.[2]

Yet there were hundreds of other entertainment entrepreneurs who did not follow this path, retaining their ties to the concert-saloon traditions and struggling to survive within the competitive world of New York amusements. An uneasy alliance of the police department, the mayor's office, private moral reform societies, and neighborhood groups kept up a continuous cultural surveillance of entertainment spaces that included dime museums, concert saloons, and vaudeville and burlesque houses. Obtaining and keeping a license from the mayor's office proved a key not only to staying in business, but also for moving into a more profitable realm in the continuum of amusement respectability. To thrive, an entrepreneur had to negotiate a treacherous terrain held by autocratic police captains, ever-vigilant moral reformers, outraged clerics, and organized neighborhood citizens. No one, finally, could say with any certainty what constituted a theater, or what the difference was between a theater and a concert hall. Indeed, many entrepreneurs sought both theater and concert licenses since the city charter authorized the police department to permit the sale of liquor in concert halls.

An 1875 "List of Theatres, Halls, Concert Rooms" counted fifty-seven licensed places for that year, a figure which remained basically constant for the next two decades. These were about evenly divided between places presenting straight drama, opera, music concerts, and circuses and the newer concert saloons and variety theaters. They were clustered mainly in three entertainment districts: the Bowery and Lower East Side; 14th Street and Union Square; and "the Tenderloin," roughly from 23rd to 42nd Streets, between Sixth and Eighth Avenues. By this time several newer private groups, such as the Society for the Suppression of Vice, the Society for the Prevention of Cruelty to Children, and the Society for the Prevention of Crime, had joined the SRJD in making active interventions in the licensing process.[3]

Consider, for example, the Belvidere Variety Theatre at 23 Bowery, licensed by the city since at least 1875. Its owner, John Schroeder, probably opened it first as a saloon room, adding a small stage with rough scenery facing tables and chairs. Upon orders of the local police captain in early 1879, Schroeder erected a seven-foot-high wooden partition to separate the barroom from the stage area, thus technically complying with the law requiring separation of theatrical performance from the serving of alcohol. In April 1879 two agents for the recently formed Society for the Suppression of Vice (SSV), founded by Anthony Comstock, visited the Belvidere and filed depositions with the mayor's office, protesting a renewal of license. One described the scene as follows:

At the tables were seated about twelve girls and women with a number of men, engaged in drinking and conversation. . . . On entering the saloon deponent seated himself near the door and was soon approached by one of the women and asked what [he] would have to drink and if she could drink with him. Seating herself at the table the drinks, lager beer and lemonade, were brought by a waiter. While drinking the woman asked deponent to go with her to one of the rooms on the side of the stage. Deponent consented and going to the room was again asked to treat which he did. In the course of the conversation which followed the woman urged deponent to take her into one of the rooms up stairs, which was more private and had better accommodations, and where they could have a bottle of wine together and would only cost three dollars. Upon deponent's remarking that it cost pretty high and whether anything else was given for the money, the woman replied that they would have a good time, that she would give him a nice diddle, pulled up her dress, showed her leg above the knee, made use of every persuasion and said she would get one dollar of the money and the other two dollars would go to the proprietor—the whole of which offers the deponent declined.[4]

In response, Schroeder vigorously denied the "false, malicious, and untrue" statements in the SSV depositions, claiming that "such practices are not permitted on the premises." He defended the arrangements in his place, stressing the makeshift wall separating barroom from theater as "similar to the front partitions used at Miner's Theatre, Volks Garden, and theatres of like character on the Bowery." He admitted that "the greater portion of the upper part of the building is let out weekly to male lodgers and the balance thereof to transient lodgers of the same sex." Schroeder also submitted a supporting petition from eight neighboring businessmen. These clothing merchants, hatters, and picture framers all affirmed that the Belvidere was not disorderly, "nor is it the source of disturbance or annoyance to us during the day or night or in our Judgement the cause of annoyance or grievance to the travelling public."

Like so many other places on the Bowery, in Union Square, and in the Tenderloin, the Belvidere continued to operate for years, a protean urban space defined and redefined by various elements of the metropolis. It qualified as a legitimate entertainment enterprise as long as John Schroeder coughed up regular tribute to the local police captain. He maintained the Belvidere as a legal and moderately successful business, catering to local working people and tourists, and providing employment for musicians and other variety performers. At least some of the women found there earned money by hustling drinks from customers and splitting the money with Schroeder. Whether they received a wage is unclear. Some of them may have also engaged in casual prostitution with customers looking for that. But as both police and private investigators found, one had to agree to move through a series of coded encounters first: letting a woman sit with you, treating her, moving to a side room, treating again, allowing her onto your lap, moving upstairs to a private room. Even there, the real profit resulted from using sex to sell liquor rather than the reverse. For the Society for the Suppression of Vice, the Belvidere was a low "dive," frequented only by thieves and prostitutes. It was "disorderly" precisely because it blurred the boundaries between respectable and unrespectable social behavior.[5]

During its infancy, roughly from 1896 to 1906, the motion picture established itself largely within venues more respectable than the Belvidere. Movies became the single most popular act in American vaudeville, the latest in a long line of visual novelty acts—"living picture" tableaux, lantern slides, shadowgraphy—that could be fit neatly into an established format organized around discrete, unrelated "turns." Vaudeville managers aggressively promoted brief travelogues, "local actualities," news films, and the occasional comedy or drama to gain an edge over their competitors. Hundreds of vaudeville theaters across the country provided the most important market for the fledgling, mostly undercapitalized moviemakers.[6]

Beginning around 1905 the rapid growth of "nickelodeon" theaters, devoted exclusively to exhibiting motion pictures, created the industry's first great boom. As Charles Musser has argued, "It is not too much to say that modern cinema began with the nickelodeons." These were usually penny arcades, empty storerooms, or tenement lofts converted into rude theaters devoted to continuous shows of motion pictures. Film historians have identified several factors that contributed to the "nickel madness," including the development of longer, more sophisticated "story films," a general expansion in popularly priced entertainment forms between 1905 and 1908, and the aggressive commercial exploitation of movies by urban immigrant exhibitors. Nickelodeons attracted a tremendous rush of entrepreneurial energy. In 1907, the not untypical Golden Rule Hall nickelodeon on the Lower East Side's Rivington Street reported a weekly take of $1,800. Fixed expenses of about $500 left the proprietor with a net weekly profit of $1,300. In 1910, in Manhattan alone, weekly movie attendance reached approximately 900,000 at about four hundred theaters.[7]

The sudden explosion of storefront theaters in New York created a complex political and cultural crisis, making plain the deep contradictions surrounding the popularity and regulation of the movies. Subject to two very different licensing procedures, movies fell between the cracks of the ambiguous theater laws. Where motion pictures were coupled with vaudeville acts, exhibitors were required to take out a theater or concert license, issued by the police department, at an annual fee of $500. Where entertainment consisted of motion pictures alone, with no stage performances, only a so-called common-show license, costing $25 and granted by the mayor, was needed. In addition, the city's building code required that any space intended for public entertainment with audiences over three hundred had to comply with certain very specific and stringent regulations involving exits, fireproofing, size of stage, lighting, and so on. Not surprisingly, therefore, the large majority of early movie houses operated under common-show licenses and kept their capacities below three hundred. In 1910, as a systematic study done for the mayor's office revealed, about 450 movie houses operated under common show licenses, another 290 held theatrical or concert licenses, and around 600 had a seating capacity under three hundred.[8]

The strategy pursued by many of the ambitious, small-time, immigrant showmen, all trying to stake claims in the new amusement Klondike, seems clear: stay beneath the surveillance of the police and the reform agencies traditionally interested in regulating the city's theatrical world. They kept their shows small and short, with only a minimal investment in a hastily refurbished penny arcade or storefront. They could obtain a common-show license for as brief a period as three months and thought nothing of packing up and moving to another part of the city as soon as business went bad. By late 1906 several established theatrical managers had protested to the police department because they were compelled to live up to expensive licensing requirements, while the itinerant movie shows were not. At the same time, complaints from clergymen and moral reformers against movies began to mount, centering on four issues: the running of Sunday shows, the large numbers of children in the audience, the screening of immoral films, and the threat of fire. But while the tremendous popularity of the movies brought forth demands for stricter regulation, these calls extended to a whole range of plebeian entertainments.[9]

Police Commissioner Theodore Bingham attempted to bring some order to the situation by reasserting his department's authority over the realm of entertainment licensing. An arrogant, tactless former army officer and federal bureaucrat, with a violent temper, Bingham had been appointed to lead the police in 1906 by Mayor George B. McClellan, Jr. He had little knowledge of New York City, and his three-year reign as commissioner would be marked by constant bickering with the mayor and controversies occasioned by Bingham's anti-Semitic and nativist pronouncements on the causes of crime. In April 1907 Bingham ordered police captains to furnish a descriptive list of all places of amusement in their precincts, especially noting penny arcades and cheap theaters, and he promised to review every application for license renewal personally. This survey counted over four hundred "'penny arcades' and similar places where phonographs, moving pictures, and mechanical pianos furnish the entertainment." By July Bingham recommended that Mayor McClellan revoke the licenses held by scores of penny arcades, nickelodeons, and cheap vaudeville houses because they admitted children unaccompanied by parents, showed obscene pictures, or violated building and fire regulations.[10]

The Children's Aid Society, founded in 1853 by Charles Loring Brace, supported Bingham's efforts by charging that these places menaced the morals of children under sixteen. The society brought suits in 1907 against several movie exhibitors. After being raided by society agents, George E. Watson, proprietor of a nickel show on Third Avenue near 34th Street, was fined $100 in special sessions on a charge of imperiling the morals of young boys by showing a Lubin film called *The Unwritten Law,* based on the sensational Stanford White–Harry Thaw murder case of the previous year. Judges viewing the film decided that two of its scenes, depicting the drugging of Evelyn Nesbit by Stanford White and the shooting of White on the roof garden, were unfit for children. In a similar case, William Short, who ran a movie house on West 116th Street, was arrested for exhibiting a film portraying the interior of a Chinese opium den. The police magistrate hearing this case remarked, "If any man should show that picture to my child I would kill him. The town is full of these sort of places and they are doing incalculable harm. The police should close every one of them."[11]

The movie boom also galvanized a renewed campaign by elements of New York's Protestant clergy for stricter enforcement of the law banning Sunday stage performances. Since the early 1880s theatrical blue laws had been honored mostly in the breach, as vaudeville and burlesque houses routinely offered "sacred concerts" on Sundays, consisting only of singing and monologues, and supposedly free of all scene shifting, costumes, makeup, and acrobatic acts. Although these tamer Sunday performances had become a New York institution over the years, complaints about Sabbath-breaking occasionally brought a flurry of arrests and threats to revoke licenses, usually against the smaller and poorer theaters along the Bowery and around Union Square. In the fall of 1906 Rev. F. M. Foster, a Presbyterian minister, and Canon William S. Chase, a Brooklyn Episcopal minister, organized the Interdenominational Committee for the Suppression of Sunday Vaudeville. They wrote Mayor McClellan that "whatever requires a license on other days of the week is forbidden on the first day of the week" and warned him that "the public has a right to hold you responsible for the violation of the law."[12]

In typical language, Rev. Percy S. Grant of the Episcopal Church of the Ascension charged that those favoring Sunday shows were mostly "of a race who have no use for our Sunday, and I don't know that they have any use for their own." He denounced the spread of Sunday entertainments, especially those he saw developing "along the lines open to us by the poorer class of vaudeville and other shows. It would not only degrade our religious nature, but our minds." In December, responding to this campaign, police closed a number of Bowery and Harlem burlesque and vaudeville houses on Sunday, as well as a popularly priced Italian opera concert. Significantly, though, when the Interdenominational Committee, with the support of Bingham and the city's Corporation Counsel, made plans to bring a test case to court on the Sunday law, they chose not one of the lesser Bowery or Harlem theaters, but William Hammerstein's Victoria theater, a big-time vaudeville house at Broadway and 42nd Street, in the heart of the emerging Times Square theater district.[13]

Meanwhile, the movie exhibitors looked for ways to defend themselves legally and politically. In June 1907 a group of about sixty formed the Moving Picture Exhibitors Association (MPEA). These were mostly Jewish and Italian showmen holding common-show licenses and ready to exploit their close ties to the Tammany Hall machine. The MPEA succeeded in getting a New York Supreme Court justice to grant an injunction preventing the mayor and his Bureau of Licenses from revoking their licenses. Significantly, their counsel was

Florence Sullivan, who was not a lawyer, but a Tammany district leader on the Lower East Side and a cousin of Timothy D. "Big Tim" Sullivan, the most powerful Democratic politician in Manhattan. It is important to note, too, that the MPEA's first president, Nicola Seraphine, defended the movie business with domestic imagery that would echo throughout film history. "A great majority of the moving pictures," he told an interviewer, "retain something connected with the home. The human heart goes out to these pictures because they recall scenes that are dear to the poorest patron of these shows. . . . The moving picture exhibitions are rapidly multiplying and are so easy of access and reasonable in price of admission that they are really a part of the home life of Greater New York."[14]

Amidst all this contention a legal bombshell landed on December 3, 1907, shaking the foundations of New York show business. Ruling on the Sunday test case, Supreme Court Justice James A. O'Gorman revoked the license of the Victoria theater for violating an old 1860 state ban on Sabbath entertainment. Ignoring the enormous changes in the city's population and leisure patterns over the past five decades, O'Gorman asserted that "the Christian Sabbath is one of the civil institutions of the state and that for the purpose of protecting the moral and physical well-being of the people and preserving the peace, quiet, and good order of society the Legislature has authority to regulate its observance." Police Commissioner Bingham welcomed this clear, definite order. "Everything in the way of Sunday theater is to be closed," he announced. "That covers Carnegie Hall as well as the one and five cent vaudeville and moving picture shows." Few decisions in the history of New York courts touched so many people. The prohibition would affect twenty-seven vaudeville and burlesque theaters; numerous opera houses, symphonies, and other concert halls; and Sunday-night plays given in German, Yiddish, and French. The combined audience for these events ran to perhaps 150,000 on an average Sunday, and if the summer seaside resort shows were included, to over half a million.[15]

For two "blue Sundays" in a row the police enforced O'Gorman's ruling, creating an eerie stillness in the city's theaters, while large throngs moved through Broadway, the Bowery, Union Square, Times Square, and other main avenues in "crowds that reached almost election night proportions." A very vocal, large, and diverse opposition immediately put pressure on the Board of Aldermen to exercise its power to give the city its own Sunday amusement law. The city's press largely opposed the blue law, invoking cosmopolitan diversity as their own standard and class bias as that of their enemies. The *World* argued that with three-quarters of all New Yorkers of foreign parentage, "repeal or non-enforcement is its inevitable fate, hastened by every attempt to revive its outworn and outgrown severity. . . . The people's Sunday belongs to the people." A mass meeting of 2,500 members of the United German Societies, representing roughly 300,000 people, called for bringing the laws of the state "into harmony with the present conditions and wants of the people." Delegates to the city's Central Federated Union, representing 250,000 members of organized labor, attacked the ruling for creating "a class distinction by permitting a certain few to follow their particular pursuit of happiness while denying the same rights to a large majority." The Tammany-dominated Board of Aldermen responded to all this pressure by quickly passing an ambiguously worded ordinance relaxing the Sunday law. It allowed for "sacred or educational, vocal or instrumental concerts," provided that these entertainments "shall be given in such a manner as not to disturb the public peace or amount to a serious interruption of the repose and religious liberty of the community."[16]

For the motion picture industry, the 1907 uproar over Sunday theater proved a turning point. Since movie exhibition was not part of the nineteenth-century entertainment equation, it had never been subject to blue laws. A revitalized Moving Picture Exhibitors Association took advantage of the legal chaos to mark out its own space, separate from the older theatrical interests, and to flex its growing political muscle. The MPEA was now led by William Fox, an intense, twenty-nine-year-old Hungarian Jewish immigrant who had invested the profits from his small cloth-inspecting company in the entertainment business. Fox had successfully converted several Brooklyn penny arcades and burlesque theaters into movie houses, and by 1907 he had opened a film distribution business and gained control of more theaters in Manhattan. He later emerged as the prototypical movie mogul, a pioneer, along with Adolph Zukor, in vertically integrating movie exhibition, distribution, and production. In his early New York days Fox was unique for his shrewd and effective use of Tammany Hall connections in building both his economic base and his influence with other movie men. His attorney and partner, and the new counsel for the MPEA, was Gustavus Rogers, a Jewish, City College–educated lawyer. Rogers had made himself useful to the Sullivan machine, and by 1903, at age twenty-seven, he had served as both legal counsel and corresponding secretary for Tammany Hall.[17]

The only theaters open in the city during the two December blue Sundays were nine Fox nickelodeons. Rogers had obtained a court injunction preventing police from closing them, successfully arguing that the phrase "or any other entertainment of the stage" (contained in the charter provision) did not apply to moving picture shows "because they do not require the use of a stage as that word is understood." Newspapers noted that, amidst the Sunday amusement drought, Fox's Harlem Comedy Theatre did an enormous business, giving performances every fifteen minutes, all day, to three hundred eager patrons, each paying a nickel. Motion pictures were not mentioned in the new city ordinance, but the corporation counsel claimed they were illegal.[18]

Moving quickly to protect all 110 members of the MPEA, controlling some five hundred movie houses, Rogers argued that movies could not be prosecuted under the new city statute because it did not mention them; nor could an older state law forbidding Sunday "public sports, exercises, or shows" be invoked because movies were not presented out-of-doors. On December 28, 1907, he won a temporary blanket injunction, later upheld, from Supreme Court Justice Samuel Greenbaum, restraining police from harassing any Sunday movie shows. As the trade paper *Moving Picture World* noted, "Nearly all the promoters of moving picture entertainments availed themselves of the injunction privilege and their houses were packed. . . . The real sufferers were the vaudeville managers. They were forced to make up their bills of singing, talking and instrumental acts in which the performers wore street clothes. In most cases the attendance was light and it was a lucky house which did not lose a substantial sum."[19]

Motion picture exhibition, now on a more secure legal footing with the court victories of 1907, became an even more inviting business opportunity. Theater managers worried about the legal ambiguities surrounding Sunday performances began substituting movies for live acts. The economic downturn of 1907–8 also encouraged vaudeville and burlesque houses to convert to movies as their main attraction. In the summer of 1908, for example, William Fox startled the city's show business community by leasing two popular, centrally located theaters, the Dewey on 14th Street and the Gotham on 125th Street, and converting them to motion pictures. Since the 1890s these theaters had been controlled by Big Tim Sullivan, offering risqué vaudeville and burlesque shows that regularly attracted protests from Sullivan's political enemies. After Fox paid one year's rent of $100,000, in advance, for the two theaters, he proceeded to make tremendous profits by offering a show with five reels of film, interspersed with several live vaudeville acts, all for ten cents.

The Dewey, with its fifty employees, red-uniformed ushers, and daily changes of films, was now, according to *Variety,* "the best run and most profitable moving picture place in New York." On Thanksgiving Day, 1908, the 1,200-seat Dewey sold 12,000 tickets, a record attendance for a movie theater. More vaudeville and burlesque theaters, many of them old bastions in the city's entertainment districts, made the transition to movies at this time, including Tony Pastor's, the Unique, and the Union Square, all on 14th Street, and two big Keith and Proctor houses on 23rd and 125th Streets.[20] The policy of adding live variety acts to the show, pioneered by Fox and Marcus Loew, created what became known as "small-time vaudeville," an important transitional phase in movie exhibition. Combining the nickelodeon's cheap admission price and film program with the live acts and trappings of the more comfortable, middle-class vaudeville house, these theaters put many of the cramped, dingy storefront theaters out of business. The "small-time" format would prove ideal for the multireel "feature films," which began to appear after 1912, and they also provided the foundation for several of the largest movie house circuits, a crucial part of the vertical monopolies that later dominated Hollywood production.[21]

As the movie boom accelerated, the desire to inspect and regulate this new entertainment phenomenon intensified in several quarters. Two parallel investigations of New York's movie business, one public, one private, took place in early 1908, and together they set the agenda for movie regulation for the next decade. Mayor McClellan ordered the city police to visit and make a complete list of all the places with penny arcades or moving picture shows. Part of the impetus here came from a disastrous nickelodeon fire in Boyertown, Pennsylvania, which killed 169 people and drew cries for tighter safety codes. But the mayor also found himself inundated with complaints from clergy warning against the moral dangers posed by movies and, between the lines, afraid of the competition that this new entertainment posed.

"A number of us," wrote Rev. Michael J. Lavelle, vicar general of the Roman Catholic Archbishopric, "are very much worried by the moving picture shows, not only on Sunday but every day in the week. We are being constantly urged to do something to have them stopped. From the reports I get, brought by sensible men, in no way fanatic, they are bad and demoralizing to the youth in this city. In fact, it is commonly believed that they cannot be made to pay unless they introduce salacious pictures." Yet in summarizing the reports of investigators who toured 320 movie shows, Police Commissioner Bingham, certainly no friend of these shows or their managers, reported, "Some of the pictures bordered on the vulgar, but in no place were pictures found which could be termed lewd or salacious." The worst that could be observed were numerous pictures showing "railroad hold-ups, shootings of persons, duels, and pictures illustrating thefts, and the consequences thereof to the thieves themselves."[22]

On the other hand, for critics of movies, the pictures themselves were only part of a troubling exhibition milieu associated with cheap commercial enter-tainment: big crowds of unsupervised children, darkened spaces, gaudy adver-tisements, the large immigrant presence both in the audience and in the ticket office, and the overall fact that movies inhabited the physical and psychic space of cheap commercial urban entertainment.[23] It was precisely this larger, dis-turbing context that gave focus to the influential report, *Cheap Amusement Shows in Manhattan,* produced jointly in early 1908 by two Progressive civic groups, the Women's Municipal League and the People's Institute. This sym-pathetic analysis stressed the sudden emergence of movies as the most popular yet least regulated of the city's commercial entertainments. Movies needed to be separated from desultory penny arcades, "as a rule the gathering place of idlers," whose slot machines showed pictures tending toward "the indecent or the violent." Compared to both penny arcades and cheap vaudeville and bur-lesque houses, movie audiences evinced order, enthusiasm, and "the leavening salt of family patronage."[24]

The author of this report was John Collier, a twenty-four-year-old social worker, who played a central role in movie censorship over the next decade. Born and raised in a wealthy Atlanta family, Collier had joined the staff at the People's Institute in 1907, bringing a passionate interest in the problem of commercialized leisure in the industrial age. In Collier's eyes, the movies of-fered an unprecedented opportunity for reformers. "All the settlements and churches combined do not reach daily a tithe of the simple and impressionable folk that the nickelodeons reach and vitally impress every day. Here is a new social force, perhaps the beginning of a true theater of the people, and an in-strument whose power can only be realized when social workers begin to use it." Collier described the earliest movie shows as "often a carnival of vulgarity, suggestiveness and violence, the fit subject for police regulation." But over the last five years the moving picture already had "purified itself automatically, or has been purified by the demand of the public; it has become the resort of families and children." Movies were already the best form of cheap entertain-ment because they were "rarely, almost never, indecent." On the other hand, the fast-paced shows "over-excited" and fatigued children; sanitary and safety conditions were abysmal; and the often vulgar live vaudeville acts "put a com-mon show into the rank of a theatre," according to Collier, who wanted them eliminated. He looked forward to the People's Institute establishing an as yet unspecified cooperative plan with the movie business, "giving endorsement to the best of the shows and receiving in return the right to regulate their programs."[25]

Collier's evaluation came at a critical moment in the evolution of both film content and the movie business. The Progressive impulse to directly shape not only theater regulation but also what appeared on the screen reflected the desire to separate movie exhibition from its association with the city's plebeian theatrical world and to purge film narrative of its more sensational representations of urban life. For their subjects, early "story films" borrowed heavily from all sorts of entertainment sources, including melodrama, vaudeville and burlesque sketches, cartoons, comics, and news stories. A substantial body of popular films had drawn from and extended the commercial exploitation of urban sensationalism. Analysis of the relatively small fraction of surviving films, and their attendant publicity, reveals at least four genres in this category that must have troubled Progressive reformers the most: erotic street scenes emphasizing public displays of sexuality, depictions of New York nightlife, "slumming" comedies, and films about urban crime. All of these movies centered on voyeuristic representations of the city's underside, offering cinematic versions of *Police Gazette* cartoons, popular stage acts, and news stories about urban low life.[26]

Films about the erotic possibilities and fantasies of city street life, from a male point of view, were common in the early years. For example, two typical early Edison films, *Soubrette's Troubles on a Fifth Avenue Stage* (1901) and *What Happened on Twenty-third Street* (1902), are about breezes exposing women's bodies. In the latter, a man and woman are shown walking along a busy city street, toward a stationary camera. The film ends after a gust of air from a sidewalk grate billows the woman's skirt, reveals her underclothes, and causes her to laugh as she and her companion continue walking. By the time this short movie, described by the Edison Catalog as "a winner and sure to please," was made, that situation—indeed, the 23rd Street grate in particular—had already been illustrated in the city's more sensational newspapers.[27]

In *It's a Shame to Take the Money* (Biograph, 1905), a bootblack and policeman collude. While the boy attends a well-dressed lady, a policeman leeringly watches over a wall as she hikes her dress for the shine. The boy refuses payment and gleefully shakes hands with the cop.[28] In *Street Car Chivalry* (Edison, 1903), men in a crowded street car fall all over each other to give a seat to a pretty young woman while ignoring a stout, older matron who climbs aboard. The camera opens on a couple necking passionately in *Central Park after Dark* (Biograph, 1903). When a cop walks by, shining a light in their face, they quickly rearrange their clothing and become more circumspect. One of the most popular films of the early period was *Personal* (Biograph, 1904), about a man who takes out a personal ad for a wife and gets surrounded by ten screaming women at Grant's Tomb, who then spend the rest of the movie frantically chasing him around the city.[29]

The physically expressive dancing and sexual styles of working-class youths had been filmed and marketed as exotic "actualities" since the 1890s in movies such as *Bowery Waltz* (Biograph, 1897), *The Bowery Kiss* (Edison, 1901), and *A "Tough" Dance* (Biograph, 1902). But a more sophisticated and narratively complex group of films portrayed the theaters, dance halls, and saloons of the Bowery and Tenderloin entertainment districts, often taking the viewer backstage in the course of their narratives. Many of these assumed viewer familiarity with contemporary news accounts and scandals about these places. Biograph advertised *A Night at the Haymarket* (1903) as a "very stunning picture tho' somewhat risque," emphasizing that "the much talked of resort is reproduced exactly." If the narrative makes little logical sense, the successive scenes are meant to communicate "six lively hours at New York City's famous Tenderloin dance hall." These include the milling crowd on the sidewalk; the latest dances (including a boisterous can-can); a fight in the "wine room" that continues on the street; and, finally, a police raid in which everybody is led out, as the women hide their faces.[30] A comic version of an archetypal vision of the city forms the center of *How They Do Things on the Bowery* (Edison, 1902). A country rube carrying a cheap valise picks up a kerchief dropped by a woman walking the opposite way. She takes him into a nearby saloon, immediately lights a cigarette, orders drinks, and drugs him as he pays the waiter. As he falls unconscious she robs him and leaves, and the last scene shows him thrown out into the street by the waiter.[31] *The Gerry Society's Mistake* (Biograph, 1903) burlesques the Society for the Prevention of Cruelty to Children, much in the news for its raids on theaters. Four young actresses are shown undressing backstage when a severe-looking man and a policeman enter, shoving papers in front of the youngest woman. She produces a wedding ring from a costume trunk, presumably proving that she is not underage. The women plead with the policeman, finally removing all their jewelry and giving it to him, as they laughingly push the SPCC agent out the door.[32]

A cognate genre, the slumming comedy, gained wide popularity, combining scenes of famous New York sights with a burlesque of the tourists who hired native "guides" to New York low life. In *Lifting the Lid* (Biograph, 1905), the action begins with a group of respectable out-of-towners who travel from their midtown hotel in a large touring car advertising "Chinatown Trips." They visit a low Bowery dive and a Chinese restaurant, sample opium in a den filled with white women and Chinese men, and get drunk at a boisterous concert saloon, where they get thrown out for joining the dancers on stage. The last shot shows them returning safely to their hotel, an appropriate ending for a movie marketed by the studio as "somewhat spicy, but unobjectionable in every way."

A more sardonic version of this subject, *The Deceived Slumming Party* (Biograph, 1908), reveals the fraud behind expeditions that played upon the desire "to investigate the mysteries of that famous section of our great metropolis—the Bowery." A plainclothes cop, in cahoots with the guide and some "Chinese" friends, blackmails the tourists by threatening to arrest them after a fake suicide in a phony opium den; the Chinese restaurant serves ground-up cats and dogs; a dandy has his pocket picked during a sham murder in a saloon.[33]

The Great Train Robbery (Edison, 1903), the first movie blockbuster, had shown how to exploit stories about crime in a "western" setting. The first film treatments of the urban underworld generally evinced a world-weary, knowing cynicism about the hypocrisy of criminal justice in the city—or else they played it strictly for laughs. In *The Kleptomaniac* (Edison, 1905), a fashionable woman caught stealing in a large department store is let go by a judge, while a poor woman who robs a local grocery to feed her daughter gets no mercy. In *A Raid on a Cock Fight* (Biograph, 1906), the arresting officer pockets all the betting money. *Monday Morning in a Coney Island Police Court* (Biograph, 1908) offers a pure burlesque: the sleeping cops have to be roused by a cleaning woman; the two lawyers are baggy-pants clowns; the judge uses an oversize gavel to beat everyone on the head; and two prize-fighters bring an end to the proceedings by knocking everyone out. *The Black Hand* (Biograph, 1906), based on the actual kidnapping and rescue of a girl in Little Italy, advanced crime movies toward a more convincing social realism, anticipating films like D. W. Griffith's *The Musketeers of Pig Alley* (Biograph, 1912) and the gangster cycle of the early sound era. Still, the reality of the outside street scenes is in jarring contrast to the very contrived stage sets, which, in most of these early films, resemble a cheap stage production.

Despite continuing objections to films such as these, at the end of 1908 the ultimate questions of licensing and censorship—of the political and cultural control of the movies—remained unanswered by the courts. On Christmas Eve 1908 Mayor McClellan, acting from a complex set of motives, unilaterally revoked the common-show licenses of over five hundred New York movie houses. This bold stroke was partly a response to a steady stream of protests against movies that flowed into the mayor's office. But it was also part of a broader political strategy to expand the mayor's power and assert his independence from the Tammany machine. This unprecedented wielding of municipal authority also had enormous consequences, some unintended, for the movie industry.

The patrician, Princeton-educated son of the Civil War general, McClellan began his political career as a protégé of Tammany Hall boss Richard Croker, who aggressively cultivated wealthy "respectables" for the Democratic machine. He was made president of the Board of Aldermen at age twenty-seven in 1892 and then served five terms in the U.S. Congress. Elected mayor in 1903 with Tammany support, McClellan split with the machine after his re-election in 1905, engaging in a bitter public feud with Tammany boss Charles F. Murphy over mayoral patronage. McClellan manifested his independence by appointing many non-Tammanyites to administrative posts and actively root-ing out some of the traditional pockets of graft and corruption in city govern-ment. One of these was the Bureau of Licenses, where applicants for common-show licenses were routinely expected to pay hundreds of dollars above the regular twenty-five-dollar fee to the bureau's administrators or the policemen who performed the street-level inspections. In November 1908 McClellan forced Bureau Chief John P. Corrigan and several subordinates to resign after investigators discovered a consistent and deep pattern of extortion and bribery in the granting of common-show licenses for movie houses.[34]

Meanwhile, various religious leaders, most of them Protestant veterans of the war against Sunday vaudeville, stepped up their campaign against the movies. In petitions, letters, and public meetings, as well as private confer-ences with the mayor, they denounced not only Sunday shows, but also the content of many films and their accompanying "demoralization" of children. McClellan lent a sympathetic ear to these objections, but perhaps for selfish motives. According to his personal secretary, the mayor did not really care to close movie shows on Sunday. But he had ambitions to become the president of Princeton College, and "in order to do so, seeks to obtain the good graces of the Church people in New York City." After personally inspecting about thirty movie houses in December, during which he was appalled by the firetrap con-ditions in many of them, McClellan convened a meeting aimed at sorting out the issues of Sunday shows, censorship, and public safety.[35]

On December 23, at City Hall, the mayor heard the key arguments of the major players at a raucous, crowded, five-hour public hearing. The antimovie clerics hammered away at what they insisted was the corruption and con-tamination of youth. "Is a man at liberty to make money from the morals of people?" demanded Rev. F. M. Foster. "Is he to profit from the corruption of the minds of children? The man who profits from such things is doomed to double damnation. To show indecent pictures is a violation of the statutes and the removal of such shows from the city is clearly justifiable." In this respect, it is important to note how defenders of movies described them as "family amusement" and "family theater." Progressives such as Charles Sprague Smith, director of the People's Institute, and R. S. Symonds, supervisor of the Juvenile League, harshly denounced the clergy and other movie opponents. "Years ago," argued Symonds, "the man was in the rum shop on a Sunday night. Where do you find him now? Side by side with his children witnessing a moving picture show."

Gustavus Rogers, who by this time represented two hundred exhibitors with a collective investment of between three and four million dollars, offered the broadest and most sophisticated defense of movies. He presented petitions with tens of thousands of signatures, collected at movie houses, calling for the continuance of Sunday shows and "heartily in favor of our children visiting the said exhibitions." He invoked recent court rulings holding that Sunday shows were not in violation of the law. Significantly, Rogers addressed the issue of "indecent pictures" by describing municipal censorship in Chicago, where all films were first screened at police headquarters and approved or disapproved for showing in that city. "If this is a practical suggestion or solution we are willing to accede to it." He emphasized the need to protect the vast majority of exhibitors, "who have lived up to the statute law and the moral law. . . . There should be legislation of some kind so that there would be supervision and management exercised over these places. I take it this cannot be accomplished by wholesale revocations. I take it it cannot be accomplished by your Honor saying, 'I won't grant any more licenses.'"[36]

McClellan made his move the next day. Expressing his "firm conviction that I am averting a public calamity," McClellan revoked and annulled the license of every moving picture show in the city, some 550 in all. He directed the new chief of the Bureau of Licenses to personally inspect every movie house in the city before a new license could be granted. Although most of his statement addressed fire and safety issues, the mayor's conclusion specifically invoked the complaints voiced by New York's antimovie forces:

> Because of the serious opposition presented by the rectors and pastors of prac-
> tically all the Christian denominations in the city, and because of the further
> objections of the Society for the Prevention of Cruelty to Children and the
> Society for the Prevention of Crime, I have decided that licenses for moving
> picture shows shall only be issued hereafter on the written agreement that the
> licensee will not operate the same on Sunday. And I do further declare that
> I will revoke any of these moving picture show licenses on evidence that pic-
> tures have been exhibited by the licensees which tend to degrade or injure the
> morals of the community.[37]

In the wake of McClellan's order, the older, highly politicized, and unstable process of theater licensing began to give way to an industry-dominated procedure of censorship. In March 1909 the beleaguered Moving Picture

Exhibitors Association asked the People's Institute to organize a Board of Censorship to pass on all films shown in New York City. The institute's recent success with a voluntary censorship of live theater in New York may have influenced the MPEA's choice. Founded in 1897, the institute had attracted large numbers of working people and immigrants to the public lectures, adult-education classes, and cultural programs it sponsored at Cooper Union. Since 1907 its Dramatic Department had regularly reviewed current plays and reported on their suitability for various audiences. "An indispensable condition for acceptance," *The Theatre* magazine noted, "was that the play should possess educational and artistic features and be without moral blemish." In 1907 sixty thousand people had attended plays at reduced rates through institute-sponsored tickets, and this economic boon was not lost on theater managers. "If a play is accepted by the Institute the manager knows that he can count on selling several thousand tickets to school teachers, labor unionists, etc. The fact that managers have begun to submit manuscripts of plays to the Institute for its approval before making the production is significant enough."[38]

At first the new Board of Censorship claimed only a narrow mission: "to eliminate obscene pictures and pictures of crime-for-crime's sake from the New York moving picture show." The MPEA, which funded the administrative costs, required exhibitors to abide by the censorship or face expulsion. The People's Institute organized a governing board that included representatives from a variety of civic, educational, and religious organizations. The Executive Committee on Censorship, chaired by John Collier, performed the actual reviewing of movies, either passing a film, suggesting changes, or condemning a movie entirely. At its first meeting on March 25, 1909, the Committee on Censorship spent six hours inspecting some eighteen thousand feet of film, of which it condemned only four hundred feet. But from the beginning, the board looked to expand its influence nationally by convincing film producers to support the exhibitors' initiative. The board stressed that its censorship would be liberal and that only a small proportion of pictures were objectionable. "But it is the *occasional* offensive picture which falls into the hands of the police, arouses the protest of vigilance societies, is advertised in the newspapers, and brings the whole moving picture business in disrepute. This picture must be caught up before it is shown on the public screen. The way to get this result is to inspect the pictures before they leave the hands of the manufacturers."[39]

The key producer group was the recently formed Motion Picture Patents Company, a patent pooling and licensing organization made up of the ten major film manufacturers. The new board quickly convinced the Patents Company of the advantages to be gained by an industrywide, voluntary censorship. In May 1909 Frank L. Dyer, president of the Patents Company, wrote John

Collier, "Your proposition of a single National Censorship Board strikes me as being the only solution of the problem, admitting there must be a censorship, which I think everyone having the best interests of the business at heart must admit." In June the People's Institute announced it was establishing the National Board of Censorship of Motion Pictures (NBC), funded by exhibitors and manufacturers. Within a year most independent producers, rivals to the Patents Company group, had also joined the voluntary censorship. By 1914 the NBC claimed to be reviewing 95 percent of the total film output in the United States. Mayors, police chiefs, civic groups, and local censoring committees from all over the country subscribed to the board's weekly bulletin.[40]

As Nancy J. Rosenbloom has shown, the "effort at accommodation between the moving picture trade and reformers had a national impact and led to the establishment of a formal relationship that remained in effect throughout the progressive era." The governing board formally elected the volunteer Censorship Committee, a revolving group of lawyers, doctors, clergymen, and women activists that viewed films submitted every week by producers. Most objections centered around excesses in scenes dealing with overt sexuality, prostitution, drug use, and the too-explicit depiction of murder and robbery. The board presumed a very simple psychology at the core of the moviegoer's experience: "Every person in an audience has paid admission and for that reason gives his attention willingly. . . . Therefore he gives it his confidence and opens the window of his mind. And what the movie says sinks in." For their part, movie producers encouraged the NBC to go beyond simply stopping the obviously immoral film. "Our Licensees," the Patents Company wrote in 1911, "recommend that your basis of criticism be extended so as to condemn pictures that are unusually vulgar and offensive to good taste, and in the opinion of your committee, generally detrimental to motion picture interests, although such pictures may not be indecent, immoral, nor injurious to public morals."[41]

While the movie men looked to rationalize their business with the imprimatur of cultural respectability, the reformers saw an opportunity to uplift the cultural life of the audience. "The moving picture," John Collier noted in 1909, "is a deliberate and serious form of the theatre." But unlike live theater, movies "are produced in a wholesale manner." Only a national censorship, he argued, could curb "sensationalism" and bring "an improvement in tone and a heightening of artistic qualities in American made pictures." The NBC also encouraged creation of local boards to deal with the censorship of vaudeville and the physical conditions of theaters. Collier envisioned a local auxiliary in every community, which might eventually "become a committee for the regulation of amusements in general."[42]

In New York City the effort to codify and reform city ordinances regulating movie exhibition bogged down over the question of municipal censorship. The issue made for strange political bedfellows. Advocates of legal censorship included a group of prominent New York civic organizations, among them two of the original members of the NBC governing board, the Women's Municipal League, and the Children's Aid Society. Both withdrew from the NBC in 1911, charging that the board's work failed to protect children. The Society for the Prevention of Crime and the Society for the Prevention of Cruelty to Children echoed their nineteenth-century criticisms of plebeian live theater. They called for laws requiring segregation of the sexes in movie theaters, keeping the lights on at all times, and banning the admission of unaccompanied minors. The problem, they argued, was not with the movies: "The evil lies in the conditions under which so many are given—the dark room, filled with adults and children, absolutely without supervision, affording no protection against the evil-minded and depraved men who frequent such places."[43]

Influential Protestant clerics, defensively reasserting their waning cultural authority in the cosmopolitan city, also endorsed a municipal censorship. Tammanyites on the Board of Aldermen, looking to build their patronage base, put forth plans for legal censorship to be conducted by the Police Department or the Board of Education. Yet other machine politicians, particularly those with personal interests in movie exhibition, opposed any municipal censorship and defended a liberal policy of theater regulation favored by the majority of their Catholic and Jewish constituency. In December 1912 Mayor William J. Gaynor, a long-time supporter of motion pictures, vetoed a comprehensive movie reform bill passed by the Board of Aldermen because it contained a Tammany-sponsored amendment for a movie censorship run by the Board of Education. Gaynor made a ringing First Amendment argument against those who would "have the pictures examined in advance, and allowed or prohibited. That is what they are still doing in Russia with pictures and with reading matter generally. Do they really want us to recur to that system?"[44]

In the end, public outcry over a series of disastrous movie house fires broke the political stalemate. New York finally got its comprehensive movie regulation in July 1913. But the new law focused exclusively on improving movie exhibition and contained no provision for censorship. It set tougher safety, ventilation, and construction standards for movie houses and centralized authority over them in the Bureau of Licenses. It prohibited vaudeville in the roughly 450 storefront theaters holding only a common-show license ($50); but it also raised the seating limits on these from three hundred to six hundred. To keep live entertainment, movie exhibitors would have to comply with the stricter requirements of regular theater laws and obtain an annual theatrical license costing $500. Reformers hailed the new law for elevating both the physical and moral conditions of moviegoers. The exclusion of live performance was crucial because of "the tendency of vaudeville to become degraded, and the increased difficulty of regulating the general physical and moral conduct of the show if vaudeville is allowed."[45]

As Hollywood replaced New York as the hub of the film industry, the National Board of Censorship began to lose its influence. And the board encountered continued resistance from those who viewed its efforts as inadequate. Between 1909 and 1915 the NBC fought a losing battle against the establishment of legal censorship arrangements in numerous states and municipalities. Its change of name in 1915 to the National Board of Review made sense for an organization increasingly devoted to opposing campaigns for legal censorship. But the National Board established the basic terms of a voluntary movie censorship that would be codified by the Motion Picture Producers and Distributors Association and its leader, Will Hays.[46] The politics of performance had shifted its locus from theater licensing to movie censorship. That censorship took the regulation of representation in modern mass culture off the street, away from the police power, and out of urban politics. The site of regulation shifted from negotiations among local interests over performance space to a Hollywood-centered brokering of what was permissible on American screens. The game would now be played on a field and under rules largely defined by the movie industry itself, mediated by national interest groups working within the studio system.

NOTES

Thanks to Francis G. Couvares, Gary Kulik, and the *American Quarterly* referees for the critical comments and suggestions made on earlier drafts of this article.

1. A copy of the 1839 law can be found in *Act of Incorporation and Laws relative to the Managers of the Society for the Reformation of Juvenile Delinquents* (New York, 1855). The 1862 law, slightly amended in 1872, 1882, and 1887, is reprinted in Society for the Reformation of Juvenile Delinquents, *Act of Incorporation, Statutes, and Decisions relative to the House of Refuge* (New York, 1874). On the history of the SRJD, see Robert S. Pickett, *House of Refuge: Origins of Juvenile Reform in New York State, 1815–1857* (Syracuse, 1969), 58–134; and Raymond A. Mohl, *Poverty in New York, 1783–1825* (New York, 1971), 241–58. Neither of these works, however, deals extensively with the theatrical connection. For a longer discussion on the SRJD and the concert-saloon boom, see Daniel Czitrom, "Mysteries of the City: Theatre Licensing, Popular Entertainment, and the Underworld in Nineteenth Century New York" (paper deliv-

ered at the Modes of Inquiry for American City History Conference, Chicago Historical Society, October 1990), 4–8.

2. On Pastor, see Robert W. Snyder, *The Voice of the City: Vaudeville and Popular
Culture in New York* (New York, 1989), 13–25; and Myron Matlan, "Tony the
Trouper: Pastor's Early Years," *Theatre Annual* 24 (1968): 70–90.

3. The 1875 list is in the Mayor's Papers prior to 1898, Municipal Archives and
Research Center, New York (hereafter cited as MP), 81-WWH-25. An 1887 list (MP,
87-HAS-37) included forty-nine places; an 1897 list (MP, 90-SWL-46) had fifty-
eight.

4. Deposition of William Waite, April 2, 1879, MP, 83-CE-26.

5. Deposition of John Schroeder and supporting petition, April 2, 1879; George
Walling to Board of Police, May 1, 1879; and William Murray to George W.
Walling, November 18, 1879 (all in MP, 83-CE-26). Peter Bailey's view of the mal-
leable nature of "respectable" behavior in English music halls is relevant here: "It
may be more fruitful if for the moment we disregard respectability as the manifestation of a generalised social code or ideology, and consider its incidence in the more
limited and situational sense as the performance of a particular role." See his important study, *Leisure and Class in Victorian England: Rational Recreation and the Contest for
Control, 1830–1885* (London, 1978), 177. On the relationship between "treating"
and sexuality, see the insightful discussion in Kathy Peiss, *Cheap Amusements: Working
Women and Leisure in Turn-of-the-Century New York* (Philadelphia, 1986), 51–55,
108–14. On the dynamics of casual prostitution see Christine Stansell, *City of Women:
Sex and Class in New York, 1789–1860* (New York, 1986), 76–89.

6. For the best overview of the interaction between vaudeville and early film, see
Robert C. Allen, "The Movies in Vaudeville: Historical Context of the Movies as
Popular Entertainment," in *The American Film Industry,* rev. ed., ed. Tino Balio (Madison, Wis., 1986), 57–82; and *Vaudeville and Film, 1895–1915: A Study in Media Interaction* (New York, 1980).

7. Charles Musser, *The Emergence of Cinema: The American Screen to 1907* (New York,
1990), 417. Figures on Golden Rule Hall from *Variety,* December 14, 1907, 12. On
the development of the nickelodeon, see Eileen Bowser, *The Transformation of Cinema,
1907–1915* (New York, 1990), 1–20; Russell Merritt, "Nickelodeon Theaters,
1905–1914: Building an Audience for the Movies," in *The American Film Industry,*
rev. ed., ed. Tino Balio (Madison, Wis. 1985), 83–102; Daniel J. Czitrom, *Media and
the American Mind: From Morse to McLuhan* (Chapel Hill, 1982), 40–54; Robert C.
Allen, "Motion Picture Exhibition in Manhattan, 1906–1912: Beyond the Nickelodeon," in *Film before Griffith,* ed. John L. Fell (Berkeley, 1983), 162–75; and Robert
Sklar, *Movie-Made America* (New York, 1975), 14–40.

8. Raymond Fosdick, commissioner of accounts, "Report on Moving Picture
Shows in the City of New York," March 22, 1911, MP, GWJ-22.

9. See *New York Tribune,* December 1, 3, 7, 1906; *New York Times,* November 19,
1906, and January 29, 1907; and *Moving Picture World,* March 30, 1907, 56–57.

10. "Trade Notes," *Moving Picture World,* June 8, 1907, 214. See also "Trade
Notes," May 4, 1907, 137, and July 20, 1907, 312. On Bingham, see Harold C.
Syrett, ed., *The Gentleman and the Tiger: The Autobiography of George B. McClellan, Jr.*
(Philadelphia, 1956); and Theodore A. Bingham, "Foreign Criminals in New York,"
North American Review 188 (September 1908): 383–94, and "How to Give New York

the Best Police Force in the World," *North American Review* 187 (May 1908): 702–11.

11. "Trade Notes," *Moving Picture World,* May 11, 1907, 153, and December 14, 1907, 663. On *The Unwritten Law,* see Jay Leyda and Charles Musser, eds., *Before Hollywood: Turn-of-the-Century Film from American Archives* (New York, 1986), 132.

12. Letter to McClellan quoted in *New York Tribune,* December 1, 1906.

13. Grant quoted in *New York Tribune,* December 7, 1906. Canon Chase argued, "The open saloon is not so dangerous to our young people, for its evils are understood, as is the apparently clean and innocent Sunday show which drives out of their minds all the holy thoughts which have sanctified the day and made it a day different from all other days and a blessing to the whole community" ("The Matter of Sunday Shows," *Moving Picture World,* October 26, 1907, 539. See also *New York Dramatic Mirror,* December 14, 1907; and *New York Times,* October 27, 1907). Several of the Children's Aid Society suits also cited illegal Sunday shows. A state statute of 1860 was quite specific, prohibiting on Sundays "any interlude, tragedy, comedy, opera, ballet, play, farce, negro minstrelsy, negro or other dancing, or any other entertainment of the stage, or any parts therein, or any equestrian, circus, or dramatic performance, or any performance of jugglers, acrobats, or rope dancing" (quoted in Consolidation Act, 1882, chap. 2007, and later incorporated into sec. 1481 of the City Charter).

14. Seraphine quoted in "Association Notes," *Moving Picture World,* June 29, 1907, 270; *New York Tribune,* 14 June 1907. On Florence Sullivan and his role in the Sullivan machine, as well as the Sullivan machine's deep involvement in the early film business, see Daniel Czitrom, "Underworlds and Underdogs: Big Tim Sullivan and Metropolitan Politics in New York, 1889–1913," *Journal of American History* 78 (September 1991): 536–58.

15. *New York Times,* December 4, 1907; *New York World,* Dec. 4, 8, 1907.

16. *New York Evening Journal,* December 8, 1907; *New York World,* December 8, 1907; *New York Tribune,* December 9, 1907. On the so-called Doull ordinance, see *New York Times,* December 18, 19, 20, 1907; and *New York World,* December 18, 19, 1907.

17. For background on William Fox, see Neal Gabler, *An Empire of Their Own: How the Jews Invented Hollywood* (New York, 1988), 64–72; and the less reliable Glendon Allvine, *The Greatest Fox of Them All* (New York, 1967), 37–52. On Gustavus Rogers, see *Tammany Times,* February 3, 1902, and December 26, 1903; and *New York Times,* March 20, 1944. See also Czitrom, "Underworlds and Underdogs." Another close associate of Fox was Winfield R. Sheehan, who in 1912 left his job as secretary to New York Police Commissioner Rhinelander Waldo and went on to become a key executive at Fox Film Corporation in Hollywood.

18. *New York Times,* December 7, 1907; *New York Tribune,* December 9, 1907.

19. "Sunday in New York," *Moving Picture World,* January 4, 1908, 7. See also "Trade Notes," *Moving Picture World,* December 28, 1908, 703–4. In an appellate court decision upholding Greenbaum's decision, Justice William Gaynor, soon to be New York's mayor, wrote, "'the composite Christian mind' of the State nowhere gave evidence of a demand for a 'still' Sabbath" (*New York Times,* August 1, 1908).

20. "Dewey Theater," *Variety,* December 19, 1908, 13; "Kraus' New York Houses Desert Western Wheel," *Variety,* July 11, 1908, 7; "Trade Notes," *Moving Picture World,* February 1, 1908, 76, May 9, 1908, 4, and June 20, 1908, 527.

21. See Allen, *Vaudeville and Film,* 310–34, for a good summary of the importance of "small time." For an illustration of the workings of two such theaters, see Charles F. Morris, "A Pair of New York's Picture Theaters," *Nickelodeon,* March 15, 1910, 141–42.

22. Lavelle quoted in Theodore Bingham to George B. McClellan, Jr., June 25, 1908, MP, MGB-52.

23. For an analysis that sees the conflict over exhibition practices as "testifying to the potential of the cinema as an alternative public sphere," see Miriam Hansen, *Babel and Babylon: Spectatorship in American Silent Film* (Cambridge, Mass., 1991), 90–125.

24. [John Collier], "Cheap Amusement Shows in Manhattan: Preliminary Report of Investigation," January 31, 1908, in Subjects Papers, Records of the National Board of Review of Motion Pictures, Rare Books and Manuscripts Division, New York Public Library (hereafter cited as NBR Papers), 2, 3.

25. Ibid. See also John Collier, "Cheap Amusements," *Survey* 20 (April 11, 1908): 75–76, and "Woman's League Investigates," *Moving Picture World,* February 22, 1908, 137; and *New York Tribune,* February 10, 1908. For background on Collier, who went on to become the controversial architect of Indian policy during the New Deal, see his memoir, *From Every Zenith* (Denver, 1963); and Kenneth R. Philp, *John Collier's Crusade for Indian Reform, 1920–1954* (Tucson, 1977), 4–19.

26. All the films discussed in this section were viewed at the Paper Print Collection, Library of Congress. For background on the sources of early story film form and content, see Tom Gunning, "The Non-Continuous Style of Early Film," and John Hagan, "Erotic Tendencies in Film, 1900–1906," both in *Cinema 1900/1906: An Analytical Study,* comp. Roger Holman (Brussels, 1982), 219–29, 231–38; John L. Fell, "Motive, Mischief, and Melodrama: The State of Film Narrative in 1907," in Fell, *Film before Griffith,* 272–83; John L. Fell, "Dissolves by Gaslight: Antecedents to the Motion Picture in Nineteenth-Century Melodrama," *Film Quarterly* 23 (spring 1970): 22–34; and Jeanne Thomas Allen, "Copyright and Early Theater, Vaudeville, and Film Competition," in Fell, *Film before Griffith,* 176–87.

27. See, for example, "The Open Grating," in *Tenderloin,* November 19, 1898; and "Playful Pranks of March Breezes," the *Police Gazette,* reprinted in Edward Van Every, ed., *Sins of New York* (New York, 1930), 130; *Edison Films,* September 1902, 36. For a feminist reading of *What Happened on Twenty-third Street* ("a story whose punchline is the sight of the female body caught unaware"), see Judith Mayne, "Uncovering the Female Body," in Leyda and Musser, *Before Hollywood,* 63–67.

28. For a variant on this theme from the 1880s, see "Golly, Missey, Biz is Gettin' Good," *Police Gazette,* in Van Every, *Sins of New York,* 292.

29. Two virtual duplicates of this film were also produced in 1904: *How a French Nobleman Got a Wife through the New York Herald Personal Column* (Edison) and *Meet Me at the Fountain* (Lubin).

30. For the advertising of this film, which remained popular for several years, see *Biograph Bulletin* 9 (August 29, 1903) and 55 (November 27, 1905). These are reprinted in Kemp R. Niver, comp., *Biograph Bulletins, 1896–1908* (Los Angeles, 1971).

31. A very similar story was told in *The Tenderloin at Night* (Edison, 1899).

32. For similar burlesques of clerical and police authority, but with less logical

narrative lines, see, for example, *In a Raines Law Hotel* (Biograph, 1905) and *Soubrettes in a Bachelor's Flat* (Biograph, 1903).

33. *Biograph Bulletin* 55 (November 27, 1905) and 157 (July 31, 1908). See also, for example, *Rube Brown in Town* (Biograph, 1907) and *The Heathen Chinese and the Sunday School Teachers* (Biograph, 1904).

34. On the Bureau of Licenses scandal, see Office of the Commissioners of Accounts, "Charges of Incompetency and Misconduct," November 4, 1908, MP, MGB-120, and Affidavit of Roger DiPasca, May 25, 1908, MP, MGB-41; *New York Times,* October 13, 1908; and *Motion Picture World,* October 10, 1908. For background on McClellan's career and his split with Tammany, see Syrett, *Gentleman,* 9–39, 199–243; and Theodore J. Lowi, *At the Pleasure of the Mayor: Patronage and Power in New York City, 1898–1958* (Glencoe, Ill., 1964), 88–92.

35. The connection between McClellan's Princeton aspirations and his policy toward movies is related by Frank Moss in the Executive Committee Minutes, May 17, 1909, Society for the Prevention of Crime Papers, Columbia University. On the anti-movie activities of the Interdenominational Committee for the Suppression of Sunday Vaudeville, see *New York Times,* December 1, 3, 21, 1908.

36. Foster quoted in *New York Times,* December 24, 1908; all other quotes from Transcript of Hearing in Mayor's Office (fragment), December 23, 1908, MP, MGB-51.

37. *New York Times,* December 25, 1908.

38. Francis Oppenheimer, "New York City's Censorship of Plays," *The Theatre* 8 (May 1908): 135. The printed evaluation forms filled out by institute theater censors closely resembled those later used for movies. On the MPEA request of the People's Institute, see John Collier to Gustavus Rogers, March 1, 1909, Subjects Papers, NBR Papers.

39. Circular letter, John Collier to Manufacturers of Motion Pictures, March 15, 1909, Document File, Motion Pictures, Edison Archives, Edison Historic National Site, West Orange, N.J. (hereafter cited as Edison Archives). On the first day of the Board of Censorship, see *New York World,* March 26, 1909; and *New York Times,* March 26, 1909.

40. Frank L. Dyer to John Collier, May 7, 1909, Edison Archives. See also "Passed by the National Board of Censorship," *Review of Reviews* 50 (December 1914): 730–31; and John Collier, "Censorship and the National Board," *Survey* 35 (October 2, 1915): 9, 73. On the Motion Picture Patents Company, see Robert Jack Anderson, "The Motion Picture Patents Company" (Ph.D. diss., University of Wisconsin, 1983); and Ralph Cassady, Jr., "Monopoly in Motion Picture Production and Distribution: 1908–1915," *Southern California Law Review* 32 (summer 1959): 325–90.

41. Nancy J. Rosenbloom, "Between Reform and Regulation: The Struggle over Film Censorship in Progressive America, 1909–1922," *Film History* 1 (1987): 308; *The Standards of the National Board of Censorship* (New York, 1914), 3, 5; Motion Picture Patents Company (H. N. M.) to National Board of Censorship, November 16, 1911, box 6, Correspondence with Film Companies, NBR Papers. Rosenbloom offers the best account of the NBC, with especially good material on its relationship to Progressive politics. See also Daniel Czitrom, "The Redemption of Leisure: The National Board of Censorship and the Rise of Motion Pictures in New York City, 1900–1920," *Studies in Visual Communication* 10 (fall 1984): 2–6; and Robert J. Fisher, "Film

Censorship and Progressive Reform: The National Board of Censorship of Motion Pictures, 1909–1922," *Journal of Popular Film* 4 (1975): 143–56. On the day-to-day work of the NBC, see Charles W. Tevis, "Censoring the Five Cent Drama, *World Today* 19 (October 1910): 1132–39; and National Board of Censorship Reports, 1909–11, in Document File, Edison Archives.

42. John Collier to Robert B. Adams, May 6, 1909, Document File, Edison Archives.

43. Thomas D. Walsh, superintendent of the Society for the Prevention of Cruelty to Children, quoted in *New York Times,* August 2, 1911. See also *New York Times,* March 14, 16, 1911, and March 30, 1913. Between 1909 and 1913 the SPCC prosecuted 114 people in the courts for alleged crimes against children in movie houses.

44. Gaynor quoted in *New York Times,* January 1, 1913. On the political battle over reforming the city's movie theater regulations, see *New York Times,* August 2, 1911; November 8, 29, 1911; and December 17, 18, 31, 1912. See also W. Stephen Bush, "Mayor Gaynor on Censorship," *Moving Picture World,* January 11, 1913, 134–36; and Rosenbloom, "Between Reform and Regulation," 313–14.

45. National Board of Censorship, *Suggestions for a Model Ordinance for Regulating Motion Picture Theatres* (New York, 1915), 6. See also Sonya Levien, "New York's Motion Picture Law," *American City* 9 (October 1913): 319–21; and John Collier, "'Movies' and the Law," *Survey* 27 (January 20, 1912): 1628–29. For an account of a nickelodeon fire on Houston Street that killed two and injured twenty, see *New York Times,* February 3, 1913. The new law's provisions were first laid out in Fosdick, "Report on Moving Picture Shows."

46. Rosenbloom, "Between Reform and Regulation," 315–22, documents the NBC's fight against legal censorship and the decline of its influence. On the NBR's persistent but losing effort to maintain its influence within the Hollywood film community, see the correspondence of W. D. McGuire, executive secretary of the National Board of Review, 1916–1923, in Correspondence with Film Companies, boxes 6, 7, NBR Papers.

Passions and the Passion Play

Theater, Film, and Religion in America, 1880–1900

CHARLES MUSSER

In September 1880 theatrical impresario Henry E. Abbey announced plans to produce a passion play at Booth's Theater in New York City. Abbey soon faced organized protests by outraged clergy, opposition from influential members of the theatrical community itself, and a threat by city officials to close down his playhouse. On Saturday, November 27, after more than two months of controversy and less than two weeks before its scheduled premiere, Abbey canceled the production.[1] Yet scarcely a few days after this reputed sacrilege was to have opened, lecturer John L. Stoddard gave a lantern-slide exhibition entitled *Oberammergau's Passion Play*, including fifty slides of the famed passion play, which had been produced in Bavaria that summer. Clergy attended in substantial numbers, and the evening's program, repeated often in other cities, helped to make Stoddard the foremost travel lecturer of his day. This paradoxical juxtaposition was only one of several twists in the history of the passion play as presented in the United States between approximately 1880 and 1900. The very intensity with which Protestant clergy and established arbiters of American culture favored certain types of presentations while opposing others suggests that dearly held values were at stake in these representations. A look at struggles over representation in the 1880s and 1890s may therefore provide a significant backdrop for the "culture wars" that have recurred throughout the twentieth century.[2]

The story of Christ's sufferings from the Last Supper through his death provided nineteenth-century exhibitors in the United States with one of their most vibrant genres.[3] Although the passion play originated and has endured as a drama, it was rarely staged as a theatrical performance. While Abbey's misfortune was enough to deter other theatrical producers over the next two decades, nonprofessionals and immigrant groups—often with the support or sponsorship of the Catholic Church—made repeated efforts to stage some version of the Passion, all of which encountered strong opposition. The passion play flourished instead within the framework of screen entertainment, where the absence of the actors' physical presence and the lantern's long-standing educational associations provided crucial distinctions that authorized these representations. This careful delineation between stage and screen operated implicitly before 1880 and explicitly for more than fifteen years following the Abbey debacle. The incorporation of motion pictures into screen practice after 1895, however, quickly destabilized this status quo.

The passion play provides a starting point for exploring the dynamic interrelationship between two cultural practices—the theater and the screen—that remained vital far into the twentieth century. The comparison between theater and film was, in fact, a focus of theoretical exploration throughout cinema's silent period and beyond. In *The Photoplay: A Psychological Study* (1916), Hugo Münsterberg systematically contrasted the two from functional and aesthetic perspectives. By recording a performance and showing multiple copies of it repeatedly, Münsterberg believed, film might democratize the theater by increasing access to the show. On the other hand, motion pictures were "surely only the shadow of a true theater, different not only as a photograph is compared with a painting, but different as a photograph is compared with the original man."[4] This quality of removal, also known as the "absence of presence," was the necessary starting point for Münsterberg, as it would be into the 1950s for film theorists such as André Bazin and others. Yet Münsterberg appreciated the many new features cinema had introduced (close-ups, editing, and so forth) and concluded that the photoplay had to be seen as an artistic practice in its own terms.[5]

In turn-of-the-century America, film seemed to many Christians to possess an ambiguous power. On the one hand, it might demolish the sacred authority of cherished stories and rituals. On the other, it might become a new way to proselytize the religiously uncommitted. Which forms of performance were both effective and acceptable to the faithful? This question was frequently and urgently asked by religious and other educated folk, not only about screen and stage performances, but also about literature, which occupied a middle ground between the "educational" devices such as the magic-lantern show and stereopticon, and the stage, which was frequently seen as a force for sensuality and sin.

In the realm of book publishing, biblical fiction was a relatively recent and still developing phenomenon. American writers and publishers avoided focusing their biblical fiction on Christ because such a product could be seen as a challenge to the Bible's authority and ran the risk of being condemned as sacrilegious.[6] Novelists and commercial publishers only began to offer creative recountings of Bible stories after about 1830, and it was not until 1880, with the publication of Lew Wallace's *Ben Hur: A Tale of Christ,* that such a story became a bestseller. As David S. Reynolds has pointed out, Wallace dared not focus on the story of Christ—despite the subtitle of his book—but concentrated instead on the clash between the Jewish hero Ben Hur and the Roman Messala.[7]

This world of late nineteenth-century public culture was strongly shaped by two Protestant groups, whose interests sometimes, though not always, coincided. Well-to-do members of mainstream Protestant denominations held generally liberal views and dominated genteel culture in the United States; in contrast, most Methodists and Baptists, along with a broad range of other evangelical Americans—who would eventually be styled "fundamentalists"— were suspicious of many forms of public culture, particularly theater, dancing, horse racing, cardplaying, and drinking. Remaining distant from many aspects of genteel culture, these evangelical groups directed most of their energy to opposing the vibrant commercial popular culture that seemed to threaten the orderly, austere values that had shaped their lives, their congregations, and their communities. Both groups were increasingly confronted by the rise of the large, impersonal city, with its increasingly alien religious and ethnocultural practices. In response, these groups sought to control the production and distribution of culture through organizations such as the YMCA and the New York Society for the Suppression of Vice as well as through the continued application of informal rules and prohibitions by book editors, authors, theatrical producers, and newspaper publishers.[8]

Although these efforts to determine the terms of representation generally centered on the depiction of crime and licentious activities, one area of great sensitivity, in which the Protestant evangelicals were particularly influential, involved depictions of religious subjects, especially the life of Christ. By the early 1900s some Protestant clergy were beginning to advocate the theatrical depiction of the Christ story. Evolutionary models of explanation do not adequately account for this shift towards liberalization. Rather, the introduction of a new medium—viz., the motion picture—and the resulting transformation of existing cultural practices disrupted a system that cultural arbiters had sought to portray as stable. In this regard, motion pictures occupied a cultural ground between the stage and the lantern show, between the theatrical and the educational.[9] Aligned alternately with one cultural practice and then the other, and buttressed by its own positive associations with science and technology, the cinema not only broke down but ultimately redefined the lines of acceptable representation for screen *and* stage.[10]

Exhibitions that recount the life of Christ go back to the earliest stages of screen practice, to the 1640s and 1650s, when Athanasius Kircher and his contemporaries first used projected images as a form of cultural enlightenment.[11] The Christ story continued to be a popular subject for magic-lantern shows in Europe and the United States. During the mid- and late nineteenth century, Protestant groups often sponsored lantern programs of religious subjects for presentation in their churches. Beginning around 1870, even after photographic lantern slides had become common, images were typically based on, if not actually taken from, religious paintings. In 1883 James W. Queen and Company offered seventy-one slides based on biblical paintings such as Leonardo da Vinci's *The Last Supper* and Benjamin West's *Christ Healing the Sick*.[12] In the 1890s the Riley Brothers sold sets of slides for programs of this type: *The Life of Christ* (950 slides) and *The Passion of Our Lord* (34 slides).[13] In these instances, the lantern-slide lecture was closely associated with the illustrated Bible.[14] The use of painting rather than staged scenes using "life models" added an important level of mediation and distancing between the story and its representation: no individual assumed the role of Christ. When photographic techniques were used, travel lectures proved a popular way of presenting on the screen the story of Christ's final days. During the Civil War, an evening program at the First Baptist Church in Brooklyn consisted largely of "a gigantic series of illuminated New and Old Testament views with a TOUR IN THE HOLY LAND, portrayed with a POWERFUL CALCIUM LIGHT."[15] An early example of the linking of travel and tourism with religion, the magic lantern enabled spectators to take a vicarious pilgrimage to the Holy Land. Before long, the projected image, like the illustrated Bible, had become a conventional way to tell the story of Christ.

Putting the passion play on the stage, in contrast, encountered strong resistance that was rooted in long-standing religious opposition to theater of any kind. In the mid-eighteenth century, theatrical presentations were forbidden in every colony except Virginia and Maryland.[16] By the nineteenth century, many of these prohibitions had given way, but tension between the amusement industry and the religious community remained.[17] If what Jonas Barish has called the "anti-theatrical prejudice" was on the wane in the late nineteenth century,[18] many evangelical Protestants saw resistance to live performances of the Passion as a last stand. To let the passion play on the boards was to accept defeat in the battle against the sinful stage. Moreover, some Protestants viewed acceptance of the passion play as a victory for rival Catholicism, for Catholics often reenacted the Passion, preferring such staging to the illustrated lectures that found favor among Protestants.[19] Since, as Alan Nielsen and others have pointed out, the late nineteenth-century American working class was becoming increasingly Catholic, while social elites were concentrated among the Protestant denominations, religious and class conflict became intertwined in controversies over the representation of the Passion.[20]

In early 1879 Thomas Maguire, manager of San Francisco's Grand Opera House, announced that Salmi Morse's *The Passion: A Miracle Play in Ten Acts* would be presented as a special event for the coming Lenten season.[21] Morse (1826–84), also known by his given name of Samuel Moss, was a German Jew who converted to Christianity in the 1850s. A self-styled businessman and entrepreneur, Morse had developed strong ties to San Francisco's theatrical community in the late 1870s.[22] In an effort to win support for his play from the religious groups, Morse had provided a private reading for San Francisco clergy. Representatives of the Catholic Church attended and offered their enthusiastic support. The Most Reverend Joseph S. Alemany, Archbishop of California, not only sanctioned the script but "inserted several passages into the text with his own sacerdotal hand."[23] Protestant ministers, however, refused to attend the event and thus set the terms and framework for a subsequent confrontation. The local press became a battleground for differing viewpoints. Though the *San Francisco Chronicle* made some effort to emphasize the reverent nature of the production by citing Morse's extensive study of the miracle plays, it quickly characterized the undertaking as a sacrilege that had "shocked the sensibilities of every citizen who reverences the religion which, under various forms, we all profess to respect."[24] In successive articles the newspaper compared the Morse play to others in medieval England and to the passion play of Oberammergau in Bavaria and found it woefully lacking.[25]

Two groups of Protestant ministers—a general meeting of the Protestant Episcopal Church and the Ministerial Union—met and passed resolutions that condemned the "outrage," urging members and all good citizens not to attend. City supervisors James O. Roundtree and E. Danforth met with manager

Maguire, asking him to cancel the performance. When that failed, they pressured the city government to ban Morse's passion play. On the day the play was scheduled to open, the Board of Supervisors met and unanimously passed a resolution requesting the district attorney to suppress the production "or any other play illustrative of scriptural subjects or characters, the same being subversive of good morals and an outrage upon religion, making it subject to ridicule and contempt."[26] Roundtree also introduced a bill making it a misdemeanor to exhibit "any play, performance and or representation, displaying or intending to display, the life and death of Jesus Christ . . . or tending to profane or degrade religion."[27]

Despite strong protest, the Morse play debuted before a large audience on March 3, 1879. James O'Neill, father of Eugene O'Neill, played Christ; David Belasco supervised the production. As Belasco later recalled it,

> The entire performance was given with a simplicity that amounted to grandeur. All was accomplished by fabrics and lighting, and when O'Neill came up from his dressing room and appeared on the stage with a halo about him women sank on their knees and prayed, and when he was stripped and dragged before *Pontius Pilate,* crowned with a crown of thorns, many fainted.
>
> I have produced many plays in many parts of the world, but never have I seen an audience awed as by "The Passion play." The greatest performance of a generation was the *Christus* of James O'Neill.[28]

Maguire, Belasco, and O'Neill initially presented an abridged version that included only the first six acts, narrating Christ's life up until the eve of his crucifixion. The last four acts, which depicted the crucifixion, resurrection, and ascension, were omitted in anticipation of strong opposition from Protestant groups,[29] and the performance ended with Christ being turned over to Pontius Pilate. On the drop curtain, however, was painted "a distant view of Calvary, with the three crosses in relief against a lurid sky."[30] The crucifixion was thus the culminating moment to which each scene pointed.

Despite the objections of some Protestant clergy, "The Passion Play" opened to mixed though appreciative reviews. The *San Francisco Examiner* offered the sharpest criticism, declaring that Morse's prose "scarcely rises once above the dead level of puerile bombast" and comparing it unfavorably to the New Testament—"one of the finest and most lasting instances of the power and beauty of our language." The review nonetheless concluded, "We can truthfully say that in the manner in which [the passion play] was performed last night at the Grand Opera House, there was nothing, in our opinion[,] to shock the religious feeling of any one but the most bigoted of Christians."[31] The *San*

Francisco Chronicle, which had denounced the production before it opened, admitted, "The leading characters were admirably portrayed. . . . The scenery was artistic and the groupings very elaborate, and the entire production was worthy of great praise, especially the music, that with its beautiful chants and choruses imparted so sacred a character to this, the first production of The Passion Play."[32] However, the *Chronicle's* reviewer concluded, "It cannot be accepted that a theater is the proper place for a Passion Play."[33]

The *Chronicle* offered a revised and more supportive perspective on the play in the week following its premiere. "Let us enter without prejudice and judge for ourselves whether or not we are benefitted by a representation of this character," the paper's critic suggested. On the night he attended, the audience was composed of "curious people, reverent people and irreverent people." A slight tendency to levity, coming from the gallery, faded as spectators became "solemn witnesses of a solemn tragedy presented with the utmost solemnity." The scene in which Christ appears and teaches his disciples by the brook of Cedron provided "a lesson of wisdom and of love. It is an assumption of such sweet humility that the divine humanity of the master commands the almost reverential attention of the audience." The reviewer concluded, "We have heard him deliver the word of life more impressively than it has ever been our lot to hear it delivered from the pulpit."[34] Predictably, the column elicited an angry response from a Congregationalist journal, which accused the *Chronicle* of furthering a "Romish" conspiracy.[35] However, in the end, the play proved a commercial and critical success, and its run was extended.[36]

The Passion Play closed after a two-week run and reopened on the Tuesday of Holy Week, April 15. Accompanied by 120 choristers and forty instrumentalists, it now featured eight of the ten scenes in Morse's original play script, including "The Descent from the Cross" and "The Ascension" but still omitting "The Crucifixion."[37] This time the city government was ready to intervene, and on April 16 the police arrested O'Neill for personating Christ. Fined fifty dollars, Morse and O'Neill appealed to the municipal court, claiming the ordinance was illegal and void. On April 21 the court convicted Morse, O'Neill, and various theatrical personnel associated with the play. O'Neill was forced to pay his fifty-dollar fine, while the others were fined five dollars.[38] The play closed less than a week after its revival. Either during the run or shortly after its forced closing, the play script was published by a San Francisco printer, Edward Bosqui & Co. In printed form it apparently aroused little controversy.

Although the San Francisco production had met with only mixed success— but plenty of publicity—Henry E. Abbey decided to back a New York production of Salmi Morse's play. Abbey later explained, "I was so impressed by the subject and treatment by him that I signed a contract for its production at Booth's under his personal supervision."[39] O'Neill was again cast as Christ, while Belasco chose to avoid further involvement. To defuse anticipated opposition, Abbey planned to forego the crucifixion scene and forbid applause during the performance.[40] When Abbey announced his future production in September 1880, opposition from religious groups and the press surfaced immediately. Within a week, the *New York Herald* and the *New York Sun* had condemned the project in the strongest terms.[41]

One perhaps unexpected opponent of the Morse play was Harrison Grey Fiske, editor of the nation's leading theatrical journal, the *New York Dramatic Mirror.* He wrote:

> The question that interests the dramatic profession with reference to this matter is this: will its production in New York and other cities cast discredit upon the stage, and still further strengthen or revive the prejudices that exist or existed in the theater? Should this be the case, *The Mirror* would most decidedly take a stand against the proposal and beg Mr. Abbey to reconsider his intention before it be too late.[42]

By querying various ministers and church officials, Fiske quickly established that opposition to the approaching performance was indeed broad and strongly felt. Thereafter, he joined those demanding that the production be canceled, using the pages of his trade paper to elicit and reprint numerous pages of impassioned opinions. Fiske was convinced that the antitheatrical prejudice that remained strongly rooted in Protestant thought and doctrine would be reenergized around this issue. The theatrical community's long struggle toward respectability would then suffer a serious reversal. By throwing his weight, and that of actors and other theatrical figures, against Abbey's production, Fiske hoped to avoid a war between the theatrical and religious communities. Ultimately, his concern was for the reputation of the theater, or in blunt terms, its profits.

Several arguments against the staging of the Salmi Morse passion play appear in the *Dramatic Mirror*'s interviews with ministers and in reprinted editorials. Perhaps the most insistent point made by the critics concerned the incompatibility of religious and commercial values. The theatrical community, it was felt, should not make money from religion's most sacred story. A priest at the Greek-Russian Chapel in New York City contended the Morse production "seems to me a different thing from the Ober-Ammergau play. As given by the peasantry it is not a money making affair[;] here[,] it is."[43] Others noted that the theater would inevitably sensationalize the passion play, if only by virtue of the profane context of the performance.[44] As one commentator suggested, "The Oberammergau performance is softened and sanctified by the associations of time, the conditions under which it was instituted, and the simple and innocent piety of the people from whom the performers are selected. To transplant such a representation away from its surroundings is to denude it of all that can make it acceptable to the public mind, and bring out its sacrilegious elements in the strongest colors."[45] And the *New York Herald* editorialized, "The Passion Play in New York would have around it the sanction of no religious feeling, nor would it be part of religious ceremony. The actors would go into their work with the same feeling with which they would perform Jack Sheppard or Toodles or Robert Macaire. . . . For sheer gain it is proposed to bring the holiest episode of our civilization down to the level of a negro minstrel show."[46] The very act of attempting to reenact or depict Christ and his suffering, according to critics, was sacrilegious; for an actor to play the son of God was blasphemous. Rev. Dr. John Phillip Newman, pastor of the Central Methodist Church, asserted: "The last request of the Redeemer to His people was to remember his death and not to reenact it; to cherish His memory, and not to perpetuate the triumph of his foes."[47]

With the exception of one rabbi's charge that the play would "stir up the embers of religious hate,"[48] most of the arguments against Morse's play refined seventeenth-century polemics that the Puritans had made against the theater in general.[49] Abbey tried to counter these charges in various ways, announcing his intention to donate the profits to charity and not to publicize the names of performers. Such efforts only became the source of further ridicule, proof that even Abbey knew the project was suspect.

Fiske and the *Dramatic Mirror* drafted a petition asking the Board of Aldermen to enact a law making it illegal "for any person to exhibit or take part in exhibiting in any theater or other place where money is charged for admittance, any play, performance, or representation displaying, or tending to display, the life and death of Jesus Christ, or any play, or performance or representation calculated or tending to profane or degrade religion."[50] The petition was signed by church officials of diverse affiliations and by people from the business, professional, and theatrical communities. As editorials and protests proliferated, the Board of Aldermen voted, with only one dissenter, to do everything possible to ban the production.[51] The Baptist Ministers Conference, noting the general outcry among Protestant leaders, condemned the "sacrilegious use of the most sacred things of our religion."[52]

Abbey and Morse undoubtedly hoped to wait out the storm of protest, as Maguire had done in San Francisco. Finally, on the Saturday before its scheduled opening, Abbey withdrew the play. Ministers quickly altered their sermons to reflect the new situation. Reverend Newman reiterated "the impossibility of an actor projecting himself into the character of Christ according to the requirements of his art." Newman praised the many newspapers, community leaders, and even the "best" theatrical managers and actors, whose opposition prevented the play from being produced.[53]

In a desperate and final effort to turn the tide, Morse gave a reading of his play, accompanied by especially arranged music, before 100 people at Cooper Union on December 3. The *New York Times* reprinted portions of the text, praised the music, found the playwright to be of reverential spirit, and then called it a "painful burlesque of sacred mysteries":[54] "In Justice to him it should be said that he treats his theme in a perfectly reverential spirit. The objection to the Passion Play is not to its sentiments, but to the outrage to Christianity which any stage treatment of the agony of Christ is calculated to produce."[55] Ending on such a note of defeat and disillusionment, the fiasco of Morse's passion play remained indelibly imprinted on the memory of every amusement entrepreneur in the United States for years to come.

While Americans from New York to California debated and decried the staging of the Passion in the United States, new attention turned to comparisons with the renowned passion play mounted every decade in the Bavarian village of Oberammergau. The 1880 production won a highly favorable reception from a wide range of American religious and cultural groups. The *New York Times,* for example, ran a half-dozen enthusiastic articles focusing on the event.[56] Moreover, according to one observer, American and English tourists made up the majority of patrons for the passion play itself.[57] The American tourists undoubtably came from the wealthier, more liberal Protestant denominations rather than from the more strenuously evangelical ones, a fact that helps to explain the travelers' enthusiasm for the performance. Moreover, a range of other factors may explain the favorable response of ministers and other Protestant observers to the spectacle: the oft-cited simplicity and devotion of the Oberammergau peasants; the traditional, church-sponsored nature of the production; and perhaps the unstated fact that the ritual was performed on distant soil, away from the culture wars back in the United States.

Americans lauded the Oberammergau performance most strikingly for the detailed realism of the crucifixion scene. As reported in the *New York Times,*

> The scene was very effective and beautiful, and was performed in a really wonderful manner. The audience was almost breathless with the seeming reality of the representation. The figure looked as if it was actually nailed on the cross.

Blood was on both hands and feet, and even with a good opera glass one could not possibly detect how Josef Maier could remain so long in this position. The crucifixion scene lasted 21 minutes, and was carried out in every detail, even to the piercing of the breast with a spear, blood rushing out of the wound.[58]

The very scene that had aroused the most controversy and had been consistently excluded from the San Francisco performance was, under different circumstances, hailed as the high point of the drama.

Despite Morse's failure, entrepreneurs did not stop trying to capitalize on the appeal to American audiences of the Bavarian spectacle. In 1880 John L. Stoddard mounted an illustrated travelogue entitled *Ober-Ammergau's Passion Play,* which proved especially successful. Paradoxically, Stoddard's show opened in the same city as Morse's aborted drama and only four days after its scheduled premiere.[59] A version of this lecture with its accompanying illustrations was subsequently published in book form. Stoddard began his exhibition with brief introductory remarks, noting,

> I hardly need add that the so-called "Passion Play," which, in obedience to public sentiments, has been recently withdrawn from the New York stage, has nothing whatever to do with this Play at Ober-Ammergau. That was a purely modern drama written by Mr. Salmi Morse, and possessing neither the music nor the text of the Bavarian play, nor even the arrangement of its parts, while it was of course wholly lacking in its remarkable religious traditions and historical associations.[60]

The illustrated portion of Stoddard's lecture began with a slide of the railway leading into Oberammergau. Taking his audience on a tour of the village and introducing the principal actors going about their everyday lives, he argued that these villagers were not rude peasants but primitive artists. Joseph Maier, who played Christ, was a woodcarver by trade, a deeply sincere and religious person:

> I can truly say that I never saw a man more unaffectedly modest and simple than Joseph Maier. The secret is, that he is *thoroughly sincere.* There is no doubt of this. It is not only the greatest conceivable honor of his life to represent the character of Jesus, it is also *the most solemn of all religious duties;* and this exalted thought keeps him above the taint of vanity.[61]

Stoddard disputed unfavorable reports of Maier's private life (which accused him of excessive beer drinking) that appeared in New York papers, concluding his defense with an account of Maier returning from the play to embrace his young children.[62] Although Catholic, Maier and other villagers were portrayed as pre-Reformation folk whose timeless simplicity endowed them with a native capacity to commune directly with God.

After establishing the milieu from which the play sprang, Stoddard showed fifty stereopticon slides of the performance, providing a detailed account of the drama's progress.[63] At its high point, as Christ dies on the cross, Stoddard dissolved from one lantern slide to the next. The two slides gave an illusion of movement as Christ's head dropped to his breast.[64] At this moment Stoddard narrated the following words: "Finally it is evident that the end draws near. With a loud voice he cries at last: 'Father, into thy hands I commend my spirit.' The head droops wearily upon his breast. It is finished."[65] Coming at the moment of greatest realism and emotion in the play, Stoddard's brilliant visual effect heightened the drama in a way that some might have considered sensational. Stoddard had taken the bold step of showing a photographic representation of a man playing Christ. This move constituted a potentially hazardous departure from earlier lantern shows of the passion, which relied on paintings, for in those, no one could be said to be playing the role of Jesus. But Stoddard's lecture was widely praised and significantly enhanced his reputation. What accounts for his success, in contrast to Morse's failure, in winning over respectable opinion?

In promoting his production, Stoddard constantly emphasized the ways in which the arguments used against the Morse play did not apply to his visual record of the one in Oberammergau. As a traveler-observer-lecturer, Stoddard maintained a degree of distance that allowed him to claim objectivity; that is, without any claims to personal authorship of the play or performance (the case with Abbey and Morse), he was able to disassociate himself from the theatrical presentation itself. By emphasizing the uniquely devout and traditional character of the Bavarian performance, moreover, he disarmed those who might have sought to discredit it as a mere stage play. In the end, these arguments permitted people who had objected so strenuously to the Salmi Morse play to attend and approve Stoddard's program.

Stoddard returned to Oberammergau in 1890 to produce a second evening-length documentary on the subject. As in 1880, he emphasized, "In any other place the Passion Play would be offensive. Like a wild mountain flower, it would not bear transplanting to another soil."[66] Like his 1880 production, the new one took the form of a first-person narrative tracing Stoddard's journey to the town, this time including his reflections on the changes that had occurred in the intervening ten years.[67] Stoddard also introduced a new character to the narrative, his photographer, cast as an uninitiated companion, whose skepticism about the propriety of the show allows Stoddard to reiterate many of the now-familiar arguments in its defense. Gradually, Stoddard's skeptical companion is won over and convinced of the unique qualities of the villagers and their play. In the 1890 production, Stoddard made good use of photographs of hundreds of choristers and actors in impressive tableaux. But, even more than its predecessor, the new production made Maier, the portrayer of Christ, the star of the show. In his narration, Stoddard assesses at length the personal qualities of the man who plays Christ, defending him against his critics and concluding that he is "a thoroughly refined, modest, sensitive man, pure and blameless in life, unselfish, and devoted to his family."[68] Analyzing a scene of Christ in the temple, he lingers on the actor's performance: "Advancing slowly, and with an indescribable mien of sadness and majesty, he pushes aside the tables, not in hasty anger, but rather as though their presence were pollution."[69] As the show ends, Stoddard concludes, "To-day, although four thousand miles from that idyllic village on the heights, its influence is with me still, and even now, whenever I recall those gentle features [of Maier, playing Christ], I feel as if some spirit from a better world were breathing on my soul its benediction."[70]

In addition to bringing out the star quality of his leading player, Stoddard introduced a new note of self-conscious playfulness into the 1890 production. On their way through the village, for example, the two travelers are shown meeting one of the "characters" in the play—a horse that will be ridden by a Roman centurion. Journeying farther, they encounter more articulate actors, as well:

> I made a sign to my photographer, and pulled the driver's coat-tail, as a hint
> for him to stop. The youth approached. His face was an agreeable one. His hair
> parted in the middle and fell to the right and left upon his shoulders.
>
> "Pardon me," said one of our party, "but I am told that you will assume this
> year the part of St. John."
>
> "Yes," he replied, his face flush with pleasure.
>
> "But," I continued, "the programme states that your name is Rendl. Are
> you the son of Thomas Rendl, who acted the part of Pilate so admirably ten
> years ago?"
>
> "I am," was the reply; "and he will personate that character again this season."
>
> "Some of us had the pleasure of meeting your father in 1880," I rejoined, "and,
> if agreeable, we should like to call on him to-morrow."

Meantime I glanced inquiringly at the photographer.

"All right," he murmured.

This signified that "St John's" portrait had been taken unawares, and in a moment more we were driving on.[71]

The portrait, posed informally, but hardly caught "unawares," was shown as part of the illustrated lecture.

Stoddard retired after the 1896–97 season and designated E. Burton Holmes his successor. Holmes attended Oberammergau's passion play every ten years and each time used it as the basis for a new lecture on the subject. Stoddard's many genteel followers accepted the designate, although they were well aware of the many differences in style between the two. Holmes—the son of a banker—was less verbally sophisticated and intellectual, but his images were more plentiful and stylistically varied. Moreover, he took his own photographs and in 1897 acquired a 60 mm Gaumont motion picture camera, which his lantern operator, Oscar Depue, used to take films. Holmes and Depue attended the 1900 Oberammergau performance, where they shot still and motion pictures of the townspeople and periodically appeared in these images themselves.[72] Like other exhibitors, Holmes was not allowed to photograph or film the play but purchased official lantern slides of the performance.

Stoddard and Holmes demonstrated ways in which the life of Christ could be successfully presented within the travelogue genre, as a documentary account of a sacred performance. Many of the same objections raised against the Morse passion play could have been applied to these documentaries: Stoddard's lectures were delivered for money, in a profane space, and without religious sponsorship. By dwelling on the crucifixion, Stoddard could have been accused of inciting religious hatred or unnecessarily upsetting his audience. Yet even his 1880 lectures proceeded without protest and were heavily patronized by clergy. Several important qualities distinguished Stoddard's lectures from the American theatrical performances: His account of the life of Christ was mediated both photographically and through the personal lecture, which made the passion play narrative subordinate to the account of his visit to Oberammergau. Unlike a theatrical production, Stoddard's passion play lecture was not an attempt to reenact the last days of Christ; it was dominated by the medium of photography, not that of performance. The images did not show actors in the process of actual performance; moreover, the illustrated lecture was understood to involve primarily the unfolding of language not of images. The travel lecture, finally, presented the passion play in a context different from that of the stage. Travel lectures were usually presented to genteel audiences in churches, whose members disapproved of idle amusement in any form. Such lectures were customarily understood to transport spectators to a distant place for the purpose of inspiring or educating them. The local theater, on the other hand, was seen as importing the exotic, the foreign, and the sensational to titillate its patrons and stimulate their desires and fantasies. As will become clear below, these highly superficial but widely observed distinctions would allow film-makers far greater freedom than either literary or theatrical storytellers in the years to come.

The nineteenth century came to a close at the very moment in which the motion picture was being invented, and opposition to theatrical presentations of the passion play seemed to intensify, especially in New York and Boston, where ethnocultural conflict between Catholics and Protestants was at its highest pitch. James O'Neill tried to revive the Morse passion play in 1889, 1891, and 1896, each time without success.[73] Other devotees of the drama sought vehicles that might circumvent the reasons for suppressing the Morse play, but without success. The desire to produce the passion play in some form persisted, particularly among Catholics, even as attempts were repeatedly frustrated. Avoiding actors altogether, or using nonprofessionals in conjunction with a church-sanctioned staging, seemed to make little difference. Protestants deemed the illustrated lecture to be the only safe and acceptable form of proselytizing and managed to keep religious subjects off the stage.

After the 1890 performance at Oberammergau, many itinerant exhibitors gave screen presentations that closely followed Stoddard's lectures on the subject. The arrival of cinema and Stoddard's success in using the screen to tell the passion tale seemed to offer new possibilities for the use of motion pictures in addressing such subjects. While preparing for the vitascope's commercial debut, Thomas Armat imagined such an undertaking.[74] Apparently, so did the Lumières,[75] whose American representative, Charles Smith Hurd, saw a performance of another Bavarian passion, the Horitz village play, in 1896.[76] He immediately approached the theater group about making a film and negotiated a contract limiting exhibition to non-German-speaking countries. With permission in hand, Hurd looked for a producer to finance the production, exhibit the films, and share the profits.

Hurd's search for financing ended when his proposition was accepted by theatrical producers Marc Klaw and Abraham L. Erlanger. They placed Dr. Walter W. Freeman in charge of the project, while Charles Webster and the International Film Company were hired to do the cinematography and lab work.[77] This group spent much of the following spring and summer in Horitz as Freeman supervised the taking of slides and at least fifty "films" totaling five thousand feet in length.[78] The villagers of Horitz in Bohemia had performed miracle plays for centuries, and their passion play, first mounted in 1816, had become an elaborate production by the early 1890s. A major tourist attraction, and attended by royalty, the play still used local actors but had a professional staff.

These motion pictures of the Horitz play clearly bore a much closer resemblance to a theatrical performance than had the individual photographs used for most lantern shows. As the discourse of motion pictures at the time emphasized, their lifelike qualities and their ability to provide a perfect visual simulacrum unfolding in time distinguished cinematic images from all other forms of representation. Counting on this sense of legitimacy, yet well acquainted with New York's reaction to the Salmi Morse production, Klaw and Erlanger chose to tour *The Horitz Passion Play* to other cities before arriving in the nation's theatrical capital.[79] The program's premiere on November 22, 1897, at Philadelphia's Academy of Music featured projected slides and films, accompanied by a lecture, organ music, and sacred hymns.[80] The lecturer was Ernest Lacy, a local playwright and scholar who taught at Philadelphia High School. He began the evening with a scholarly address on the history of miracle and passion plays. The illustrated portion of the lecture commenced with Lacy's discussion of the village and residents of Horitz. The actors were shown working as stone carvers and grain harvesters. Moving on to the play itself, the film depicted ten scenes from the Old Testament and twenty-two from the New Testament. The *Philadelphia Record* considered the results to be the "most notable, and certainly the most noble use to which that marvelous invention, the cinematograph, has yet been put." The review continued:

> Endless lectures on Ober-Ammergau have not been able to give so vivid an
> idea of that more famous Passion Play as last night's spectators at the Academy
> gained as they sat in silent and all-absorbed attention before these scenes. The
> Horitz drama is much more marked by primitive simplicity than that of Ober-
> Ammergau. There is a decidedly more naive and child-like treatment of these
> great sacred themes and episodes. Without the life-like movement of these
> views it would have been impossible to have appreciated anywhere near to the
> full the unquestioning, credulous simplicity of this theatrical representation.
> In these pictures, however, we actually see the half-naked Adam and Eve run-
> ning about in a quaint little Garden of Eden, with invading devils lurking un-
> der the Tree of Life, and an odd-looking Serpent of Evil leaning its flat head
> out of the boughs. Cain kills the kneeling Abel, but one sees how the pretense
> of realism is not so necessitous but that the bad brother brings his club down
> unmistakably far away from Abel's head. The Flood scene, with its swimmers
> in the immovable scenic waves, affords also a queer spectacle.[81]

Reviews were enthusiastic even though they noted—but finally downplayed—both dramatic flaws and such technical imperfections as blurred images and flicker.

Freeman and Lacy gradually polished their exhibition. They reduced the number of films, particularly those from the Old Testament. Hand-tinted lantern slides replaced individual films in some cases, for instance, when introducing the actors through portraits. Organ music accompanied the lecture from the outset, and the producers soon added three singers.[82] Certain moments were heightened, notably the crucifixion, by halting the projection of a film and freezing the image for a few seconds.[83] After the first week, *The Horitz Passion Play* moved to Philadelphia's Horticultural Hall, where it remained for an additional two weeks. The producers then booked two-week runs in Boston in January and in Baltimore in February.

The program provoked little controversy, in part because of the careful way it was promoted. The exhibitions were announced only a few days before they were to be given, allowing potential opposition little time to organize. Publicity emphasized Ernest Lacy's reputation as a guarantee of high quality. Alluding to his Philadelphia appearance, the *Boston Herald* informed Bostonians that "a finer or more reverent piece of word-painting has seldom been heard."[84] In Baltimore clergymen offered their endorsements. Before the first public performance in that city, W. W. Freeman arranged a special afternoon screening for Cardinal James Gibbons and others prominent in the Catholic Church. Gibbons was subsequently quoted as endorsing the pictures as "wonderfully realistic and deeply religious."[85] Through active publicity, Klaw and Erlanger also won support from Protestant clergy.

In Lacy's lecture and through newspaper publicity, the Klaw and Erlanger group sought to win over audiences and potential critics. They promoted the Horitz actors as the Austrian Oberammergau Company and imposed a format on *The Horitz Passion Play* that inevitably recalled Stoddard's famous lecture, at the same time going to great lengths to promote the authenticity of their own production.[86] Lacy argued: "The Horitz production is nearer to nature, in that the players who perform the various parts are untutored, unread peasants, with nothing but their faith to guide them. . . . The Oberammergau production is more up-to-date as it were, and the effect of sincerity is not so deeply impressed on the mind as in the Horitz production."[87]

Initial publicity also distinguished the exhibition from a regular theatrical performance. "There will be no 'real' actors, no living personages in the presentation of this most sacred and sublime of the world's tragedies," the *Boston Herald* assured its readers. Similarly, the Philadelphia *Observer* had noted "something so extraordinary, so unearthly, so fascinating in the strange, silent pictures with their moving, gesticulating, yet voiceless crowds, that the absence of flesh and blood only made the conception more spiritual and relieved it from the touch of irreverence."[88] Film had, according to these commentators, a spiritual capacity. It could cleanse the subject of potential blasphemy: "A machine like that used last night disposes forever of the objection of irreverence," concluded the *Boston Herald* reviewer.[89]

These exhibitions seemed to have all the power of a theatrical performance yet none of its drawbacks. In fact, there were ways in which filmic mediation facilitated the viewer's imagination and response to the program. The lack of presence was not only necessary for religious reasons, it was desirable for aesthetic ones. At first aware that the images were only representations of a representation, the *Boston Herald* critic soon began to feel himself in the presence of the actors themselves: "The thought that one is gazing at a mere pictorial representation seems to pass away and in its place comes, somehow or other, the notion that the people seen are real people, and that on the screen there are moving the very men and women who acted the 'Passion Play' last summer in the Bohemian forest."[90] Finally, this viewer reached a stage in which the image transported him to another time and place entirely:

> Then the players begin to depict the birth and life of Christ, and with this change of subject there comes a new change of mental attitude. So absorbing becomes the interest of the pictures that the onlooker, from merely regarding the figures of the real, live people who acted the play in Bohemia, begins to forget all about what was done in Bohemia and henceforth is lost in the thought that the faces and forms before him are the real people who lived in Palestine 2000 years ago, and with their own eyes witnessed the crucifixion of Christ.[91]

The aesthetic and the religious merged to create a powerful effect.

Publicity had the desired results. As in Philadelphia and later in Baltimore, Boston's opening night was attended by "a splendid audience, including in its numbers not only regular theater-goers but a considerable contingent of people who are much oftener to be found at church than attending a play."[92] Yet despite such repeated success, Klaw and Erlanger proceeded cautiously. Only a single set of Horitz films were available for exhibition as late as April 1898.[93] The program was given for four days during late February in Rochester, New York, before opening in New York City at Daly's Theater on March 14 as a Lenten lecture.[94] By that time any possibility of controversy had dissipated—not merely because of the positive reactions generated in other cities, but because a similar type of exhibition had already opened at New York's Eden Musee.

Opened in late March 1884, New York's Eden Musee, on 23rd Street west of Madison Square, appealed primarily to a well-to-do clientele by cannily mixing an "educational" approach with sensationalism. Waxworks and musical concerts were its key programming elements until December 18, 1896, when films were first projected in the Musee's Winter Garden. Once motion pictures proved popular with patrons, Musee president Richard Hollaman committed his institution to featuring them among its attractions.[95]

Hollaman had been eager to acquire the film rights for *The Horitz Passion Play* and felt betrayed when Hurd assigned them to Klaw and Erlanger.[96] Nevertheless, Hollaman and an associate, Frank Russell, attended the Philadelphia premiere. They were impressed and, seeing an opportunity, embarked on their own production, which, for promotional purposes, was said to be based on the Oberammergau staging. While photographs and drawings from that famous rendition may have provided some guidelines, and the Horitz version was occasionally pilfered for striking scenes or effects, Salmi Morse's play was dusted off and generally performed the role of scenario.[97] In six weeks Hollaman's crew shot twenty-three scenes on a roof in New York and produced about nineteen minutes of screen time.

The Eden Musee created the films in great secrecy for fear that reports of an actor playing Christ for money might create a public outcry.[98] Hollaman was uncertain how to publicize the resulting *Passion Play of Oberammergau*. *The Horitz Passion Play* had gained public acceptance in part because it was performed by simple Bohemian peasants. The reaction to Hollaman's project, if its actual production circumstances were known, could not be predicted. The producer therefore emphasized the show's connections with Oberammergau while concealing the fact that it was a reenactment.

At a press screening on Friday, January 28, it was precisely Hollaman's attempt to misrepresent his production as authentic that journalists condemned, not the show's potential for religious sacrilege. "All the preliminary announcements of this exhibition have tended to convey the impression that this is a genuine reproduction of the celebrated passion play at Oberammergau," the *New York Herald* protested.[99] The confusion revolved around the meaning and definition of "reproduction"—an ambiguous term with which critics, theorists, and audiences still struggle. In the face of such criticism, Hollaman beat a strategic retreat, admitting that the show was a reenactment and avoiding any mention of Salmi Morse's play.

Despite the flurry of criticism, by 1898 the screen presentation of religious subjects had become so familiar that even the Musee's awkward handling of the press failed to harm the program's reception. The show did even better than Hollaman had expected.[100] Among the many visitors were ministers and church people, all of whom applauded the moral benefits of the passion play pictures. "The 'Passion Play' might well be said to give those who see it a personal and loving acquaintance with the Divine One. After the exhibition was over I left feeling like living a better life, becoming a better man, trying to follow the teachings of One whom I now know as I never knew before," a prominent lawyer told the Musee manager.[101] A short time later, Rev. R. F. Putnam wrote the editor of a prominent magazine:

> The performance of this play in New York by living actors and actresses was prohibited by the conscientious sentiment of the people, the influence of the press and the action of the authorities. But to the rendition of it by these pictures there can be no objection. One might as well object to the illustrations of Dore and other artists in the large quarto Bibles. Intensely realistic they are, and it is this feature which gives them truthfulness and makes them instructive. Painful they are necessarily to sensitive and sympathetic souls, and so are many of the pictures which surmount some of the altars of our churches. . . . I cannot conceive of a more impressive object-lesson for Sunday school scholars.[102]

Devout Protestants thus saw *The Passion Play of Oberammergau* as an effective way to convert those who were not religious and inspire the faithful. For such audiences the Musee must have seemed like a church, an effect enhanced by the presence at times of choir boys chanting anthems.

The immense popularity of the passion play led the Musee to send out traveling companies to present two-hour shows in other cities. Almost immediately, however, the Musee found itself in competition with a nearly identical rival. For reasons involving Edison's legal proceedings against purported infringers on his motion picture patents, films of the Eden Musee's production were quickly sold on the open market. One Professor Wallace, a Boston-based exhibitor of lantern slides and films, opened a program called *The Passion Play of Oberammergau* at Poli's Wonderland vaudeville theater in New Haven, one week before the Musee version was to play at the Hyperion. Poli charged ten-cents and twenty-cents admission—much less than the Hyperion had intended. The show appealed not only to Poli's regular, often working-class and Catholic clientele, but was crowded with "audiences representing the best people of the city."[103] To ensure decorum and thus reassure the latter audiences, the exhibitor advertised, "During the performance of the play no passing to and fro will be permitted, and the doors will be closed against newcomers."[104]

The Passion Play of Oberammergau thus drew a diverse audience that included evangelical Christians, sophisticated frequenters of more refined theatrical entertainments, and plebeians in search of cheap amusement.

After its commercial runs, *The Passion Play of Oberammergau* was shown regularly in churches and for religious groups. Col. Henry H. Hadley, a noted Methodist evangelist, bought at least some of the films, combining them with scenes from other sets of passion play pictures. In 1898 he showed them in a tent at Asbury Park, New Jersey, and at evangelistic meetings in a Methodist church in Danbury, Connecticut.[105] Other versions of the passion play were shown in the United States, including one narrated by Thomas Dixon, Jr., future writer of *The Clansman* (which became the basis for D. W. Griffith's *The Birth of a Nation*). Sigmund Lubin, a Jew who, like Morse, had converted to Christianity, made his own version of *The Passion Play of Oberammergau* in May 1898, selling it for twenty cents per foot, substantially less than either *The Horitz Passion Play* or the Eden Musee's *Passion Play of Oberammergau,* which were marketed by the Edison Manufacturing Company and its licensed agents. A set of twenty-five films, possibly part of Pathé's 1902–4 film, *La Vie et la Passion de Jesus-Christ,* was also available in this country, probably through William Selig.[106]

In the end, it was the exhibitor who determined not only the actual shape of the narrative but the status of claims to authenticity made by producers of various films. Although the Horitz and Eden Musee passion play films were initially offered to exhibitors only in complete sets, exhibitors demanded their own selection from the outset. By the publication of its 1901 catalog, the Edison Company was officially selling passion play films on a scene-by-scene basis so that exhibitors could purchase and then organize individual scenes into any combination they desired. In some cases, exhibitors used films made by more than one producer, purchasing the scenes they liked best and adding to their collections as finances permitted. No two programs were exactly alike; the showman exercised a creative role, selecting the moving pictures and stereopticon scenes, placing them in an order, writing and delivering a narration, and providing incidental music. He had to know his audience well enough to avoid either boring them or offending their religious sensibilities.

Clearly, religious subjects were an important genre for the early film industry. Watching them came to be regarded as a desirable Sunday-afternoon activity for growing numbers of Christian viewers. For many showmen, religious subjects were a way to evade Sunday blue laws. In the end, entrepreneurs exploited religious subject matter for their own commercial purposes, ultimately assimilating them into the emerging culture of mass amusements. In the process, they gradually wrested greater control over the construction of these images and narratives, even as the clergy who made or showed them sought to use them to evangelize the masses. Throughout the nineteenth century, in fact, religion and popular culture constantly renegotiated the appropriate ways to narrate the life and passion of Christ as well as other religious subjects.[107] Such negotiations were particularly confrontational in the 1880s and early 1890s as evangelical Protestants opposed theatrical entrepreneurs on one hand and Catholics on the other. By 1898, with the introduction of motion pictures, these oppositions had abated, even though the detente was short-lived. Catholics along with Protestants, evangelical reformers and purveyors of amusements, all seemed for a time to find a new sphere of compatibility in the motion picture.[108] A reverent person could find religious inspiration at a vaudeville house in 1900—something very much in question only ten years earlier. The religious and the cinematic turned toward each other in the late 1890s and remained on friendly terms for almost another decade.

In the early 1900s filmmakers and exhibitors continued to exploit the "absence of presence" that had given the magic lantern and stereopticon their special status. In these years the French studios Pathé and Gaumont made ambitious films of the life of Christ that were fictional in their approach to representation. The mediation of documentary methods—in which the author necessarily maintains a critical distance from his filmic subject—no longer seemed necessary or even desirable. These changes, in turn, reverberated in the theatrical world as the differences between stage and screen diminished. With the absence of presence becoming increasingly the principal difference between the two practices, the prohibition against staging the passion play seemed pointless and old-fashioned. In May 1902 a popular new dramatic journal, *Theater Magazine,* published an article entitled "The Passion Play on the American Stage." Written by Rev. Percy Stickney Grant of the Church of the Ascension in New York, it reviewed the traditional arguments against putting the passion play on the stage and found them to be surmountable. Grant concluded: "I should like to see a Passion Play on the American stage, under proper conditions. I do not believe it would cheapen the Christian religion. Christian people must not shut their eyes to anything which tends to give greater reality to the story of Christ through fear that it will shaken their faith."[109]

Historian Tom Gunning indicated that a passion play was staged at the 1904 Louisiana Purchase Exposition in Saint Louis.[110] Other local productions of the passion play were staged in San Francisco; Paterson and Union City, New Jersey; Columbus, Ohio; and Bronxville, New York.[111] Nevertheless, although it had become acceptable to put the passion play on the American stage by the early twentieth century, the theater never rivaled the screen in the frequency of such depictions. From *The Passion Play* (Pathé, 1907), to *King of Kings* (deMille, 1927), to *The Last Temptation of Christ* (Scorsese, 1988), the life of Christ has remained a cinematic staple for almost a century. Even as raucous debates erupted over how the life of Christ should be depicted, the very legitimacy of attempting such a depiction became, by 1900, a moot issue. Within a decade after the introduction of the motion picture, a complex system of rules and prohibitions in regard to the representation of Christianity's most sacred story had been literally turned on its head. The Protestant clergy, which had called the dramatization of the passion sacrilegious a few years earlier, soon advocated it as a desirable means for instilling faith. On one hand, they emphasized the obvious continuities between the magic lantern and the cinema, thus legitimating filmed versions of sacred narratives. On the other, coming to recognize that the cinema was in many ways much like the theater, they gradually abandoned their prejudices against dramatic enactments of the Passion in any form. This remaking of rules and prohibitions surrounding religious narrative underscores the ways in which a new mode of representation such as the cinema can alter and destabilize not only specific cultural forms of which they are a part, for example, screen practice, but the broader cultural landscape.

As I have discussed elsewhere, the powers of photographic mediation took the "curse of presence" off many types of amusements when presented on the screen.[112] Even condensed vaudeville acts and excerpted theatrical farces could be sponsored by a church group as long as they were presented in cinematic form. Indeed, for many evangelical Christians, cinema became a means of sanitizing popular culture and holding on to the straying faithful. Although film did not make the profane sacred, it could avoid charges of blasphemy or obscenity in its treatment of religious subjects. Such developments inevitably evoke Walter Benjamin's famous essay of the 1930s, "The Work of Art in the Age of Mechanical Reproduction," which noted that all art had its basis in religious ritual, the location of its original use value. Cinema did much to disrupt the relationship between religion and certain cultural practices.

Around 1900 technical reproduction had reached a standard that not only permitted it to reproduce all transmitted works of art and thus to cause the most profound change in their impact on the public; it also had captured a place of its own among the artistic processes. For the study of this standard nothing is more revealing than the nature of the repercussions that these two different manifestations—the reproduction of works of art and the art of the film—have on art in its traditional form.[113]

First photography and then cinematography extracted these presentations from their religious setting and so "emancipate[d] the work of art from its parasitical dependence on ritual," resulting in the "liquidation of the traditional value of the cultural heritage."[114] The fight over the passion play in nineteenth-century America was precisely a fight over its ritual significance. Evangelical Protestants refused to accept the Passion as a suitable subject for dramatic treatment, concerned that what Benjamin would have called its "aura" or "authenticity" would be blasphemized. As reproductions of a religious-based ritual, these films freed the passion play from the weight of tradition and soon enabled it to function both in the artistic sphere and beyond it. It allowed avatars of urban commercial popular culture to appropriate a subject that had previously resisted easy incorporation into a capitalist economy and modern culture.

And yet, however much the cinema eased tensions between evangelists and various forms of popular culture, the interests of showmen and evangelists were too divergent for peace to last for long. As cinema became a form of mass entertainment with the proliferation of specialized motion picture theaters after 1906, evangelical Christians quickly began to see these nickelodeons as "schools for crime."[115] They led efforts to censor the "orgies of obscenity"[116] that made their way to the screen, insisting that values beyond those of the marketplace should regulate the new medium. The absence of presence no longer provided protection. From the Woman's Christian Temperance Union, to the Legion of Decency, to the Moral Majority, this Christian assault has seemed at times to reject the media of mass communication altogether. Such now-familiar attitudes make the acceptance and even the embrace of motion pictures by evangelical groups in the late nineteenth century all the more remarkable.

NOTES

A draft of this article was first presented at the Domitor Conference on Film and Religion in Quebec City, Canada, in June 1990. I appreciate the comments and shared ideas of that occasion, which greatly facilitated my subsequent revisions. Thanks also to Francis G. Couvares, Tom Gunning, Jon Butler, Richard Abel, and Gary Kulik for their assistance in shaping this final essay. André Gaudreault helped with a French translation that appeared in Roland Cosandey, André Gaudreault, and Tom Gunning, eds., *Un Invention du Diable? Cinéma des Premiers Temps et Religion* (Sainte-Foy, 1992), 145–86. In the interim, I have had the pleasure of reading Alan Nielsen's impressive book, *The Great Victorian Sacrilege: Preachers, Politics and the Passion, 1879–1884* (Jefferson, N.C., 1991) on Salmi Morse and his play, *The Passion* (1879). Nielsen is a theater historian whose exhaustive research from this perspective easily surpasses, and complements, my own research into screen practice (magic lantern and early film). While our concerns are very similar, our analyses and conclusions are somewhat different.

1. Abbey's failure to open Morse's *The Passion* and its relevance to film history was first discussed in Terry Ramsaye, *A Million and One Nights* (New York, 1926), 366–77.

2. In this respect, recent counterparts to debates around the passion play have often focused on Martin Scorsese's *The Last Temptation of Christ* (1988); see the essay in this volume by Charles Lyons.

3. As Eileen Bowser has pointed out, genres in early cinema were extremely narrow in their range, when compared to later motion picture genres such as the western or the musical ("Preparation for Brighton: The American Contribution," in Roger Holman, comp., *Cinema 1900–1906* [Brussels, 1982], 1:3–29).

4. Hugo Münsterberg, *The Photoplay: A Psychological Study* (1916; reprint, New York, 1970), 12–13.

5. André Bazin, "Theater and Cinema," pt. 2, *Esprit,* July–August 1951, in *What Is Cinema* (Berkeley, 1967), edited and translated by Hugh Gray. The absence of presence as an impoverishment but also as a liberation was likewise addressed by Walter Benjamin, who saw it as destructive of an art object's aura and of tradition. I will return to these insights in my conclusion, for the history of the passion play on stage and screen exemplifies the issues that concerned Benjamin in his essay, "The Work of Art in the Age of Mechanical Reproduction," in *Illuminations,* edited and with an introduction by Hannah Arendt (New York, 1969), 219–20.

6. For a recent analysis that explores the compatibilities and interpenetration of religion and the mid-nineteenth-century culture industry, see R. Laurence Moore, "Religion, Secularization, and the Shaping of the Culture Industry in Antebellum America," *American Quarterly* 41, no. 2 (June 1989): 216–42.

7. David S. Reynolds, *Faith in Fiction: The Emergence of Religious Literature in America* (Cambridge, Mass., 1981), 203.

8. Paul Boyer, *Purity in Print: The Vice-Society Movement and Book Censorship in America* (New York, 1968), 1–22; Abe Laufe, *The Wicked Stage: A History of Theater Censorship and Harassment in the United States* (New York, 1978), 13–23.

9. For a discussion of the distinctions between old and new middle class, see Harry Braverman, *Labor and Monopoly Capital: The Degradation of Work in the Twentieth Century* (New York, 1974).

10. The historiography on movie censorship has generally paid little attention to the period before 1907, that is, before cinema became a form of mass entertainment. See, for example, Annette Kuhn, *Cinema Censorship and Sexuality, 1909–1925* (London,

1988); and Richard S. Randall, *Censorship of the Movies: The Social and Political Control of a Mass Medium* (Madison, Wis., 1968). Historians have also paid relatively little attention to the relationship between censorship of motion pictures and other cultural practices, such as theater. Exceptions include Dorothy Knowles, *The Censor, the Drama and the Film, 1900–1934* (London, 1934); and Thomas Cripps, *Slow Fade to Black: The Negro in American Film,* 1900–1942 (London, 1977), 41–69.

11. Athanasius Kircher, *Ars magna lucis et umbrae,* 2d ed. (Amsterdam, 1671), 768–71.

12. Xenophon Theodore Barber, "Evenings of Wonders: A History of the Magic Lantern Show in America" (Ph.D. diss., New York University, 1993), chap. 9.

13. Riley Brothers, brochure for *Bunyan's Pilgrim's Progress* (ca. 1890).

14. For subsequent (if less direct) methods of relating screen images to Bible illustrations, see Herbert Reynolds, "From Palette to Screen: The Tissot Bible as a Sourcebook for *From Manger to Cross,*" in Roland Cosandey, André Gaudreault, and Tom Gunning, eds., *Un Invention du Diable? Cinema des Premiers Temps et Religion* (Sainte-Foy, 1992), 275–310.

15. *Brooklyn Eagle,* March 10, 1863, 3.

16. Garff B. Wilson, *Three Hundred Years of American Drama and Theater: From Ye Bare and Ye Cubb to Chorus Line,* 2d ed. (1973; Englewood Cliffs, N.J., 1982), 8–9.

17. Moore, "Religion," 222.

18. Jonas Barish, *The Antitheatrical Prejudice* (Los Angeles, 1981).

19. Barber, "Evenings of Wonders," chap. 9.

20. Nielsen, *Great Victorian Sacrilege,* 41, 130.

21. Salmi Morse, *The Passion: A Miracle Play in Ten Acts* (1879); "Footlights," *San Francisco Chronicle,* February 23, 1879, 2; advertisement, *San Francisco Chronicle,* February 24, 1879, 4.

22. Nielsen provides an excellent biographical sketch of Morse in *Great Victorian Sacrilege,* 29–49.

23. William Winter, *The Life of David Belasco* (New York, 1918), 1:116. These amendments appear in Morse, *Passion,* 67–69.

24. "A Threatened Sacrilege," *San Francisco Chronicle,* February 26, 1879, 2.

25. "The Passion Play," *San Francisco Chronicle,* March 2, 1879, 1; "Footlights," *San Francisco Chronicle,* March 2, 1879, 2.

26. "Board of Supervisors," *San Francisco Examiner,* March 4, 1879, 3.

27. Ibid.

28. Cited in Winter, *Life of David Belasco,* 124–25.

29. "The Passion," *San Francisco Chronicle,* March 4, 1879, 3.

30. "The Passion Play," *San Francisco Chronicle,* March 7, 1879, 2.

31. "Amusements," *San Francisco Examiner,* March 4, 1879, 3.

32. *San Francisco Chronicle,* March 4, 1879, 3; see also Lise-Lone Marker, *David Belasco: Naturalism in the American Theater* (Princeton, 1975), 26–27.

33. *San Francisco Chronicle,* March 4, 1879, 3.

34. "The Passion Play," *San Francisco Chronicle,* March 7, 1879, 2.

35. San Francisco *Pacific,* quoted in *San Francisco Chronicle,* March 16, 1879, 2. Jews seemed incidental to this antagonism between Protestants and Catholics. Yet

according to David Belasco's biographer, William Winter, the "ignorant Irish who witnessed it were so distempered that, on going forth, some of them, from time to time, assaulted peaceable Jews in the public streets." If these street disturbances occurred, however, they went unreported in the local press. See Winter, *The Life of David Belasco,* 1:117.

36. "Amusements," *San Francisco Chronicle,* March 14, 1879, 3.

37. Advertisement, *San Francisco Chronicle,* April 14, 1879, 4.

38. "The Passion Play," *San Francisco Chronicle,* April 17, 1879, 4; "The Passion Play," *San Francisco Chronicle,* April 18, 1879, 4; "The Passion Play," *San Francisco Chronicle,* April 22, 1879, 4.

39. "Mr Abbey's Decision," *New York Times,* November 28, 1880, 7.

40. "The Passion Play at Booth's," *New York Dramatic Mirror,* September 25, 1880, 7.

41. Quoted in *New York Dramatic Mirror,* September 25, 1880, 7.

42. "The Passion Play at Booth's," *New York Dramatic Mirror,* September 25, 1880, 7.

43. "The Proposed Passion Play," *New York Dramatic Mirror,* October 30, 1880, 7.

44. *Celtic Monthly,* October 1880, quoted in *New York Dramatic Mirror,* October 9, 1880, 9.

45. "A Shock of Repulsion," *Andrews American Queen,* reprinted in *New York Dramatic Mirror,* October 9, 1990, 9.

46. *New York Herald,* reprinted in *New York Dramatic Mirror,* October 30, 1880, 7.

47. *New York Dramatic Mirror,* November 6, 1880, 7, where he was apparently improperly identified as J. W. Newman. John Phillip Newman (1826–1899) was a major figure in the Methodist Episcopal Church, having served as chaplain to the U.S. Senate from 1869 to 1874 and as General Grant's spiritual adviser during his terminal illness. Newman also established two colleges, a church journal, and three Methodist conferences.

48. "The Proposed Passion Play," *New York Dramatic Mirror,* October 30, 1880, 7.

49. Barish, *Antitheatrical Prejudice,* 80–131.

50. "The Passion Play," *New York Dramatic Mirror,* November 27, 1880, 7.

51. "Aldermanic Virtue Aroused," *New York Times,* November 24, 1880, 8.

52. "The Passion Play Denounced," *New York Times,* November 16, 1880, 2.

53. "Pastors to Their Flocks," *New York Times,* November 29, 1880, 2.

54. "The Passion Play Read," *New York Times,* December 4, 1880, 2, and editorial on 4.

55. Ibid. William Winter (*Life of David Belasco,* 122) completes the history of Morse's efforts to have his play produced. Morse made a final attempt to present the play in February–April 1883, which resulted in the author being brought before Judge George C. Barrett of the New York Supreme Court. On February 22 of the following year, Morse committed suicide by drowning in the Hudson River.

56. *New York Times:* March 8, 1880, 2; "The Old Miracle Plays," May 16, 1880, 2; "The Ober-Ammergau Drama," May 31, 1880, 2; "The Passion Play," May 31, 1880, 3; "Joseph Mayer's Acting," June 3, 1880, 2; "The Actors in the Passion Play," June 5, 1880, 2.

57. *New York Times,* May 31, 1880, 2.

58. *London Daily News,* quoted in *New York Times,* May 31, 1880, 2.

59. For background information on John L. Stoddard, see Charles Musser, "The Roots of Travel Cinema: John L. Stoddard, E. Burton Holmes and the Nineteenth-century Illustrated Travel Lecture," *Film History* 5, no. 1 (March 1993): 68–84; and Musser, *The Emergence of Cinema* (New York, 1990), 38–41, 209–10, 221–22.

60. John Stoddard, *Red Letter Days Abroad* (Boston, 1884), 62.

61. Ibid., 86.

62. Ibid., 59.

63. "Ober-Ammergau's Passion Play," *New York Times,* December 12, 1880, 5; "The Lecture Platform," *New York Tribune,* December 12, 1880, 2. Actual photographs of the play had been taken for the king of Bavaria.

64. Daniel Crane Taylor, *John L. Stoddard: Traveler, Lecturer, Litterateur* (New York, 1935), 98.

65. Stoddard, *Red Letter Days Abroad,* 98.

66. John L. Stoddard, *John L. Stoddard's Lectures* (Boston, 1902), 4:230.

67. Ibid., 232–34.

68. Ibid., 268.

69. Ibid., 294–96.

70. Ibid., 335.

71. Ibid., 243.

72. E. Burton Holmes, "Oberammergau in 1900," in *The Burton Holmes Lectures,* 10 vols. (Battle Creek, Mich., 1903), 3:117–224.

73. Nielsen, *Great Victorian Sacrilege,* 229.

74. Thomas Armat to Raff and Gammon, February 24, 1896, exhibit, *Animated Photo Projecting Company v. American Mutoscope Company,* no. 7130, filed December 31, 1898, U.S. Circuit Court, District of Southern New York.

75. *Boston Herald,* January 2, 1898, 10.

76. Zdenek Stabla, *Queries concerning the Horice Passion Film* (Prague, 1971), 10–16. Hurd is usually given the initials "W. B.," but the only source for this appears to be Terry Ramsaye (*Million and One Nights,* 367). It is likely that Ramsaye or his informant was misinformed, because a Charles Hurd was in Horitz during the filming and subsequently involved with contractual matters involving the Horitz play. Of course, there may have been a W. B. as well as a Charles Hurd, but no contemporaneous evidence of this has been found.

77. *The Phonoscope,* November–December 1897, 9.

78. "The Passion Play," *Boston Herald,* January 2, 1898, 10; *Philadelphia Record,* November 21, 1897, 16.

79. Ramsaye, *Million and One Nights,* 368.

80. Kemp Niver, with Bebe Bergsten, *Klaw and Erlanger Present Famous Plays in Pictures* (Los Angeles, 1976) includes useful information about the exhibition of *The Horitz Passion Play* and reprints several complete reviews.

81. "Passion Play Tableaux," *Philadelphia Record,* November 23, 1897, 6.

82. "The Passion Play," *Philadelphia Inquirer,* November 23, 1897, 5; "The Passion Play at Daly's," *New York Herald,* March 15, 1898, 13.

83. "The 'Passion Play' at Daly's," *New York Herald,* March 15, 1898, 13.

84. *Boston Herald,* January 2, 1898, 10. Ernest Lacy delivered the lecture in Baltimore, as he would in New York and Brooklyn. When the program was given in less prominent locations, such as Rochester and Pittsburgh, Lacy was spelled by another speaker.

85. "'Passion Play' Scenes," *Baltimore Sun,* February 8, 1898, 7.

86. *Philadelphia Inquirer,* November 23, 1897, 5.

87. *Boston Herald,* January 2, 1898, 32.

88. "Entertainments," *Philadelphia Public Ledger,* November 23, 1897, reprinted in Niver, *Klaw and Erlanger,* 12.

89. "The 'Passion Play,' Given Here in Boston," *Boston Herald,* January 4, 1898, 6.

90. Ibid.

91. Ibid.

92. Ibid.

93. Thomas Edison, Marc Klaw, Abraham L. Erlanger, Walter W. Freeman, William Harris, and Franck Z. Maguire, contract, April 7, 1898, Edison National Historic Site, West Orange, New Jersey.

94. *Rochester Post-Express,* February 22, 1898, 7.

95. For more information on the Eden Musee, see Charles Musser, *Before the Nickelodeon: Edwin S. Porter and the Edison Manufacturing Company* (Berkeley, 1991), 116–42.

96. Ramsaye, *Million and One Nights,* 367–68.

97. "Scenes on Bible Subjects," *New York Tribune,* January 29, 1898, 9.

98. Any public attention in regard to the filming of *The Passion Play of Oberammergau* also would have alerted Klaw and Erlanger, who might have then preempted the Musee's New York debut.

99. "The Passion Play," *New York Herald,* February 1, 1898, 7, reprinted in Ramsaye, *Million and One Nights,* 373.

100. "Crowds at the Musee," *New York Mail and Express,* February 5, 1898, 15.

101. "Passion Play at the Eden Musee," *New York Mail and Express,* February 1, 1898, 3.

102. Rev. R. F. Putnam to the editor, *Home Journal,* February 15, 1898, reprinted in *Moving Picture World,* February 22, 1908, 133.

103. *New Haven Journal-Courier,* March 8, 1898, 3.

104. *New Haven Journal-Courier,* March 7, 1898, 6.

105. Ramsaye, *Million and One Nights,* 374–76.

106. *Films of the Passion Play or Life of Christ* (n.d. [1903]). Found among the Selig material in the Charles Clarke Collection at the Academy of Motion Picture Arts and Sciences, this unidentified catalog does not seem to represent an entirely new and unknown passion play since information about such a production would have almost certainly emerged in archival documents, trade journals, or other sources.

107. Michel Foucault, "What Is an Author?" in Paul Rabinow, ed., *The Foucault Reader* (New York, 1984), 101–20.

108. John Higham argues that the late 1890s was a period of confidence that undermined American nativism, while the post-1907 period saw its resurgence (*Strangers in the Land: Patterns of American Nativism, 1860–1925* [New Brunswick, N.J., 1955], 106, 158).

109. Rev. Percy Stickney Grant, "The Passion Play on the American Stage," *Theater Magazine,* May 1902, 12.

110. Tom Gunning, "World's Fair as Technological Microcosm: Cinema and Other Space/Time Technologies at the Louisiana Purchase Exposition, St. Louis, 1904" (paper delivered at the Domitor Conference, New York University, June 16, 1994).

111. Nielsen, *Great Victorian Sacrilege,* 228–29.

112. Charles Musser, with Carol Nelson, *High-Class Moving Pictures: Lyman Howe and the Forgotten Era of Traveling Exhibition* (Princeton, 1991).

113. Benjamin, "Work of Art," 219–20.

114. Ibid., 220, 221.

115. *New York Herald,* February 8, 1909, 1.

116. Ibid.

Mothering the Movies

Women Reformers and Popular Culture

ALISON M. PARKER

The Woman's Christian Temperance Union, best known as an antialcohol organization, had a broad censorship program directed at a wide range of cultural production. One of its targets was film. An examination of the WCTU's movie censorship campaigns reveals significant aspects of the middle-class response to the development of film and to other perceived changes in American popular culture. The union's complaints against movies had social power inasmuch as they represented a coherent synopsis of public fears concerning the "evils" of film. This critique gained the support of many Americans at key moments of crisis for the industry, finally forcing it to agree to stricter self-censorship in 1934.[1]

The WCTU waged its battle for movie censorship with the rhetoric of child-saving. Its members fought for federal censorship, promoted and created "educational" films, and strictly controlled their own children's access to movies under the rubric of safety for youths. The organization supported federal regulation in part because it believed that the impact of motion pictures, especially on impressionable children, was too strong to allow the emerging movie industry to remain unregulated.[2] The WCTU put forth an agenda that drew upon its role as exemplar of womanly virtues in public action. Perceiving a spatial and moral threat to their role as guardians of youths, WCTU members made concerted attempts through the 1930s to fight for censorship of motion pictures.[3]

Charting movie attendance rates, the WCTU argued that youths were in greater danger of becoming "addicted" to watching movies than they were of becoming addicted to alcohol. Like some Progressive educators, the WCTU concluded that movies now served as "the greatest factor in the education of youth."[4] The WCTU's Department for the Promotion of Purity in Literature and Art (later the Motion Picture Department) promoted and produced independent antialcohol films for schools and community groups, as well as censored and regulated films produced by the movie industry.[5] Its desire to offer a "pure" version of American culture to replace the "impure" made the WCTU's dual goals—of censorship, on the one hand, and of the promotion of educational and "pure" movies for youths, on the other—complementary, not incompatible.

News of motion pictures projected onto large screens in nickelodeons reached middle-class reformers early. The Woman's Christian Temperance Union published articles about reforming the five-cent theaters in 1906, only one year after they opened.[6] Until about 1910 some hopeful reformers believed that the local movie theater could vanquish the local saloon.[7] The General Federation of Women's Clubs, for instance, claimed that saloons "have found the competition of the motion picture a more serious foe than the W.C.T.U. or any anti-saloon or anti-cigarette league."[8] The WCTU, not surprisingly, rejected this view of commercial movies, pointing instead to their potential to corrupt youths as surely as alcohol would. The WCTU's first published condemnation of movie content demonstrates its fundamental concern for morality in cultural productions. This *Union Signal* editorial of 1906 criticized the "sensational" aspects of movies, which undermined traditional values: "Natural modesty receives its first shock. Crime is made 'interesting,' 'romantic,' 'exciting,' —everything but criminal. Deformities of the human frame are made laughable. Age is represented as a target for youthful scorn and laughter."[9] Depictions of crime and immodesty had been a central part of the Department for the Promotion of Purity in Literature and Art's definition of "impure" culture since the 1880s. But observations regarding ageism were specific to the new genre and highlighted the appeal of movies to youths.[10]

The Department for the Promotion of Purity in Literature and Art noted in 1907 disturbing increases in the number of children in movie theater audiences and unwelcome new theater locations.[11] *Union Signal* editors observed that increasing numbers of young girls went to the movies right after school and that wage-earning girls went when they got off work; boys ("hoodlums") often frequented the theaters in the evening, as well. Citing the importance of control over children's activities, the editors solemnly declared, "Eternal parental vigilance is the price of unsullied young womanhood and manhood."[12] Not only were children increasingly attending the movies, but "from the downtown districts and cheaper business streets," it was noted, "these nuisances are invading the better class residence portions of the city."[13]

WCTU activists entered local campaigns for movie regulation using rhetoric consistent with Progressive educators' and social scientists' commitment to reforming children's health and hygiene. A focus on popular "progressive" issues such as health and safety provided the organization with another argument in favor of regulation. The issue of health and safety was a serious one in the early nickelodeon years. Historian Douglas Gomery concludes that theaters were dangerous places, especially because of the risk of fire.[14] Concern for the physical safety of movie viewers, particularly children, locates the WCTU and like-minded reformers squarely within Progressivism. Some early state laws governing movies restricted the attendance only of youths because, as labor-protection laws of the era exemplify, it was easier for the courts to accept laws based on protecting children or women, thereby excluding adult men from regulatory consideration. New York and New Jersey had passed laws by 1909, for example, making it illegal "to admit to a kinetoscope or moving picture performance or to any place of entertainment injurious to *health or morals,* any child under the age of 16 years, unless accompanied by parent or guardian."[15]

Various rationales for censorship appeared in WCTU publications. Subjects appropriate for adults and cultivated people might be dangerous, and thus "obscene," it was argued, when seen by youths or the uncultivated and should therefore be banned altogether. In a more positive vein, the department praised serious movie dramas that demonstrated moral lessons. "Realistic" movie plots derived from respectable novels or the Bible were recommended over "unrealistic" westerns, comedies, or gangster movies with sensational action, crime, or sexually titillating themes. Realistic portrayals of urban crime could be useful, however, if used to "document" and condemn the evils and dangers of alcohol use. Drunkenness, seduction, or even violence might be acceptably portrayed in motion pictures to teach youths the danger of such activities, as long as the terrible fates of wayward characters were consistently emphasized throughout. In the mid-1930s the WCTU produced its own films, for instance, with titles such as *The Beneficent Reprobate,* which purposefully showed the worst results of drinking and smoking to dissuade people from engaging in these activities.[16]

For the WCTU, the power of film resided in its status as a visual medium that made people, especially children, vulnerable to suggestion. Watching movies could produce in youths "unwonted elation" and an "ungovernable spirit."[17] The WCTU reported in 1910 that a child arrested on burglary and assault charges told a judge that he had learned how to break into homes from watching the movies, and that another boy had copied a "self-murder" by gas asphyxiation he had seen at a motion picture show.[18] The judge's account suggests that the WCTU's discussion of the impact of movies on youths' subsequent behavior was part of a larger discourse of social science, to which juvenile court judges as well as evangelical laywomen subscribed.

WCTU directors cited studies by social scientists and reformers to demonstrate that the movie industry had consolidated its monopolistic power and gained, by the 1920s and 1930s, large, passive audiences full of youths. "The Motion Picture houses of this Country," it insisted, "are frequented daily by great numbers of people, including boys and girls of whom it has been estimated 75% are under twenty-four years of age."[19] Union members believed that in the hands of the consolidated movie industry, a medium with much positive educational potential was instead teaching cultural and moral relativism, thereby alienating youths from the older, Victorian generation. "You are disgusted and stay away from the movies," it warned parents, "but your children and grand-children are becoming perhaps oblivious to the degrading tendencies of the movies and cease to distinguish good from evil."[20] At best, movies were creating an amoral, if not wholly immoral, rising generation. WCTU state reports asked suggestively, "To what extent are 'movies' responsible for the 'crime wave' and the wet political situation?"[21] Through the 1930s, department directors cited increasing "evidence" of the responsibility of movies for inducing youths to antisocial behavior, such as six "well authenticated cases of crime, misdemeanor or delinquency due to influence of motion pictures" and "four runaway marriages resulting from the influence of motion pictures."[22] To women moral reformers, the evidence suggested a significant loss of maternal control over their children's behavior as youths spent more and more leisure time in motion picture theaters.

The WCTU's condemnations of the impact of movies were usually broad and inclusive, rarely mentioning specific titles. The New York *Annual Report* of 1917, however, provides us with uncharacteristically specific information regarding the movies it both approved and opposed:

Appreciative letters [were] sent to the Worlds' Film Company commenting on clean, wholesome pictures shown, especially, "The Man Who Taught." Protested against the film, "Intolerance," and other vulgar films. . . . Mrs. Lindsay, Mrs. Dennison and others of the county [Albany] called up the mayor and chief of police and protested against the exhibition of "Twilight Sleep," in the actual birth of a child. This latter part was omitted.[23]

In the case of *Twilight Sleep,* a WCTU director atypically took the time to specify the reason for the union's protest: a relatively graphic portrayal of childbirth. WCTU members implicitly made distinctions between "good" realism and "bad." The latter included such things as urban crime, prostitution, and the violation of women's privacy in childbirth. Another account described the nature of the cuts made in the offensive scene to satisfy the WCTU: "'Twilight Sleep' was advertised greatly but owing to strong opposition from county union instead of an actual birth being shown with nurse and doctor in attendance, only the faces of two mothers were shown, one in quiet sleep, the other showing traces of suffering."[24] WCTU members interpreted the scene as disrespectful of the sanctity of motherhood and demanded that it be eliminated. Respect for women's purity as mothers, they believed, could be jeopardized by allowing men and youths to watch voyeuristically an honored and private female act. Their protests against *Twilight Sleep* were based on scenes they interpreted as disruptive of social conventions. In contrast, WCTU complaints against D. W. Griffith's *Intolerance* owed less to scenes of immodesty or decadence than to his belittling and critical portrayal of female social-purity reformers, who were, it seemed, caricatures of WCTU members. In the film, the interference of the women reformers destroys the life of a woman and her child.[25]

Historians who discuss Progressive-era rhetoric about the morality and movies often assert that reformers' emphasis on youths masked their prejudice against immigrants, who entered the United States at an unprecedented rate in the early twentieth century. Lary May, for instance, suggests that Progressive reformers wanted to manage and control the introduction of immigrants to American culture and hoped simultaneously to halt a perceived "revolution" in morality. Robert Sklar contends that the procensorship "moralists" (as he deridingly refers to them) focused on youths merely as a way to disguise their class-based agenda.[26] The WCTU's regulatory stance was, indeed, partially motivated by its desire to assist immigrant youths in becoming law-abiding citizens. In this context, the WCTU framed its requests for procensorship activism in terms of citizenship. "You are asked to help mobilize public sentiment," a Kentucky report beseeched, "until all motion pictures will reflect a wholesome attitude toward life and will help to make patriotic citizens instead of creating false ideals and helping to nullify respect for law and order."[27] The WCTU's interest in youths as citizens can be tied to its class-based fears of immigrants, who, to the organization's members, often represented the poorest and most alien of the urban classes.[28]

Yet the WCTU's intentions were more complex than this interpretation suggests. In focusing upon youth, the WCTU was putting on its traditional maternal mantle as the protector of children, displaying a tangle of gender, ethnic, and class concerns and, importantly, legitimizing women's participation in the political public sphere. The organization campaigned against "immoral" movies because they were more accessible to children than "obscene" literature. WCTU activists identified their movie censorship goal as the salvation of youths and referred to their censorship efforts as campaigns to "'mother the movies.'"[29] In fact, some local unions actively recruited mothers by "sending out 5,800 pages of motion picture literature to seven hundred new mothers."[30] Most unions publicized statistics on children's high movie-attendance rates to dramatize the urgent need for all women (as nurturers and mothers) to take action. Although censorship demands appeared as part of women's unselfish desire to help children, not themselves, the WCTU's focus on youths was also an integral part of its justification of women's political activism.

American women reformers tried to increase pressure for censorship at home through their focus on children around the world. Consequently, the WCTU's fight for the purity of the child viewer was carried on at an international level, as well as at the state and federal levels.[31] The WCTU was prompted to give its censorship campaign an international focus by the fact that by the 1920s the United States produced approximately "85 per cent of the pictures shown around the world."[32] Noting that complaints about American movies had been heard "in the Orient," Mexico, Canada, and Europe, the organization called for regulation of all films for international commerce.[33] In 1926 New York's director of motion pictures, Helen A. Miller, explicitly warned her colleagues that it was important for the United States to present a consistent moral image for American religious missionaries to succeed in gaining converts abroad:

> Countries we have long characterized as "heathen" have taken active steps against the American movies. Even Turkey has forbidden children under fifteen years of age to attend the movies "to protect young Turks from the demoralizing effects of American-made films." The infidel nation is aroused to save its children against the Christian nation. . . . Will Hays said in a recent

speech in Berlin "the world-wide distribution of films fill an important part in making people in different lands understand each other," but Sir Hesketh Bell [former governor of Uganda] says, "Nothing has done more to destroy the prestige of the white man among the colored races, than these deplorable pictures." . . . Our missionary magazines are full of the subject and our church bodies are continually calling our attention to the enormity of it.[34]

For Miller, the need of heathens to censor American movies revealed that Will Hays's promovie propaganda was superficial and false.[35]

The WCTU's negative view of America's domination of the global film market was linked to its advocacy of pacifism. It condemned films that made war seem exciting to young people, especially after the horrors of World War I. WCTU reformers characterized American movies as "one of the greatest obstacles to World Peace, inasmuch as they create international misunderstanding."[36] The WCTU established the Peace and Arbitration Department after World War I and, like many other women's groups, believed in the importance of international alliances in preventing another devastating war. In the 1930s the department protested against newsreels and feature-length films with jingoistic themes: "By inculcating the war spirit through news reel episodes which glamorize the use of military force as the solution of international problems and through numerous feature pictures which make war seem a glorious adventure, the screen continues to present war as an honorable phase of present-day life."[37] Fears about glamorizing and glorifying war heightened the WCTU's desire to teach youths to be pacifists.

Articles in the *Union Signal* such as one entitled "Recent Publicity concerning Film Censorship" reported on the foreign response to Hollywood films. A reporter accompanying president-elect Herbert Hoover to South America in 1928 quoted a Uruguayan editor, who claimed that American movies were a "main obstacle to the proper understanding and esteem between the United States and the South American countries" because they showed only the "cabaret life, the sins of society and crime. The news is filled with bank robberies, Hollywood divorces, gunmen and lynchings."[38] Reports such as this reinforced the claim that popular culture produced in the United States threatened to jeopardize the prestige of the nation and destabilize international relations. Returning from a 1930 national convention of the Federal Motion Picture Council, department director Maude Aldrich expressed racial biases that, at least in part, motivated her call for federal censorship: "The films that are *undermining the ideals of the youth of all lands,* causing the colored races of the world to distrust the leadership of the white race, and spreading international misunderstanding, are made in America."[39] If the "colored races of the world" saw evidence of lynchings, vigilante justice, adultery, and crime in the United States, they might judge white Americans to be hypocritical, immoral racists. Asserting the need to maintain the prestige and power of North American leadership over South America, the WCTU argued that the United States could not convincingly assert its moral and political influence if its popular culture pictured a society whose people disregarded its laws—including, of course, the WCTU's prized prohibition law, the Volstead Act.

WCTU concern for the effect of movies on youths not only led the organization to look beyond the borders of the United States, it also encouraged stronger appeals for national censorship and regulation. Agreeing on the dangers of movies to youths within the United States as well as without, the Department for the Promotion of Purity in Literature and Art organized a series of local campaigns designed to convince theater managers to show better movies, to close on Sundays, and to schedule special children's matinees. The department often targeted theater managers, since they were vulnerable to local community pressure. Reformers argued that even though exhibitors were locked into nationwide movie distribution contracts, they could be flexible regarding what types of movies they showed during those hours and days when the largest numbers of children attended the movies:

> Isn't it time to demand of local theater managers that pictures shown on Friday nights and Saturday afternoons be chosen carefully? A committee representing the General Federation of Women's Clubs, and similar organizations found that of 800 feature pictures only 39 were fit for children to see, and only 80 fit for any person under twenty to see.[40]

Agreeing that only a small number of Hollywood films were suitable for children's viewing, the General Federation of Women's Clubs and the WCTU, among others, attempted to regulate more closely children's access to commercial leisure activities.[41] Locally based movie censorship attempts often involved investigations of "doubtful" movies followed by complaints to local authorities, such as the chief of police or the mayor.[42] WCTU members also influenced town and municipal elections. For instance, WCTU records show that as the result of special elections, Sunday movies were forbidden in various communities in North Dakota, New Jersey, Ohio, Florida, Illinois, and Pennsylvania in the late 1920s and early 1930s.[43]

Some women's organizations, including the WCTU, had favored strong federal movie censorship from the first and joined with religious and moral reform groups to call for strict regulation.[44] From 1914 through the 1930s, the state and local unions heeded the national WCTU's call for government regulation of motion pictures and put tremendous energy into lobbying United States congressmen and senators for a series of laws ranging from legislation regulating the relationship between studios and local exhibitors to bills demanding full movie censorship. WCTU state departmental reports indicate that these national campaigns often took priority over campaigns for local or state censorship:

> This department [Northern California] has made its major work along legislative lines, principally flooding the United States legislators from California with resolutions and through them urging both houses of Congress to support the Motion Picture bills H.R. 2999, H.R. 4757 by Culkin and H.R. 6472 by Pettingill and later when introduced in the Senate, S-3012 by Neely.[45]

Federal motion picture censorship was never achieved, but the WCTU's persistent dedication to such a difficult national campaign makes sense in the context of its participation in other national legislative battles. One director sanguinely explained, "That is the way we gained the 18th and 19th amendments."[46] The department further argued that in light of the large number of movies produced and distributed each year, national censorship would be more efficient and effective.[47]

Affirming its interest in maintaining children's good morals, the Department for the Promotion of Purity in Literature and Art supported the first proposed federal movie censorship law, the Smith-Hughes Picture Censorship Bill of 1914. Written by Rev. Wilbur Crafts of the International Reform Bureau, this bill created the Federal Motion Picture Commission as part of the Bureau of Education. The commission's duty was "to censor all films, endorsing the good and condemning those which come under the specifications of what is 'obscene, indecent, immoral, inhuman, or those that depict a bull-fight, or a prize-fight, or that will corrupt or impair the morals of children or incite to crime.'"[48] The department was confident that if educators were appointed as censors, their moral-reform agenda would be similar to its own. It also believed that the above list of taboo subjects—including anything "inhuman"—was broad enough to improve the movies. The WCTU opposed early movies of prizefights, for example, as a sport that encouraged male brutality and illegal betting, incited violence in its audience, and worse, resulted in an "ungovernable spirit" in youths.[49] The WCTU urged its members, as well as other reform and religious organizations, to endorse the bill by sending letters, telegrams, resolutions, and petitions to Washington.[50] Four months after their initial calls for action, however, union leaders reported that "very few petitions" had been received in Congress and that the bill would probably be indefinitely held up in the House Committee on Education.[51] At this early stage, it seems, the WCTU could not successfully rally its large membership to the movie censorship cause, even by petitioning, a technique at which it had become so adept. The extraordinary effort WCTU members were giving at that time to woman's suffrage, war work, and the passage of national prohibition diverted their attention from the movie issue, which, they judged, would take years of further public agitation before a consensus was created.[52]

The WCTU interpreted as a victory for children the Supreme Court's first ruling on censorship and motion pictures in 1915. The judges decided that movie censorship was not in violation of the First or Fourteenth Amendments of the Constitution because movies were not art, but merely commercial products made for profit and open to regulation as "a business pure and simple." This ruling was important because it legitimized prior restraint, allowing a movie to be evaluated by a governmental agency before it was seen by the public.[53] Subsequent WCTU reports reiterated and supported the Court's decision: "[The movie producers'] goal—self stated, is 'profit.' 'Does It Pay' is their slogan. All is grist that comes to their mill—children, youth, foreigners who are trying to learn the meaning of Christian civilization, as well as the thronging adults who are ever looking for the latest thrill."[54] The movie industry's status as a money-making business was used to suggest that it had no regard for the moral ramifications of its products. Ironically, this attack on the profit motive constituted a critique of capitalism that came from within the very middle classes that promoted it.

Agitation for federal regulation of the movie industry gained momentum only in the early 1920s, after World War I had ended, and Prohibition and woman's suffrage had been achieved. A series of scandals over the dissipated life-styles of famous actors and actresses—accompanied by a noticeable proliferation of "sex pictures"—helped precipitate the first of two major crises for the movie industry. A noticeable decrease in middle-class movie attendance and more calls from the public for national movie censorship forced a response from the movie industry. In 1922 the Motion Picture Producers and Distributors of America hired the former postmaster general, Will Hays, to oversee the upgrading of morals in the movies.[55] Reform groups interested in protecting children such as the WCTU, the General Federation of Women's Clubs, and the National Congress of Parents and Teachers were initially optimistic that Hays would stand by his pledge to make "progress in 'ESTABLISHING AND MAINTAINING THE HIGHEST POSSIBLE MORAL AND ARTISTIC STANDARD OF MOTION PICTURE PRODUCTION.'"[56] Nevertheless, the WCTU downplayed the industry measures as temporary because they were noncompulsory and insisted, "We feel impressed with the need of a Federal law for the control of the motion picture business of the whole country."[57]

The national WCTU's increasing belief that movies had become the central cultural influence for youth prompted it in 1925 to officially rename its Department for the Promotion of Purity in Literature and Art: it became the "Motion Picture Department" to underscore its ongoing fight for movie censorship laws. This renaming reflected the department's steady shift of focus away from books and paintings and toward movie censorship in the second decade of the twentieth century.[58] Equally important, after the successful passage of Prohibition, movie censorship came to be seen by WCTU leaders as a political reform cause that might provide the national organization with a new and broader justification for its existence. The fight for movie censorship legislation became part of a national WCTU strategy to increase membership by highlighting this popular reform issue of the 1920s and 1930s.[59]

The final report of the national Department for the Promotion of Purity in Literature and Art, written by Director Harriet Pritchard in 1925, stressed that the department had worked to produce and support "pure" temperance movies for children since 1914:

> We believe the respectable shows [antialcohol and other educational movies in schools] will counteract the desire in the hearts of the children for the sensational and dangerous pictures that are now being presented to them in the public movies. It is ten years since we made arrangements to have moving pictures used, knowing that they would be helpful in Scientific Temperance Instruction.

Pritchard's report emphasized the WCTU's growing conviction that "the movies constitute much of the education of many."[60] She offered a vision of the power of movies over youths that not only justified but also demanded the creation of the Motion Picture Department:

> Shall this [movie industry] education produce graduates of the type of the 14 year-old girl murderers, of the Leopold-Loeb super-intellectuals criminal breed, of the flapper who is a potential mother and may reproduce more of the same, of the foreigner, the fool and the traitor who consider the 18th Amendment a joke and laugh at the Stars and Stripes?

This dramatic rhetorical question affirmed that much was at stake in the WCTU's support of movie censorship. Indeed, the regulation of literature, art, and even popular journalism seemed far less important than that of motion pictures, for "an evil incident in a newspaper does not have, perhaps, one-tenth the bad influence upon human conduct as would ensue if the same story were depicted in motion pictures."[61]

The work of the new Motion Picture Department began with its leaders testifying to Congress against self-regulation by the movie industry. The national department director, Maude Aldrich, reported that she and Mary Caldwell, the state director for Tennessee, attended the 1926 hearings on federal regulation held by the House Committee on Education, where Caldwell "gave a very convincing testimony as to her efforts to co-operate along lines suggested by the Motion Picture Industry, and of her failure to get better pictures, or to check the showing of the worst ones by the co-operation."[62] As the WCTU's voice on this issue, Maude Aldrich became a nationally visible procensorship leader. This visibility gained her positions as a lecturer for and member of the board of directors of the Federal Motion Picture Council in America, an organization instrumental in working for censorship both nationally and internationally.[63] In 1926, for instance, Aldrich gave "some 300 addresses," more than five per week, to various organizations.[64] She also published her views in periodicals such as the *National Grange Magazine, Woman's Missionary Friend,* and *Twentieth Century Progress,* as well as the *Union Signal.*[65]

The Motion Picture Department organized its procensorship fight around an attack on the motion picture industry's purported predominance in American popular culture—in effect, its cultural hegemony.[66] Aldrich began her department's campaign with a series of articles in the *Union Signal:* "What the People Want," "What the Exhibitor Wants," "Moral Standards of Motion Pictures," and "Endorsing Motion Pictures." Each article explained a different aspect of the industry's increasing control of motion pictures, such as the requirement that local exhibitors book a block of twelve to fifteen films at a time, sight unseen (the practices known as "block booking and "blind selling").[67] These practices particularly hampered any potential cooperation between sympathetic distributors and local procensorship citizen groups.[68] WCTU activists stressed that federal censorship laws were imperative because the motion picture industry was now "a great trust" that had to be controlled centrally to ensure effective regulation in the public interest.[69] By distributing concrete information about the economic power of the movie industry, Aldrich galvanized WCTU members to join in the Motion Picture Department's crusade.

The Hays Office became adept at deflecting reformers' critiques by promising with great fanfare to "clean up the industry." These announcements temporarily assured many reformers and the larger public that their protests were making an impact.[70] In response to the WCTU's protests during Prohibition against films that showed people drinking with impunity, it issued—and widely publicized—guidelines requiring the industry to "make certain that into no picture there be allowed to enter any 'shot' of drinking scenes, manufacture, or undue effects of liquor."[71] Although these guidelines were not systematically observed, the Hays Office's apparent acceptance of them served in the short term to dissipate the force of the WCTU's complaints. Indeed, hiring Will Hays was a brilliant public relations move by the movie industry rather than a real commitment to reform the content of motion pictures.

A 1928 article submitted to the *Union Signal* by Jason Joy, industrial relations director for the MPPDA, illustrates the public relations maneuvers of the industry.[72] Joy's article, entitled "How Women Can Help for Better Films," began with a flattering statement about how the industry was "eager" for the WCTU's opinion and dependent on its support. Next, he presented WCTU members with a "plan of co-operation." This proposal mimicked the industry-approved strategy of 1916–20 adopted by the National Committee for Better Films (and sponsored by the National Board of Review of Motion Pictures), calling for the WCTU to publicize those films it approved of, while remaining silent about those films of which it disapproved.[73] Joy took the opportunity to chide WCTU activists' practice of making vocal protests against particular films: "Therein lies the greatest obstacle to successful club work with motion pictures—this eternal looking for flaws."[74] Whereas other women's groups affiliated with the Committee for Better Films had refrained from fighting for legal censorship, focusing instead on inducing local exhibitors *voluntarily* to schedule proper movies for children, the WCTU had repeatedly forced the issue into the legal and political spheres by fighting for regulatory laws.

Maude Aldrich, of the national Motion Picture Department, responded sardonically to Joy's letter: "This would, indeed, be a most excellent cooperation in their own interest, for if we will advertise the good pictures they will advertise the bad ones and in this way get the largest possible gate-receipts from both."[75] Members of the WCTU, she explained, were dedicated to acting as surrogate parents, to help "neglected" children, "who most need protection from undesirable films and . . . are the ones who receive the least protection through indorsed {sic} lists of films." Endorsed lists would only be read by responsible parents and so would not help children who attended movies without guidance. The utility of such endorsements was clearly limited.[76] In spite of Joy's attempts, legal censorship remained the national WCTU's goal.

Remaining unconvinced of the virtues of the movie industry, department officials claimed that as the public waited patiently for self-regulation, the industry had produced "hundreds of the most artistic underworld films which the mind of man can devise."[77] By negatively characterizing Hollywood productions as representing the "artistic underworld," they obliquely identified the movie industry with a drug culture, as well as with a bohemian culture that ostensibly subverted America's moral and aesthetic standards through an obsession with sensuality, an overexposure of the female form, and a reliance on romantic plots that included adultery. Hollywood producers were charged with manipulating young audiences: "Low standards of life and conduct and excessive dependence upon thrill tend to empty a human life and the emptier a life is the more dependent it is upon stimuli from without." In criticizing unregulated movies of the 1920s, the WCTU characterized motion picture viewers as dependent, soulless addicts, devoid of any true aesthetic sensibility, and movies themselves as suppliers of empty thrills rather than "pure" ideals.[78] This image of the viewer as addict was common among progressive academics and reformers. The WCTU took for granted, however, that its own members would not become addicts; they could objectively view and then critique any movie without suffering from its otherwise harmful effects.

The WCTU's Motion Picture Department achieved its greatest credibility and political and organizational strength in the late 1920s and early 1930s. Its most sophisticated national procensorship campaign, in 1930, grew out of the movie industry's attempt to increase audience attendance during the early years of the depression, when movies again became more openly "impure." The new "sex pictures" generated another backlash within large segments of the public, which threatened to result in federal censorship.[79] To initiate its campaign, the department sent a resolution to Congress asserting that the motion picture industry had been given ample time to demonstrate its dedication to "clean" films and had failed to do so:

> WHEREAS, Present-day methods have proven entirely inadequate to meet the situation, and many pictures shown on the screen depict crime and immorality, scoff at Prohibition and establish false standards of social life, thus signally *failing to transmit the best, Therefore Be It Resolved,* That we respectfully request that your honorable body enact a law for the federal supervision of motion pictures, establishing higher standards before production for films that are to be licensed for interstate and international commerce.[80]

Emphasizing the necessity of preproduction intervention, the resolution was distributed in triplicate copies to state directors by national director Maude Aldrich "with a request that they not only encourage the unions to send in these resolutions but that they enlist every other organization possible to assist in the task."[81]

The political savvy and organizational skills of WCTU members produced results. Aldrich noted with satisfaction one news report that within a few weeks of the campaign's launching, "resolutions were reaching Congress from many organizations. The article said, 'apparently some organization is back of the movement.' Our WCTU leaders were actually mobilizing the organizations of the nation."[82] The WCTU saw itself—somewhat grandiosely—as the leading organization within the broader procensorship movement.[83] Demanding federal censorship of motion picture production, WCTU activists asked for and received signed resolutions from a wide variety of middle-class clubs and organizations:

> Churches, Missionary Societies, Bible study groups, Sunday schools, Men's Forums, Brotherhoods, Parent-Teacher Associations, D.A.R.'s, Daughters of Confederacy, Women's Clubs, Mother's Circles, Legion Auxiliaries, Rebecca Lodges, Business Men's organizations, Granges, Epworth Leagues, Y.P.B.'s [Young People's Branches of the WCTU], Girl's schools, and many other groups.[84]

As national director, Aldrich was clearly pleased by the widespread response of state and local WCTUs and other organizations to the procensorship resolution. In 1931 so many religious organizations "enlisted in the movement for federal supervision" that Aldrich modestly stated, "We would not as an organization claim credit for enlisting these great and influential groups in this vitally important movement, but we rejoice in their fellowship together with us and find renewed courage and inspiration in their action."[85]

Even in the year of its greatest failure, the revocation of the Eighteenth Amendment in 1933, the 355,000-member WCTU still commanded enough strength to organize another national petition drive for censorship.[86] Aldrich presided over this procensorship campaign when she "turned in to the United States Congress with personal letters to Congressmen over 100,000 names of persons petitioning for federal supervision."[87] Unwilling to acknowledge that much of its power had indeed ended with the repeal of Prohibition—yet recognizing a need to shift priorities after this defeat—the WCTU tried to deemphasize the importance of alcohol to its existence as a women's reform organization:

> Motion pictures are having a far more injurious effect upon public morals in general than the saloon ever had. The saloon touched a few millions of people directly and these were in the main adults. The motion picture touches every man, woman, and child in the whole country directly and its character molding effect is appalling.[88]

This position reflects both an intellectual shift and an organizational strategy that had emerged in the 1920s, whereby movies became the union's new lead-

87

ing enemy and a new reason for being. Alcohol, the WCTU explained, had indirectly affected the child through the actions of a drunk parent, but movies directly affected each child's character. The "scoffing" at Prohibition in movies, moreover, helped provide the WCTU with a scapegoat for its earlier failure and a spur to its new campaign.

The period of the WCTU's greatest strength as an organization working for movie censorship was 1925 to 1933.[89] The censorship efforts of the WCTU and other Protestant organizations, however, were overshadowed in 1934 by the Catholic Legion of Decency. While the WCTU pushed for federal regulation, a measure that was completely unacceptable to the movie industry, the Catholics, out of greater concern for the separation of church and state, advocated consumer boycotts. To spur Catholic parents into action, the legion used tactics familiar to WCTU members such as focusing rhetorically upon the dangers movies presented to youths: "What a massacre of innocence of youth is taking place hour by hour!"[90] Aldrich noted the legion's role in forcing the movie industry to strengthen its self-censorship mechanisms:

> The year [1934] has been notable for the creation of the "Legion of Decency," which has given unusual publicity to the character of the films being exhibited and to the need for more wholesome motion pictures. The immediate effect of this movement, originated in the Catholic church and *now equally shared by Protestant denominations,* has been to cause considerable activity among the Motion Picture Producers in selecting a number of splendid books and dramas as motion picture themes. They have also made deletions or stopped production in the case of a few films.[91]

Aldrich acknowledged the positive results of the industry's increased efforts toward self-censorship, specifically its commitment to produce movies based on "splendid books," but also insisted upon the WCTU's continued dedication to passing a federal movie censorship law.[92]

The movie industry inaugurated stricter self-censorship in creating the Production Code Administration (PCA) in 1934. Lea Jacobs's thoughtful study of self-censorship, *The Wages of Sin,* argues that 1934 did indeed mark a decisive turning point in the operation of the Hays Office. The PCA demanded more thoroughgoing revisions of plot and narrative structure, rather than the mere imposition of facile moralistic endings that had characterized the industry's earlier self-regulatory efforts.[93] The new restrictions enabled some WCTU directors to modify their view of the immediate danger presented by the movies.[94] The department's New Jersey director acknowledged improvements in 1938, noting that the "indecent picture is almost a thing of the past and drinking to some extent has been eliminated, as well as other undesirable features." Yet she felt compelled to modify her approval: "However, the work must go on, and every woman at her post is necessary. We have our movie-mad children and the powerful influence of the screen with us, as well as block booking and blind selling, which has been an agitation for the last ten years and which has not yet been definitely settled at Washington."[95] The sheer number of young viewers, all "mad" about movies, signaled to her that the American public could never rely on the movie industry's self-control but rather must continue to lobby for federal legislation. Her insistence reflects a bias in the WCTU against the effectiveness of "self-restraint" and in favor of legal restraints. Paradoxically, federal censorship was much less likely to win the support of politicians after 1934, for the industry could point with greater sincerity to its "cleaned up" films as proof that further regulation was unnecessary.

The WCTU's phrase, "mothering the movies," offered a justification for the activism of members, who felt compelled to protect all children, their own and others. "Mothering the movies," also a paradigm for WCTU members' conceptualization of the relationship between motion pictures and audiences, is therefore representative of their choice of solutions to the problems of the movies. Concerns about children were consistently linked by WCTU reformers to their understandings of evangelical internationalism, pacifism, and race, and to their views of the moviegoer as addict. The WCTU's censorship activism was tied, therefore, to its temperance activism. Its members believed that moviegoers were, like children and "heathens," eminently corruptible; like drunkards, they were incapable of self control. The WCTU's lack of faith in self-restraint applied to all moviegoers, but especially youthful ones. "Immoral" movies, in effect, drugged them. The organization had consistently argued that neither drunkards nor drink-sellers could exercise self-control; there was, by extension, no reason to expect that moviemakers or moviegoers could restrain themselves. Insisting "that every public amusement should be not only a pleasure but a moral uplift to humanity," the WCTU asserted that all movie viewers were in need of women's, or mothers', protection and that reforming women could make all forms of cultural consumption safe.[96]

At the turn of the century and today, censorship advocates have found their most common ideological ground on the subject of the vulnerability of youths. Reformers, judges, and legislators of the Progressive era focused on the susceptibility of youths when deciding what to censor and how to regulate youths' access to books, newspapers, and movies. Laywomen's rhetoric, defining censorship campaigns as programs to "mother the movies," led to high

ALISON M. PARKER

levels of grass-roots activism amongst the very women who advocated traditional values for themselves and their families. Today, new right and feminist antipornography activists also speak of protecting children as a means to reform culture. Indeed, much of the American public supports laws restricting the access of youths to pornographic films and supports harsh actions against those who create child pornography. The only adult pornography now subject to legal governmental regulation is that which is deemed by "community standards" to be without literary, social, or scientific value.[97] Like earlier reformers, the new right argues that censorship is necessary to protect children and traditional "family values."

Woman's Christian Temperance Union members welcomed experts and celebrated every legislative and regulatory advance as a victory for mothers and their children. Whereas some women defined themselves in hostile relation to child-study experts, union members tried to make innovative use of expert knowledge and apply it to their own concerns.[98] Historian Molly Ladd-Taylor asserts, "Motherhood was a central organizing principle of Progressive era politics. . . . [B]etween 1890 and 1920 it became an overtly political concern, inextricably tied to state-building and public policy."[99] Certainly this generalization is true of the WCTU's agenda. The union's appeal to the state to protect traditional values is ironic given government's reconstructive role: WCTU members, as women, did not consider the possibility that their maternal role as moral caretakers of the family might be usurped by a federal government with expanded regulatory powers. Rather, they believed they could achieve their goals more efficiently through the state. This belief was founded on the assumption that people like them would set the terms of censorship by proposing specific wordings of laws and appointing like-minded reformers and educators to censorship boards. In the long run, however, a centralized government proved corrosive of the very emphasis on volunteerism and individual moral effort that had been the hallmark of WCTU reform. The WCTU's grass-roots style of political action, which functioned so well through the use of petitions and local voluntary actions, was ultimately undermined by its call for government regulation, which removed the site of "mothering" ever farther from the home.

NOTES

1. This essay has been adapted from a chapter in *Purifying America: Women, Censorship, and Cultural Reform, 1873–1933*, forthcoming from the University of Illinois Press, in its Women in American History series. For discussions of early film, see

Eileen Bowser, *The Transformation of Cinema, 1907–1915* (New York, 1990); and John Fell, ed., *Before Hollywood: Turn-of-the-Century American Film* (New York, 1987).

2. For discussions of youths, progressive reformers, and the movies, see Miriam Hansen, *Babel and Babylon: Spectatorship in American Silent Film* (Cambridge, 1991), 320; Richard deCordova, "Ethnography and Exhibition: The Child Audience, the Hays Office, and Saturday Matinees," *Camera Obscura* 23 (1990): 103; Garth Jowett, *Film: The Democratic Art* (Boston, 1976), 77; and Robert Sklar, *Movie-Made America: A Social History of American Movies* (New York, 1975).

3. For further discussion of the local movements for child matinees, see deCordova, "Ethnography and Exhibition," 91–106.

4. Alta B. Norton, "Motion Pictures," *Ohio State Annual Report,* 1930, 127 (hereafter, annual reports of the WCTU are cited by state and the abbreviation *A. R.*). Mary Sayers, "The Crusade for Clean Movies," *Pennsylvania A. R.,* 1930, 108. All WCTU materials are at the Frances E. Willard Memorial Library in Evanston, Illinois, the national headquarters of the WCTU.

5. The WCTU's commitment to science and reform represents a fusion of Progressive-era faith in technology and its moral-reform goals.

6. Movies in vaudeville shows represented a middle stage of motion picture presentation, familiarizing a middle-class audience with movies before the growth of nickelodeons (Robert Allen, *Horrible Prettiness: Burlesque in American Culture* [Chapel Hill, 1991]).

7. Roy Rosenzweig, *Eight Hours for What We Will: Workers and Leisure in an Industrial City, 1870–1920* (New York, 1983), 190–93.

8. The National Board of Censorship was financed by the movie industry. The board created the Committee on Children's Pictures and Programs, run mainly by women from the General Federation of Women's Clubs, to urge parents to control their children's movie-viewing experience rather than fight for censorship (Charles Matthew Feldman, *The National Board of Censorship (Review) of Motion Pictures, 1909–1922* [New York, 1977], 194).

9. "Five Cent Schools of Crime," *Union Signal* (hereafter cited as *Signal*), October 18, 1906, 8.

10. For a discussion of America's emerging fascination with a popular youth culture, see Paula Fass, *The Damned and the Beautiful: American Youth in the 1920's* (New York, 1977).

11. The year 1907 marked the "first movie censorship ordinance ever passed in this country," in Chicago (see Ira H. Carmen, *Movies, Censorship and the Law* [Ann Arbor, 1965], 186).

12. "Five Cent Schools," 8.

13. "The Nickel Theater," *Signal,* April 25, 1907, 8.

14. Douglas Gomery, *Shared Pleasures: A History of Movie Presentation in the United States* (Madison, 1992); and Douglas Gomery, "The Movies Become Big Business: Publix Theaters and the Chain Store Strategy," *Cinema Journal* 18, no. 2 (spring 1979).

15. *National Minutes of the WCTU* (hereafter cited as *Minutes*), 1909, 334 (emphasis added). Also see Helen W. Barton, "Motion Pictures," *New York A. R.,* 1939, 86–88.

16. WCTU-produced or -endorsed movies were discussed as early as 1919 in leaflets such as "Making Our Own Motion Pictures" (see *Minutes,* 1919, 190; and "Motion Pictures," *Pennsylvania A. R.,* 1938, 99).

17. See Emilie D. Martin, "Promotion of Purity in Literature and Art," *Minutes,* 1897, 449; Emilie D. Martin, "Purity in Literature and Art," *Minutes,* 1899, 283; Mrs. H. H. Hubbart, "Report of the Department of Purity in Literature and Art," *Pennsylvania A. R.,* 1905, 214; and "Prize Fight Moving Pictures," *Signal,* July 21, 1910, 8.

18. *New York A. R.,* 1910, 170–71.

19. This estimate is probably higher than the average of children's movie-attendance rates (M. Evelyn Killen, "Motion Pictures," *Delaware A. R.,* 1931, 87; and Helen Andruss Miller, "Motion Pictures," *New York A. R.,* 1926, 161).

20. Norton, "Motion Pictures," 127; Sayers, "Crusade," 108.

21. Norton, "Motion Pictures," 127.

22. Maude M. Aldrich, "Motion Pictures," *Minutes,* 1930, 174–75; and Mary Sayers, "Department of Motion Pictures," *Pennsylvania A. R.,* 1929, 103.

23. Harriet S. Pritchard, "Purity in Literature and Art," *New York A. R.,* 1917, 139.

24. Harriet S. Pritchard, "Purity in Literature and Art," *Minutes,* 1916, 309.

25. Pritchard, "Purity," *New York A. R.,* 1917, 139.

26. Lary May, *Screening Out the Past: The Birth of Mass Culture and the Motion Picture Industry* (New York, 1980); and Sklar, *Movie-Made America,* 124.

27. Cora B. McGregor, "Motion Pictures," *Kentucky A. R.,* 1931, 107.

28. Also see "Resolutions Adopted by the Jubilee Convention," *Signal,* November 27, 1924, 8.

29. Jessie L. Leonard, "Motion Pictures," *Massachusetts A. R.,* 1928, 84.

30. Miller, "Motion Pictures," 162.

31. For a detailed account of the world's WCTU, see Ian Tyrell, *Woman's World/Woman's Empire: The Woman's Christian Temperance Union in International Perspective, 1880–1930* (Chapel Hill, 1991).

32. Maude M. Aldrich, "Motion Pictures," *Minutes,* 1926, 176; and "Motion Pictures," *Signal,* October 23, 1926, 14.

33. President Obregón of Mexico imposed an embargo on all films from the United States in 1922 (Ruth Inglis, *Freedom of the Movies: A Report on Self-Regulation from the Commission on Freedom of the Press* [New York, 1974; original copyright 1947], 99).

34. Helen Andruss Miller, "Motion Pictures," 162; and "Motion Pictures," *New York A. R.,* 1932, 136. See Patricia Hill, *The World Their Household: The American Woman's Foreign Mission Movement and Cultural Transformation, 1870–1920* (Ann Arbor, 1985), for an account of women's missionary work. Also see Peggy Pascoe, *Relations of Rescue: The Search for Female Moral Authority in the American West, 1874–1939* (Oxford, 1990).

35. For a discussion of colonialism and censorship, see Ruth Vasey's contribution in this anthology.

36. Miller, "Motion Pictures," 1926, 162; Harriet S. Pritchard, "Purity in Literature and Art," *New York A. R.,* 1922, 99; Harriet S. Pritchard, "Purity in Literature

and Art," *New York A. R.,* 1925, 160; and Maude M. Aldrich, "Motion Pictures," *Minutes,* 1928, 156–59.

37. Lulu Heacock, "Motion Pictures," *Southern California A. R.,* 1938, 94. In New York, newsreels were not subject to state and local censorship regulation after 1927 (Carmen, *Movies,* 142–43).

38. "Recent Publicity concerning Film Censorship," *Signal,* March 30, 1929, 14. Maude M. Aldrich, "Motion Pictures," 1926, 176; and "Motion Pictures," *Minutes,* 1925, 192.

39. Maude M. Aldrich, "The Motion Picture Problem," *Signal,* January 25, 1930, 12 (emphasis added). See Terry Ramsaye, *A Million and One Nights: A History of the Motion Picture* (New York, 1925), 642–43; and *Minutes,* 1917, 194.

40. Mrs. Bristol French, "Motion Pictures," *Missouri A. R.,* 1933, 90.

41. Barton, "Motion Pictures," 86–88.

42. Maude M. Aldrich, "Moral Standards of Motion Pictures," *Signal,* October 6, 1928, 13. See Emilie D. Martin, "Higher Standards for Women in Literature and Art," *Signal,* June 22, 1911, 11; *Minutes,* 1916, 309; *Minutes,* 1908, 362; and Ida Mabel Apgar, "Motion Pictures," *New Jersey A. R.,* 1933, 105.

43. Maude M. Aldrich, "Motion Pictures," *Minutes,* 1929, 174; Lulu Freeman Larry, "Motion Pictures," *Illinois A. R.,* 1929, 82; Sayers, "Department of Motion Pictures," 103; Aldrich, "Motion Pictures," 1930, 174–75; Norton, "Motion Pictures," 127; and Millie C. Munson, "Social Morality," *New Jersey A. R.,* 1921, 67.

44. For an exploration of women's role in the National Board of Censorship, see Andrea Friedman, "'To Protect the Morals of Young People, and Likewise Womanhood': Women and the Regulation of Obscenity in Early Twentieth-Century New York" (paper presented at the Berkshire Conference on Women's History, Rutgers University, June 1990). See also Feldman, *National Board of Censorship.*

45. Carrie A. Clark, "Motion Picture Department," *Northern California A. R.,* 1936, 83. See also Jessie L. Leonard, "Motion Pictures," *Massachusetts A. R.,* 1933, 79.

46. Jennie M. S. Laird, "Motion Picture Department," *Nebraska A. R.,* 1931, 51.

47. For problems with enforcement, see Florence Havens Ayres, "Motion Pictures," *New Jersey A. R.,* 1938, 97.

48. Harriet S. Pritchard, "A Federal Motion Picture Commission," *Signal,* May 21, 1914, 10.

49. Ramsaye, *Million and One Nights,* 286–89. For other work on early film, see John L. Fell, ed., *Film before Griffith* (Berkeley, 1983); Anthony Slide, *Early American Cinema* (New York, 1970); and Tino Balio, ed., *The American Film Industry,* rev. ed. (Madison, Wis., 1985). Hansen, *Babel and Babylon.*

50. Margaret Ellis, "Motion Picture Censorship Bill Should Pass," *Signal,* June 25, 1914, 2.

51. "Hughes-Smith Censorship Bill Needs Help," *Signal,* October 1, 1914, 9; and Harriet S. Pritchard, "Work for the Promotion of Purity in Literature and Art," *Signal,* March 2, 1916, 10.

52. Harriet S. Pritchard, "Purity in Literature and Art," *New York A. R.,* 1916, 175. See Nancy F. Cott, *The Grounding of Modern Feminism* (New Haven, 1987).

53. For discussions of these issues, see Carmen, *Movies,* chap. 1; and Murray

Schumach, *The Face on the Cutting Room Floor: The Story of Movie and Television Censorship* (New York, 1964).

54. Helen A. Miller's image of the movie producers as obsessed with profit may have been part of a veiled anti-semitism that was sometimes directed at the movie industry (Miller, "Motion Pictures," 1926, 161). See Neal Gabler, *An Empire of Their Own: How the Jews Invented Hollywood* (New York, 1988).

55. For descriptions of the scandals, see Slide, *Early American Cinema,* 146–47; and Ramsaye, *Million and One Nights,* 803–21. Leonard J. Leff and Jerold L. Simmons document resistance from film directors to "cleaner" pictures in *The Dame in the Kimono: Hollywood, Censorship, and the Production Code from the 1920s to the 1960s* (New York, 1990).

56. "Cleaning Up the Movies," *Signal,* July 13, 1922, 9.

57. See Harriet S. Pritchard, "Purity in Literature and Art," *New York A. R.,* 1923, 121; Cora McGregor, "Motion Pictures," *Kentucky A. R.,* 1928, 93; Lillie R. Stone, "Purity in Literature and Art," *Massachusetts A. R.,* 1922, 80; and Pritchard, "Purity," 1922, 98. Also see Ramsaye, *Million and One Nights,* 308.

58. State unions had separate Departments for the Promotion of Purity in Literature and Art as late as 1927 (see Katherine L. S. Goddard, "Purity in Literature and Art," *Massachusetts A. R.,* 1927, 83).

59. Lulu Freeman Larry, "Motion Pictures," *Illinois A. R.,* 1931, 78; Jessie L. Leonard, "Motion Pictures," 1928, 83; and "Motion Picture Department," *Massachusetts A. R.,* 1927, 77.

60. Pritchard, "Purity," *New York A. R.,* 1925, 160.

61. Ibid., 161.

62. Aldrich, "Motion Pictures," 1926, 175.

63. Aldrich, "Motion Pictures," 1925, 192; and Mary Sayers, "Motion Pictures," *Pennsylvania A. R.,* 1927, 104–5.

64. Aldrich, "Motion Pictures," 1926, 176.

65. Maude M. Aldrich, "Motion Pictures," *Minutes,* 1932, 182.

66. The problems of popular culture and cultural hegemony are addressed by Lawrence Levine, *Highbrow/Lowbrow: The Emergence of Cultural Hierarchy in America* (Cambridge, 1988); John Fiske, *Understanding Popular Culture* (Boston, 1989); and Allen, *Horrible Prettiness.*

67. Block booking was not prohibited by the Supreme Court until 1946. For information on the legal history of block booking, see Michael Conant, *Antitrust in the Motion Picture Industry: Economic and Legal Analysis* (Berkeley, 1960); "Congressional Proposal Prohibits Blind and Block Booking of Films," *Signal,* May 10, 1930, 2–3; Maude M. Aldrich, "The Motion Picture Problem," *Signal,* January 25, 1930, 12; and Maude M. Aldrich, "What the Exhibitor Wants," *Signal,* May 28, 1925, 6.

68. Aldrich, "Moral Standards," 12.

69. Miller, "Motion Pictures," 1926, 161; Sayers, "Crusade," 107.

70. Maude M. Aldrich, "What the People Want," *Signal,* March 5, 1925, 6.

71. "Do the Liquor Dealers Control Censorship of Moving Pictures?" *Signal,* April 20, 1916, 3; "Department of Motion Pictures," *Signal,* January 1, 1927, 10. "Motion Picture Producers Adopt Policy of Support of Prohibition Law," *Signal,* July 24, 1926, 3.

72. Joy was a retired official of the American Red Cross and had worked in the War Department (Inglis, *Freedom of the Movies*, 103).

73. The WCTU's Department of Social Morality had experimented with a version of this "boost the best" plan in 1920 but had quickly disavowed its utility (Gertrude S. Martin, "What About the Movies?" *Signal*, March 25, 1920, 5).

74. Jason S. Joy, "How Women Can Help for Better Films," *Signal*, June 2, 1928, 15.

75. Maude M. Aldrich, "Motion Pictures," *Signal*, December 5, 1925, 12.

76. Maude M. Aldrich, "Indorsing Motion Pictures," *Signal*, October 27, 1928, 15.

77. Aldrich, "Moral Standards," 12.

78. Ibid.

79. June Sochen, *Mae West: She Who Laughs, Lasts* (Arlington Heights, 1992). For an "unauthorized" account, see Kenneth Anger, *Hollywood Babylon* (New York, 1975), 259–70.

80. Helen Andruss Miller, "Motion Pictures," *New York A. R.,* 1930, 164.

81. Aldrich, "Motion Pictures," 1930, 173.

82. Ibid.

83. In 1929, Aldrich, as national director, spoke to a wide variety of religious conventions, such as the national convention of the Disciples of Christ, the New York Synod of the United Presbyterian Church, and the Methodist Episcopal Church, and successfully convinced them to pass "resolutions for federal supervision of motion pictures providing higher standards at the source of production" (Aldrich, "Motion Pictures," 1929, 173; and Sayers, "Department of Motion Pictures," 103).

84. Maude M. Aldrich, "Motion Pictures," *Signal*, December 13, 1930, 12.

85. In spite of the WCTU's professed concerns about "race hatred," Aldrich unproblematically reported that among the approximately two thousand resolutions sent to Congress in 1931, the "Women of K.K.K." had registered its approval of censorship along with the Rotary Club and the Girl Scouts (Maude M. Aldrich, "Motion Pictures," *Minutes,* 1931, 116).

86. Joseph R. Gusfield, *Symbolic Crusade: Status Politics and the American Temperance Movement* (Urbana, 1963), 162.

87. Maude M. Aldrich, "Motion Pictures," *Minutes,* 1933, 176.

88. Alice W. Mann, "Department of Motion Pictures," *Pennsylvania A. R.,* 1932, 108.

89. Maude M. Aldrich, "Motion Pictures," *Minutes,* 1934, 171; and "Motion Pictures," *Pennsylvania A. R.,* 1938, 99.

90. Quoted in Jowett, *Film,* 248. For a more extensive discussion of the role of Catholics in the censorship movement, see contributions by Francis Couvares in this anthology.

91. Aldrich, "Motion Pictures," 1934, 172 (emphasis added).

92. Ibid.; LuAnna Wilson, "Motion Pictures," *New York A. R.,* 1934, 122.

93. Lea Jacobs, *The Wages of Sin: Censorship and the Fallen Woman Film 1928–1942* (Madison, Wis., 1991).

94. Jowett, *Film,* 254.

95. Ayres, "Motion Pictures," 97.

96. Harriet S. Pritchard, "Moving Pictures as Educators," Literature and Art Leaflet No. 5, 1911, 4–5, Willard Memorial Library.

97. See Edward De Grazia, *Censorship Landmarks* (New York, 1969).

98. Ruth Bordin, *Woman and Temperance: The Quest for Power and Liberty, 1873–1900* (Philadelphia, 1981); Barbara Epstein, *The Politics of Domesticity: Women, Evangelism, and Temperance in Nineteenth-Century America* (New York, 1981).

99. Molly Ladd-Taylor, *Mother-Work: Women, Child Welfare, and the State, 1890–1930* (Urbana, 1994), 43. For more extensive discussions of maternalist discourse, see Seth Koven and Sonya Michel, eds., *The Origins of Welfare States* (New York, 1993).

"To Prevent the Prevalent Type of Book"

Censorship and Adaptation in Hollywood, 1924–1934

RICHARD MALTBY

As a literary study in stark realism and exposition of animal passions running wild, the novel has considerable merit. . . . As a screen proposition, *An American Tragedy,* with its shameless wallowings in the sex gutters, its debauchery and insistent dwelling on the baser sides of human nature, would seem impossible of conversion into anything resembling wholesome or appealing entertainment for the majority of picture followers.

Harrison's Reports, April 18, 1931

In June 1932, furious at Paramount's travesty of his most recent novel, Theodore Dreiser denounced "The Real Sins of Hollywood" to readers of Bernarr Macfadden's *Liberty* magazine. Producers, he reported, were quite uninterested in transferring an author's ideas to the screen and would be much happier if they had to pay for only the title of a play like Eugene O'Neill's *Strange Interlude.* Then they could have their writers fashion a movie script with a plot bearing only the vaguest resemblance to the original. When asked to justify this defamation, they claimed that the play itself was "far above the head" of the average moviegoer, who in any case knew no more about it than that a play of that title had been a big success in New York. Such barbaric treatment of literature, concluded Dreiser, "spells the end of art, does it not?"[1]

Dreiser's familiar scenario is one of Hollywood's most frequently told tales, a genre piece in its own right. Few eastern writers seemed to feel that their profitable sojourn in Hollywood was complete until they had published an account of their mistreatment at the hands of studio executives or their scenario

97

Clyde Griffiths (Phillip Holmes) is interrogated by District Attorney Orville Mason (Irving Pichel) in the trial scene of *An American Tragedy*. Photo courtesy Paul Ballard Collection, Academy of Motion Picture Arts and Sciences.

departments. In 1930 Stephen Vincent Benét rejected his agent's suggestion that he write such a piece, saying "I'd rather be the person who went there and didn't." O'Neill, who embodied the commercial success of the creative artist on Broadway, was a recurring icon of such pieces. Robert E. Sherwood suggested in 1929 that if a studio could hire him, they would doubtless turn O'Neill loose on *Rebecca of Sunnybrook Farm.* Another staple ingredient of the genre was a denunciation of the way Hollywood adapted the author's material so that, as Leda Bauer explained in the *American Mercury* in 1928, the original story was completely rewritten: "When there is no longer any connection with the story on which the screen play was based, it is pronounced perfect, the title is changed to something short, spicy, and completely inapplicable, and the original story is resold to another company to go through the same process."[2]

1

Conventional criticism of Hollywood's practices of adaptation has also been preoccupied with assessing a movie's adequacy to its source material. A metaphor of failed or inverted alchemy recurs in this criticism: whatever the quality of the original material, Hollywood's apprentice sorcerers are seldom credited with producing anything but "disappointing lead." This critical discourse operates at a relatively untheorized level, assuming that the literary work possesses a stable, transhistorical meaning. A movie's fidelity to its original source is conventionally measured by how well it captures the "letter and the spirit" of the text, as though adaptation was, in critic Dudley Andrew's phrase, "the rendering of an interpretation of a legal precedent."[3]

At a number of distinct discursive levels the critical examination of adaptation has privileged the authority of the precursor text, endorsing the attitudes of writers who derived their idea of the profession of authorship from the New York literary marketplace. What Barbara Herrnstein Smith has called "evaluative authority" has been conferred on their opinions of Hollywood's procedures. Claiming to speak from the cultural center, they have been called upon "to devise arguments and procedures that validate the community's established tastes and preferences, thereby warding off barbarism and the constant apparition of an imminent collapse of standards." Herrnstein Smith suggests that those who possess evaluative authority represent their opinions as "a consensus based on objective value" and pathologize other positions as deficient: "suffering from crudenesses of sensibility, diseases and distortions of perception, weaknesses of character, impoverishment of background-and-education, cultural or historical biases, ideological or personal prejudices, and/or underdeveloped, corrupted, or jaded tastes."[4] Eastern writers, and the critics who have followed them, would endorse every term of this description as an accurate representation of the experience of adaptation in Hollywood. The villains of their scenario have almost always been a combination of philistine producers and picayunish industry censors, the "Self-Regulators" of the "Hays Office," bowdlerizing Art in the name of the innocence and ignorance of the great American public.[5]

On the assumption that the Hays Office's function was to prevent particular kinds of representations from reaching the screen, industry censors have been blamed almost as frequently as the producers for Hollywood's failure to transcend itself. Describing the Alfred Hitchcock/David O. Selznick adaptation of Daphne Du Maurier's *Rebecca,* for example, Robin Wood declares, "We know that the change from the novel was dictated by the Motion Picture Production

Code, not anyone's actual desire."[6] Wood characterizes the Production Code and its administrators as dictatorial, but neither desiring nor desirable; they are credited with no intention other than the repression of meaning. The discursive framework of "censorship" has been one of the mechanisms by which Hollywood has been blamed for what it was not, rather than blamed, endorsed, or simply acknowledged for what it was. But those who have castigated Hollywood as imitative rather than innovative, conservative rather than progressive, repressed rather than liberating, have seldom explained how it could have occupied any location in American cultural topography other than its assigned place as the primary instrument of the mass culture against which modernist cultural leadership and innovation defined itself.

By way of contrast to these accounts, which assume that what motivated Hollywood's practice of adaption was a form of aesthetic ineptitude, this article describes that practice as belonging to a conscious ideological project. Through its trade association, the Motion Picture Producers and Distributors of America, Inc. (MPPDA), the American film industry deliberately sought to "prevent the prevalent type of book and play from becoming the prevalent type of picture." This project, documented in detail in the case files of the Production Code Administration (PCA) and its precursor, the Studio Relations Committee (SRC), arose from the particular public position in which the industry found itself as a purveyor of fictions for mass consumption. In a speech the MPPDA often quoted, its president, Will Hays, argued, "When you buy a book by a certain author, you have at least a general idea of what it is about and of what sort of psychology is going to be offered to you." But while novelists and dramatists appealed to "a more or less limited group" of "sophisticates," motion pictures had "a following infinitely more numerous," made up of "the vast majority of Americans, who do not fling defiance at customs and conventions, but who cling with fine faith and devotion to the things that are wholesome and healthy and who live lives similar to those of their forefathers, who made America what it is."[7]

Hays, the Hoosier Presbyterian elder who had masterminded Warren Harding's election campaign of 1920, had an apparently inexhaustible supply of such rhetorical homilies. Underlying them, however, and disguised by their banality, was a recognition that the industry's practice of adaptation formed an important part of its defensive posture toward those civic and religious groups such as the General Federation of Women's Clubs who had designated themselves as parentally in charge of the nation's culture. Although sophisticates might object to the effect of censorship "befuddling . . . what has gone not only unchallenged but approved in literature and on the stage,"[8] the industry did not recognize the cultural authority of New York's literati, nor did it adopt their evaluative criteria. It merely paid them wages. The seemingly endless story conferences that eastern authors found so objectionable in Hollywood's practices of adaptation and narrative construction were the occasions on which, as Jeffrey Sconce has put it, the economic capital of the studio was used "to convert the cultural capital of the novel back into the economic capital of a successful motion picture." The production company's interest was satisfied if the source material was adapted to the conventions of its movie genre and the expectations of the audience: "While such an adaptation might inspire a few people to return to the novel, the chief concern was that it enticed them to return to the moviehouse."[9] The *Variety* review of Paramount's adaption of *An American Tragedy* stated the point bluntly: "Critics will see two sides to this film—as a picture and as an adaptation of the novel. The latter phase is not as important to the trade as whether it's going to do any business."[10] Beyond such commercial vulgarities, the industry's concern was, equally, less with the adaptation of a work than with its adaptation to a set of external political conditions. The regulations it devised to render "objectionable" books or plays "unobjectionable" sought both to maximize commercial advantage and to distribute an affirmative cultural vision Hays shared with the clubwomen. "The manhood and womanhood of America is sound and wholesome," Hays declared in 1925, "and it wants wholesomeness in its entertainment in accord with the wholesomeness in its life."[11]

2

What Hays called the "organized industry"—the major vertically integrated companies constituting the industry's oligopoly power and comprising the dominant membership of the MPPDA—maintained a consistent attitude toward the practices of adaptation and regulation throughout the 1920s and 1930s. The fundamentals of its position had been established in the previous two decades. Since Chicago's first censorship ordinance of 1907, the public debate over movie content had always been conducted around the question of whether the motion picture industry was morally fit to control the manufacture of its own products. In a 1915 decision that determined the constitutional status of the medium for the next thirty-seven years, the Supreme Court had declared that motion pictures were "mere representations of events, of ideas and sentiments, published and known" and therefore not to be afforded the protection of the First Amendment. The Court's decision did more than establish the constitutionality of prior censorship. In declaring that the motion picture industry was "a business pure and simple . . . not to be regarded . . . as part of the press of the country, or as organs of public opinion," the Court confirmed a widely held Progressive opinion that "pure" entertainment—amusement that was not harmful to its consumer—was a commodity comparable to the pure meat guaranteed by the Food and Drug Administration, and its manufacture and distribution just as liable to the incursions of government regulation.[12]

Led by its exhibition sector, the industry had recognized the economic sense of maintaining its own procedures for the regulation of content since the formation of the Motion Picture Patents Company in 1908. The National Board of Censorship, financed through industry trade associations but staffed by volunteers from civic groups, had performed this regulatory function with some success until its effectiveness was severely damaged by the public controversy over *The Birth of a Nation* in 1915. Two other short-lived trade associations had subsequently sought to resist the implementation of federal and state censorship legislation by pledging themselves to voluntary codes of practice over screen content. The MPPDA was established in 1922 to safeguard the political interests of the emerging oligopoly, and while censorship and the regulation of content were important aspects of its work, the association's central concern was with the threat of legislation or court action to impose a strict application of the antitrust laws to the industry. It pursued policies of industrial self-regulation in matters of arbitration and intraindustry relations as well as film content, and Hays firmly attached the movies to the "associative state" fostered by Herbert Hoover's Department of Commerce. In pursuit of its avowed intent "to establish and maintain the highest possible moral and artistic standards of motion picture production," the association also constructed an elaborate public relations operation by which it established contact with nationally federated fraternal, educational, and religious organizations to make them "a friendly rather than a hostile critic of pictures."[13]

In its scale and its apparent openness, the MPPDA's public relations policy was indicative of the larger project of culturally legitimating the amusement industry it represented. This strategy presumed a degree of cultural consensus about appropriate behavior and appropriate texts, or what Hays called "fundamental agreement about what is right and what is wrong."[14] One site where such agreement did not exist, however, was on the Broadway stage of the mid and late 1920s. Another was in the fiction best-selling lists. In both, cultural conventions were being challenged with varying degrees of maturity and durability. Works like *The Plastic Age, The Green Hat, Elmer Gantry, Bad Girl,* or *An*

American Tragedy provided the industry with a considerable problem. Their financial success made them commercially desirable and culturally appropriate for adaptation, but their content made that adaptation extremely problematic.

The studios relied on what was called "pre-tested" material—novels, short stories, and plays—for something over half of their output, particularly of prestige and big-budget productions. Adaptations from Broadway successes, best-selling novels and nonfiction, and short stories from the mass-circulation magazines offered the best guarantee of commercial success, substantially outweighing the cost of their acquisition. Because well-known properties had already achieved public recognition, their copyright status was relatively easy to clarify, and companies could avoid the legal hazards sometimes attendant on unsolicited original material. The studios spent considerable sums on source acquisition, and by 1925 the motion picture rights of novels were worth an average of $5,000, while a successful play would sell for $20,000. Prices rose in the second half of the decade: by the early 1930s Warners spent an average of $600,000 a year on purchasing source material, and in the 1933–34 production season, the industry as a whole bought 200 novels and nonfiction books at a cost of $2 million. Purchasing power on this scale made the industry an important source of revenue for both writers and publishers. Income from the sale of subsidiary rights, including movie rights, was commonly much larger than that from royalties. The publicity value of a film could also add to book sales: the movie edition of *All Quiet on the Western Front* sold 200,000 copies in two months.[15]

For both material and ideological reasons, the industry's position made it difficult to reject source material that had already proved commercially successful in another medium, but a significant proportion of both the novels and plays of the 1920s contained "unsuitable" material. The industry purchased more material than it could use, regarding the excess expenditure as an inevitable waste cost in an industry governed by fashion. There might be a variety of reasons for not producing a film from a book: a decision about the script's lack of entertainment value, the absence of a suitable star, or the failure to solve a fundamental scripting problem in condensing a novel's plot, for instance. The requirements of censorship were another such reason, one that the administrators of the Production Code understood as a generic pressure, comparable to the pressure of convention in, for example, a romantic comedy. The conversion to sound presented additional problems by increasing the industry's dependence on pretested sources for dialogue, particularly in a period when the Broadway stage was itself threatened with state censorship and denounced by Cardinal Patrick Hayes, Roman Catholic archbishop of New York, as "reeking with filth." Early in 1927 the New York police closed three plays dealing with homosexual themes. Shortly thereafter, the Wales Padlock law prohibited the representation of "sex degeneracy or sex perversion on the stage." Producer John Golden wrote in *Theatre Magazine* that Broadway was "passing through an epidemic of sex and filth . . . due this time, they tell us, to the war, to women's rights (whatever they are), to frank talk, jazz and close-proximity dancing, short skirts, open work in clothes and open work between the sexes."[16]

The MPPDA's first regulation of motion picture content was instituted in June 1924 and dealt exclusively with the problem of adaptation. The Formula, as it was known, was a formalization of existing practice by which studios were discouraged from picturizing a book or play containing "salacious or otherwise harmful" subject matter for fear that it might have "a deleterious effect on the industry in general." The procedure was instituted because of complaints from civic groups about the adaptation of a number of novels in the 1923–24 production season, among them *Flaming Youth, Three Weeks, Black Oxen,* and *West of the Water Tower.* It was a relatively crude mechanism, effectively operating a blacklist of works not to be filmed. In 1925 Hays claimed that the Formula had kept 160 "prevalent books and plays" with picturization rights worth $2–3 million from the screen.[17]

Not surprisingly, the Formula provoked the hostility of both publishers and writers. In February 1924, for instance, Ethel Smith Dorrance accused Hays of being responsible for Universal's decision not to produce an adaptation of her novel *Damned.* Although he denied that the association had made any statement against the book, Hays acknowledged that it had been discussed by the association's Board of Directors, who felt that "a picture following the book with the same title would merit very severe criticism." The Authors' League of America took up the case, asking that Hays "state specifically the objections" to Dorrance's scenario adaptation of her book, which had partially sanitized the plot. They suggested that Hays was being unfair in condemning the adaptation "on the basis of the advertising, title, or contents of the book." Hays persuaded them that they had no case against the association, but they pursued the issue with Universal, arguing that it was "detrimental to an author's reputation if a picture based upon the author's work is not produced," and that a company's purchase of picture rights committed them to produce it. In reply, Universal's president, Carl Laemmle, bluntly asserted his property rights: "The matter of the producing or not producing of *Damned* is one which I alone can determine and, of course, I cannot subscribe to your statement that 'production must be considered as part of the compensation to the author.'" Laemmle also warned Hays that other producers should be dissuaded from accepting any contract provision "which could be construed as any right on the part of the author to force the producer to produce any story bought." Subsequently, the league threatened the MPPDA with an antitrust suit, and negotiations between them produced a revised version of the Formula in December 1927. This now permitted the author of a rejected story to provide a new story, with a new title that "in no way suggests the old title, containing all that is suitable in the original story and omitting all that is unsuitable for the screen. If the story is accepted and produced it will be advertised as an entirely new story and will not be presented as an adaptation or revised version of the rejected story. In none of the publicity or advertising will mention of the rejected book or play be made."[18]

By 1927 the association had extended its mechanisms for the regulation of content by compiling a code to govern production, administered by its Studio Relations Committee in Hollywood. The "Don'ts and Be Carefuls," as this code was familiarly known, synthesized the restrictions and eliminations applied by state and foreign censors. Two years later Hays initiated a further elaboration of the code, which after prolonged internal discussion emerged in April 1930 as *A Code to Maintain Social and Community Values in the Production of Silent, Synchronized and Talking Motion Pictures.* The industry's internal debates over the implementation of the Production Code revealed the extent to which producers were primarily concerned with the problems of adaptation, particularly given the new possibilities offered by sound. MGM's head of production, Irving Thalberg, who had chaired the committee responsible for compiling the "Don'ts" in 1927, argued that "a character may speak delicately and exactly of subjects which he could by no stretch of the imagination indicate in pantomime." Such movies could "tread on more delicate ground" and deal "with perfect propriety . . . with human elements the silent picture was forced to shun." The additional possibilities provided by spoken dialogue therefore made it legitimate "to use any book or play which has attained wide notice or attracted general interest even though the book or play borders on the censorable," provided that in preparing it for production the story was "cleaned up so as to be appropriate for exhibition." Regarded purely as a social influence, Thalberg argued, "the decent presentation of an interesting but originally questionable story theme would do much to counteract its former unfavorable influence."[19]

In its practice of adaptation the industry had to steer a narrow course between the restrictive requirements of vocal public opinion and accusations from authors and audiences that they were attempting to obtain "attendance by deception" through "misleading, salacious or dishonest advertising." The agreement with the Authors' League, the apparently preposterous process by which a story was rewritten, retitled, and then sold on the basis of the value of what was no longer in it, was an attempted solution. On one hand it provided for a commercially equitable relationship between the culture industries of publishing and motion pictures. On the other, by concealing the fact that *A Woman of Affairs* was adapted from Michael Arlen's *The Green Hat,* or *The Story of Temple Drake* from Faulkner's *Sanctuary,* it tried to answer the complaint of civic groups that, however much the content of films based on "salacious" sources was modified, their existence would encourage readers to turn to the corrupt original to discover the real story. The project sought to maximize mutual commercial advantage at the same time that it overtly declared itself as an exercise in the ideological recuperation of "unsuitable"—that is, culturally unsettling—literary material. Although the producers claimed to be "fully sympathetic" toward authors' objections to "the distorting of stories" and of authorial intentions in the process of adaptation, they maintained, "This was a condition that has always existed and . . . cannot be avoided." "Radical changes" to the author's original story arose inevitably from "the exigencies of production as well as the demands of the public [and] censorship conditions." The Formula was a means of offering authors material compensation in exchange for their abandonment of any equity rights over the picturization of their original material.[20]

In practice, the Formula seldom obscured the origins of adaptations, and while the MPPDA disingenuously claimed that filmmakers were taking the responsible course and protecting the innocent from corrupting or disturbing information, their critics argued that they were cynically encouraging a sophisticated mode of audience response that involved reading through the action on the screen to identify deliberately displaced meanings. In *A Woman of Affairs,* for example, the explanation for the husband's suicide on their wedding night was changed from his having syphilis to his having perpetrated a bank fraud: whether audiences, particularly those members alert to the connotations of the book, accepted this somewhat arbitrary substitution was a matter of some debate.[21] Contrary to Thalberg's expectation that sound would expand the possibilities of delicate expression, its immediate effects were to disrupt the silent cinema's mechanisms of ambiguity and visual innuendo and to render the objectionable more explicit. As the complaints of civic and religious groups grew ever more strident after 1929, however, Hays came increasingly to feel that the assimilation of contemporary literature was far more trouble than it was worth. In 1933 he bluntly told producers,

Most of the trouble in Code observation, censorship and public disapprobation of this business grows out of bad source material. Much could be prevented if we did not start out on a bad story. Very few instances have there been where the result was worth the trouble. . . . The minute you buy a story like *Sanctuary* until this time next year when it is played in the last outpost, there is trouble. There has not been a day in the last three months when this office has not had some repercussions about *Sanctuary*—not a day.[22]

After 1933 even the Nobel Prize offered no protection: Sinclair Lewis's *Ann Vickers,* widely condemned in the Catholic press, did not escape the Production Code until its characters had been ritually denounced and burdened with a conventional morality, and its thematic and narrative coherence muddied to a point of internal contradiction. Three years later, MGM simply abandoned an investment of $200,000 in Lewis's *It Can't Happen Here.*

By refusing to concede equity rights to authors, the Authors' League Agreement also registered the extent to which the industry regarded literature as property. The "proper property rights of authors and dramatists" were firmly distinguished from other rights they might claim, a question that was legally laid to rest over the adaptation of Dreiser's *An American Tragedy* in 1931. The novel was exactly the kind of literary object that presented the industry's adapters with its most difficult problems. Its burdensome length (Sergei Eisenstein spoke of "Dreiser's Niagara flow of words and descriptions") was a relatively minor issue. The substance of the problem lay in the fact that both its detailed actions and its thematic concerns were inappropriate to an affirmative medium. But the book's notoriety (it was banned in Boston at least three times in the 1920s) made it as attractive as it was impossible.[23] Famous Players–Lasky bought the movie rights in 1926 for $90,000 but made no attempt to produce it immediately, in part because of the protests it received from Women's Clubs and Better Film organizations. The project was, however, regularly suggested to newly arrived European émigrés: in 1930 Eisenstein prepared a script only to have the studio reject it. David O. Selznick reported that reading it had made him "so depressed that I wanted to reach for the bourbon bottle. As entertainment, I don't think it has one chance in a hundred." The studio should not finance a project, he said, "that cannot possibly offer anything but a most miserable two hours to millions of happy-minded young Americans." The MPPDA, one of whose officials described the book as being as much "a symbol of everything objectionable" as Roscoe "Fatty" Arbuckle, was anxious to delay production until after the meetings of state legislatures in early 1931. However, Paramount was committed to the production, having invested a further $60,000 in the dialogue rights, and with much consultation the studio prepared a script "shifting the emphasis of the story from the seduction, attempted abortion, murder, and execution to a relationship of Clyde and his mother" that was basically acceptable to the MPPDA.[24]

Not surprisingly, Dreiser objected strenuously to Paramount's attempt to turn *An American Tragedy* into what Sergei Eisenstein had described as "'just another'. . . story of 'boy meets girl,' without going into any 'side issues.'"[25] In a letter of protest to Jesse Lasky, Dreiser argued that the film could not "possibly fail to give the impression to the millions of people throughout the world who will see this picture, that the novel on which it is based is nothing short of a cheap, tawdry, tabloid confession story which entirely lacks the scope, emotion, action and psychology of the book involved. Here is an inequitable infringement of a vested property."[26] Dreiser claimed that his contract obliged Paramount to "use its best endeavors to accept such advice, suggestions and criticisms" as he made, and that there was nothing in his contract that indicated that Paramount had the right to change "the structure, or what I may better call the ideographic plan" of his book. He recruited a jury of literati to view the film in New York and determine whether the picture "sufficiently carries out the ideology of the book as to hold me free from any personal or artistic harm before the world." Not surprisingly, the jury concurred with Dreiser's opinion that it was not "an intelligent interpretation of the logic of the book." With that support Dreiser sued to enjoin Paramount from showing it on the grounds both of the terms of his contract and of what he called "a new principle" of "author's equity."[27]

Dreiser was asking the courts to grant him (and, he later claimed, the "thousands of authors who haven't had a square deal in having their works belittled for screen exploitation") a legal right over movie adaptation comparable to those granted authors by law and custom on Broadway and in Manhattan's publishing houses. The New York literary marketplace of the 1920s operated under a consensual conception of the profession of authorship, which recognized authors as the creators and owners of their literary property and granted them creative control of the entire production process. An element in this authorial creative control involved the publisher affording the author some protection from the vicissitudes of the market. A publisher, insisted Scribner's editor-in-chief, Maxwell Perkins, "must not try to get the writer to fit the book to the conditions of the trade. . . . It must be the other way around."[28]

This definition of the profession of authorship had already come into conflict with the brute economics of Hollywood on several occasions in the 1920s. Attempts by Samuel Goldwyn and Adolph Zukor to lure "Eminent Authors" to

Hollywood in the early 1920s had ended in recriminations against "the old sausage machine" and the "entrenched bureaucracy" of scenario departments. No one, Elinor Glyn discovered, "wanted our advice or assistance, nor did they intend to take it. All they required was the use of our names to act as shields against the critics." On a more material level, the Authors' League Agreement was itself in part a response to the threat posed to the writer's traditional identity by Hollywood's more mechanized and bureaucratic approach to aesthetic manufacture. A comparable agreement was reached between the Dramatists' Guild and 152 New York theatrical producers in 1927, in part provoked by the intrusion of Hollywood money into theatrical production in the mid-1920s. The Minimum Basic Agreement guaranteed royalty and rights income and gave playwrights right of approval over basic casting, direction, and set-design decisions. "In short," Richard Fine suggests, "the Guild agreement granted playwrights roughly the same basic legal rights and privileges as prevailed for authors in the publishing industry."[29]

Dreiser was arguing for an extension of this relationship and its definition of the profession of authorship to the different economic conditions of Hollywood. In *Liberty* he argued that the major companies owed part of their monopoly power and profits "to the artistic development of the film." As part of this debt, they should make "a genuine effort . . . now and then to portray a masterpiece of literature . . . in some such fashion as to widen [its] appeal." The basis of his critique was that whereas previously art had always and necessarily been the province of the artist as an individual, the motion picture had turned art into "an industry, along with coal, iron and steel." For the first time, "an art, so called, is discussed as representing an investment."[30] Dreiser's analysis was hardly original and not without its own contradictions, but among New York literati the claim to an author's equity right in the determination of meaning was uncontentious enough.

It did not prove to be so in court, however. In a trial marked by heated exchanges, during which Justice Graham Witschief threatened to have Dreiser removed from the court, the author lost. The judge's legal aesthetics privileged viewers over authors: "Whether the picture substantially presents the book or not depends on one's point of view. . . . [T]he producer must give consideration to the fact that the great majority of people composing the audience before which the picture will be presented will be more interested that justice prevail over wrongdoing than that the inevitability of Clyde's end clearly appear."[31]

Dreiser's ire was provoked by this judicial rejection of his authorial privilege. For his readers in *Liberty* he catalogued twenty movies condemned for "not truly portraying their originals" by reason of their "failure to catch the spirit of the author, his real meaning or mood!" In a reply to Dreiser, *Liberty*'s editor-in-chief, Fulton Oursler, quoted the judge as saying that Paramount had "submitted the opinions of an impressive list of critics, who find that the picture is a true representation of the letter and spirit of the book."[32] Witschief's language employed the legalistic terminology of fidelity discussed by Dudley Andrew, but the legally determining issue was a matter of who had authority over the adapted text, and in that respect Dreiser had no case.[33] Outside the court, however, in the critical consensus of where evaluative authority ought properly to lie, the studio had no defense, and no account of Hollywood the destroyer of writers is complete without a reference to Dreiser's case as "voicing the frustration of every novelist before and since who has found the film image of his work beyond recognition."[34]

Yet Dreiser's analysis, however commonplace (it shares a set of untenable assumptions about Hollywood's production practice with auteur criticism, for instance), was not particularly penetrating. This may have been because he acquired his perspective on the industry through his contact with its production branch, with whom he incorrectly understood his dispute to be. Dreiser directed his hostility principally at the movie's director, Josef von Sternberg, whom he held responsible for the "distorted" and "belittling interpretation of a work which is entitled, on its face, to a far more intelligent and broadening conception of the inscrutable ways of life and chance." As Lea Jacobs has observed, it is somewhat ironic that Dreiser, embroiled as he so frequently was in battles over the censorship of his literary production, failed to recognize the involvement of the MPPDA's censors in a picturization that he felt "might as well have been deliberately calculated to misinterpret not only my character and powers as a novelist, but my mental and artistic approach to life itself." This in turn may have resulted from a misperception of the differences in the organization and power structures of publishing and the motion picture industry. Given Dreiser's political persuasions, a further layer of irony is added by his failure to acknowledge the operation of economic determination in the last instance. In his *Liberty* article, he recognized the hegemonic role of the MPPDA in uniting the major companies in a "purely commercial and . . . business-minded . . . tyranny over a new and even beautiful art form," but he did so in only the most general terms. Not only was he, as Jacobs argues, "never able to confront the actions of industry censors directly," he seems also to have misunderstood the relationship within Paramount between Sternberg and "those who provide directors with their authority."[35]

The case did not lead either eastern authors or the motion picture industry to reconsider their understanding of the position of the individual creator: for

Before Dreiser's storm, Paramount released this publicity photograph of the producers of *An American Tragedy* admiring both the book and its screenplay adaptation. The picture was captioned: "Paramount's decision to produce a motion picture based on Theodore Dreiser's sensational novel and stage success, *An American Tragedy,* has been hailed as one of the outstanding examples of the unlimited possibilities of the talking screen, as compared with the silent film. The enthusiasm of Josef von Sternberg, director of the picture, over the story in talking picture form is shared by Jesse L. Lasky (right), first vice-president of the Paramount Publix Corporation, and B. P. Shulberg, managing director of west coast production." Photo courtesy Paul Ballard Collection, Academy of Motion Picture Arts and Sciences.

Dreiser the sin of which Hollywood was guilty was precisely that of pursuing the industrial logic of responding to consumer demand rather than championing a heroic creative individualism.[36] In Hollywood, heroic individualism existed only inside its fictions, not in its boardrooms. Writers repeatedly accused producers of timidity and conformism in their dependence on convention, but in doing so they made little acknowledgment of the legal constraints on the industry, understanding them only as questions of taste and evaluation.

It could be argued, however, that the industry's practices of adaptation conformed to the legal definition imposed by the Supreme Court in 1915, by which the American cinema did not originate or innovate. The existence of legal censorship effectively denied producers authorial control over their product as it finally appeared before the public. As proprietors of what the Court had called "a business pure and simple," the producers were concerned to limit their legal liability for shaping public sentiments when they were at the same time denied the legal redress accorded other expressions of opinion.

The studios' heads of production developed a number of strategies by which they attempted to evade authorial responsibility for the moral standards of their output. "We do not," maintained Thalberg, "create the types of entertainment; we merely present them." In February 1930, when the studio heads discussed the adoption of the Production Code, Jesse Lasky proposed that, given the industry's dependence on source material, responsibility for the moral standards of what was depicted in motion pictures properly lay in "the hands of the men and women writing the current fiction, the literature of the day. They are our reporters and they are the ones that set the standards for the present type of entertainment."[37] Thalberg himself, arguing that the civic groups demanding reform exaggerated the effect movies had on their audiences, insisted,

> The motion picture does not present the audience with tastes and manners and views and morals; it reflects those they already have. . . . People see in it a reflection of their own average thoughts and attitudes. If the reflection is much lower or much higher than their own plane they reject it. . . . The motion picture is literally bound to the mental and moral level of its vast audience.[38]

Whatever individual studio employees might have claimed about their own motives, the distribution and exhibition executives in the industry's center in New York and the political operatives who ran the MPPDA's public relations machinery required a far more complex understanding of the relationship between movies and their multiple audiences than writers, directors, or even Hollywood producers, since an important part of their function lay in maintaining the motion picture and its industry in the ideologically neutral space of entertainment. The industry's policymakers were neither so naive as to believe that their products merely reflected a preexistent public opinion, nor, as Eisenstein clearly understood, so subversive that they sought to produce forms of expression challenging the status quo.[39] Hays and his assistants were perpetually engaged in persuading their employers that whether we like it or not, we must face the fact that we are *not* in that class of industries whose only problem is with the customer. Our public problem is greater with those out of than those in the theatre. We could commit no greater folly than to ignore the classes that write, talk, and legislate, on the basis that the mass public, as reflected by the box-office, is with us in any event. Reform elements outside, not inside, the saloon, enforced prohibition upon the country.[40]

The industry's blunt commercial interest was in occupying what was both a mediating position between authors and audiences and a cultural median point, in being a subject of interest but not of concern, a topic for conversation but not action. Were they to slip from that median to a point provocatively nearer the position of negation that post-Romantic cultural theory identifies as the locus of art, they would also likely move from the periphery of the political agenda toward a place closer to the center of attention.

In his analysis of Eisenstein's adaption of *An American Tragedy,* Keith Cohen suggests,

Adaptation is a truly artistic feat only when the new version carries with it a hidden criticism of its model or at least renders implicit . . . certain key contradictions implanted or glossed over in the original. Of prime interest, therefore, in Eisenstein's scenario is not so much its imitative fidelity or even its cinematic approximation of specifically literary effects, as its pointed distortion, reorientation of Dreiser's work.[41]

Yet despite the opinions of Paramount's tame critics, precisely the same argument could be made for the adaptation directed by Sternberg. The subversion of the precursor text came from a very different ideological location from Eisenstein's, however. In his account of the case, Harry Alan Potamkin stressed the fact that Paramount had drawn the court's attention to Dreiser's "high regard for the Soviet Union" and Eisenstein's "Bolshevist affiliations." For Potamkin, "the question involved in the conversion of a social novel into film is one of the treatment of an experience in which 'society has an equity,'" by which he meant "our common right to any re-incorporation of what the social entity, or any living part of it, has apprehended *textually.*" The fight for the integrity of this experience, he argued, was not personal to Dreiser, nor primarily to do with the rights of authorship. "It is a struggle against the debasing of the intellectual and social level of an experience," and in that struggle, "the New York Supreme Court has decided to the disadvantage of the socially critical idea."[42]

From their entirely different ideological perspective, the MPPDA might well have accepted Potamkin's conclusion even as it endorsed the court's decision. The association remained quite unrepentant about its role in the project; indeed, it regarded its involvement as a success because the film occasioned no public outcry. In an article in the MPPDA magazine *The Motion Picture, An American Tragedy* was offered as an example of the fact that "because a book or play is objected to as a book or play does not mean that it will be objectionable on the screen, for one of the obligations of producers under the Production Code is to make sure that the 'objectionable' becomes unobjectionable." The article quoted letters of praise from club women who had originally protested the adaptation, one of whom felt, somewhat ambivalently, "as though I had been at the trial of a son of my best friend." Another reported,

> When I heard this picture . . . was to be made, I rather regretted it, as I felt the book was not of sufficient value to be brought before the public. The picture has made me change my mind. I so wish many parents of our youth of today could see this picture! I have been a great believer that the parents of today are more to blame for the lack of discipline and respect of our youth than the youth itself.[43]

3

Rendering the objectionable unobjectionable was not unique to the movies; rather, it was a feature of the complex negotiations involved in the dissemination of a culture of consumption. The new commodities of that culture required that the bounds of public discourse be revised, but in such a way that the commodities themselves not be blamed by cultural conservatives for the consequences of those revisions. For the movies, even before the implementation of the Formula, these negotiations often involved questions of adaptation and were as much concerned with the likely attitudes of audiences inside and outside the movie theater as they were with content. For the movies to offer the maximum pleasure to the maximum number at the maximum profit, they had not only to provide a satisfactory level of entertainment for their diverse audiences, but also to offend as small a proportion of the society's cultural and legislative leadership as possible.

In January 1923 a Universal Studios publicity release signed by Carl Laemmle and sent to newspaper editors throughout the country declared that he was "going to commit a crime that will probably bring a storm of criticism and indignation down upon my head. . . . I am going to take liberties with

Victor Hugo!" Hugo, continued Laemmle, had written *The Hunchback of Notre Dame* "for an age which licked up raw meat. So he packed his story full of lust and blood and thunder and gruesome, grisly, ghoulish, to say nothing of gory, stuff. . . . Today's conditions are slightly different. The public still likes dripping red meat in its literature and even on its stage, *but not on its screen.*" Adapting *The Hunchback* to "today's screen taste" without losing "all the power and virility of Hugo's masterpiece" was a "delicate surgico-screeno-literary operation." Although Laemmle acknowledged that some critics might think it criminal to take liberties with Hugo, he thought it was "better to present a classic in a palatable form than in an undigestible mass! . . . His story will still be there, but some of the drippiest morsels of his red meat will be parboiled or even discarded entirely." There was, however, an entirely different subtext to these carnivorous metaphors. Hugo's *Notre Dame de Paris* was, like *Les Misérables,* on the Roman Catholic Index of Prohibited Books. Laemmle's statement was designed to ensure that any discussion of the film's variations from the novel would center on the safely aestheticized subject of whether "it was better to delete offensive things from classics rather than never to attempt to produce them at all" and avoid revealing the accommodations made to Catholic sensibilities in the adaptation, in case anti-Catholic editors "made the wrong use" of the information.[44]

Organized Catholicism was a prominent influence on the mediation of film content from the early 1920s. The activities of the Legion of Decency in 1934 are properly understood not as a sudden outburst of indignation but rather as the culmination of a close relationship between the church and the MPPDA. Throughout the 1920s the Motion Picture Bureau of the International Federation of Catholic Alumnae (IFCA) ran a reviewing service that by 1929 provided capsule moral evaluations of 200 films a month for forty-two newspapers, 113 Catholic newspapers, and seven radio stations. Moreover, through the MPPDA it exercised a degree of direct influence on motion picture content, not limited to specifically Catholic issues. In her monthly radio broadcast in May 1929, Rita McGoldrick, secretary of the IFCA's bureau, complimented Universal on "their willingness to cooperate with the public groups toward the ideal of better pictures" in adapting *Show Boat,* "that highly elaborate, lovely story of the Mississippi." She praised Carl Laemmle for his courage in making "a sincere effort to raise the standards of screen entertainment." Realizing the difficulty that the miscegenation theme would present in many sections of the country, "he *did not hesitate* to sacrifice what would ordinarily have been splendid motion picture material, alive with suspense, dramatic emphasis and moments of emotion."[45]

115

The adaptation of *Show Boat* addressed a recurrent industry concern in attempting to ensure that its product was acceptable to audiences in all parts of the country and abroad. In such concerns the sensibilities of white southerners received disproportionate attention. *The Hunchback* was a less likely instance of the industry's fundamental problem in adaptation. If part of the literary function, as understood by Dreiser or suggested by Hugo's anticlericalism, was to provide a critique of the dominant culture, part of the motion picture industry's cultural function was quite consciously "to exercise every possible care that only books or plays which are of the right type are used for screen presentation." Although it was seldom expressed explicitly, Hays conducted the "organized industry" in a broad ideological project, concisely identified by Lary May as transferring "the old moral guardianship of the small city and town to the movie corporations," making films "passionate but pure" by containing the titillations they offered their audiences within morally conventional narratives.[46] Metropolitan cynics saw Hays's job as being to "consecrate" the industry's "perfect formula" of "five reels of transgression followed by one reel of retribution." Commenting on the announcement of the Production Code in 1930, an editorial in *The Nation* declared that, leaving aside any question of art, Hays's attempts to keep the movies sexually clean had in practice left them "completely drenched with sex."

> The suggestion of everything which he has attempted to suppress has diffused itself through every scene, and the mind of the audience is encouraged to play about every idea that cannot be stated. Perhaps if an occasional film "justified adultery" or admitted that otherwise respectable girls sometimes have illegitimate children it would not be necessary for every film to deal with seduction arrested at the bedside.[47]

But the movies were, in this respect, little different from the majority of American theater, castigated by Elmer Rice in 1932 for its "timid, conventional, orthodox, and banal" treatment of sexuality, for its "canonization of bodily purity and the triumph of the institution of wedlock." Three years before, Joseph Wood Krutch had argued in similar terms that the real center of American drama was located at "that spiritual crossroads where Broadway intersects with Main Street." Popular successes like *Night Hostess*, "half-baked rather than hard-boiled . . . just naughty enough to seem sophisticated," encapsulated the superficial naïveté of the provincial village. But these plays were neither penetrating nor sincere, and they appealed "to an audience which still hankers after the sticky delights of romantic fiction at the very moment when it is playing at wickedness."[48] Theater critic Benjamin de Casseres's review of the 1926 stage version of *An American Tragedy* coincided with Rice's general judgment on the treatment of sex in modern drama. Describing it as "the typical American crime and sex play of last season," he observed, "I wanted to cheer when Clyde Griffith went to the chair—one American sentimental sex-idiot less."[49] This was a dramaturgy of transgression rather than transcendence, but the gulf that separated Michael Arlen's *The Green Hat* from MGM's adaptation of it as *A Woman of Affairs* was far more material than the merely aesthetic considerations that distinguished it from *Strange Interlude.* In however debased or circumscribed a manner, "the prevalent book or play" occupied the cultural position of negation, which Hays described as a "revolt from Victorianism." His account of the "lost generation" of writers expressing "a distrust in everything, including themselves" was in every sense conventional, including that of its disapproval:

> There was no God. The world was rotten. A fist was shaken at every convention of society. The sole aim of life was to get as much pleasure as possible out of it. The teachings of Freud, which in their popular conception not only stressed the importance of sex on human thought but which questioned the wisdom of all sex repressions advocated by conventional society, added confusion to thinking. . . . The cat-and-dog fight over prohibition communicated itself to other laws, with the result that there was a general decline in respect for all law. Drinking became a mark of defiance, and we found that the ancient temptation to steal apples we had been forbidden was still strong in us.[50]

The affirmative role that the motion picture industry negotiated with the bourgeois institutions of cultural politics was not only different from but incompatible with the position of contemporary cultural critic occupied by the readership of the *American Mercury.* Part of the hegemonic role that the industry shared with the weekly mass periodical press and advertising was quite literally to contain the spread of an urban, sophisticated culture that failed to provide an affirmative cultural vision acceptable or at least tolerable to the dominant cultural ideology. It had, therefore, to be "prevented," and adaptation was one device for its prevention. Hollywood's cultural function was in part to contain and recuperate the negation of Art into the affirmation of entertainment. The industry was not defensive about this practice of cultural paternalism. Hays reminded the "thoughtful women of Philadelphia" that "this present period has witnessed a . . . defiance of the rules and conventions under which the world has operated for ages." In print and on stage there was "extremely free discussion of topics which, previous to this particular era, were discussed in whispers, if at all."[51]

The revolt from Victorianism was by no means confined to deliberate acts of provocation in books and on stage, however. Elmer Rice pointed out that in women's magazines, which were, like the movies, a site of affirmative culture, it was the advertisements that broke cultural taboos rather than the "innocuous and infantile fiction in the adjoining columns." Frequently cast in semidramatic form, they dealt with "such distasteful subjects as bodily odors, menstruation and 'female hygiene,' the mere mention of which will, no doubt, arouse in the reader a feeling of disgust." No theatrical performance had yet attempted "to repeat upon the stage the 'confidences' which are so publicly exchanged by the heroines of the advertising pages or to reproduce the window displays of any corner drugstore." Even in its semidramatic form, advertising, the most affirmative aesthetic form of a consumer culture, occupied a cultural location far removed from artistic aspirations to either autonomy or social criticism, a location in which the breaking of a taboo might lead to a liberating purchase. Rice's list of distasteful taboos indicated that the culture of consumption was identified by its promoters and critics alike as feminine: it offered "a therapeutic renovation of sensuality," "self-realization through emotional fulfillment . . . the need to construct a pleasing 'self' by purchasing consumer goods." As Jackson Lears has suggested, advertising, "ceaselessly open to aesthetic novelty," had by the 1920s "begun to assimilate the allegedly rebellious impulses of aesthetic 'modernism'" and in this act of appropriation incorporated its adversarial stance in the promotion of "a leisure world of intense private experience."[52]

What advertising was doing to Cubism or *Fortune* magazine to photography —putting aesthetic autonomy to work—the motion picture industry was doing to "those books and plays which boldly flaunt their wares under the sacred name of realistic literature": circumscribing their challenge to social convention by adapting them to narrative, generic, and regulatory conventions.[53] In terms of movie content, the residue of such encounters between the Production Code and the "prevalent type of book" was most frequently the sexual suggestiveness of which *The Nation* complained. Sexual explicitness was, however, not in itself the problem. As was happening in advertising, a properly commodified sexuality was in the process of satisfactorily negotiating the boundaries of its expression, as readily susceptible to adjustment to the fashions of the moment as a hemline. The issue was less one of content than of audience, less to do with authorial intent than with likely variations in reception.[54] As Lamar Trotti, then a publicist for the MPPDA, argued in 1927,

A book that you and I, as adults, may well read and enjoy—a book that has dubious situations and words, perhaps, but which will not affect us in any wrongful fashion—may be altogether wrong for someone else with a different background and a different understanding. We may view the form of a nude figure—you and I—and be uplifted by it, inspired and made better men and women, while to the man with whom we are rubbing elbows, it may convey another and altogether distorted meaning.[55]

If it was not the young or "morons" who needed the MPPDA's parental protection, it was "the folks who represent the intelligentsia in the country towns and small cities," who, according to Carl Milliken, secretary to the MPPDA and in charge of its public relations program, were "not yet prepared to view with approval a long series of scenes including close-ups which show the heroine clad only in breechclout and brassiere." Advertising its appeal to an undifferentiated market, Hollywood's ideological self-positioning obliged it to address cultural common denominators in an affirmative vision of national community, inventing the consensus that it claimed to be addressing. Unlike books and music, declared the Production Code, films could not be confined to only certain classes of people. "The exhibitor's theatres are built for the masses, for the cultivated and the rude, mature and immature, self-respecting and criminal. . . . Hence the larger moral responsibilities of the motion pictures."[56]

Quite overtly at issue in the industry's internal discussions about self-regulation was a definition of entertainment as a social function, and an argument about the means by which the ideological apparatus of representation would be policed. The movies themselves were textual manifestations of that debate as well as the textual evidence around which it was conducted. The content of movies inevitably became the site of dispute, but the forces impelling the debate were not generated by the ideological superstructure of movie content. In this debate, the producers did not have the sole or even the dominant voice, because it was also being conducted throughout the American press, among religious, educational, and civic groups, and in legislatures. Since the producers consistently denied their responsibility for creating public taste in entertainment, they made themselves subservient to a hegemonic definition of what it was they should be producing. As Hays was almost infinitely fond of saying, the motion picture business was everybody's business. But when he said, "The fact is, motion pictures are yours rather than ours. It is for you indeed to say what they shall be like and how far forward they may go toward their limitless possibilities. We who have the physical control of them are ready to do your bidding," he was addressing not a small metropolitan elite

represented by the likes of Dreiser or the Algonquin Round Table, but the organized and culturally assertive component of those whom H. L. Mencken
called the "booboisie," the club women and the PTAs.[57] Much of the running
public debate over the regulation of the industry concerned itself with how effectively Hays had made good on his promises, but the industry had very early
accepted that it needed to convince these politically influential groups of its respectability. By 1930 the producers' attempts to put limits on the social responsibility of motion pictures were in retreat, in part because of the new
problems created by sound, and in part because their own position in the debate almost invited activists to claim the authority to offer that definition. In
his draft version of the Production Code, Father Daniel Lord, the leading figure
in the revival of the Catholic Sodality youth movement, insisted on the industry's responsibility for the moral correctness of the entertainment it produced:

> The moral importance of entertainment is something which has been univer-
> sally recognized. It enters intimately into the lives of men and women and af-
> fects them closely; it occupies their minds and affections during leisure hours;
> and ultimately touches the whole of their lives. A man may be judged by his
> standard of entertainment as easily as by the standard of his work.[58]

This notion of "correct entertainment" as that "which tends to improve the
race, or at least to re-create and rebuild human beings exhausted with the realities of life," was the common assumption of all the groups concerned with
reforming the movies in the early 1930s. However reluctantly, the industry accepted its definition as "recreation," as "the period in which a man rebuilds
himself after his work . . . during which he gets the chance to rebuild himself
physically . . . morally, spiritually, and intellectually."[59] A concomitant of the
movies' affirmative cultural function lay in their incorporation of other cultural objects, from interior decoration to literature, into that mode. In considering the draft script for *An American Tragedy,* Hays observed, "If this production is justified at all, it is as a picturization of a terrible possibility for any boy,
a picturization in fact of what is one of the tragedies often actual and always
potential among the youth. . . . This whole project is going to cause real criticism. Our problem is to make certain that that criticism is not justified." If the
picture was to make "a real contribution" to understanding "our social problems in America," then

> the lovemaking certainly does not have to be salacious. There need be, in my
> opinion, only the slightest reference to the pregnancy. Every opportunity
> might be sought to leave the impression that the boy was fundamentally of

good character save only this trouble (if this is so the Great American Tragedy is still a Greater Tragedy). There should be no reference to abortion and only the slightest reference to the idea that they "had done everything." There need be no use of the words that per se will draw fire such as "seduce." Certainly there need be no reference to a "weak clergyman." If the chaplain is shown he should be a stronger character and a credit to his profession. . . . I think we should strive to avoid every single criticism except that which comes from the treatment of the theme at all.[60]

In the movie, as well as in the court, the virtues of entertainment and moral rectitude triumphed over the vices of Dreiser's determinism. If *An American Tragedy* did, indeed, represent "the prevalent type of book," it had been deliberately prevented from becoming the prevalent type of picture. Insofar as that represented a conscious project to contain the spread of a metropolitan, "sophisticated" culture that rejected the dominant, affirmative cultural vision, the project of adaptation was not so much one of bowdlerization as of recuperation, in the name of a hegemony that understood American tragedies in terms very different to those of Dreiser. Speaking in 1932 for an increasingly vocal Catholic cultural influence on that hegemony, Father James Gillis, editor of *Catholic World,* advised Dreiser, and more importantly his readership, to "snap out of it. . . . Look up at the sky, take a squint at the sun, go out on the hillside and inhale deeply. Get out of the gutters. Come up from those sewers. Be decent, be clean, and America will not seem so tragic."[61]

NOTES

This essay was originally delivered as a paper at the annual meeting of the American Studies Association, New Orleans, in November 1990. My thanks to Kate Bowles for her many helpful comments during the process of revision.

1. Theodore Dreiser, "The Real Sins of Hollywood," *Liberty,* June 11, 1932, 6–11. Audiences might also remember that *Strange Interlude* had been banned in Boston in 1929 (Morris Ernst and Alexander Lindey, *The Censor Marches On: Recent Milestones in the Administration of the Obscenity Law in the United States* [New York, 1940], 69).

2. Stephen Vincent Benét to Nannine Joseph, February 20, 1930, quoted in Richard Fine, *Hollywood and the Profession of Authorship* (Ann Arbor, 1985), republished as *West of Eden: Writers in Hollywood, 1928–1940* (Washington, D.C., 1993), 1; Robert E. Sherwood, "Renaissance in Hollywood," *American Mercury* 16 (April 1929): 434; Leda Bauer, "The Movies Tackle Literature," *American Mercury* 14 (July 1928): 294. Richard Fine cites a number of representative instances of the genre, including those of Mary Roberts Reinhart and Elinor Glyn. See also Ian Hamilton, *Writers in Hollywood, 1915–1951* (London, 1990).

3. George Bluestone, *Novels into Film: The Metamorphosis of Fiction into Cinema* (Baltimore, 1957), 219; Dudley Andrew, *Concepts in Film Theory* (New York, 1984), 100.

4. Barbara Herrnstein Smith, "Contingencies of Value," *Critical Inquiry* 10 (September 1983): 17–18.

5. Former postmaster general Will H. Hays was president of the film industry trade association, the Motion Picture Producers and Distributors of America, Inc. (MPPDA), commonly known as the Hays Office, and also referred to in this article as the association. Among its responsibilities was the administration of the Production Code, or "Hays Code." In his account of the workings of the code, Jack Vizzard reports the reservations of a fellow code administrator in the 1940s: "I don't think it's so good to be called a self regulator. It sounds like someone who plays with himself" (*See No Evil: Life inside a Hollywood Censor* [New York, 1970], 56).

6. Robin Wood, *Hitchcock's Films Revisited* (New York, 1989), 244.

7. Will H. Hays, *Motion Pictures and the Public: An Address before the Women's City Club of Philadelphia, April 20, 1925* (New York, 1925), 2.

8. Wilton A. Barrett, secretary of the National Board of Review of Motion Pictures, testimony before the Committee on Education, House of Representatives, 69th Cong., 1st Sess., on "Bills to Create a Commission to be Known as the Federal Motion Picture Commission, and Defining Its Powers and Duties, 1926" (Washington, D.C., 1926), 337.

9. Jeffrey Sconce, "Narrative Authority and Social Narrativity: The Cinematic Reconstitution of Brontë's *Jane Eyre*," *Wide Angle* 10, no. 1 (1988): 47, 61.

10. On this point, the reviewer was not optimistic. Those who had read the book would find it "a disappointing transposition." They were more likely to "simply decide there is no relation" between book and film. "But the film has this in its favor—not many film fans have read the book. If they had, there wouldn't be so many tabloid newspapers in the country. The public at large has neither the inclination nor the patience to delve into any double-volume novel" (*Variety*, August 11, 1931).

11. Hays, "Motion Pictures," 10.

12. *Mutual Film Corporation v. Industrial Commission of Ohio*, 236 U.S., 230 (1915), reprinted in *The Movies in Our Midst: Documents in the Cultural History of Film in America*, ed. Gerald Mast (Chicago, 1982), 142. See also Garth Jowett, "'A Capacity for Evil': The 1915 Supreme Court *Mutual* Decision," *Historical Journal of Film, Radio and Television* 9, no. 1 (1989): 59–78.

13. Ellis W. Hawley, "Herbert Hoover, the Commerce Secretariat, and the Vision of an 'Associative State,'" *Journal of American History* 66, no. 1 (June 1974): 116–40; "Certificate of Incorporation of Motion Picture Producers and Distributors of America, Inc.," March 10, 1922, quoted in Raymond Moley, *The Hays Office* (Indianapolis, 1945), 226; *The Open Door*, MPPDA pamphlet (New York, 1924, 1927).

14. Hays, "Motion Pictures," 5.

15. Clara Beranger, "The Story," in *Introduction to the Photoplay*, ed. John Tibbetts (1927; reprint, Shawnee Mission, Kans., 1977), 137; Richard Koszarski, *An Evening's Entertainment: The Age of the Silent Feature Picture, 1915–1928* (New York, 1990), 108; William James Fadiman, "Books into Movies," *Publishers' Weekly*, September 8, 1934, 753. See also Robert Gustavson, *The Buying of Ideas: Source Acquisition at Warner Bros., 1930–1949* (Ann Arbor, 1983); Fine, *Hollywood*, 33, 68; and *Publishers' Weekly*, September 20, 1930, 1266.

16. *Literary Digest,* October 25, 1930, 20. John Golden, "The Decadent Stage—Clean It or Kill It!" *Theatre Magazine* (March 1927), 7. An excellent account of the cultural politics of Broadway in the late 1920s can be found in Mary Beth Hamilton, "When I'm Bad I'm Better: Mae West and American Popular Entertainment" (Ph.D. diss., Princeton University, 1990).

17. MPPDA memo, November 20, 1924, 1924 Meetings–Scenarios file, Motion Picture Association of America Archive, New York (hereafter cited as MPA); Ethel Smith Dorrance to Hays, February 29, 1924, 1924 *Damned* file, MPA; 1925 Public Relations Committee file, MPA.

18. Originally published in 1923, *Damned* told the story of a "girl who was so beautiful that she meant ruin for any man who beheld her—even for Satan himself." The novel described a series of affairs leading to her death. In Hell, in imitation of *One Thousand and One Nights,* she relates her adventures to Satan (Ethel Smith Dorrance, *Damned: The Intimate Story of a Girl* [New York, 1923]). Hays to Dorrance, February 29, 1924; Eric Schuler, secretary, Authors' League, to Hays, April 25, 1924; Schuler to Carl Laemmle, June 10, 1924; Laemmle to Schuler, Laemmle to Hays, June 11, 1924, 1924 *Damned* file, MPA; Authors' League agreement, 1927, in Moley, *Hays Office,* 239.

19. "General Principles to Govern the Preparation of a Revised Code for Talking Pictures," reporter's transcript of a meeting held at the offices of the Association of Motion Picture Producers, Los Angeles, February 10, 1930, 1930 Production Code file, 139. For a full discussion of the development of the 1930 Production Code, see Richard Maltby, "The Genesis of the Production Code," *Quarterly Review of Film and Video* 15, no. 4 (1995): 5–32.

20. Although it was accepted within the publishing industry that in theory the economic rights, including subsidiary rights, to a literary property resided with the author, it was also accepted that when a publisher contributed to the success of an author's work, the publisher was entitled to a share of the income, often on a fifty-fifty basis. Negotiations over screen rights seldom involved authors directly, being handled by agents, publishers, or theatrical producers. MPPDA Resolution, June 24, 1924, in Moley, *Hays Office,* 239; Fine, *Hollywood,* 33, 68; "Memorandum of Conference between Leroy Scott, C. B. DeMille, Jesse Lasky, Irving G. Thalberg, and Edwin J. Loeb," August 21, 1928, 1928 Books and Plays file, MPA.

21. In contravention of the Formula agreement, advertisements for *A Woman of Affairs* had identified its literary source.

22. Hays, speech to studio executives, ca. April 20, 1933, 1933 Production Code file, MPA.

23. Sergei Eisenstein, *Immoral Memories: An Autobiography,* trans. Herbert Marshall (London, 1985), 156. Mark Fenster traces a remarkably similar recent instance in his article "Containment, Excess, Ambivalence: The Adaptation of *Less than Zero,*" *Velvet Light Trap* 28 (1991): 49–64.

24. Thomas Strychacz cites the sale price as $80,000 in 1926 and $55,000 in 1931 ("Dreiser's Suit against Paramount: Authorship, Professionalism, and the Hollywood Film Industry," *Prospects* 18 [1993]: 200 n. 3). David O. Selznick, *Memo from David O. Selznick,* ed. Rudy Behlmer (New York, 1973), 55–56. Eisenstein's script is printed, along with an account of its production, in Ivor Montagu, *With Eisenstein in Hollywood* (New York, 1969). Other accounts of the Eisenstein project can be found in Sergei

Eisenstein, *Film Form: Essays in Film Theory* (New York, 1969), 95ff.; and Jay Leyda and Zina Voynov, *Eisenstein at Work* (London, 1982), 52–59. Jason Joy to Maurice McKenzie, September 19, 1930; Lamar Trotti, memo, February 24, 1931, *An American Tragedy* file, Production Code Administration Archive, Margaret Herrick Library, Academy of Motion Picture Arts and Sciences, Los Angeles (hereafter cited as PCA).

25. Eisenstein, *Immoral Memories,* 156. Dreiser seems subsequently to have been more permissive about adaptations of *An American Tragedy.* "In 1936 he reviewed four different dramatizations (one French, one German, one Russian, one American), each with a different approach to the 'moral'" of his novel, and found virtues in them all, including the Russian, which emphasized the duty of labor, the rights and godlike status of the worker, etc. 'Unfortunately,' he added, 'this dramatization is not nearly as well done as one might have hoped'" (Ellen Morris, *Two Dreisers* [New York: Viking, 1969], 287.

26. There is an account of Dreiser's reaction to the Josef von Sternberg version in Hamilton, *Writers,* 53–55, and a detailed account of the court case and Dreiser's attempt to assert his intellectual property rights and "mental equity" in Strychacz, "Dreiser's Suit," 187–203. Robert H. Elias, ed., *The Letters of Theodore Dreiser,* vol. 2 (Philadelphia, 1959), 527. Dreiser chose to ignore the qualifying phrase in the contract that required Paramount to accept his suggestions only "insofar as it may, in the judgment of the Purchaser consistently do so."

27. Among the jury were George Jean Nathan, Floyd Dell, Carl Van Doren, Patrick Kearney, psychoanalyst A. A. Brill, and Hermann S. Oelrichs, who described the picture as "a succession of banal intrigues, sure fire courtroom scenes and how sorry mother is" (Strychacz, "Dreiser's Suit," 189; Elias, *Letters,* 530; Dorothy Spensley, "Dreiser Looks for a Fight," *Motion Picture Classic,* June 1931, 36).

28. Fine, *Hollywood,* 69, 14; Maxwell Perkins to Marjorie Kinnon Rawlings, March 26, 1936, quoted in A. Scott Berg, *Maxwell Perkins: Editor of Genius* (New York, 1978), 299.

29. Elmer Rice, *Minority Report: An Autobiography* (New York, 1963), 179; Elinor Glyn, *Romantic Adventure* (New York, 1937), 291; Fine, *Hollywood,* 36; Alfred L. Bernheim, *The Business of the Theatre: An Economic History of the American Theatre, 1790–1932* (New York, 1932), 115.

30. Dreiser, "Real Sins," 6. Asserting that Paramount's version of *An American Tragedy* was "an utter misrepresentation and libellous distortion of Mr. Dreiser's book," Dreiser's lawyers argued, "Unless a motion picture producer is prepared intelligently to reproduce a novel which requires time and space, the company should not buy it. . . . [W]hen a motion picture company buys a novel, there is an implied agreement that it will present that novel and not something else. When a writer grants his name, reputation and the title of one of his greatest works to a motion picture company, he does not expect to be wholly misrepresented to his public" (Arthur Garfield Hays and Arthur Carter Hume, "An American Film Tragedy. Film Version. Pending Legal Contest," quoted in Strychacz, "Dreiser's Suit," 194). A 1946 article quoted Dreiser as arguing that although producers bought "the right of reproduction, they don't buy the right to change it into anything they please. The word reproduction means what it says. They can't make a piece of work that is inimical to my standards and picture me as writing something I never in the world would have writ-

ten" (H. S. Kraft, "Dreiser's War in Hollywood," *Screen Writer* 1 [March 1946]: 12, quoted in Strychacz, "Dreiser's Suit," 191). Strychacz's textual analysis of the court case takes a more sympathetic view of Dreiser's argument than the present essay and argues that the case was significant in promoting a model of authorship and evaluative authority based on the expertise of professional writers and readers. The juries called by both Dreiser and Paramount anticipated "the power of professional critics within the university system to legitimate opinions about literature—opinions that can never be legally verified or stabilized, but that nevertheless possess an objective authority as they are institutionalized within the profession of literary studies" (Strychacz, "Dreiser's Suit," 188, 198).

31. Elias, *Letters,* 562. After the trial, Paramount added new opening and closing scenes, apparently in an attempt to appease Dreiser. There is a detailed account of textual changes proposed by both the MPPDA and Dreiser in Lea Jacobs, *"An American Tragedy:* A Comparison of Film and Literary Censorship," *Quarterly Review of Film and Video* 15, no. 4 (1995).

32. Paramount's jury included Broadway producers John Golden and Louis E. Gensler, critics Charles Brackett and Corey Ford, publisher George Palmer Putnam, and authors Owen Johnson, Robert E. MacAlarney, and George S. Vierreck. Several of Paramount's witnesses also claimed that Dreiser had on a number of occasions objected to scenes or dialogue in the picture which were reproduced from the novel (Strychacz, "Dreiser's Suit," 198; 202 nn. 21, 25).

33. Paragraph 2 of the contract granted Paramount "sole and exclusive rights to use, adapt, translate, change, subtract from and add to said story." As Thomas Strychacz notes, the effect of the clause permitting Dreiser to offer advice on the adaptation was to demote the author "to a position of professional *consultant* whose main task was to offer opinions" (Strychacz, "Dreiser's Suit," 192).

34. Bluestone, *Novels,* 217 n. 3.

35. According to the deposition of Paramount executive William T. Powers, Sternberg told Dreiser that Paramount "had to consider its reputation and the requirements of the various censorship boards. Mr. Dreiser said he was not concerned either with the reputation of the Corporation or with censorship problems and that he definitely insisted that the picture should display and emphasize all of the violent attacks against society and religion which he had, he claimed, carefully developed in the writing of the book" (quoted in Strychacz, "Dreiser's Suit," 201 n. 5). Elias, *Letters,* 528–29; Jacobs, *"An American Tragedy,"* 154; Dreiser, "Real Sins," 7. In 1929, it was reported that Dreiser was contemplating writing an exposé of the motion picture industry, using a fictionalized Will Hays as its centralized character and "divulging a lot of the inside facts on the political activities of the Hays organization over the country and especially in Washington" (*Motion Picture News,* October 19, 1929).

36. According to Keith Cohen's analysis, "Dreiser insists throughout *An American Tragedy* on the individualistic values and motives that inform Clyde Griffith's character." In conversation with Eisenstein in 1927, Dreiser insisted on the importance of the drama of the individual, "since only through the individual could the mass and its dreams be sensed and interpreted" (Keith Cohen, "Eisenstein's Subversive Adaptation," in *The Classic American Novel and the Movies,* ed. Gerald Peary and Roger Shatzin [New York: Ungar, 1977], 254).

37. "General Principles," 96.

38. Ibid., 138–39.

39. Ivor Montagu reports that Eisenstein understood Lasky's proposal that he adapt *An American Tragedy* as "a sentence of final doom" on his expedition to Paramount. "It would never be permitted to foreigners, some even Russians, to make *An American Tragedy* in the way we were bound to make it. . . . [It] could never be allowed by a firm with responsibilities to the social setup such as are owed by an organization of the magnitude of Paramount" (Montagu, *With Eisenstein,* 113–14).

40. Hays, draft of 1932 annual report of the MPPDA, Will H. Hays Archive, Department of Special Collections, Indiana State Library, Indianapolis.

41. Cohen, "Eisenstein's Subversive Adaptation," 245.

42. Harry Alan Potamkin, "Novel into Film: A Case Study of Current Practice," in *The Compound Cinema: The Film Writings of Harry Alan Potamkin,* ed. Lewis Jacobs (New York, 1977), 186–87.

43. "The 'Objectionable' Becomes UNobjectionable," *Motion Picture Monthly* 7, no. 6 (September–August [*sic*] 1931): 3, 8. Such testimony did not prevent *Harrison's Reports* from both denouncing the film and reveling in its box office failure. "Mr. Hays may be able to convince some simple-minded women that 'An American Tragedy' is 'Unobjectionable.' But Paramount is finding out that the great majority of the American people take a different view of it; the box office is telling the tale. . . . [P]icture-goers revolted at the sight of a young man cold-bloodedly planning to murder the poor girl he had seduced so as to make himself free to marry a wealthy girl. The decency hidden within even the morbidly and sexually inclined persons revolted at the very thought of being offered as entertainment a picture showing such a dastardly act" (*Harrison's Reports,* September 26, 1931, 156; and May 20, 1933, 77).

44. Robert Cochrane to Will Hays, January 22, 1923, Will Hays Papers, University Publications of America (microform), 1988, pt. 1, reel 8, frames 646–48.

45. "Endorsed Motion Pictures," broadcast by Rita McGoldrick, May 9,1929, 1929 IFCA file, MPA. See also Francis R. Walsh, *"The Callahans and the Murphys* (MGM, 1927): A Case Study of Irish-American and Catholic Church Censorship," *Historical Journal of Film, Radio and Television* 10, no. 1 (1990): 33–45.

46. MPPDA Board of Directors resolution, June 24, 1924, quoted in "Agreement Executed between the Authors' League of America, the Dramatists' Guild of the Authors' League, the Authors' Guild of the Authors' League and the Motion Picture Producers and Distributors of America Inc., December 15, 1927," in Moley, *Hays Office,* 239; Lary May, *Screening Out the Past: The Birth of Mass Culture and the Motion Picture Industry* (New York, 1980), 205.

47. "Virtue in Cans," *The Nation,* April 16, 1930, 441.

48. Elmer Rice, "Sex in the Modern Theater," *Harper's,* May 1932, 665; Joseph Wood Krutch, "Our Hard-Boiled Plays," *Theatre Magazine,* February 1929, 20.

49. Benjamin de Casseres, "The Debasement of Crime, Sex and Money in Current Drama," *Theatre Magazine,* September 1927, 16. A similar opinion was expressed by Emanuel Eisenberg, "From the Front Page," *Theatre Magazine,* May 1930, 31. Ellen Morris reaches a comparable conclusion about the novel's relation to contemporary moral standards: "Dreiser appeared in his novel to take little account of the postwar revolution in sexual mores. . . . The murder trials that caught the fancy of the news-

paper public, such as the Snyder-Gray and the Hall-Mills affairs, were those that dramatized the new rather than the old sexual code. They involved crimes of adultery, in which a faithless wife or husband was murderer or victim. But Dreiser's murders were crimes of ambition, dating from a time when the bonds of sexuality were so strong that they could be broken only by violence" (Morris, *Two Dreisers,* 210).

50. Hays, annual report of the MPPDA, 1931, Will Hays Papers. For instances of similar rhetoric, see *Selected Articles on Censorship of the Theater and Moving Pictures,* ed. Lamar T. Beman (New York, 1931), 280–84 passim.

51. In Father Daniel Lord's draft version of the Production Code, which eventually became the text of "The Reasons Supporting the Code," he suggested that one necessity for the code was that "small communities, remote from sophistication and from the hardening process which often takes place in the ethical and moral standards of larger cities, are easily and readily reached by any sort of film" ("General Principles," 120). See also Stuart Ewen, *Captains of Consciousness: Advertising and the Social Roots of the Consumer Culture* (New York, 1977), 42, 54, 190; Richard Butsch, "Introduction: Leisure and Hegemony in America," in *For Fun and Profit: The Transformation of Leisure into Consumption,* ed. Richard Butsch (Philadelphia, 1990), 3–27; Michael Denning, "The End of Mass Culture," in *Modernity and Mass Culture,* ed. James Naremore and Patrick Brantlinger (Bloomington, Ind., 1991), 253–68; Roland Marchand, *Advertising the American Dream: Making Way for Modernity, 1920–1940* (Berkeley, 1985), 341; and Will H. Hays, "Motion Pictures," 10.

52. Rice, "Sex," 670; Marchand, *Advertising,* 16–24, 52–61, 206–34, 344–6; T. J. Jackson Lears, "From Salvation to Self-Realization: Advertising and the Therapeutic Roots of the Consumer Culture, 1880–1930," in *The Culture of Consumption: Critical Essays in American History, 1880–1980,* ed. Richard Wightman Fox and T. J. Jackson Lears (New York, 1983), 27–28, 22. See also Martin Pumphrey, "The Flapper, the Housewife and the Making of Modernity," *Cultural Studies* 1 (May 1987): 179–94; Andreas Huyssen, "Mass Culture as Woman: Modernism's Other," in *Studies in Entertainment: Critical Approaches to Mass Culture,* ed. Tania Modleski (Bloomington, Ind., 1986), 188–206; and Gaylyn Studlar, "The Perils of Pleasure?: Fan Magazine Discourse as Women's Commodified Culture in the 1920s," *Wide Angle* 13 (1991): 6–33.

53. Lamar Trotti, "Screenwriting," draft of article, 1927 Trotti file, MPA. Marchand, *Advertising,* 140; Jeffrey L. Meikle, *Twentieth Century Limited: Industrial Design in America, 1925–1939* (Philadelphia, 1979), 9, 17; Daniel Bell, "Modernism Mummified," in *Modernist Culture in America,* ed. Daniel Joseph Singal (Belmont, Calif., 1991), 163. Lears describes the process by which art is assimilated into advertising as requiring "the ascendance of formalism and professionalism . . . the rejection of all romantic dreams of transcendence, the dismissal of any vestigial sense of higher purpose, the acceptance of art as primarily a set of formal problems to be solved" (T. J. Jackson Lears, "Uneasy Courtship: Modern Art and Modern Advertising," in Singal, *Modernist Culture,* 180).

54. The development of a commodified sexuality directed toward a female audience is discussed in Janet Staiger, *Interpreting Films: Studies in the Historical Reception of American Cinema* (Princeton, 1992) 124–138; and Miriam Hansen, *Babel and Babylon: Spectatorship in American Silent Film* (Cambridge, Mass., 1991), 243–94. See also

Richard deCordova, *Picture Personalities: The Emergence of the Star System in America* (Urbana, 1990), 117–47.

55. Trotti, "Screenwriting."

56. The MPPDA, for instance, participated actively in Americanization programs run by a variety of voluntary organizations (Milliken to Hays, October 9, 1929; PCA *Applause* file; Marchand, *Advertising,* 4–5; "General Principles," 119, 121).

57. Hays, "Motion Pictures," 3.

58. "General Principles," 116–17.

59. Ibid., 116, 11.

60. Hays to Jason Joy, February 9, 1931, *An American Tragedy* file, PCA.

61. James Gillis, "Sursum Corda," *Catholic News,* February 6, 1932, quoted in William M. Halsey, *The Survival of American Innocence: Catholicism in an Age of Disillusionment, 1920–1940* (Notre Dame, 1980), 106.

Hollywood, Main Street, and the Church

Trying to Censor the Movies before the Production Code

FRANCIS G. COUVARES

The Legion of Decency's sensational campaign of movie boycotts and the movie industry's inauguration of self-censorship in response to that campaign in 1934 remain signal events in both the scholarly and popular memory of depression-era Hollywood.[1] As film historian Garth Jowett has noted, however, "The unanswered question is why . . . did the Catholic Church suddenly decide to bring its massive influence to bear on the problem of motion picture immorality?"[2] This essay will argue that the Catholic Church did not turn so suddenly toward Hollywood. It will also argue that the encounter of church and movie industry was in some degree less a struggle than a mutual embrace, motivated by an urge on the part of both movie moguls and Catholic clerical and lay leaders to defend their institutional interests and achieve respectability and cultural authority in twentieth-century America.

This essay will further suggest that Hollywood's difficulties with censorship and consumer boycotts were part of a far wider *Kulturkampf,* the chronological boundaries of which span the years approximately from the 1870s to the

1940s. In that cultural struggle, the social accompaniments of industrializa-tion—immigration and ethnic conflict; urbanization and the rise of commer-cial "mass culture"—set off a series of skirmishes over public morality that pit-ted native against stranger, Protestant against Catholic, Christian against Jew, "modernist" against "fundamentalist," small town against city, and at one time or another, most of these groups against the "merchants of leisure," who seemed capable of subverting the moral lessons of family, church, and tradi-tion. Thus, when in 1934 the Catholic Legion of Decency defended "Ameri-can" traditions of morality against Hollywood's commercial greed and "alien" values, it was varying a familiar theme, already well developed by several gen-erations of American cultural critics. Even more than earlier commercial amusements such as vaudeville and burlesque, the penny press, and the dime novel, the movies threatened to gain control over the representation of crime and punishment, of class and ethnicity, and especially of familial and sexual re-lations.[3] However inflated such claims, in trying to control the content of movies from the 1910s to the 1930s, critics and moviemakers entered an es-sentially political contest over the locus of cultural authority in the modern United States.

In late 1921 Paul Bern, Samuel Goldwyn's scenario editor, ordered his en-tire staff to spend one full day reading nothing but newspapers from small towns in order, he explained, to get stories of "real life."[4] Like many of the public statements of Goldwyn and his fellow movie moguls, these words are nothing so much as a gesture of mock piety toward the "folk," understood to be Protestant, small-town Americans. The gesture was designed to reassure publics, regulators, investors, and perhaps the moviemakers themselves that with a little effort and a little education, Hollywood and Main Street could ef-fect a meeting of the minds.

Although ritualistic and self-serving, such pious rhetoric was indulged in repeatedly from the 1910s through the 1930s because it reflected a reality about the movie industry and its relation to its market. To gauge the audi-ence's tastes and standards accurately was for the producers an objective both highly desirable and largely unattainable. The problem was not simply that they were mostly Jewish arrivistes trying to amuse the Daughters of the Amer-ican Revolution. It was also that the cultural insiders themselves—the main Protestant churches and the secular civic and reform organizations of Protes-tant America—failed miserably to agree on what they liked or tolerated.

As early as the 1910s, middle-class Protestant critics of the movies found themselves antagonizing some part of their natural constituency whenever they presumed to speak for the constituency as a whole. Nowhere was this difficulty clearer than in the National Board of Censorship. The board was founded in 1909 by the People's Institute, a reform organization composed largely of Protestant, upper-middle-class New Yorkers after Mayor George B. McClellan, Jr., had closed all the movie theaters in New York in response to numerous complaints about indecency on the screen. Despite its name, the board had no legal authority, but everyone—the members of the board, the press, the politicians, and the movie producers and distributors—presumed that the respectable "censors" would readily arrive at acceptable standards of screen morality and straightforwardly communicate those standards to the moviemakers. Before long, however, it became clear that the board was not sure what it stood for or whose values it represented.[5]

Within the board's own committees, the arbiters of morality found themselves disagreeing strenuously over what was permissible in several types of movies, especially white slavery films and other "sex problem photoplays."[6] Such disagreements sometimes expressed themselves in terms of gender, with the volunteer women on the ground-level censoring committees finding themselves overruled by the board's professional staff or the General Committee, both of which were composed almost entirely of men. More often, disputes divided people who were indistinguishable sociologically, but who assumed positions on an ideological scale that ranged from Victorian traditionalist to cosmopolitan modernist. However, even those officers of the board most sympathetic to traditionalist values were often frustrated by the very middle-American, Protestant constituents for whom they believed they spoke. Many of the latter let the board know that its moral standards were far too liberal and metropolitan. Confounded by bitter criticism from his midwestern flank, one of the board's officers, Orrin Cocks, railed against "those rampant people in the West" who were making it nearly impossible for him or anybody else to articulate the Protestant point of view on movie morals. As one board committee member admitted, New York, where the board worked (and where many films were still being made in the years just preceding World War I), could not make standards "for the country as a whole."[7]

When in 1915 the National Board of Censorship became the National Board of Review, it acknowledged the central difficulty for those hoping to define mainstream morality and translate it into rules for censoring movies: even Protestant, middle-class Americans could not agree on the proper limits to the representation of sexuality and other controversial matters.[8] On the one hand, the leading representatives of Protestant America—the spokesmen for the major denominations and the Federal Council of Churches—were becoming generally, though not uniformly, more liberal in both theology and social morality. On the other hand, most of those who were coming to be called "fundamentalists," along with many of the faithful in the leading denominations, rejected the latitudinarian ambiguities of such shepherds of the faith.[9] Unfortunately for Hollywood, it was just these shepherds whom it recruited in the 1920s to win over the small-town critics of movie morality.

The Motion Picture Producers and Distributors of America (MPPDA) was founded in 1921, in the wake of several lurid Hollywood sex scandals and just after New York became the sixth state to institute a board of movie censorship.[10] The MPPDA tried assiduously to court organized reformers who had taken or might be expected to take a public position in favor of legal censorship of the movies.[11] Will Hays, who took over the MPPDA in 1922, had good reason to believe that many, perhaps most, of those reformers would be happy to find a middle ground between the "too liberal" and "indulgent" standards of the National Board—which allowed a "stream of filthy films" to flow into America's communities under the guise of art—and the alternative of governmental censorship, which threatened to dam the flow of free expression.[12] Most of those Hays hoped to court were connected to the mainstream Protestant churches or groups whose social morality was a secularized or "progressive" version of Protestant values. Among the former were the Federal Council of Churches itself, the umbrella national association of the main Protestant denominations, and such Protestant service organizations as the YMCA and YWCA. Among the latter were the General Federation of Women's Clubs, the National Congress of Parents and Teachers, the National Education Association, the Boy Scouts of America, the Daughters of the American Revolution, and the Campfire Girls. The most secular of the organizations were the Russell Sage Foundation and the National Recreation Association, both of which were closely identified with progressive politics and the emerging disciplines of the social sciences. In its public relations work, the industry also established relationships with the International Federation of Catholic Alumnae and the National Catholic Welfare Conference, both of which would prove increasingly important as the 1920s wore on.

In the early 1920s, however, it was Protestant America that seemed from the view of the studios most in need of courting. The installation of Will Hays as "Czar of All the Rushes" in 1922 was a sign of Hollywood's apprehension over the condemnation of movies by spokesmen for Protestant, small-town America. One leading mid-western critic, Rev. Wilbur Fiske Crafts, revealed the vehemence and the quality of that condemnation when he called upon citizens to "rescue the motion pictures from the hands of the Devil and 500 unChristian Jews."[13] Few Protestant critics spoke with the passion or prejudice of

On assuming his duties as movie "czar," Will Hays (left) poses with studio executive Jesse Lasky in 1922. Photo courtesy of the Museum of Modern Art Film Stills Archive.

Crafts, but most assumed that they were defending Christian America against alien influences. In this context, Hollywood's appointment of Hays to head the industry trade association seemed a master stroke. A native of Indiana, an elder in the Presbyterian Church, and a major figure in the national Republican Party, Hays might have been chosen by a skillful Hollywood casting director for his role. By 1920, when he ran Warren Harding's presidential campaign and chaired the Republican Party, Hays's "evangelical political rhetoric earned for him the dubious title, 'Billy Sunday of the Republican Party.'"[14] He was the ideal man to reassure the hometown critics that one of their own would be riding herd on the untrustworthy aliens who ran the movie business.

As one of his first projects, Hays established formal relations with as many religious and reform organizations as possible. He presented himself to the critics as their man on the inside of Hollywood. He offered them the opportunity to affiliate themselves with his campaign for "film betterment" by joining the Committee on Public Relations. The message to the affiliated organizations was simple: oppose legislated censorship and the movie industry will allow you, through participation in the Committee on Public Relations, to collaborate actively in the great work of improving the "democracy of entertainment." Hays offered to finance nationwide mailings of any movie-related literature produced by affiliated organizations, including film-betterment handbooks, movie reviews, and surveys of viewer preferences. Committed as they were to spreading the gospel of film betterment as opposed to film censorship—that is, to praising the good rather than condemning the bad products of Hollywood—officers of these affiliated organizations were given the royal treatment by Hays's office. Over the years, Hays's public relations operation arranged and financed for those officers numerous nationwide speaking tours and trips to Hollywood to meet the stars and visit the studios.[15]

As Ruth Inglis has noted, the result of all this attention was that Hollywood's "'open door' became a kind of trap door for criticism."[16] Charges of cooptation had been leveled at the Hays Office since its start by such unwooable critics as Reverend Crafts, who died soon after the creation of the Committee on Public Relations, and Canon William S. Chase, pastor of one of the largest Episcopal churches in Brooklyn, head of the Lord's Day Alliance, and general secretary of the influential Federal Motion Picture Council. Both clerics were ardent proponents of federal censorship. In his critique of Hollywood's alien influence over Christian America, however, the more sophisticated Chase combined a quieter anti-Semitism with a quasi-progressive distrust of the ethics of the marketplace. Cognizant also of the power exercised in big cities and industrial states by immigrants and the institutions that represented them, men such as Crafts and Chase saw the federal government alone as capable of reimposing moral authority on a dangerously fragmented nation.[17]

For a time, the Committee on Public Relations seemed successful in moderating the critics. Hays worked particularly hard to win over the "club women," whose most distinguished leader, Mrs. Thomas G. (Alice Adams) Winter, accepted a prominent place on the committee. For most of the decade Winter was simultaneously president of the General Federation of Women's Clubs, a noted magazine author and lecturer, and—unbeknownst to her public—a paid consultant to Will Hays.[18] Whatever the effect of such payments, the relationship between Hays and the committee was not free of conflict. When Hays announced the end of the ban on Fatty Arbuckle's films in December 1922, members of the committee protested their exclusion from the decision and forced Hays to back down. In this and other ways the members of the committee appeared to win several victories over Hollywood. For example, at their urging Hays won commitments from Eastman Kodak and several studios to participate in efforts by the National Education Association and the Federal Council of Churches to produce noncommercial, "educational" films.[19] More important, in the press and from many pulpits and lecterns, the opinion seemed widespread that Will Hays had made a difference in Hollywood, that the movies were slowly getting better under his tutelage.

In the mid-1920s, however, several controversies frayed the bond between Hays and his affiliated groups. In 1924 and 1925 Hays found himself subject to bitter attacks from many of his allies. One cause of these attacks was an industry effort once again to rehabilitate Arbuckle. Another was the release of a Famous Players–Lasky film entitled *West of the Water Tower,* which portrayed small-town life as petty and repressed, and included the character of a "dissolute clergyman." In line with the newly promulgated "Formula," designed to keep daring fictional and theatrical material off the screen, members of the committee had explicitly vetoed the idea of making a movie of *West of the Water Tower.* Predictably, when the movie was made and released, several of them reacted sharply both to the studio's defiance of the committee and to Hays's inability to do anything about it. Led by the National Congress of Parents and Teachers and the General Federation of Women's Clubs, many organizations withdrew in protest from the Committee on Public Relations, effectively bringing its existence to an end. Thereafter Hays incorporated the committee's work into his own office in the form of the Department of Public Relations, to which he appointed as chair Col. Jason Joy, former national secretary of the American Red Cross. Joy, who had also chaired the committee, wooed back most of the departed organizations and expanded the office's outreach activities.[20] Once again Hays's public relations machine appeared to be rolling, but deeper ruts in the road lay just ahead.

One precipitant of the collapse of Hays's good relations with Protestant America was, ironically, a film designed to win its wholehearted support, Cecil B. deMille's 1927 release, *The King of Kings.*[21] What went wrong, among other things, was that George Reid Andrews, Hays's most prominent ally in Protestant America, suddenly turned against him. Respected clergyman, author, and leader in the Federal Council of Churches, Andrews had served as Hollywood's favorite Protestant stamp of approval. Within the Hays Office he was cited for his uncensorious "consultations" and his "cooperative effort" in steering moviemakers away from objectionable material. Hays's subsidy to Andrews's Church and Drama Association was money well spent. In 1926 Andrews was a script consultant for the filmed version of *The Scarlet Letter,* a production he praised publicly even after it drew the condemnation of many fellow clerics and reformers. In print and before numerous church-related and philanthropic meetings, Andrews reassured his constituency that movies were partaking in "the best developments in the theatre."[22]

After working closely on *The King of Kings,* Andrews apparently came to see his paid consultancy with deMille as the beginning of an even more lucrative and permanent arrangement with the motion picture industry. When Andrews failed to win from the Hays Office a commitment to finance his Church and Drama Association at the level he deemed adequate, he turned against the industry. Andrews may also have been stung by growing suggestions by religious associates that he had become an apologist for Hollywood. In any event, he commenced speaking publicly against the industry and in the process inspired many liberal Protestants to condemn the friendly arrangement which Hays and Joy had so carefully nurtured in the Department of Public Relations. By the end of the decade, both the Episcopal *Churchman* and the liberal *Christian Century* were calling for an investigation by the Federal Council of Churches into the manipulation of Protestant leaders by the Hays Office. And increasingly the call for a federal censorship law—never far from the surface in Protestant circles—sounded more and more loudly. In Protestant religious journals and the general press, the charge that Andrews and many other respectable Protestants had been used as "catspaws" by Hollywood was hardly debatable by the end of the decade.[23]

It should be noted that neither *The King of Kings* nor any other Hollywood event singlehandedly generated this crisis of conscience in Protestant America. By mid decade, frustration over the failure of Prohibition to accomplish its reformative purposes, the rise of spectacular criminality associated with resistance to Prohibition, and the emergence of a more vocal fundamentalist dissent from the cosmopolitan attitudes of the mainstream church leadership had prepared the ground for Hollywood's new troubles with Protestant America.[24] Moreover, the "youth culture" of the 1920s—of which "flappers," drinking gin, dancing to jazz, and making love in automobiles were only the most sensational elements—seemed to many middle-class Americans living proof of the breakdown of family values and the need for reasserting fundamental Christian standards.[25]

As relations between Hays and the Protestant churches took a turn for the worse, so did Hollywood's broader political fortunes. From all quarters, it seemed, the honeymoon between Hays and the hometown critics was ending. In Congress, legislators filed several bills providing not only for federal censorship but also, more ominously, for increased taxes on the movie business and federal regulation of distribution. In forty-four states, meanwhile, over one hundred bills were on file calling for new or tightened state regulation and censorship. From those whom Hays charged with keeping track of public attitudes toward the industry, especially his indefatigable chief counsel, C. C. Pettijohn, the movie czar was hearing that small-town distaste for the urban and alien values portrayed on the screen was growing, and that 1927 would "give us more trouble and more hard fighting than any two years in the past."[26]

Reacting in particular to films that seemed to condone violations of conventional sexual mores and challenged the authority of family, church, and civil government, even long-time enemies of censorship began to call for governmental protection of children and other "impressionables." Among the most notable of these was William Randolph Hearst. In 1923 his *Los Angeles Examiner* had editorialized against censorship, quoting with approval a labor leader's call to "uproot the whole idea of censorship" and all other "European methods of repression." Four years later, however, Hearst concluded in a letter to Hays that government coercion was necessary since the producers would "never reform voluntarily." In a signed editorial published in October 1927, Hearst assured his readers that, although state censors had proved "discouragingly unintelligent," a federal censorship commission would recruit only "intelligent, educated, experienced men and women, with moral but liberal minds."[27]

In response to the growing clamor, in 1927 Hays assigned Jason Joy to the newly created Studio Relations office in Hollywood. From the start, Joy saw his job as translating into clear guidelines for the Hollywood studios the innumerable eliminations and alterations demanded by state and local censors in the past and prodding producers into following those simple guidelines for the sake of their own best interest. To this end Joy extracted from the producers reluctant approval of "Eleven Don'ts and Twenty-six Be Carefuls," a list of rules that studios could follow to avoid the censors' wrath. The "Don'ts" included references to "white slavery," "sex perversion," childbirth, venereal disease, profanity, "ridicule of the clergy," "wilful offense to any nation, race or creed," and the like, while the "Be Carefuls" expanded on these matters and included many references to the depiction of criminal activity.[28]

Since the Studio Relations office could not enforce the Don'ts and Be Carefuls, Joy's role was that of benign hector. He sought to institutionalize what Samuel Goldwyn had impulsively ordered in 1921: a Hollywood effort to find out what "they" wanted. The producers might, through the agency of Joy's office, learn just what pleased and what offended their audiences, thereby avoiding costly censorship. Joy marshaled evidence to prove that his advice was sound, that "the sequences which we told the companies would be eliminated, have been eliminated by the Censor Boards—and usually nothing else has been cut out." He never tired of insisting that "audience reactions in communities far removed from the 'Hollywood idea' should be known."[29]

Joy's information was not the only news that Hollywood was receiving from the grass roots. No one in Hollywood doubted that the box office spoke loudly, albeit not always clearly, about what America wanted. But while extraordinarily good or bad receipts probably spoke for themselves, it was generally the local exhibitor who interpreted for the studios the response of audiences to what appeared on the screen. Communication was not always successful. Just as respectable reformers in the National Board and mainstream Protestants in the Federal Council of Churches could be charged with having lost touch with Christians in the heartland, so Hollywood was frequently charged with having lost touch with the exhibitors in the neighborhood theaters. Since the exhibitors represented Hollywood's front line in the culture wars being waged in America at the time, managing relations with them became a central concern of the Hays Office.

From the very earliest days of the movies, exhibitors were the first to sense trouble over movie content from patrons and others in the local community. They were also exposed earliest to the effects of censorship, boycotts, and obscenity prosecutions. After the shutdown of movie theaters in New York City just before the Christmas holiday in 1908, William Fox, leader of the citywide exhibitors' league, acted quickly to resolve the political crisis. He appealed to the People's Institute to organize a board of censorship so that politicians and concerned citizens might be reassured that the movies would be morally policed.[30] Like Fox, other leading representatives of exhibitor interests such as W. Stephen Bush of *Moving Picture World* and Martin Quigley of *Exhibitors Herald* (later *Motion Picture Herald*) strenuously preached a gospel of self-regulation. As one of Bush's successors at *Moving Picture World* warned in 1927, the industry had to clean up the movies "before the civil authorities are moved to action."[31]

At the same time as they sought to police their own industry, many exhibitors battled against local and state censorship campaigns. In 1921, for example, the exhibitors of North Carolina sponsored a tour by Louise Connolly of the National Board of Review to explain "the utter fallacy of legalized censorship" to the leading women's clubs in the state.[32] Although exhibitor, distributor, and producer seemed to have a common interest in fighting censorship, however, the exhibitors were in fact understood by all to be the least reliable link in the chain of industry solidarity. Some theater managers undoubtedly shared their patrons' dislike of sex, profanity, and crime on the screen; others simply feared the retribution of local citizens outraged by such showings.[33] Whatever the cause, in some cases, theater owners and managers could be found coming perilously close to—and sometimes frankly embracing—the practice of censorship on the local and state level.

Sometimes exhibitors simply had to accede to political pressures for self-censorship. Thus in Indianapolis in 1911, the mayor's Public Morals Commission gave local exhibitors the good news that it would not recommend municipal censorship and the bad news that it expected them to form a committee to review complaints about films and, if necessary, to "suppress" them.[34] In New York, the "decent fellows that [were] running the family houses" gladly acquiesced in the licensing commissioner's campaign to withhold licenses from exhibitors who showed "indecent" pictures because they saw it as an alternative to the imposition of prior censorship by a state board.[35] In other cases exhibitors seemed to need no prodding to move toward prior censorship. In Ohio in the 1910s, the state's exhibitors proved to be the most vocal and best-organized proponents of a state censorship law. Indeed, one of their number proudly accepted a position on the subsequently constituted board of censorship.[36] In 1913 the Motion Picture Exhibitors' League of America condemned the National Board of Review for passing pictures that predictably ran into trouble with local police or censoring committees and voted instead for state censorship as the only means of guaranteeing exhibitors a measure of peace in their home communities.[37] It is not surprising, then, that in 1921, when the industry rallied the National Board of Review, leaders of the American Federation of Labor, the New York State Conference of Mayors, and a host of other leaders and opinion makers in an effort to defeat the censorship bill before the state legislature, the exhibitors were conspicuously absent from the coalition.[38] By the mid-1920s exhibitors all over the country were cooperating with local and state censorship, expecting, as in the case of the Philadelphia censorship committee, to fill a seat reserved for them, alongside those reserved for women's club members, churchmen, educators, or others, depending on the political pressures operating in a particular locale or state.[39]

The exhibitors often found themselves caught between the righteous indignation of local officials and reformers and the aggressive marketing practices of producers and distributors. They had to sign a standard exhibitor's contract, which informed them that they would "not be relieved of the obligation to pay for any feature by reason of any act . . . by any board of censors, . . . or act of any official in any . . . community that shall prohibit or prevent the exhibition" of any movie they had booked.[40] Confronted with such exacting contractual conditions, the exhibitor could not doubt that the people who paid Will Hays's salary had shifted liability in the censorship wars to the foot soldiers who ran the movie houses. On the other hand, the local exhibitors sometimes heard kind words from reformers and legislative critics of Hollywood, who cast them in the role of victims of the movie monopoly. The critics decried the "stranglehold" such contracts exercised over the small proprietor, whose profit was "exceedingly small" and whose power to bargain exceedingly limited.[41] Similarly, when reformers recommended putting exhibitors on local censoring committees, they characterized such a move as a form of exhibitor empowerment vis-à-vis the producers and distributors. Thus, in recommending local action against bad movies, Charles N. Lathrop, writing for the Federal Council of Churches in 1922, argued that one tactic was "always wrong. That is, to launch immediately a crusade *against* the picture exhibitors. They are part of a big system for which they are only partly responsible. They are also members of the community. . . . All efforts should be positive and constructive."[42]

By 1927—the year of *The King of Kings*—the Protestant reformers whom Will Hays had hoped to co-opt were increasingly promoting federal anti-block-booking legislation as the only way to give local exhibitors, and therefore local communities, the power to keep out movies they found offensive. If enacted, such a measure would strike at the very heart of the Hollywood oligopoly system that Hays had been hired to safeguard. Block booking was designed to establish the major studios' monopoly over exhibition by foreclosing entry into the market by independent distributors. Along with blind selling, which required exhibitors to book studio features with little or no advance knowledge of their content, block booking also guaranteed a steady market for studio products, no matter how variable their quality. Block booking gave the major studios a measure of control over the independent theaters that was in some ways as great as that exercised over their own chain theaters. While the majors made deals with one another guaranteeing that only the best of their productions would be shown in chain theaters, they required independents to purchase exclusively from one distributor, sight unseen, a very large block of films. Among these films were many B films that could not be expected to draw crowds, but could be used on slow nights or as second features.[43]

Treated so peremptorily, exhibitors plausibly claimed impotence when accosted by citizens who demanded to know why films offensive to local sensibilities were being shown. It is not surprising that some of them, like one "Miss Decker, representing exhibitor interests of Cincinnati neighborhood theatres, blamed block-booking for all exhibitor shortcomings." Her charge was recorded by Carl Milliken, second in command to Will Hays, who heard it while attending a convention of social workers. It was, he reported, "well received by the minority 'anti-everything' part of the audience." However small that minority, it clearly worried Milliken enough to ask one major producer, "Would it be possible for our distributing companies to make two blocks of their pictures, one to supply neighborhood houses and one for metropolitan theatres?"[44]

As secretary of the MPPDA, Milliken had to respond to many letters similar to the anguished one sent to his boss, Will Hays, by C. L. Rosen, proprietor of the Ringling Theatre in Baraboo, Wisconsin, in 1927. Noting that he "cater[ed] to general family trade," Rosen asked Hays to help him "guarantee against showing a single item that could possibly offer the remotest offense." Presented by his customers with so stringent a criterion of acceptability, the exhibitor had no choice but to plead with his only supplier to save him from the wrath of the locals. No producer who pondered this letter, argued Milliken to studio head Hal Roach, could doubt for a moment just why the industry needed the Don'ts and Be Carefuls.[45] As grass-roots criticism of Hollywood's products and practices sharpened, these modest restraints on studio prerogatives seemed more necessary than ever. If Jason Joy's department properly administered the new standards, and if the producers faithfully respected them, less offense might be given to local viewers, especially to those small-town, mid-western, Protestant viewers of whom manager Rosen was so solicitous. And perhaps, therefore, neither such viewers nor such managers would be driven to repudiate the system of self-regulation administered by the Hays Office and to turn instead to censorship or antitrust legislation.

Alas for Hays and Hollywood, the introduction of sound in the late 1920s added the sexual double entendre to the list of offenses guaranteed to arouse middle America.[46] At the same time, the considerable costs of installing sound technology threatened the survival of the independent exhibitors and led them to found their own trade association. Known as the Allied States Association, the new organization promptly joined the already aroused voices of mainstream Protestantism in calling for the liberation of small-town and neighborhood America from the clutches of the movie trust by ending the system of block booking.[47] Indeed, as early as 1925, when the major studios were moving rapidly to acquire large chains of theaters and thereby complete the vertical integration of the industry, independent exhibitors had perfected the strategy of linking their struggle against the economic power of New York corporations with the moral crusade to protect Main Street from the "Hollywood idea." Even the Motion Picture Theatre Owners of America (MPTOA), which was more sympathetic to producer interests, declared that it was "unfair to the public as well as contrary to every honorable American business process to have such important community institutions as Motion Picture Theatres owned or directed by Producers who live in New York and have no interest in the localities where these trust-operated Theatres are conducted."[48]

As individual independent exhibitors and entire state chapters left the MPTOA, which had come to be dominated by the Hollywood studios, the Hays Office had an increasingly difficult time obscuring the contradiction at the heart of its relations with exhibitors. Its stout assistance in campaigns against censorship and blue laws seemed less and less valuable to an independent exhibitor about to be gobbled up—or driven out—by a theater chain owned by one of Hays's bosses.[49] By early 1928 C. C. Pettijohn was struggling mightily to keep regional exhibitor organizations from endorsing the Brookhart antitrust bill, under consideration at the time in the U.S. Senate. And the liberal congressman from New York, Emanuel Celler, despite strong reservations about censorship, was introducing Senator Brookhart's bill into the House, "to renew discussion concerning the unfair trade practices and monopolistic tendencies of film producers."[50]

While Will Hays's experiment in self-regulation seemed to be staggering under assaults from both grass-roots Protestants and exhibitors, a powerful ally appeared from the unlikeliest quarter—the Catholic Church. The church hierarchy included some of the bitterest critics of Hollywood movies, but at the same time it also opposed vigorously both legislated censorship and antitrust legislation. The church demanded reform of movie content along lines of its own devising, but it promised to oppose legislated censorship, especially in those states in the industrial Northeast and Midwest where its influence was greatest, as well as on the federal level. Neither the church nor organized lay Catholics were strangers to Hollywood or the Hays Office. The National Catholic Welfare Conference (NCWC) and, most significantly, the International Federation of Catholic Alumnae (IFCA) had been part of Hays's public relations and "movie-betterment" campaigns from the start. Indeed, for Hays and his colleagues, Catholic clergy and organizations appeared increasingly to be the ideal collaborators in the great task of uplifting—as opposed to censoring or restructuring—the movie business.

Founded during World War I as a relief organization, the NCWC staked out a position clearly on the left of Catholic opinion regarding questions of social justice and welfare. The organization's guiding spirit was Father John A. Ryan. The son of an Irish nationalist, ardently prolabor, and a Populist in his early years in Minnesota, Ryan authored in 1919 the "Bishops' Program of Social Reconstruction." This far-reaching manifesto advocated laws guaranteeing a minimum wage and minimum working age; the right to organize; public housing; old age, health, and unemployment insurance; and regulation of utilities and other monopolies, as well as worker stock ownership and worker-management cooperation. As one Catholic historian noted, "The progressive secular press expressed 'incredulous delight' with the document; liberal Protestants responded favorably, as did labor leaders. Upton Sinclair called it nothing less than a 'Catholic miracle.'"[51] On questions of free speech, however, Ryan did not differ from most Catholic intellectuals or the church hierarchy, whose Thomist political philosophy led them to assert that "error has not the same rights as truth."[52]

For the movie moguls this Catholic certainty about "principles of eternal and unchanging truth" had its attractions because, unlike Protestants, Catholics linked their moral certainties with a firm rejection of state action to control opinion. The origins of this squeamishness about censorship lay not in theology but in social history. Engaged in continuing tribal rivalry with Protestants throughout the country over Sabbath observance, the enforcement of Prohibition, and other questions, American Catholics could not help feeling that they were still regarded as aliens by much of Protestant America. What the Al Smith campaign would reveal nationally in 1928 was already perfectly clear on the local level: anti-Catholicism was alive and well and politically potent.[53] In most big cities Catholics wielded considerable political power and expected their church and their cultural institutions to be taken seriously. But as their sights turned upward they sensed the limits of their power and status. Federal or state legislation to control movies, like any other kind of blue law, therefore, struck Catholics as an unattractive solution to the problem of movie morality. There is very little evidence of serious clerical or lay Catholic involvement in campaigns to pass censorship laws in the United States in the first four decades of the twentieth century. Self-regulation, not censorship, was the settled policy of Catholic America, and it was uttered in terms nearly identical to those employed by Will Hays and the studio moguls.[54] By the end of the 1920s, therefore, as prominent Protestant voices were calling for measures that portended doom for the economic order of Hollywood, the apparently nonpolitical moralism of American Catholicism seemed to fit the industry's needs.

Even before the decisive events of the early 1930s, when Catholics formulated and, to a large extent, implemented the industry's Production Code, Hays and Hollywood found it easier to deal with Catholics than Protestants. When Charles A. McMahon of the NCWC complained in 1926 about the misuse of sacramental symbols in *The Merry Widow* or the impropriety of women masquerading as nuns in *Bobbed Hair,* both his complaint and the Hays Office's prompt reply indicated a genial meeting of the minds.[55] When the

IFCA sharply castigated two 1927 releases from Universal as "so disgustingly vulgar" that they deserved to be withdrawn, Jason Joy immediately reminded the producer that federation women had been "very helpful in averting Federal Regulation by appearing at the hearing in Washington." Moreover, he noted, they had sent out to their "enormous membership" repeated mailings on the theme of the improving quality of movies and the wrongheadedness of censorship and other legislative interventions into the movie business.[56] The studio got the message and withdrew the offending releases from circulation.

Just when the *King of Kings* fiasco was beginning to sour relations with Protestant leaders, Will Hays found it "rather a comfort" to read an editorial in the Catholic *Extension Magazine* entitled "In All Things Charity." The editorial sympathized with Hollywood's dilemma in attempting to treat sensitive subjects on the screen. The "tender sensibilities . . . of a man's nationality and his religious beliefs" could make it impossible for moviemakers to treat any controversial theme. In fact, the writer went on, Will Hays had done a "commendable" job of avoiding "ridicule, gossip and slander" while insisting that "sham, injustice, insincerity and greed are still legitimate objects of attack." Indeed, Hollywood's success in this regard was but one sign of the times, which promised a "millennium of peace and good will" among all peoples and nations.[57]

A better puff piece could not have been written by Will Hays himself. Nor could Cecil B. deMille have asked for a better religious consultant than Father Daniel A. Lord, who had joined Protestant George Reid Andrews (though on a nonpaying basis) on the set of *The King of Kings* in 1927. Unlike Andrews, Lord, a professor of dramatics at Saint Louis University, seemed to have no private agenda and confined his collaboration to matters of religious practice, persuading deMille not to use the distinctly Protestant version of the Lord's Prayer; and to matters of rather obvious bad taste, persuading the director to cut most of a scene wherein Mary Magdalene performs a sexually suggestive dance before an impassive Christ. Distinctly the supporting actor to Andrews's leading part, Lord may have found it easier to relax into his role as religious adviser. But he seems also to have sympathized strongly with the efforts of deMille and Hays to make *The King of Kings* what he called "a real awakening of interest in religious pictures."[58] After a few months of collaboration, Lord's stock was rising in Hollywood. Lord had been "very helpful, constructive in his attitude," asserted Will Hays, in the process of passing on the priest's suggestion that Hollywood produce a version of the Catholic children's fable, "Tom Playfair."[59]

The history of warm relations with Catholic organizations and the recent

Irish of "the old school" disport themselves in *The Callahans and the Murphys* (MGM, 1927). Photo courtesy of the Museum of Modern Art Film Stills Archive.

blossoming of good will between Father Lord and Hollywood did not prevent trouble from erupting in 1927. An MGM comedy of that year called *The Callahans and the Murphys* raised a storm of protest in Catholic America.[60] The controversy showed that however stout Catholic opposition was to censorship and antitrust legislation, Hollywood's alliance with the church would prove difficult and dangerous.

Upon its release in June 1927, *The Callahans and the Murphys* drew protests over its alleged ethnic slurs from Irish American organizations (and not initially, it should be noted, from Catholic clerics or lay organizations). By early July E. J. Mannix of MGM was writing to representatives of "the different Irish societies that called upon us," reassuring them that many cuts had been made in response to their criticisms and promising "in all future pictures which deal in any way with Irish characters, to submit scenario[s] for discussion."[61] But a week later the storm had not subsided, and the problem had reached the desks of MGM's New York officers and Will Hays. W. D. Kelly of MGM's home office sent a telegram to Mannix in Hollywood announcing that "objections now have reached stage where we must do something." Both the Hays Office and the "entire home office," Kelly insisted, saw only one course of action: "MEET IRISH DEMANDS." Whereas Mannix had tried earlier to make minimal cuts while reassuring protestors that the studio meant "to please all and to offend none," and to give all people, Irish and others, nothing but "a hearty good laugh," he was now directed clearly to edit the film further in accordance with the recommendations of the Hibernian Society and the Catholic Theatre Guild, to whom the Hays Office had referred the matter. Specifically, he was to cut all scenes wherein "degraded Irish" were shown drinking, fighting, striking women, working as ditchdiggers, bootlegging, or disporting themselves unrespectably on Saint Patrick's Day. One scene in particular, showing "mothers drinking and drunk at Irish picnic[,] proved absolutely objectionable to Father Kelly [of the Theatre Guild] and . . . has been the butt of most of the Irish societies' complaints."[62]

Within a few weeks Mannix was able to assure the home office that nearly every one of the cuts had been made. Furthermore, a new opening title had been created to respond to protests that "our younger Irish" were offended by burlesque treatments of the Irish "of the old school." The new title would read: "This is the story of the Callahans and the Murphys both of that fast fading old school . . . to whom the world is indebted for the richest and rarest of wholesome fun and humor."

Nevertheless, Mannix made it clear that he considered the Irish demands "just another instance of the societies trying to censor our pictures."[63] But if Mannix saw no difference between censorship and pressure group tactics, neither the home office nor the Hays Office made the same mistake. As far as they were concerned, there was a world of difference between managing public opinion (in connection with which they had developed considerable expertise) and submitting to government regulation, whether of movie content or, more ominously, distribution practices. It was this very distinction between organized public pressure and governmental action, which many Protestants seemed to confound, that both the Catholic Church and the Hays Office insisted on drawing very sharply.

By the last week of July the Hays Office appeared to be managing the crisis successfully. It was circulating letters from several of the chief faultfinders, who now expressed satisfaction that the film had been properly reedited in response to their protests. Mannix wrote to Jason Joy with the good news that, after personally rescreening the film for nearly twenty representatives of Irish groups, only one objectionable drinking scene remained, which was to be cut immediately. The storm seemingly over, a chastened Mannix saw fit to apologize to "Colonel" Joy and "General" Hays: "I am extremely sorry that this has caused you this trouble."[64]

On the very day the genie seemed to have been stuffed back into the bottle, however, the NCWC issued a press release that blew the lid once more. Written by the head of the NCWC motion picture bureau, Charles A. McMahon, the editorial blasted *The Callahans and the Murphys* in the most uncompromising terms. The picture "reeks from start to finish with vulgarity and indecency," the editorial thundered. Worse, it was "a gross insult, deliberate or otherwise, to the ancient fatherland culture of the Irish people." Echoing earlier critics, McMahon insisted that the "Donnybrook Irishman has long since passed from the legitimate stage. Thanks to patriotic organizations . . . he has likewise been dropped . . . [from] St. Patrick's Day cards and souvenirs. . . . Film outrages like 'The Callahans and the Murphys' can not help but make the usually tolerant and liberty-loving Irish-American as clamorous for legalized censorship as the most vocal reformer."[65] The portent of that last sentence could not have escaped the notice of Hays or the studio men, especially coming from the NCWC, whose members, as Jason Joy reminded MGM, "have been our ardent supporters . . . at congressional hearings on censorship" and in mobilizing the Catholic public to support "our praiseworthy productions."[66]

Even worse than the insult that the film had given to Irish Americans was the way in which, in McMahon's formulation, ethnic insensitivity turned into an "offense to the Catholic religion" and an attempt "to discredit the Catholic Faith." Although the film's only direct references to Catholicism seem to have been a few depictions of Irish characters in distress making the sign of the cross and the depiction of Saint Patrick's Day as an occasion for drunken revelry, McMahon chose to call attention to the film's insults to Catholics, not to the Irish, in his headline. As an officer in the church hierarchy's principal organization devoted to the secular life of Catholics, McMahon brought to his critique a quality of official religious denunciation that made the moguls and their czar shiver. Following upon his editorial, McMahon sent a letter to Joy reiterating his charges about the film's offenses "to race, religion and common decency." He advised Joy that to avoid such upsets in the future the moviemakers had only to "employ some one to see that no such material of this kind creeps into their productions."[67] Thus, more than two years before the onset of the Great Depression, which made the movie industry acutely vulnerable to organized pressure at the box office, both the agent and the form of that pressure had already emerged. Moreover, three years before Father Lord and

Martin Quigley authored the Production Code, which was a more elaborate and philosophically unified version of the Don'ts and Be Carefuls, and more than six years before the Catholic Legion of Decency began mobilizing boycotts and Joseph Breen began playing the role of code enforcer in Hollywood —that is, well before the "Catholic Crusade" made its entrance with an obvious flourish in 1934—McMahon had written a first draft of the script.

Both Joy and MGM tried one last time to fight back against the onslaught. Joy's strategy was twofold: first, to marshal a range of Irish and Catholic opinion against McMahon's appraisal of the movie; and second, to promise the critics that greater care would be taken by his office to police the studios' treatment of similar materials in the future. With respect to the latter issue, Joy recommended that MGM immediately begin to clear with the NCWC and other groups all script materials for a forthcoming production of *Bringing Up Father.* Based on a comic strip about an Irish family which had run in the Hearst papers for twenty years without protest, the proposed picture, Joy reminded the studio, would have to be handled delicately in light of recent protests.[68]

On the other hand, with Joy's help MGM defended itself to Hays. The studio noted that the production supervisor, the director, the scriptwriter, and both female leads were Irish, that the reedited version of the picture had been cleared with many Irish American organizations, and that the movie was a tribute to the Irish, full of "mother love," "clean romance," and "robust humor."[69] Meanwhile, Joy made a special effort to attend a Catholic Charities convention in Los Angeles, inviting many of the attenders to tour the studios and taking the opportunity to talk "with probably 100 different priests and nuns." He found "no one who had any objection against the industry on the ground that it offended the church." Specifically, no one had found *The Callahans and the Murphys* insulting to their religion.[70] Most important, Joy had developed a relationship with Father William Lucey, a leader in Catholic social action, who would later become archbishop of San Antonio and an ardent supporter of the CIO and the New Deal. Earlier in 1927 Lucey had been asked to offer advice and comment on *The King of Kings,* apparently on a more limited basis than Father Daniel Lord. But he had made a good impression, and now, in response to a query from Joy, he opined indignantly, "It was ridiculous to object to {*The Callahans and the Murphys*} on the ground that it was anti-Catholic." Joy immediately recruited Lucey to consult with MGM on its forthcoming *Bringing Up Father.*[71]

Whatever Lucey's value in the future, however, his support in the current controversy over *The Callahans and the Murphys* proved unavailing. Against

Father Lucey's views, those of Cardinal Dougherty of Philadelphia, who condemned the film and urged its withdrawal, weighed far more heavily. Dougherty's pronouncement convinced Hays that the battle was lost; the movie czar, in turn, finally convinced MGM to withdraw the film from circulation.[72] The NCWC bulletin gloated in triumph, declaring the withdrawal "proof of the power of public criticism rightly expressed and properly directed."[73] This was probably exactly the way Will Hays hoped it would be interpreted, as a victory for self-regulation. But Jason Joy and members of Hays's own staff read it differently. It was nothing less than a victory for "censorship," which had "established a precedent which will rise up to plague us in the future."[74]

In several ways Joy's instincts were right. First, he was correct that Catholic opinion was less uniform and rigid on matters of movie morality than the NCWC and the church hierarchy insisted. And second, Joy was correct that defeat on *The Callahans and the Murphys* had clearly put his own office at risk. In a few years he would be gone because, among other reasons, Will Hays had come to find the myth of Catholic unanimity and power indispensable. If he could prove that public opinion truly made a difference in Hollywood, he could fight off legislative intervention. Given the disarray among leading Protestant opinion makers, the confidence with which Catholic clerics seemed to speak for their very large public was nothing short of bracing. And to satisfy that newly resonant and confident voice—which seemed at once to represent the great industrial cities and an emergent force of religious respectability that might win over Protestant America to the policy of self-regulation—Hays needed one of their own. He turned, therefore, away from Jason Joy and to several Catholics: Father Lord, Martin Quigley, and, ultimately, Cardinal Mundelein's hand-picked candidate for industry self-censor, Joseph Breen.

Will Hays had, in effect, found a grass roots he could cultivate more comfortably. And, as the fate of another film made in 1927 suggests, so had MGM. The film in question, a melodrama called *The Garden of Allah,* was treated with all the A-movie respect it deserved. The book, by Robert Hichen, told of a Catholic priest who is drawn into a passionate romance with a woman but ultimately decides to return to his priestly vows. Two years prior to filming, MGM had dutifully submitted the book to Jason Joy, who sent it to Mrs. Thomas A. (Rita) McGoldrick, head of the motion picture bureau of the IFCA and a long-time supporter of the industry. She, in turn, referred it to two Catholic priests, both of whom advised that a tasteful screen realization of the story would certainly be "acceptable to Catholics." More important than these precautions, however, was the very nature of the story and its treatment. This

was not a crude B-movie burlesque, not a comedy at all, but a pious exploration of "temptation" and "renouncement." As Mrs. McGoldrick's personal
review of the film for the IFCA's reviewing service noted, the movie was "a distinguished example of restraint and good taste," and "reverently Catholic." It
was the story not of "a sensuous wanton" but of a "conscience haunted." And
in the end, the church, not the flesh, governed that conscience.[75]

Although on its release the film was denounced by an "organization
of [Irish] vigilance committees" in New York, which had been created "to
prevent any repetition of plays like 'The Callahans and the Murphys,'"
McGoldrick's organization promptly whirled into action to stem the critical
tide. She and two other national officers composed a letter affirming that "the
picture has been gloriously done" and that it was "a fine example of the good
faith the producers kept with those of us whose advice was asked in the beginning." She mailed the letter to all the important Catholic periodicals, to every
state official on her organizational list, "and to all others whose opinions might
be influenced by our decision." "Our championship in this matter," her letter
concluded, "is our return to Metro-Goldwyn-Mayer for having handled the
film in so dignified a manner."[76] A film so dignified and with such powerful backers met little resistance from Catholics, or from anybody else for that
matter.

By the end of 1927, then, with the controversies surrounding *The King of
Kings, The Callahans and the Murphys,* and *The Garden of Allah* mostly behind
him, Will Hays had discovered a new strategy for containing grass-roots assaults on Hollywood morality. He allowed the Catholics to write the Production Code a few years later, and, under great pressure from the Legion of Decency, he let them administer it, because both he and they were in search of
respectability and perfectly willing to confer it upon each other. Like Hays,
many Protestants in the early 1930s found the Catholics' appropriation of the
crusade for decency a curious but inspiring development. Accustomed for so
long to think of Catholics as neither willing nor able to become responsible
citizens, these Protestants discovered that a new generation of Catholics,
mostly of Irish and German extraction, sought as strenuously as any Son or
Daughter of the American Revolution to distance themselves from lower-class
habits and values and to prove themselves perfectly respectable Americans. "I
only wish the Protestant Church was as vigorous in this matter," admiringly
announced a minister who had long been involved in the censorship movement
in Philadelphia.[77]

The Catholics who launched the crusade against Hollywood were part of a
new generation of Catholic clerics and lay intellectuals whose ambition in-

creasingly was to speak not only for their coreligionists but also for Americans as a whole. Their confident fundamentalism in matters of morality made a strong impression at a time when neither liberal Protestantism, nor Deweyan social science, nor legal realism could restore the moral ground that most middle-class Americans had once trod with self-assurance and authority. Never having faced what historian Edward A. Purcell, Jr., called the "crisis of democratic theory," and having a "ready justification for democracy" in natural law and a "ready justification for an entire system of morality" in Thomist theology, Catholic thinkers "were much closer in their intellectual and emotional response to the great majority of Americans" in their acceptance of the American status quo.[78]

Indeed, by the 1930s Catholic intellectuals were charging that secularized Protestant Americans had lost touch with their own roots, particularly with the natural-law tradition that had produced the nation's founding documents. Setting the tone for the anticommunist conservatism that would flourish in the post-World War II period, these Catholics charged that communism and other forms of political pathology were products of moral relativism and intellectual drift. Only Catholic Americans, they averred, could save the republic from betrayal. As Wilfred Parsons, a Jesuit professor at Catholic University and an important player in the events that led up to the writing of the Production Code and the forming of the Legion of Decency, put it: "By a sort of natural affinity, the modern intelligent Catholic finds himself drawing ever more closely to American cultural origins at the same time that his fellow non-Catholic Americans are disavowing those origins with almost indecent haste." Similarly, a writer in *Commonweal* proclaimed in 1941, "I am integrally part of America, America is integrally part of me!"[79]

Like the New Deal and the CIO, the Legion of Decency and the Breen office marked a new stage in the *Kulturkampf* that began with the Industrial Revolution and intensified with the arrival of commercial mass culture. In the 1930s the victory of New Deal liberalism confirmed socioeconomic and political gains for the descendants of those disproportionately Catholic immigrants who first arrived in the late nineteenth century.[80] On the other hand, the triumph of Catholic power in Hollywood suggests that, in defense of their traditional habits and sensibilities, most Catholics were willing to cede to the church the power to police their cultural environment.

The story of efforts to control the content of movies before the Production Code reveals many of the constituent elements of a far wider struggle over cultural authority in the twentieth century. The press, popular stage, movies, radio, and, eventually, television precipitated a political contest over the representation of crime, sex, ethnicity, and other controversial matters. One element in this struggle was the drive for both economic and cultural power by corporate oligopolies and their "colonization" through the marketplace of much of the educational and recreational activity of American society. Under the rubric of hegemony theory, many historians and critics of mass culture have narrated the story of struggles over representation in terms of responses to that drive for domination in the forms of acquiescence, accommodation, resistance, evasion, and the like.[81] However, a close look at the history of movie censorship indicates that the political struggle over screen representations responded to a greater variety of social dynamics. At the very least, the story narrated above indicates that the struggle over movie censorship responded to an important shift in the internal organization of Protestant and Catholic communities and in the relative power of each within the American polity. The power of the movie oligopoly was real, but limited. Even the lowly exhibitor could, through trade association and political alliance, challenge the very existence of the oligopoly. Organized pressure from reformers and churches could force producers to accede to a series of more or less restrictive compromises in their business practices. In efforts to defend itself, Hollywood might assemble and rearrange its alliances, finding advantage where it could, but never either clearly comprehending the field of play or controlling the outcome.

In the end, the history of efforts to censor and regulate the movies is best read not as a simple tale of artistic freedom struggling against repressive moralism. Neither, on the other hand, is it a simple tale of hegemonic capitalism legitimizing consumerism and co-opting dissent. An industry largely financed by Protestant bankers, operated by Jewish studio executives, and policed by Catholic bureaucrats, all the while claiming to represent grass-roots America, resists either heroic or demystifying narrative treatment.

NOTES

Earlier versions of this essay received insightful criticism from participants in a session of the British Association of American Studies at the University of Exeter, March 1990, and from colleagues in the Five College Social History Seminar, October 1990; I thank them all, but especially Richard Maltby, Kathy Peiss, and Daniel Czitrom. Thanks also to George Billias for his comments.

1. See Leonard J. Leff and Jerold L. Simmons, *The Dame in the Kimono: Hollywood, Censorship, and the Production Code from the 1920s to the 1960s* (New York, 1990), 47ff.

2. Garth Jowett, *Film: The Democratic Art* (Boston, 1976), 247. See also his "Moral Responsibility and Commercial Entertainment: Social Control in the United

States Film Industry, 1907–1968," *Historical Journal of Film, Radio, and Television* 10 (1990): 3–31.

3. On dime novels, see Michael Denning, *Mechanic Accents: Dime Novels and Working-Class Culture in America* (London, 1987); on vaudeville, Robert W. Snyder, *The Voice of the City: Vaudeville and Popular Culture in New York* (New York, 1989); on burlesque, Robert C. Allen, *Horrible Prettiness: Burlesque and American Culture* (Chapel Hill, 1991).

4. *Moving Picture World,* December 7, 1921.

5. Francis G. Couvares and Kathy Peiss, "Sex, Censorship and the Movies: The National Board of Review, 1909–1922," unpublished paper; Nancy J. Rosenbloom, "Between Reform and Regulation: The Struggle over Film Censorship in Progressive America, 1909–1922," *Film History* 1 (1987): 307–25; Daniel Czitrom, "The Redemption of Leisure: The National Board of Censorship and the Rise of Motion Pictures in New York City, 1900–1920," *Studies in Visual Communication* 10 (1984): 2–6; Ruth A. Inglis, *Freedom of the Movies: A Report on Self-Regulation from the Commission on Freedom of the Press* (New York, 1947), 74–87.

6. See Kay Sloan, *The Loud Silents: Origins of the Social Problem Film* (Urbana, 1988), chap. 4. On "sex-problem" films, see the files on *Traffic in Souls, The Inside of the White Slave Traffic,* and *Where Are My Children?* in Controversial Films files, National Board of Review Collection, Rare Books and Manuscripts Division, New York Public Library, Astor, Lennox, and Tilden Foundations (hereafter cited as NBR). On the breakdown of board consensus concerning representations of race, see the file on *The Birth of a Nation,* NBR.

7. "Report of Meeting at Mechanics Institute," February 5, 1915, Subject Papers, NBR; "Suggestions for a Note on the National Board's Weekly Bulletin," n.d., *Where Are My Children?* file, NBR; minutes, January 15 and September 14, 1916, Committee on Films for Young People, NBR.

8. Aside from sex, the other issue that most deeply divided the board was race, most dramatically in the case of *The Birth of a Nation* (see Nickieann Fleener-Marzec, "D. W. Griffith's *The Birth of a Nation:* Controversy, Suppression, and the First Amendment as It Applies to Filmic Expression, 1915–1973," [Ph.D. diss., University of Wisconsin, 1977]; and Fred Silva, ed., *Focus on "The Birth of a Nation"* [Englewood Cliffs, N.J., 1971]).

9. On the conflict between modernism and fundamentalism in American Protestantism in the early twentieth century, see William R. Hutchinson, *The Modernist Impulse in American Protestantism* (Cambridge, Mass., 1976).

10. In order of their inauguration, the states of Pennsylvania, Ohio, Kansas, Maryland, Virginia, and New York maintained movie censorship boards. By the 1920s, well over one hundred cities empowered police or civilian boards and licensing authorities to censor movies. In addition to the states listed above, several used their licensing authority to ban films screened by bodies such as the National Board of Review or the New York state board (see Inglis, *Freedom,* 70–77; Ford H. MacGregor, "Official Censorship Legislation," *Annals* 128 [November 1926]: 163–74; and Robert Sklar, *Movie-Made America: A Cultural History of American Movies* [New York, 1975], 78–85).

11. Inglis, *Freedom,* 103–11.

12. Ibid., 78–89; Tsuchiya Hiroko, "The Making of Hard Playing Americans: The Legitimization of Working Class Leisure, 1890–1929 (Ph.D. diss., Columbia University, 1986), 310. For a critique of the National Board as too elitist and too indulgent, see New York State Legislature, *Report of the Joint Legislative Committee to Investigate the Moving Picture Industry* (Albany, 1917), 5.

13. Quoted in Terry Ramsaye, *A Million and One Nights: A History of the Motion Picture through 1925* (New York, 1926), 483. On Crafts's progressive views, see Hiroko, "Making of Hard Playing Americans," 303–4. On anti-Semitism directed toward the Hollywood moguls, see Neal Gabler, *An Empire of Their Own: How the Jews Invented Hollywood* (New York, 1988).

14. Robert Francis Martin III, "Celluloid Morality: Will Hays' Rhetoric in Defense of the Movies, 1922–1930" (Ph.D. diss., Indiana University, 1974), 9.

15. Inglis, *Freedom,* 100–4; Martin, "Celluloid Morality," 182. On Hays's public relations effort, see Federal Council of the Churches of Christ in America, *The Public Relations of the Motion Picture Industry* (New York, 1931), 66–73, 95–105; Kevin Brownlow, *Behind the Mask of Innocence* (New York, 1990), 13–17; and Paul W. Facey, "The Legion of Decency: A Sociological Analysis of the Emergence and Development of a Social Pressure Group" (Ph.D. diss., Fordham University, 1945), 19–20.

16. Inglis, *Freedom,* 111.

17. On Canon Chase, see Ramsaye, *Million and One Nights,* 482–84; Federal Council of Churches, *Public Relations,* 106–7; Inglis, *Freedom,* 80–82, 100; and Martin, "Celluloid Morality," 96–98, 221.

18. On Winter, see Inglis, *Freedom,* 106–7; and Federal Council of Churches, *Public Relations,* 83–86, 99, 101, 104, 114. On Winter's later career with the Hays Office, see Lea Jacobs, *The Wages of Sin: Censorship and the Fallen Woman Film, 1928–1942* (Madison, Wis., 1991), 68, 108–9. Hays assiduously cultivated local leaders of the General Federation (see, for example, memorandum, C. C. P[ettijohn] to Will Hays, November 5, 1926, and Lola Adams Gentry to Jason Joy, September 27, 1927, in the Will Hays Papers, Indiana State Library [microfilm edition, University Publications of America; hereafter cited as Hays Papers]). In at least one case, monetary payments were contemplated, and perhaps offered, to a women's club officer (Jason Joy to Will Hays, January 5, 1926, Hays Papers).

19. See Leo Litzky, "Censorship of Motion Pictures in the United States" (Ph.D. diss., New York University, 1947), 32–36; and Will Hays to Hal Roach, February 18, 1926, Hal Roach Collection, Archives of Performing Arts, University of Southern California.

20. Federal Council of Churches, *Public Relations,* 69–73, 116–24; Inglis, *Freedom,* 104–6; Litzky, "Censorship," 36–42. On the Formula, see Hays to Roach, May 26, 1926, and enclosed resolutions of support for the Formula dated July and August 1924 by producers, advertisers, and West Coast theater operators (Hal Roach Collection).

21. Richard Maltby, *"The King of Kings* and the Czar of All the Rushes: The Propriety of the Christ Story," *Screen* 31 (summer 1990): 188–213; *The King of Kings* file, Production Code Administration (PCA) Collection, Margaret Herrick Library, Academy of Motion Picture Arts and Sciences (AMPAS), Beverly Hills. See also Litzky, "Censorship," 54–59.

22. See MPPDA press releases, March 27, June 10, July 27, 1926, Hays Papers. Joy memo to Will Hays, January 27, 1926, Hays Papers; see also Maltby, *"King of Kings,"* 206–9.

23. Maltby, *"King of Kings,"* 207–12. See also Federal Council of Churches, *Public Relations,* 3–4, 113; and John Alan Sargent, "Self-Regulation: The Motion Picture Production Code, 1930–1961" (Ph.D. diss., University of Michigan, 1963), 45.

24. On religious fundamentalism, see Hutchinson, *Modernist Impulse,* chap. 8. On movies within the broader context of social conflict, see Sklar, *Movie-Made America,* 89–91. For a somewhat dated but still useful survey of ethnocultural conflict in the 1920s, see John P. Roche, *The Quest for the Dream: The Development of Civil Rights and Human Relations in Modern America* (New York 1963), 103–29. A more recent treatment is John Higham, *Send These to Me: Immigrants in Urban America,* rev. ed. (Baltimore, 1984), chaps. 6–9.

25. See Paula S. Fass, *The Damned and the Beautiful: American Youth in the 1920s* (New York, 1977).

26. Anonymous memo to Hays, May 20, 1926, and C. C. Pettijohn memo to Hays, February 10, 1927, Hays Papers; Martin, "Celluloid Morality," 235–36.

27. *Los Angeles Examiner,* October 8, 1923, October 13, 1927, in Clippings file, "Censorship (1924–36)," General Files, AMPAS; Martin, "Celluloid Morality," 245–46; Leff and Simmons, *Dame,* 8.

28. Federal Council of Churches, *Public Relations,* 124–40; Inglis, *Freedom,* 113–16.

29. Joy to Hays, February 4, 1928, Hays Papers. See also extensive correspondence in *Common Clay* file, and Joy to Shulberg, July 15, 1930, in *Morocco* file, PCA; and Federal Council of Churches, *Public Relations,* 126–27.

30. *Moving Picture World,* December 7, 1921.

31. See *Motion Picture World* editorial enclosed with Hays to Frank Butler, February 9, 1927, MPPA file no. 8, Hal Roach Collection. See also Richard L. Stromgren, "The Moving Picture World of W. Stephen Bush," *Film History* 2 (1988): 13–22.

32. *Moving Picture World,* November 5, 1921.

33. A national survey of 104 exhibitors conducted by the NBR in 1921 revealed that about one-third of the managers found "sex pictures" as objectionable as did their customers ("Summary of Answers to Questionnaires to Exhibitors," March 1921, NBR). Comments by and about exhibitors revealing their own attitudes and those of local audiences and citizens during the 1910s and early 1920s can be found in the NBR Regional Correspondence.

34. *New York Morning Telegraph,* December 31, 1911, clipping in Censorship (1923), General Files, AMPAS.

35. New York State Legislature, *Report of the Joint Legislative Committee to Investigate the Moving Picture Industry* (Albany, 1917), 13–14.

36. Frederick Marshall Wirt, "State Film Censorship with Particular Reference to Ohio" (Ph.D. diss., Ohio State University, 1956), 58–64, 67–68.

37. *New York Times,* July 13, 1913.

38. Inglis, *Freedom,* 87.

39. See, for example, (Philadelphia) *North American,* January 11, 1924, clipping in Censorship file, Theatre Collection, Free Library of Philadelphia. For comment on

exhibitors offering the "heartiest cooperation" with state censors, see Virginia Department of Law, Division of Motion Picture Censorship, *Report, July 1, 1927 to June 30, 1928* (Richmond, Va., 1928), 5.

40. Reproduced in New York State Legislature, *Report of the Joint Legislative Committee,* 6.

41. Ibid., 6, 9.

42. Charles N. Lathrop, *The Motion Picture Problem* (New York, 1922), 38.

43. Richard Maltby, *Harmless Entertainment: Hollywood and the Ideology of Consensus* (Metuchen, N.J., and London, 1983), 45, 98; Tino Balio, ed., *The American Film Industry,* rev. ed. (Madison, Wis., 1985), 257–59; Inglis, *Freedom,* 49–50; Federal Council of Churches, *Public Relations,* 41–44, 145–46; Mae D. Huettig, *Economic Control of the Motion Picture Industry: A Study in Industrial Organization* (Philadelphia, 1944), 116–24.

44. Carl Milliken to Hal Roach, June 2, 1927, MPPA file no. 8, Hal Roach Collection.

45. Milliken to Roach, December 29, 1927, MPPA file no. 8, Hal Roach Collection.

46. See *Exhibitors Herald-World,* November 12, 1929, for controversies in New York and Kansas over whether existing censorship laws, written to control pictures, could legitimately be applied to the control of speech.

47. Howard T. Lewis, *The Motion Picture Industry* (New York, 1933), 299–335.

48. MPTOA press release, January 29, 1925, Hays Papers.

49. See, for example, Pettijohn to Hays, November 5, 1926, and Joy to Hays, January 3, 1928, Hays Papers.

50. Pettijohn to Hays, February 3, 1928, and newspaper clipping, February 7, 1928, Hays Papers. In contrast to the grim reports from the field in 1928, see the assertion by Burt New, Pettijohn's assistant, that exhibitors were "almost without exception . . . friendly . . . toward this organization" (*Annual Report,* 1926, Hays Papers).

51. Jay P. Dolan, *The American Catholic Experience: A History from Colonial Times to the Present* (Garden City, N.Y., 1985), 344; and more generally on Ryan and the NCWC, 342–45, 402–17. See also James Hennesey, *American Catholics: A History of the Roman Catholic Community in the United States* (New York, 1981), 226–53.

52. Hennesey, *American Catholics,* 251. See also Edward A. Purcell, Jr., *The Crisis of Democratic Theory: Scientific Naturalism and the Problem of Value* (Lexington, Ky., 1973), 169–81. For Ryan's own account of Catholic political and social philosophy, see *The State and the Church,* coauthored with Moorhouse F. X. Millar (New York, 1930).

53. For a particularly rancorous example in the 1920s of Protestant Republican anti-Catholicism—and of Catholic Democratic racism—see John R. Schmidt, *"The Mayor Who Cleaned Up Chicago:" A Political Biography of William E. Dever* (DeKalb, Ill., 1989), 71–72, 160, 165–66.

54. Inglis, *Freedom,* 74; Litzky, "Censorship," 59.

55. Memo circular from Fred W. Beetson, January 28, 1926, MPPA file no. 6, Hal Roach Collection.

56. Joy to Frank Butler, 15 June 1927, MPPA file no. 9, Hal Roach Collection.

57. *Extension Magazine,* November 1927, clipping enclosed with Hays to Roach, December 7, 1927, MPPA file no. 8, Hal Roach Collection.

58. Letter from Rev. Daniel Lord to Rev. John J. Burke of the NCWC, quoted in Maltby, *"King of Kings,"* 19.

59. Hays to Roach, September 2, 1927, MPPA file no. 8, Hal Roach Collection.

60. See *The Callahans and the Murphys* file, PCA Collection, AMPAS. An excellent recent study of this film and its fate is Francis R. Walsh, "'The Callahans and the Murphys' (MGM, 1927): A Case of Irish-American and Catholic Church Censorship," *Historical Journal of Film, Radio and Television* 10 (1990): 33–45. I am grateful to Professor Walsh for allowing me to read a prepublication version of his article and commenting helpfully on an earlier version of this essay.

61. E. J. Mannix to Mrs. Donovan, July 8, 1927, and E. J. Mannix to C. F. Horan, July 14, 1927, *The Callahans and the Murphys* file, PCA Collection, AMPAS (hereafter cited as *Callahans*).

62. W. D. Kelly to E. J. Mannix, telegram, June 22, 1927, *Callahans.* On Irish protest against a "seemingly endless string of 'Cohen and Kelly' comedies," see Les and Barbara Keyser, *Hollywood and the Catholic Church: The Image of Roman Catholicism in American Movies* (Chicago, 1984), 96–97.

63. Mannix to Kelly, n.d., PCA Collection, AMPAS.

64. John Byrne to MGM, July 23, 1927; Mannix to Joy, July 25, 1927; Felix Feist to Mannix, July 25, 1927; Joy to Hays, July 25, 1927; John Crane to Father John Kelly, n.d. (all in *Callahans*).

65. Press release, "'The Callahans and the Murphys' Film Called Insult to the Catholic Faith," July 25, 1927, *Callahans.*

66. Joy to Mannix, August 8, 1927, *Callahans.*

67. Charles A. McMahon to Joy, July 30, 1927, and Joy's conciliatory reply, August 8, 1927, *Callahans.*

68. Joy to Hays, July 25, 1927; Joy to Mannix, August 8, 1927; Mannix to Joy, August 10, 1927; Joy to Milliken, September 6, 1927; Milliken to Joy, October 6, 1927 (all in *Callahans*).

69. William A. Orr to Hays, October 23, 1927, *Callahans.* See the recollections of the Irish American scriptwriter, Frances Marion, *Off with Their Heads* (New York, 1972), 153–57.

70. Joy, file memo, September 8, 1927, *Callahans.*

71. Joy, file memo, August 16, 1927, and Milliken to Joy, October 6, 1927, *Callahans.* On Lucey, see David O'Brien, *Public Catholicism* (New York, 1989), 168–69, 175–76, 184, 199.

72. In the later Legion of Decency campaign, it was Dougherty who proved perhaps the most vehement and tenacious of the Catholic bishops. In Philadelphia he organized a diocesewide boycott not only of condemned films but of all films made by studios that produced anything worthy of legion condemnation (see Facey, "Legion," 150–51; and *Time,* October 1, 1934, clipping in Censorship file, Free Library of Philadelphia).

73. Clipping, December 1927, *Callahans.*

74. "Arthur" to Joy, December 23, 1927, and Joy to Kirk Russell, January 4, 1928, *Callahans.*

75. McGoldrick to Milliken, October 2, 1927, *The Garden of Allah* file, PCA Collection, AMPAS (hereafter cited as *Garden*); copy of internal IFCA memo, October 1, 1927, *Garden.*

76. McGoldrick to Milliken, October 2, 1927, *Garden.*

77. *Philadelphia Record,* August 12, 1930, clipping in Censorship file, Free Library of Philadelphia.

78. Purcell, *Crisis,* 169.

79. Both quoted in Purcell, *Crisis,* 170–72.

80. The embodiment of such economically liberal and culturally conservative Catholic politics was Cardinal Mundelein of Chicago, who was a fervent friend of Franklin Roosevelt and played a decisive role in the establishment of both the Production Code and the Legion of Decency (see Edward R. Kantowicz, *Corporation Sole: Cardinal Mundelein and Chicago Catholicism* [Notre Dame, 1983]). Mundelein's role in bringing together Hays, Lord, Quigley, Breen, and, crucially, Wall Street financier Harold Stuart to pressure Hollywood to meet Catholic demands for clean movies is skillfully narrated by Stephen Vaughn in "Financiers, Movie Producers, and the Church: Economic Origins of the Production Code," in *Current Research in Film: Audiences, Economics, and the Law* 4 (1988): 201–17, and "Morality and Entertainment: The Origins of the Motion Picture Production Code," *Journal of American History* 77 (June 1990): 39–65.

81. See the essays in Richard Butsch, ed., *For Fun and Profit: The Transformation of Leisure into Consumption* (Philadelphia, 1990), for discussion of some of the uses and abuses of hegemony theory in the study of popular culture.

Black Films, White Censors

Oscar Micheaux Confronts Censorship in New York, Virginia, and Chicago

CHARLENE REGESTER

From the 1910s to the 1950s, motion picture censor boards dictated what could and could not be shown on the American screen. Racially provocative films regularly raised the ire of those who sought to impose "acceptable standards" on motion pictures. However, their standards of acceptability were often a reflection of the ideological disposition of censor board members themselves and, more generally, of the white majority. Motion pictures that were consistent with the censors' views regarding race were judged acceptable; those found to be inconsistent with their views were judged unacceptable.

This essay will focus on the career of African American filmmaker Oscar Micheaux. But before addressing that career, it is useful to place it in the context of the history of race and censorship in the American cinema. Censorship of motion pictures surfaced at the center of the debate over racial representation as early as 1910, when African American prizefighter Jack Johnson defeated white fighter Jim Jeffries. Al Tony-Gilmore, author of *Bad Nigger,* contends that the fight was filmed with the simple intention of increasing box office receipts. However, when "the unexpected happened"[1] and Jeffries was defeated, a national campaign was launched to prohibit the exhibition of these pictures. "First, there was an apparent sentimental desire to spare the white race the humiliation of seeing its highly-esteemed champion knocked out [by a black opponent]. Secondly, there were strong apprehensions that race riots might recur with a showing of the films."[2] Leading among those organizations wanting to halt the exhibition of these fight pictures was the United Society of Christian Endeavor (an organization boasting a membership of some four million), whose secretary, William Shaw, telegraphed the following plea to governors throughout the United States: "Race riots and murder in many places following the announcement of Johnson's victory in prize fight. These results will be multiplied many-fold by moving picture exhibitors. Will you join other governors in recommending prohibition of these demoralizing shows?"[3]

Lawmakers in 1910 justified the suppression of the Johnson fight pictures on the grounds that they were "degrading and dangerous"[4] and would incite white audiences into attacking innocent African American victims. Film historian Thomas Cripps perhaps best articulates the core of this fear: "Johnson's presence was a kind of iconic celebration of the 'bad nigger' who flaunted white values as he battered a train of white opponents."[5] Historian James Nesteby has argued that, when "black has been equated with bad, inhuman or subhuman, and soulless, and white has been equated with good, mature, pure, and civilized,"[6] a film in which the hero is black and the villain white was so inconsistent with cultural expectations that it quickly spurred efforts at suppression. Whites feared the "savage-like brute" image of Jack Johnson, an image of the African American male that had been popularized in literature and was now making its way onto the motion picture screen. On the other hand, African Americans reveled in the retelling of the Johnson-Jeffries story. Although some blacks may have feared that the film would arouse white anger, many were willing to take the chance.

In the wake of Johnson's victory, the black press quoted the provocative remarks Johnson had made prior to the fight: "If I whip that white man, he never will forget it; if that white man whips me, I'll forget it in about fifteen minutes."[7] Among other things, Johnson's statement pointed up the absurdity of the whites' racial-protection claims. Reflecting on the victory, one black journalist concluded, "It was a good deal better for Johnson to win and a few Negroes be killed in body for it, than for Johnson to have lost and all Negroes to be killed in spirit by the preachments of inferiority from the combined white press."[8] Thus, the *Chicago Defender* insisted, the film reflected the pride that African Americans felt when Johnson "fairly knocked [the] ears off" for-

mer world champion Jeffries.[9] The black press and most black leaders consequently lobbied hard for the exhibition of these fight pictures.

Racially provocative themes on the screen would again prove to be a point
of public contention in 1915 upon the release of D. W. Griffith's Civil War
drama, *The Birth of a Nation.* According to historian Peter Noble, Griffith's
"extraordinarily vicious anti-Negro" film resulted in arousing racial hostilities
that propelled a nationwide crusade to suppress the exhibition of this picture.[10]
Within the African American community, protest erupted from churches, the
African American press, and the National Association for the Advancement of
Colored People (NAACP), as well as from whites who were disturbed by such
portrayals. The African American press launched a crusade to halt the film's
exhibition and provided extensive coverage of black protest activities. Editorials denounced *The Birth of a Nation,* attacking men such as D. W. Griffith and
Thomas Dixon (whose book served as the basis of the film). Papers such as the
Cleveland Gazette, the *Freeman,* W. E. B. Du Bois's the *Crisis,* the *New York Age,*
and the *Boston Guardian* labeled the film a direct attack on African Americans,
reporting on riots and near-riots wherever and whenever *The Birth of a Nation*
was shown—in Topeka, Kansas; Lafayette, Indiana; Philadelphia; New York;
and Boston.

In Chicago the story was slightly different. Although slow in denouncing
the exhibition of the film, according to the *Chicago Defender,* the local NAACP
did finally lead an attack against its showing. The mayor of Chicago, in response to pleas from his African American constituents, refused to issue a permit to show the film in Chicago. His actions were later supported by a bill
introduced in the state legislature that banned "any lithograph, drawing, picture, play, drama, or sketch, that tends to incite race riot, or race hatred or that
shall represent or purport to represent any hanging, lynching, or burning of
any human being incited by race hatred."[11] Booker T. Washington applauded
the crusade to halt the exhibition of *The Birth of a Nation* in Chicago, urging
others to "prevent the production of the photoplay, *The Birth of a Nation,* in
any community, North or South. . . . The people in Chicago are acting very
wisely in forestalling its appearance; and this is the policy which it would be
well for every community to pursue."[12]

Film historian Thomas Cripps contends that the collective effort to halt the
exhibition of *The Birth of a Nation* was, in large part, a reaction to the "art,
technology, the advertising, the racism . . . [which] all fell together into what
Negroes took to be a malicious conspiracy."[13] Despite that conspiracy, some
African Americans sought to use motion pictures to expose racial violence and
counter what they perceived as a distorted and ugly image of African Americans

portrayed by white filmmakers. Some African Americans sensed that films had the potential to document the truth and provide a record of important historical events, as the Johnson fight film had shown. Their evolving understanding of the value of film led African American filmmakers to use film to expose racial violence and counter the distorted and ugly images of blacks on the screen.

One of the most important African American filmmakers to undertake this challenge was Oscar Micheaux. An amazing combination of writer, filmmaker, and entrepreneur, Micheaux took on the assignment—some would call it the burden—of honestly portraying African Americans on the screen. He would portray blacks neither as degraded caricatures, as white filmmakers had done, nor as one-dimensional, angelic caricatures. Furthermore, although he intended to convey the truth of racial oppression from his perspective, he also sent several other messages to his fellow African Americans about the need to expose their problems, about ways to solve them, and, above all, about constructing a racial image of which they could be proud.

Given the racial climate in early twentieth-century America, Micheaux was bound to encounter opposition. His controversial themes stirred resistance from the white censors, who wished to impose their own standards on his works, and from members of the African American establishment, who would not tolerate exposure of corruption or error within their ranks. Added to those almost insurmountable impediments was the problem of finances. Where and how could an African American raise the capital needed to produce, distribute, and promote full-length commercial films? Despite these obstacles, Oscar Micheaux managed to produce nearly fifty films between 1918 and 1948 and emerged as one of the most significant filmmakers in cinema history.

Characterizations of Oscar Micheaux are many and colorful. He has been described by Donald Bogle as a "fiendishly aggressive young entrepreneur."[14] Bogle added that Micheaux was a "charismatic, indefatigable showman with a dash of flair he no doubt felt befitted a motion picture director. . . . [He] has been remembered by the actors who worked with him as a man dedicated to his own concept of black cinema."[15] Daniel Leab referred to Micheaux as "a superb promoter."[16] Henry Sampson described him as a "skilled entrepreneur, an astute businessman and a man who was sensitive to the needs of the black film audience."[17] Richard Gehr described him as "a combination of Samuel Goldwyn and Samuel Glick who embraced the self-determination philosophies of W. E. B. Du Bois, Booker T. Washington and Marcus Garvey . . . long before."[18] James Hoberman contended, "Micheaux is America's Black Pioneer in the way that Andre Breton was Surrealism's Black Pope. His movies throw our history and movies into an alien and startling disarray."[19] Thomas Cripps as-

Portrait of Oscar Micheaux. Reprinted from *The Conquest: The Story of a Negro Pioneer* (Lincoln, Nebraska: The Woodruff Press, 1913).

serted, "Micheaux's prairie roots, querulous personality, curious racial theories, and financial ties to his own publishing firm supported him against adversity" and distinguished him from other African American filmmakers of the time.[20] Richard Grupenhoff classified Micheaux as "the quintessential self-taught grass roots filmmaker."[21] In our forthcoming biographical sketch in the *Encyclopedia of African American Culture,* Jane Gaines and I have termed Micheaux "a maverick stylist who understood but was not bound by classical Hollywood cutting style, who used precious footage economically, who was adept in his use of the flashback device, and whose 'rough draft' films were vaguely avant-garde."[22] J. Ronald Green argued that Micheaux has been "repeatedly derided . . . for being 'white,' 'bourgeois,' 'fatuous,' and 'middle class' [yet despite such labels was] not capitulating to whiteness. Rather he [was] seeking some middle ground, a vantage point from which to explore the antagonistic strength of the class war—the oppression from above and the degradation from below."[23]

Collectively, these views portray an extraordinary African American film-maker who remains as intriguing today as he was in 1918, when he began his career. Born in Cairo, Illinois, of former slaves who apparently migrated to the Midwest seeking a better life, Micheaux developed a fascination for the section of the country in which he grew up. Sent to market by his father to peddle fruits and vegetables produced on the family farm, Micheaux learned promo-tional skills that served him well when he became a novelist, a book publisher, and later, a filmmaker.[24] In the first half of his life, Micheaux left the farm, be-came a Pullman porter, and then fulfilled his lifelong dream of becoming a landowner in South Dakota. Having acquired adequate financial resources, he next launched a writing career.

Being a strong supporter of Booker T. Washington, as he revealed in his first novel, *The Conquest* (1913), Micheaux applied Washington's philosophical views to his own life. Writing semiautobiographical novels, promoting his works among white farmers in the Midwest, and establishing his own book publishing company, Micheaux deliberately set out to prove in word and deed that "a colored man can be anything."[25] With the publication of his third novel, *The Homesteader* (1917), Micheaux was lured into filmmaking when the black-owned Lincoln Motion Picture Company declined to serialize his novel on the screen. Undeterred, Micheaux proceeded to produce his first motion picture. Thus began the venture Micheaux pursued for the second half of his life. Based on events in his past, *The Homesteader* was some three hours long and became the first eight-reel film to be produced by an African American film-maker. Filmmaking provided Micheaux with the medium in which to articu-late his own ideological views and expose issues he believed had too long been ignored by the African American community. At the same time, Micheaux's first film marked the beginning of the censorship difficulties that he would en-counter throughout his filmmaking career.

Micheaux's problems with the censors can be linked both to his provocative material and his provocative style. His films often exposed intraracial and in-terracial prejudice, color consciousness, hypocritical ministers, corrupt politi-cians, interracial relationships, incestuous relationships, and vices he felt were destructive of the moral fiber of the African American community. These be-haviors included drinking, gambling, prostitution, and crime. With equal vigor, he exposed white America's racism by attacking lynching, the Ku Klux Klan, and the denial of economic and educational opportunities to African Americans. Micheaux's films reveal the intricate web of his philosophical views, some of which seemed to echo the discourse of propriety prevalent among middle-class Americans. Jane Gaines attributes the complexity of

Micheaux's films to the fact that sometimes "he was seeing . . . Black culture through the eyes of white culture."[26] Some critics charge that Micheaux sustained a double standard and an ambivalence regarding the African American community. Others accuse him of elevating the African American community on one level, yet denigrating it on another.[27] Indeed, on some level, as a black filmmaker living in white America, Micheaux needed to accommodate to the predominant values. In the end, perhaps, films, like minstrel shows, "produced a popular form in which racial insult was twinned with racial envy, moments of domination with moments of liberation, counterfeit with currency . . . and all of it compromising a peculiarly American structure of racial feeling."[28] Like minstrel shows, Micheaux's films demonstrated this twinning tendency in their ambivalences about race.[29]

On the one hand, Micheaux was skillful at reversing stereotypes popularized by white Hollywood. For example, he had actors appear in whiteface; he cast whites as the villains; he portrayed blacks as professionals and heroes. On the other hand, Micheaux's films are not without black villains, and he used language as a device to enhance his sometimes negative characterizations, for example, choosing "standard English" for admirable characters but dialect for scoundrels. However much these devices may have confused or disturbed black viewers, Micheaux's major problems came from white reactions to his films. In treating provocative themes in his films, he must have realized he would have difficulty receiving the approval of censor boards. "If black filmmakers could make movies in isolation," notes Cripps, "they still could not release them until white eyes had approved them."[30] In addressing issues considered racially provocative by white viewers, Micheaux emerges as a prime example of black filmmakers' struggle with the power of censorship.

Despite occasional mention of Micheaux's troubles with censorship, rarely have his efforts to win censors' approval been thoroughly examined. It is therefore useful to explore Micheaux's attempts to obtain censor approval, examine his efforts to comply with the demands of the censor boards, and compare decisions rendered by film censor boards in different regions of the country. An underlying assumption of this examination is that Micheaux's plight will reflect upon that of other African American filmmakers who confronted white film boards, although the extent to which Micheaux's experience is typical of that encountered by other filmmakers (black or white) can be determined only by further research.

Examining Micheaux's plight with the film censor boards of his time will expose the power that these (predominantly all-white) censor boards wielded over filmmakers (black and white), the obstacles that African American filmmakers (in particular) faced in having to comply with the boards' decisions, and the skill Micheaux employed to circumvent decisions made by these censor boards. Such skill allowed Micheaux to survive when most black filmmakers did not.

Micheaux was likely aware of the racially provocative elements in his motion pictures and, since he attempted to appeal to white audiences as well as black, aware of the impact his films might have had on white audiences as well as black ones. Cripps contends that "whites seemed to have developed a sensitivity to racial slurs that escaped the cavalier Micheaux."[31] On the other hand, it may be that Micheaux was not as cavalier as he pretended. He may rather have used the motion picture medium as a vehicle by which to attack the racial divisions that existed in American society and limited the social, political, and economic progress desired by African Americans.

Mark Reid suggests, "Micheaux's reading of the African American moviegoer anticipated by fifty years the commercial black-oriented films of the early 1970s. Moreover, the 'colored man with bricks' who defeats the Klan is a superhero, and ancestor of such heroes of the 1970s as Sweetback, who appears in Melvin Van Peeble's *Sweet Sweetback's Badasssss Song* (1971)."[32] Micheaux as a filmmaker faced the same dilemma that contemporary black filmmakers must contend with, that is, how to reveal negative aspects of African American life or culture without glorifying, glamorizing, or reinforcing them. Because their films are viewed by both African American and white audiences, black filmmakers must tread a fine line if they are to receive wide appeal.[33]

It can be argued that Micheaux's consistently sensationalist approach (using provocative themes, including sex and violence) was strategically deployed to appeal to audiences. Scantily clothed dancers, corrupt ministers with Dr. Jekyll–Mr. Hyde personae, gamblers, numbers runners, prostitutes, drug users, businessmen, dishonest physicians—Micheaux's depiction of all these types made his films targets for censor boards, but also sources of embarrassment for some of his African American viewers.[34] Nevertheless, the attendance at Micheaux's motion pictures demonstrated the existence of a viable African American cinema audience in the 1920s, 1930s, and 1940s that craved portrayals of African American life.

Micheaux's pictures also promoted self-sufficiency and self-elevation while failing to acknowledge the discriminatory practices that were in place and that limited African Americans' ability to pursue the lofty ideals they advocated. Gaines contends that the operation of "'double-consciousness' [a concept introduced by W. E. B. Du Bois] seems a fairly obvious way to explain Micheaux's offenses."[35] Micheaux was a filmmaker who, because he was operating in two worlds, one black and one white, was forced to negotiate a tenuous place between them. Being the astute filmmaker that he was, Micheaux set out to satiate the appetites of his audience, though he did so not without encountering resistance. In particular, he faced persistent resistance from white film censors.

In the early 1900s the filmed depictions of divorce, crime, drunkenness, sex, and brutality led many parents, educators, and religious and political leaders to call upon government to regulate motion pictures. Their concerted efforts resulted in the formation of municipal censorship laws, such as that first established in New York City in 1906 and 1913, and in Chicago in 1907, and state legislation regulating the censorship of motion pictures in Pennsylvania in 1911, Kansas and Ohio in 1913, and Maryland in 1916.[36] In 1921 New York established a state motion picture commission composed of three members appointed by the governor. Any films that the censors deemed obscene, indecent, immoral, inhuman, sacrilegious, or "of such a character that its exhibition would tend to corrupt morals or incite to crime" was denied a license for exhibition.[37] The New York commission's standards were similar to those adopted by other state and municipal censorship boards. Hollywood's Motion Picture Production Code, first established in 1930, mirrored the standards established by the New York motion picture commission. For example, the code prohibited scenes that glorified criminals; portrayed illicit love as attractive and beautiful; used firearms for nonessential activity; displayed drinking, childbirth, surgery, prostitution, or "white slavery"; or promoted sex in an "unhealthy" manner or a manner which stimulated the "baser element."[38] These were the standards imposed on all filmmakers, white and black alike.

Filmmaking during the censorship era, therefore, demanded a skill over and beyond that of dramatic artistry: filmmakers also had to devise ways to make their films acceptable to the censor. Although this was a problem for all filmmakers, it would prove especially difficult for African Americans in the industry. Very little has been written about such filmmakers, and scholars have made only occasional reference to the difficulties African Americans encountered with largely all-white censor boards. This study of the censoring of Micheaux's motion pictures, which were exhibited throughout the United States, is intended to redress that omission. However, since censorship records remain unavailable or inaccessible for many jurisdictions, the present examination will be limited to three whose records are available (the city of Chicago and the states of New York and Virginia) and to those films likely to have been reviewed by more than one film censor board.

Micheaux was well aware of the strictures these boards were likely to place on his motion pictures. But responding to these rules meant compromising with the (white) establishment, and this was not easy for a man as defiant as Micheaux. In addition, Micheaux wanted to produce motion pictures that sold. Although he realized that conveying racial unrest in his pictures created controversy, he also knew that such depictions appealed to his audiences. For example, *The Brute* (1920) focused on the themes of gambling and seduction. It involved a young woman who is pursued by the manager of a gambling operation, and her aunt, who attempts to rescue the niece while being accused of extorting money from the manager. The motion picture included a boxing match between a black prizefighter and a less well known opponent. In featuring former prizefighter Sam Langford on the screen with a white opponent, the story drew black audiences into the theater. Since the film does not survive, much of what can be inferred about it is purely speculation, but clearly, when Micheaux created this combat scene between a black and a white fighter, he was attempting to play upon the excitement and racial animosity that had been created by the Johnson-Jeffries fight pictures of 1910. Historian Bernard L. Peterson, Jr., contends that *The Brute* "also included . . . several scenes of racial violence, which caused the film to have difficulty obtaining censor approval in Chicago where it was produced."[39] However, since film reviews do not specifically refer to violent scenes other than the prizefight, it is certainly tenable that this scene touched a raw nerve and sparked the greatest racial resentment.

The report of censorship difficulties this film encountered are elaborated by Thomas Cripps: "In Chicago [*The Brute*'s] opening was ruined by a nasty fight with the local censor, who wanted no racial violence on the screen only months after the city had faced the worst race riot in American history."[40] When *The Brute* was submitted for review on August 9, 1920, the Chicago motion picture censors ordered as many as thirty-eight cuts, most of which had to do with questions of "morality" or crime. For example:

> *Reel II:* All scenes where money is seen on table during gambling.
> *Reel III:* Subtitle ending 'show them a dollar, and virtue is' . . . Cut Out—
> Scenes of shimmying (vulgar dancing)
> *Reel V:* 'That's easy—I'm going to kill a rat.'
> Subtitle ending, 'but remember, next time, I'll use this.'
> Close-up of gun . . .
> Scenes of Margaret as she sits on arm of chair (in very low cut gown) and as she stands near table with bottle in hand.
> *Reel VII:* 'And now . . . yes—kill all three'
> Scene where Margaret places gun in his [back] as he leaves office.

Scenes of dragging wife by hair

'I told him next time I'll use this.'[41]

These scenes were declared immoral, insulting, indecent, and tending to incite to crime. More important, the film censors recommended that the scene showing the "close view of [the] knock out"[42] be entirely deleted from the film. To what extent the film played upon the fears of racial violence can only be surmised: since the film does not survive, the manner in which Micheaux presented his ideas and developed his plot remains unknown. All that can be known, as with many of Micheaux's films, is what can be gleaned or extracted from censorship records and film reviews. And based on these records, it can be concluded that the Chicago film censors apparently found the scene in which the black prizefighter knocked out his white opponent so objectionable, and so reminiscent of the controversy created by the Johnson-Jeffries fight pictures, that they deemed it necessary to exclude it from Micheaux's work.

Although *The Brute* was exhibited in New York and perhaps in Virginia, no records reveal how film censors reacted to it in these states. We can speculate that they shared the Chicago censors' views, particularly concerning the racially provocative scenes. Reaction to Micheaux's motion picture, however, is not confined to reports provided by censor boards. It can also be found in the black press, where the film received a mixed reaction. Lester A. Walton, film critic for the *New York Age,* had a typically ambivalent response:

> As I looked at the picture I was reminded of the attitude of the daily press, which magnifies our vices and minimizes our virtues. . . . As at no time in the history of motion pictures have white producers sought to represent the Negro in a complimentary light, it is therefore the duty of our race producer to gladden our hearts and inspire us by presenting characters typifying the better element of Negroes. . . . At times there are lapses between important intervals . . . but these errors of omission are forgotten when Langford knocks out Cutler.[43]

It is interesting to note that while the white censors were concerned with the "moral" implications of the film and its treatment of the issue of race, the African American press was more concerned with the degree to which African Americans were portrayed on the motion pictures screen in an uncomplimentary manner.

The objections to *The Brute* raised by the Chicago motion picture censors did not deter Micheaux in his attempt to portray interracial strife. In his 1920 film, *Symbol of the Unconquered* (alternately titled *The Wilderness Trail*),

Micheaux continued to provoke controversy, exposing lynching and the Ku Klux Klan. Perhaps he considered this film a rebuttal to *The Birth of a Nation:* in contrast to Griffith's glamorization of the Klan, Micheaux depicted its techniques as vicious intimidation.

Symbol of the Unconquered focuses on a land speculator who, in attempting to retain a piece of valuable oil land, becomes romantically involved with a woman who is passing as white. The land speculator meets resistance from white neighbors, the Ku Klux Klan (one member of which is an African American who may have been strategically included to obtain censor approval), and an Indian villain. The mulatto and land speculator succeed in their effort to retain this valuable property and thus embody Micheaux's film title.

Symbol of the Unconquered was reviewed by the Chicago board of censors in November 1920 and approved for exhibition, but not without changes. It is noteworthy that censor records indicate that the film had been initially reviewed by only one film censor, A. J. Bowling, the sole black member of the commission. Bowling had probably been hired exclusively to review films that appealed to black audiences, and his decision regarding these works was generally accepted by the entire censor board.[44] Bowling had served on the censor board in 1915 but had apparently been discharged from the commission in April of that year for an unknown impropriety. The *Chicago Defender* reported that having corrected his "troubles," he was reinstated as the commission's sole African American member. In defining Bowling's role on the board, the *Defender* reported, "No picture which has a Negro theme can be passed by the censor board until it has been seen by Rev. Bowling."[45] A minister of the African Methodist Episcopal Church who had attended Harvard University, Bowling was clearly a product of the black bourgeoisie who played a double role. On one hand, he served as a representative of the entire African American community. On the other, he was the vehicle by which the white power structure attempted to bridge the gap between the two communities.

The commission's scanty records suggest that Bowling indeed tried to work in the best interest of his constituents by opposing *The Birth of a Nation.* In the case of *Symbol of the Unconquered,* the records suggest that the bourgeois Bowling may have been offended by Micheaux's sensationalist themes. If the Chicago censor board really did follow Bowling's recommendations concerning African American films, then it was Bowling who specified the following substantial changes in *Symbol of the Unconquered:*

> *Reel II:* Sub-title—ending: 'That they had often lynched his kind for a smaller offense . . . talking to a white girl on the street.'

Cut all scenes of colored man holding white girl's hand in [love scenes]. . . .
Reel IV: All scenes of Englishman looking at Colored girl after subtitle
'Strongly desirous'
'Why should you worry, he is nothing but a Negro'
Change Subtitle—'Old Darkeys to Old Negro's [*sic*]'
Reel V: 'She is nothing but a Negress'
Reel VI: 'He is one of those arrogant educated Negroes' . . . Cut close view of
2nd warning
'The Ride of Midnight' etc.
'The Symbol of the Unconquered Race'[46]

Micheaux's film had managed to disturb both blacks and whites. A film that featured a black character passing as white,[47] an interracial relationship, unfavorable depictions of the Ku Klux Klan, and scenes that made retaliation against the Klan seem admirable would certainly offend white audiences. From the earliest local censorship laws to Hollywood's Production Code, miscegenation was considered objectionable without question. Although specific reaction to miscegenation in *Symbol of the Unconquered* by New York and Virginia censors remains undocumented, Micheaux's subtle reference in this film to an interracial relationship between a black woman and white Englishmen would probably have been disturbing to film censors regardless of whether the censor or the filmmaker was white or black.[48]

Black audiences were likely to be offended by elements of the film's dialogue such as, "She is nothing but a Negress," "Old Darkey," and "educated arrogant Negroes." Micheaux probably did not intend to devalue African Americans, but rather to demonstrate how they are devalued by others. Yet, when taken out of context, such words could provoke anger in black viewers, as they obviously did in A. J. Bowling. It is also possible that Micheaux was deliberately insulting African Americans, hoping to awaken their sensibilities and heighten their race consciousness. Such a strategy, however, misfired and invited black resentment, thereby exacerbating his problems with the largely white censor boards.[49]

Many of Micheaux's motion pictures could be characterized as message films. *The Dungeon* (1922), a murder mystery, contains a subplot that portrays African American politicians as hypocrites. It focuses on Gyp Lassiter's attempt to obtain political office by agreeing to abstain from voting on a bill that would make residential segregation permanent.[50] By also casting the hypocritical politician as a murderer, Micheaux heightens his critique of black leadership.

Powerful in its message, *The Dungeon* disturbed film censors. Denied a license on May 20, 1922, by the New York Motion Picture Commission, the censors summarized the film as follows:

The story treats of Gyp Lassiter, a villainous wretch, who employs a drug fiend to hypnotize a woman who he wants to get possession of. The drug fiend brings the woman to Gyp who marries her while she is in a state of hypnotic condition. Gyp then takes her to a house which has been the scene of a murder of eight of his previous wives. By nature a killer, he then proceeds to asphyxiate her in a dungeon. From the clutches of death, she is rescued by a former lover who then kills Gyp. The film is of such a character that, in the opinion of the Commission, it is inhuman, immoral, and would tend to corrupt morals and incite to crime.[51]

It is noteworthy that the censors emphasized the film's sensationalism and its offenses to conventional morality, especially its treatment of women. In portraying a woman who was exploited by a man, enticed by a drug fiend, and later asphyxiated, the film would almost certainly have offended one Mrs. Burton, the only woman on the New York censorship commission and thus the representative of women's clubs and church groups, which supported censorship with particular zeal.[52]

Despite *The Dungeon*'s rejection in New York, Micheaux submitted the film for exhibition in Chicago, an act that demonstrated his insistence on having the film shown to black audiences. In March 1923 the Chicago motion picture censors reviewed the film and approved it for exhibition. However, they ordered Micheaux to eliminate such scenes as:

Reel I: All three scenes of girls shimmying. Scene of man giving girl check and sub-title 'Paid her off.'
Reel VI: 'The most notorious woman in town and right now she is lying in some other man's arms.' One scene of girl shimmying and scene following girl 'swaying body in dance.'
Reel VII: Man choking woman. Three . . . scenes of woman on floor of dungeon where blood is coming from her mouth. Three scenes of gas pouring from pipe in dungeon.[53]

Many of the objections raised by the Chicago censors were similar to those offered by the New York Motion Picture Commission. Both film censor boards were concerned with the physical assault on a woman by a man, the portrayal of a woman as sexually promiscuous, the graphic display of an attempted murder, and the method of murder (exposure to poisonous gas). If Micheaux wanted his picture approved, he had to accede to these deletions, even though they would reduce the impact of his intended message: politicians should be judged both for their political integrity and for their moral character. It was an ambitious attempt, but unfortunately, the deletions that film censors ordered resulted not only in diluting his message but also in reducing the sensational-ism that might have lured audiences into the theater.

Although *The Dungeon* was not as racially provocative as some other Micheaux films, it did portray whites who sought to bribe an African Ameri-can into supporting residential segregation, an act that most African American viewers would have seen as a betrayal of their right to be fully integrated into American life. In this case, since Micheaux was clever enough to introduce such issues in subtle ways, he managed to avoid the censors' wrath. However, in many other instances, the power and impact of his message were minimized by film censors.

In Micheaux's own experiences as a novelist and filmmaker, he had encoun-tered resistance from whites, in part because of his treatment of racial issues, in part because he attempted to elevate himself socially, politically, and econom-ically. When Micheaux produced uncomplimentary portrayals of African Americans (for example, the ministers in *The Homesteader* and *Body and Soul*), he again provoked outrage—in these cases, from members of his own commu-nity who resented such depictions. It seems logical that Micheaux would an-ticipate criticism from both blacks and whites again in response to his 1924 film *Birthright*, which portrayed an African American Harvard graduate who met with both interracial and intraracial prejudice.

Birthright was approved for exhibition by the New York Motion Picture Commission in January 1924, but only with the following eliminations:

Reel I: Eliminate underlined word from subtitle: 'How the *hell* can he arrest him when he just hit down.'
Reel III: Eliminate subtitle: 'Legal—hell—anything a white man wants to pull over on a nigger is legal.'
Reel IV & V: Eliminate all but one scene in each reel of shooting craps. . . . The reason for above eliminations are that they are 'sacrilegious' and would 'tend to incite to crime.'[54]

Micheaux, in compliance with the film censors' recommendations, changed the word *Hell* to read H———L. Such a tactic allowed him to keep the word in the film, as well as his remark about the exploitation of blacks by whites. Micheaux had dared to suggest on the screen what many African Americans clearly thought but were afraid to express publicly. He further cut the line "You ain't no black Jesus" and agreed to portray the crap game only once, con-ceding that his attempt to expose immorality might have the effect of rein-forcing stereotypes of the African American on the motion picture screen.[55]

Birthright faced its strongest opposition when it was reviewed by the

Virginia film censors. In February 1924, according to reports provided by the Virginia State Archives, Micheaux was exhibiting his motion picture in theaters in Virginia without a license.[56] Micheaux probably knew that his film would encounter censorship difficulty in this state and tried to show it in theaters without receiving the board's approval. When the board became aware that the film was being exhibited without a license, it issued letters to the mayors of Portsmouth, Norfolk, Lynchburg, Roanoke, Newport News, and other cities warning them of the impending danger that such exhibition posed for theater operators or owners and for the general public:

> The exhibition of *Birthright* is an audacious and inexcusable violation of the Censorship Act. This board has neither examined nor licensed the film in question, and if it bears the Virginia seal, fraud of the most questionable sort has been committed. . . . We have reason to believe that it bears upon the race question and embodies scenes and sub-titles which this board would find most objectionable.[57]

The film censors then forwarded a letter to Micheaux warning him of this violation and stated,

> We are more than surprised that your concern, which has been treated with all courtesy by this Board, should be a party to what appears to be a deliberate violation of the censorship act. I believe, too, that before you are done with this business, you will have occasion to regret the seemingly questionable methods to which your concern appears to have resorted.[58]

Micheaux argued that he had not intentionally exhibited the film, but because theaters had already been booked and he had made arrangements to advertise the film, rather than lose money needed for the production, distribution, and promotion of the films, he decided to show it in a few theaters and seek censor approval at a later time. In appealing to the commission, he not only reminded members of his previous good relations with them but also explained that his extensive recent travel had been complicated by his having to ride "in cinder ridden Jim Crow cars all night."[59] Micheaux was fined twenty-five dollars for violating the state censorship act. Having accepted Micheaux's apology and his payment of the fine, the chairman of the commission told the auditor of public accounts,

> [Micheaux] admitted the offense charged but told a somewhat pathetic story of financial difficulties, mismanagement on the part of his subordinates, and par-

tial ignorance of the law. Furthermore, he expressed a willingness to pay the penalty for his offense provided the Board would recommend a fine that would not absolutely cripple his concern.[60]

Micheaux was clearly playing upon the stereotypical impressions whites held of African Americans by suggesting that his employees were either inadequate, incompetent, or ignorant of their duties and responsibilities, an explanation that he hoped would clear him of wrongdoing associated with exhibiting his picture without censor approval. Nevertheless, although Micheaux was skilled at manipulating those people involved with every aspect of the film business, especially the power block that the film censors and the theater owners represented, it is not certain that *Birthright* was ever rescreened and approved for exhibition by the Virginia film censors.

Micheaux submitted *Birthright* for review to the Chicago censors three years later, in 1927. The film was approved for exhibition only after fourteen cuts were required, including:

> *Reel II:* 'Every time a Pecker wood' etc.
> 'Legal—hell, everything a white man wants to put over on a spade,' etc.
> *Reel IV:* 'Peter, it's hard to be nice in Niggertown'
> *Reel VII:* Sub[title]—'Naked.' Second scene of the Negro in bushes where gun shows 'and coming out of bushes and holding up other man.'
> All but one scene of man threatening man as they walk down the street.
> She didn't shoot craps—she don't bootleg—nor—[61]

The Chicago motion picture censors apparently found that these scenes and dialogue were immoral, would tend to incite to crime, and were racially offensive. Two white women on the commission, Cora Doolittle and Edith E. Kerr, were offended by the uncomplimentary portrayal of women in the film.[62] And since the film focused on African American women, a similar response might have been anticipated from the especially well-organized black women's clubs of Chicago.

Although *Birthright* is another film that does not survive in its early version, it seems clear that, because it featured racially provocative material on the screen, it was certain to raise the ire of most film censors, who feared aggravating racial hostilities between blacks and whites. In view of the way film censors had historically reacted to racial issues on the motion picture screen, Micheaux no doubt anticipated that his use of epithets in referring to both whites and blacks would be deleted. Therefore, the historian must ask whether Micheaux aimed to educate, entertain, or provoke his viewers, or simply to use sensationalism to promote his motion pictures. His strategy seems to have included all four modes at one time or another, and sometimes simultaneously. Unfortunately, virtually any combination invited negative reactions from film censors and audiences.

Having exposed the malicious tactics employed by the Ku Klux Klan in *Symbol of the Unconquered,* Micheaux would revisit this theme in his motion picture *A Son of Satan,* produced in 1924. The New York commission rejected *A Son of Satan* in September 1924, stating,

> This picture is filled with scenes of drinking, carousing and shows masked men becoming intoxicated. It shows the playing of crap for money, a man killing his wife by choking her, the killing of the leader of the hooded organization and the killing of a cat by throwing a stone at it. There are many scenes of crime. The film is of such character that in the opinion of the Commission, it is "inhuman" and would "tend to incite to crime."[63]

There is reason to question whether the principal cause for rejecting the film was its depictions of carousing or its uncomplimentary portrayal of the Ku Klux Klan. What seemed most disturbing to the board was the scene in which the leader of the "hooded organization" is killed. This scene might indeed have been racially provocative, but Micheaux inserted it even knowing it would cause him problems. In appealing the commission's decision, Micheaux argued that he had already eliminated certain scenes that had allowed it to obtain censor approval in Pennsylvania and other states. He informed the censors that all the characters were played by black actors and his film would be shown in three theaters catering only to black audiences in New York,[64] perhaps in an attempt to minimize the negative reactions of the white censors. However, Micheaux's ploy did not work entirely, and he was still required to edit his film. Following a reexamination by the New York Motion Picture Commission of a revised version of the film, Micheaux was awarded a license in October 1924.[65]

In July 1924 Micheaux submitted *A Son of Satan* to be reviewed by the Virginia censors, whose rejection read (in part):

> The central figure in the plot is a mulatto whose villainies justify the significant title of the photoplay. By implication, at least, the audience is led to believe that the criminal tendencies of the man are inherited from his white forefathers.
>
> *A Son of Satan,* at best, is unwholesome as it touches unpleasantly on miscegenation.
>
> In some of the scenes—notably that showing the "fashionable" dance where

a white orchestra furnishes music for blacks—there is an intermingling of the two races which would prove offensive to Southern ideas.

The most serious feature of the picture, however, is the series of race riots incited by *A Son of Satan,* who uses a white man as his tool. . . .

A Son of Satan is rejected on the ground that it might tend to corrupt morals or incite to crime.[66]

Virginia film censors reacted strongly to the implication that the criminal tendencies of the mulattoes could be attributed to the "white blood" that flowed in their veins. In this implication, Micheaux directly confronted white filmmakers' portrayals of mulattoes in such films as *The Birth of a Nation* and, in later years, *Imitation of Life* (1934). Both films gave the impression that mulattoes would be socially acceptable and less prone to illicit behavior were it not for their "black blood." Virginia motion picture censors were also disturbed by the perception that Micheaux's depiction of race riots might provoke them in actuality. The Virginia censors considered such depictions too dangerous and disruptive to be shown on the screen.

To ensure that the film would not be exhibited in Virginia, and remembering that Micheaux had previously exhibited *Birthright* without receiving censor approval, the censors notified theaters throughout the state that *A Son of Satan* was rejected "in toto."[67] However, Micheaux proceeded to advertise his picture at the Attucks Theatre in Norfolk, which resulted in the manager being notified by the censorship board that he was in violation of the censorship law.[68]

In October 1924 Micheaux submitted a revised version of *A Son of Satan* to the Virginia censors, indicating that he had eliminated scenes of the race riot. Micheaux added that New York and Pennsylvania had approved the film following these deletions.[69] The Virginia film censors then awarded *A Son of Satan* a license, stating, "It was with some hesitation that we decided to reconsider this picture, since your corporation for many months past has shown but little disposition to observe our law. Our final conclusion, however, was that you erred more through ignorance than through willfulness, and so we decided to be lenient."[70] Arguably, Micheaux "manipulated" the censors by playing on their sense of generosity and in allowing them to think his errors in judgment were due to lack of knowledge of the law.[71]

Micheaux's sensationalism did not prevent but perhaps enhanced his ability to address some of the most volatile questions in the United States at the time. Among these questions was that of the dynamics of racial identity. Interracial sexual relationships, especially those involving one partner passing for white, fascinated Micheaux as social, filmic, and personal issues. In his semiautobiographical works, *The Conquest* and *The Homesteader,* he contends that, as a black farmer living in the West, he was involved in an interracial relationship, one that he refused to consummate due to his allegiance to his own racial heritage. Micheaux's films suggest that the rationale for passing is simply that blacks seek access to the same opportunities afforded whites. Furthermore, they expose the false logic at the core of racism: if whites can so easily be deceived by "passing" blacks, the discrimination based on skin color loses all meaning.

Micheaux addressed the issue of passing in *The House behind the Cedars* (1923), based on Charles W. Chesnutt's novel. In this film Rowena, a mulatto, leaves home to live with her brother, an attorney. They both pass as white. Rowena becomes romantically involved with a white southern aristocrat (Tryon). Forced to return home when her mother becomes ill, she is reunited with a former suitor (Wain), who is unaware that she had passed as white. The white southerner remains steadfast in his pursuit of her even after her true identity is revealed. In 1925 the Virginia censors rejected *The House behind the Cedars.* In an effort to ensure that Micheaux had been treated fairly, they gave the film a second review with additional examiners, including a group of "public-spirited women," the state labor commissioner, a representative of the Department of Public Welfare, the head of the State Bureau of Vital Statistics, and Maj. Earnest Sevier Cox, an ethnologist and author of *White America.* These reviewers agreed that the film should be licensed after considerable deletions had been made. In their summary the Virginia censors made clear that the film's treatment of miscegenation made it unacceptable for public exhibition in its original form:

> The *House Behind the Cedars* . . . touches even more dangerous ground—the intermarriage of the two races. Its plot is based on a love affair between a white man (described in the film as the scion of an aristocratic North Carolina family) and a colored woman who masquerades as a white. Even after the woman has severed her relations with the man he is pictured as still seeking her society, nor does his quest end until she has become the wife of a dark-skinned suitor. . . .
>
> In the opinion of the Va. Board of Censors, this film, whatever its good points, should not be displayed in this state—especially in negro houses for which it is intended—since many of its scenes, as well as sub-titles, are liable to cause friction between the races and might therefore incite to crime. Furthermore the picture . . . indirectly contravenes the spirit of the recently enacted anti-miscegenation law which has put Virginia in the forefront as a pioneer in legislation aimed to preserve the integrity of the white race.[72]

Virginia censorship records indicate that Micheaux made a reconstructed version of the film, which included the following eliminations:

Reel I: Eliminate words 'And my wife was—' from sub-title in which Warwick tells about his marriage and child. The implication is that he marries a white woman.

Reel II: Eliminate sub-title reading in substance as follows 'You are going away and will pass as white and marry a fine white man.'

Reel IV: Eliminate sub-title containing Doctor's reference to trifling negroes and to the 'pretty women along the borderline' of the race.

Reel VII: Eliminate scene in which Tryon sees Wain attempting to embrace Rowena; also all scenes of pursuit. Eliminate Tryon's letter to Rowena; also Tryon at P.O. Box awaiting answer; also Rowena's reply; also scene in which Tryon reads communication from the girl.[73]

Micheaux complied with the requests of Virginia film censors, but nonetheless dared to express his displeasure regarding their objections and to turn the tables by attacking *The Birth of a Nation:*

I do not agree with you relative to the supposed white man following Rowena after she had returned to her dark skinned lover—that is, I do not consider this worthy of eliminating and question whether you would have ever taken it seriously had your feelings not been aroused over what you saw in the second reel.

I must also add that you are unduly alarmed as to how my race is likely to take even the discussion in the second reel. There has been but one picture that incited the colored people to riot, and that still does, that picture is *The Birth of a Nation.*[74]

Micheaux later attempted to appease the Virginia censors by calling them the most liberal censors that he had encountered—a backhanded compliment, if read carefully. Despite the filmmaker's attempts to smooth relations, the board still required him to conform to their standards, even in regard to racial issues he felt better qualified to judge than they. By so conforming, he was able to show a censored version of his film.

In Chicago Micheaux was required to eliminate the following from *The House behind the Cedars:*

Reel I: Cut subtitle ending 'poor old negguh'

Reel II: Cut subtitle . . . 'Walker's son not only of questionable birth etc.'

Cut subtitle 'You are black and you are not free' etc.

Reel V: Cut subtitle 'marry a yankee and she's too white for it.'

Reel VII: Cut subtitle ending '. . . with virus of Etteopina.'[75]

The Chicago motion picture censors were concerned with the film's implication that one character was of "questionable birth." Certainly, the suggestion of illicit sex leading to illegitimate birth clearly violated the codes of film censorship. In addition, Micheaux's graphic reference to a sexually transmitted illness was bound to cross the line of moral rectitude as defined by film censors. However, most disturbing to Chicago film censors was the portrayal of northerners, which had not been a problem for the Virginia motion picture censors. The Chicago censors were disturbed by Micheaux's racial epithets and his subtle implication that although blacks were "free," this freedom remained nominal. They also seemed upset by the film's implication that northerners particularly rejected light-complexioned African Americans.

Micheaux used his motion pictures as a vehicle not only to attack injustice but also to criticize those aspects of the African American community that he viewed as dangerous and hypocritical. *Body and Soul* (1925) focuses on a minister who deceives his following and ultimately deceives himself. While he professes to be a man of the gospel, at the same time he gambles, drinks hard liquor, and commits assault, rape, and murder. Probably anticipating the criticism he was likely to receive from the African American community, Micheaux revealed at the film's end that this story was merely a dream. Nevertheless, in casting Paul Robeson as both the villain and hero, Micheaux encouraged audiences to make comparisons between the two and thereby made it difficult for them to distinguish easily between good and evil. The film's message was similar to that of *The Dungeon,* in which Micheaux suggested that audiences should be skeptical of leaders who appear to be the pillars of the African American community, yet who may actually be deceptive, immoral, and hypocritical.

Although Micheaux completed *Body and Soul* in 1924, he did not submit it for review to the New York censorship board until 1925. The commission denied him permission to exhibit the film, explaining its action in a letter to Micheaux:

> *Body and Soul* is the story of a man, minister of the gospel, whose habits and manner of life are anything but the life of a good man. He associates with the proprietor of a notorious gambling house, extorts money from him, betrays a girl of his parish, forces her to steal from the bible her mother's savings, forces the girl to leave home, and finally kills the girl's brother when he comes to the sister's protection. . . . The film is of such a character that in the opinion of the Commission it is sacrilegious, immoral, and would tend to incite to crime.[76]

Micheaux's appeal argued that, because a photograph and some titles were missing from the print submitted for review, the censors had misunderstood the film. He added that he had not intended to portray the main character in a manner that would be insulting to the clergy. He hoped to make it clear that his protagonist was a master of deception with many aliases and was not in fact an ordained minister.[77]

In response to Micheaux's appeal, the New York Motion Picture Commission rescreened *Body and Soul* but again denied the film a license.[78] Refusing to give up, Micheaux edited the film once more and resubmitted it to the New York censors. He contended that in reediting the film, he had altered the theme by transferring the villainy associated with the minister to another character and presented the minister in a light that in no way would reflect negatively upon the clergy. Adding to these changes, he inserted new title cards in the film that were designed to lessen the impact on audiences of the film's negative portrayal of the African American minister.[79]

Micheaux's strategic editing apparently proved successful. Since, in silent film, the meaning of a scene can be altered through the insertion of new title cards, Micheaux was able to respond to most of the complaints of the censors without shooting new scenes. The combination of cuts and new title cards also mollified members of the African American community, who feared that his portrayal of the minister would be seen as a direct attack upon one of the most respectable elements in the community. The commission reviewed the revised print and approved the film for exhibition.[80] However, it also stipulated that all scenes of drinking and gambling were to be eliminated.

The extent to which the film was censored by Virginia film censors remains unknown. But when *Body and Soul* was reviewed by the Chicago film censors, it was rejected "because it is criminal and exposes to contempt and obloquy a minister of the Protestant Church."[81] Apparently resubmitted in a revised version, the film was then approved for exhibition contingent upon some twenty-eight cuts being made. Scenes that offended film censors included those containing epithets such as "darkies," lines spoken by an African American minister who says "damned nuisance," and a scene as well as dialogue ("shut yer yellow mouth") involving a chase that occurs prior to the minister's rape of his victim.[82] The Chicago censors viewed Micheaux's portrayal of the African American minister as offensive, especially those scenes involving the minister's sexual exploitation of a young woman. The commission labeled such scenes immoral and likely to incite to crime.

In reflecting on Micheaux's censorship experience, it is important to remember that all U.S. filmmakers of the early 1900s were subject to the whims of censor boards. But African American filmmakers had to overcome special additional hurdles—those of racism and cultural difference. Even with the best of intentions (a characteristic in short supply on the boards), censors could not fully understand or sympathize with black filmmakers' messages; neither could they overcome their fears of how such films might be received by African American audiences. Black filmmakers found themselves at a distinct disadvantage in dealing with censors, some of whom were racially biased, most of whom were racially insensitive. Micheaux had to contend not only with largely white film censor boards but also with the opinions of middle-class African Americans, especially representatives of churches and prominent organizations, who were offended by what they saw as slurs upon their hard-won image of "respectability." Perhaps the conservative opinions of middle-class African Americans were not much different from those held by whites. Micheaux, himself, could easily identify with and share in the opinions of the black middle class because in some respects he held many of these same class-oriented views.

Where Micheaux differed ideologically from most middle-class African Americans was on whether or not his films should depict only those actions that were a "credit" to the "Race" to the exclusion of those that were an "embarrassment." Micheaux summed up his career as follows:

> I have always tried to make my photoplays present the truth, to lay before the Race a cross-section of its own life, to view the colored heart from close range. My results might have been narrow at times, due perhaps to certain limited situations which I endeavored to portray, but in those limited situations the Truth was the predominant characteristic. It is only by presenting those portions of the Race portrayed in my pictures in the light and background of their true state that we can raise our people to greater heights. I am too much imbued with the spirit of Booker T. Washington to ingraft false virtues upon ourselves, to make ourselves that which we are not. Nothing could be a greater blow to our own progress. The recognition of our true situation will react in itself as a stimulus for self-advancement.[83]

Micheaux's relationship with censorship was difficult at best, crippling at worst. Because he saw himself as a man with a message for African Americans, he sometimes infused his films with themes that would elevate the African American community. His stories proposed that African Americans should become landowners, adhere to higher moral codes of conduct, not be intimidated by the Klan, and not be deterred by interracial or intraracial prejudice. He urged African Americans to pursue success even when at times it required more courage and effort than seemed justified by meager rewards. But for Micheaux, the production of an authentically uplifting message required him to address themes from which others shied away. His films warned African American audiences that they should be aware of moral corruption within their own community, in their politicians and religious leaders. Thus Micheaux courted opposition both among both those who regulated his texts and those who consumed them.

At the same time, in their intentionally provocative and stubbornly unrespectable sensationalism, Micheaux's films can be interpreted as a form of resistance to white containment. Because of this ambiguity, the censor boards simply did not understand—or perhaps they understood all too well and refused to approve of—his works in their original form. The scrutiny to which Micheaux's films were subjected illustrated the dilemma that all filmmakers faced, but which African American filmmakers in particular had to contend with. African American filmmakers had to realize that if their films were to be exhibited they would, in the words of Thomas Cripps, bear "white fingermarks."[84]

Micheaux often succeeded in distributing versions of his films by outwitting largely white censor boards. Although the censors often succeeded in diluting or altogether suppressing Micheaux's messages, by skillfully acceding to some of the censors' demands, he managed to reach his audience. The recent recovery of many of his motion pictures and the available documentation of his struggle to exhibit his works shed light on an important phase of American cinema history—and African American cinema history, in particular—in the early twentieth century.

NOTES

1. Al Tony-Gilmore, *Bad Nigger: The National Impact of Jack Johnson* (New York, 1975), 75.

2. Ibid.

3. Ibid., 76.

4. Ibid., 80.

5. Thomas Cripps, *Slow Fade to Black: The Negro in American Film, 1900–1942* (New York, 1977), 18.

6. James Nesteby, *Black Images in White Films, 1896–1954* (Washington, D.C., 1982), 2.

7. Ibid.

8. Ibid.

9. Tony Langston, "James J. Jeffries," *Chicago Defender*, March 11, 1916.

10. Peter Noble, "The Negro in *The Birth of a Nation*," in *Focus on "The Birth of a Nation*," ed. Fred Silva (Englewood Cliffs, N.J., 1971), 125.

11. "Maj. Jackson's Telling Speech Passes Important Bill," *Chicago Defender*, May 22, 1915.

12. Booker T. Washington, "Time to Fight Bad Movies Is before They Are Shown," *Chicago Defender,* May 22, 1915.

13. Thomas Cripps, "The Reaction of the Negro to the Motion Picture, *Birth of a Nation,*" in *Focus on "The Birth of a Nation,"* ed. Fred Silva (Englewood Cliffs, N.J., 1971), 113.

14. Donald Bogle, *Toms, Coons, Mulattoes, Mammies, and Bucks* (New York, 1973), 109.

15. Donald Bogle, *Blacks in American Film and Television: An Illustrated Encyclopedia* (New York, 1988), 422.

16. Daniel Leab, *From Sambo to Superspade: The Black Experience in Motion Pictures* (Boston, 1975), 78.

17. Henry Sampson, *Blacks in Black and White: A Source Book on Black Films* (Metuchen, N.J., 1977).

18. Richard Gehr, "One-Man Show," *American Film* 16 (May 1991): 34.

19. James Hoberman, "Bad Movies," *Film Comment* 16, no. 4 (July–August 1980): 11.

20. Cripps, *Slow Fade,* 183.

21. Richard Grupenhoff, "The Rediscovery of Oscar Micheaux, Black Film Pioneer," *Journal of Film and Video* 40 (winter 1988): 46.

22. Jane Gaines and Charlene Regester, "Oscar Micheaux," in *Encyclopedia of African American Culture and History* (forthcoming).

23. J. Ronald Green, "Oscar Micheaux's Darktown Revue: Caricature and Class Conflict," in *In Touch with the Spirit: Black Religious and Musical Expression in American Cinema,* ed. Phyllis R. Klotman and Gloria J. Gibson-Hudson (Bloomington, Ind., 1994), 73.

24. Oscar Micheaux, *The Conquest: The Story of a Negro Pioneer* (Lincoln, Nebr., 1913), 14–15.

25. Ibid., 145.

26. Jane Gaines, "Fire and Desire: Race, Melodrama, and Oscar Micheaux," in *Black American Cinema,* ed. Manthia Diawara (New York, 1993), 66.

27. Hoberman, "Bad Movies," 11.

28. Eric Lott, "The Seeming Counterfeit: Racial Politics and Early Blackface Minstrelsy," *American Quarterly* 43, no. 2 (June 1991): 227.

29. Some scholars suggest that Micheaux reedited *Body and Soul* (1924) to double-cast Paul Robeson as the despicable minister and the minister's brother, who is of impeccable character. These scholars think this duality was an afterthought created to minimize the offensive negative portrayal of the African American minister and forestall further objection from black audiences and film censors.

30. Cripps, *Slow Fade,* 192.

31. Ibid.

32. Mark A. Reid, *Redefining Black Film* (Berkeley, 1993), 14.

33. According to Henry Louis Gates, Jr., because African American filmmakers themselves are products of the middle class, their films' commercial appeal feeds upon the appetite among middle-class whites and blacks for portrayals of the life of the black underclass ("Disturbing Themes Link Black-Oriented Films," *Richmond Times-Dispatch,* March 8, 1992). Thus, while Micheaux was condemned for criticizing

the black middle class, contemporary African American filmmakers are criticized for exploiting the black underclass.

34. Hoberman, "Bad Movies," 11.

35. Gaines, "Fire," 66.

36. Garth Jowett, *Film: The Democratic Art* (Boston, 1976), 108–38.

37. "Motion Picture Division," *Twenty-Fourth Annual Report of the State Department* (Albany, 1928), 309–16.

38. Janet Maslin, "When Hollywood Could Be Naughty," *New York Times,* February 4, 1994.

39. Bernard L. Peterson, Jr., "A Filmography of Oscar Micheaux: America's Legendary Black Filmmaker," in *Celluloid Power: Social Film Criticism from "The Birth of a Nation" to "Judgment at Nuremburg,"* ed. David Platt (Methuchen, N.J., 1992), 121.

40. Cripps, *Slow Fade,* 189.

41. Censors Report, *The Brute* file, August 9, 1920, Chicago Board of Motion Picture Censors, Illinois Regional Archives Depository, Northeastern Illinois University (hereafter cited as CBMPC).

42. Ibid.

43. Lester Walton, "Sam Langford's Wallop Makes *The Brute* a Screen Success," *New York Age,* September 18, 1920.

44. Cripps reports that in earlier years a Rev. A. J. Carey had served on this board, where he assumed a similar role (*Slow Fade,* 42). The *New York Age* also reported that Reverend Carey in 1914 served as "the colored member of the board, who occupies a strategic position and can render the race invaluable service" (Lester Walton, "Chicago Censor Board Rejects *One Large Evening:* Ridiculing the Race," *New York Age,* April 9, 1914).

45. "Race Again Has Member on Movie Censor Board," *Chicago Defender,* May 8, 1915, 1.

46. Censors Report, *Symbol of the Unconquered* file, November 18, 1920, CBMPC.

47. Peterson, "Filmography," 122.

48. Edward de Grazia and Roger Newman, *Banned Films: Movies, Censors, and the First Amendment* (New York, 1982), 31.

49. Chairman, Virginia State Board of Motion Picture Censors to G. W. Kessler, March 18, 1924, Virginia State Archives (hereafter cited as VSBMPC). Reactions to *Symbol of the Unconquered* by New York and Virginia censors remain unknown, although there is some evidence that the film was approved for exhibition in Virginia.

50. "Regent: *The Dungeon,*" *Afro-American,* June 9, 1922, 4.

51. New York State Motion Picture Commission to Micheaux Films Corporation, May 20, 1922, New York State Archives (hereafter cited as NYSMPC).

52. See the essay by Alison Parker in this volume.

53. Censors Report, *The Dungeon* file, March 20, 1923, CBMPC.

54. NYSMPC to Oscar Micheaux, January 16, 1924, NYSMPC.

55. Oscar Micheaux to NYSMPC, January 16, 1924, NYSMPC.

56. VSBMPC to C. C. Collmus, Jr., February 25, 1924, VSBMPC.

57. Chairman, VSBMPC, to the mayor, city of Portsmouth, February 28, 1924, VSBMPC.

58. Chairman, VSBMPC, to Oscar Micheaux, February 28, 1924, VSBMPC.

59. Oscar Micheaux to VSBMPC, October 14, 1924, VSBMPC.

60. Chairman, VSBMPC, to C. Lee Moore, auditor, November 10, 1924, VSBMPC.

61. Censors Report, *Birthright* file, March 2, 1927, CBMPC.

62. Ibid.

63. NYSMPC to Oscar Micheaux, September 20, 1924, NYSMPC.

64. Oscar Micheaux to NYSMPC, September 27, 1924, NYSMPC.

65. License, *A Son of Satan* file, October 1, 1924, NYSMPC.

66. Censors Report, "Reasons for Rejection," signed by Evan R. Chesterman, R. C. L. Monroe, and Dr. Mastin, *A Son of Satan* file, July 22, 1924, VSBMPC.

67. Chairman, VSBMPC, to "All Coloured Theatres in Virginia," July 22, 1924, VSBMPC.

68. VSBMPC to Oscar Micheaux, October 27, 1924, VSBMPC.

69. Oscar Micheaux to VSBMPC, October 6, 1924, VSBMPC.

70. VSBMPC to Oscar Micheaux, November 10, 1924, VSBMPC.

71. Censors Report, *A Son of Satan* file, March 31, 1927, CBMPC. *A Son of Satan* was not submitted to approval in Chicago until 1927. Chicago censors approved it with sixteen cuts, including scenes that violated racial codes and those more conventionally described as immoral or indecent:

> *Reel II:* Subtitle 'He crushed the life out of her with his two hands.'
> *Reel IV:* Cut subtitle—containing the word 'spade.'
> Cut all scenes of hooded men (of order) in room around table except 1st scene as they came into the room. . . . This to include subtitle 'Exalted Cyclops which comes out.'
> *Reel VI:* Choking of girl not shown—Shooting of man is cut.

72. Censors Report, *The House behind the Cedars* file, VSBMPC.

73. Ibid.

74. Oscar Micheaux to VSBMPC, March 13, 1925, VSBMPC.

75. Censors Report, *The House behind the Cedars* file, December 1, 1925, CBMPC.

76. NYSMPC to Micheaux Film Corporation, November 9, 1925, NYSMPC.

77. Oscar Micheaux to NYSMPC, November 9, 1925, NYSMPC.

78. NYSMPC to Oscar Micheaux, November 10, 1925, NYSMPC.

79. Oscar Micheaux to NYSMPC, November 11, 1925, NYSMPC.

80. NYSMPC to Micheaux Film Corporation, November 12, 1925, NYSMPC.

81. Censors Report, *Body and Soul* file, February 21, 1927, CBMPC.

82. Censors Report, *Body and Soul* file, February 18, 1927, CBMPC.

83. *Billboard,* December 27, 1924, 49.

84. Cripps, *Slow Fade,* 192.

Goodness Had Nothing to Do with It

Censoring Mae West

MARYBETH HAMILTON

Bystander: You're a fine gal, Lady Lou, a fine woman.
Mae West: One of the finest women that ever walked the streets.
She Done Him Wrong

Mae West is best remembered as Hollywood's most colorful victim of censorship. In 1933, with her first two starring pictures, *She Done Him Wrong* and *I'm No Angel,* West achieved a truly phenomenal popularity, becoming, in the words of the trade journal *Variety,* "the biggest conversation-provoker, free space grabber and all-around box office bet in the country. She's as hot an issue as Hitler."[1] But in 1934, after a nationwide campaign against film immorality with which West's name became virtually synonymous, she was subjected to the constraints of the Production Code Administration (PCA), the film industry's self-regulatory body, and her popularity began a steady decline. In 1938 Paramount dropped her from her studio contract, only six years and eight films after she began.

Other performers survived the Production Code Administration. Mae West did not. West herself gave a straightforward explanation of her troubles: she was a freewheeling sexual libertine victimized by a punitive censorship body staffed by a group of Victorian prudes. West's biographers have echoed that analysis; so, more subtly, have many historians. For Robert Sklar, the pre-1934 West was raw, acerbic, even sexually revolutionary, precisely because she was uncensored. She was an exemplar of Hollywood's "Golden Age of Turbulence," exploding on screen with unfettered power before the censors killed her off.[2]

Yet the censorship files of the Motion Picture Producers and Distributors of America (MPPDA), more popularly known as the Hays Office, call that analysis into question. First, they make clear that Mae West was never "uncensored." Well before the founding of the PCA, West was subjected to Hays Office scrutiny. *She Done Him Wrong* and *I'm No Angel* underwent extensive revision by the PCA's precursor, the Studio Relations Committee (SRC), a systematic procedure applied to every Hollywood production well before the cameras began to roll.

At the same time, the files make clear that this censorship was a complex process and that the Hays Office was no simple body of prudes aiming to repress all sexual content. On the contrary, as Lea Jacobs has argued, Hollywood censors played a constructive role in shaping sexual expression and meaning.[3] West's experience was no exception. Before 1934, in fact, censorship helped create Mae West as we know her, shaping her persona far more effectively than West herself would ever admit.

In the final months of 1932 *She Done Him Wrong* went into production at Paramount and immediately fell under the scrutiny of the Hays Office. The studio received extensive advice from Dr. James Wingate, head of the SRC, the Hays Office's West Coast representative charged with administering the Production Code in detail. Wingate scrutinized every stage—each successive script draft, all the song lyrics, and the finishing touches for the release print. His suggestions, most of which Paramount implemented, dealt far more in pragmatics than morals. Through advice on dialogue, characterization, setting, and "atmosphere," he guided the studio in shaping controversial material so as to safeguard its investment and protect the film against costly deletions by state censor boards.

It was no easy endeavor. Mae West presented special problems, though not because, as West herself maintained, she "was the first [film star] to bring sex out into the open."[4] While the SRC was wary of sexual topics, it was also accustomed to dealing with them. The years 1931 and 1932 had seen the release by all major studios of a cycle of what the Hays Office dubbed "sex films": *Back Street, Possessed,* and *Blonde Venus,* among others, tales of the transgressions of beautiful and willfully modern young women. Though such films had caused the censors no end of headaches, they were a familiar commodity. The peculiar troubles that West presented, in contrast, were rooted in her Broadway origins and her reputation for urban "realism," for providing a glimpse of authentic underworld vice.

In 1932 Mae West's national reputation rested on two events. The first was her arrest on obscenity charges in 1927 after producing two Broadway plays: *Sex,* a tale of prostitution, and *The Drag,* a "comedy-drama of homosexuality." The second was her follow-up to the arrest, the 1928 hit play *Diamond Lil,* on which *She Done Him Wrong* was based. The tale of an 1890s Bowery madam who bewitches the preacher who sets out to reform her, the play capitalized on West's notoriety, tantalizing audiences with a chance to "go slumming" with a convicted pornographer who would guide them down "the most wicked street in the world."[5]

Diamond Lil's claims to underworld authenticity ought to be taken with a large grain of salt. Set in a picturesque Gay Nineties tavern peopled with comical Bowery barflies, *Lil* was a sentimental slumming excursion, a fond look back at a caricatured past. It was a sharp contrast to West's earlier plays, whose tone was leering and confrontational, whose style was rooted in underworld theater, and whose "urban vice" came across as uncomfortably real. *Lil* abandoned such blatant sensationalism to cultivate a chuckle of bemused nostalgia and highlight the bewitching persona newly developed by its star. Oozing through the play in her floor-length gowns, writhing and wriggling with every step, West made an amiably implausible period piece, a tabloid headliner in a whalebone corset. Every word, every gesture, exuded a good-humored irony. As one critic described it, "She seems to recoil with an almost gun-like precision after each of her more tawdry speeches, and makes her own comment . . . upon them, even while she continues to play them seriously."[6]

What *Diamond Lil* offered was slumming made comfortable, the lure of the forbidden with the rough edges smoothed off, and as historians such as Lewis Erenberg have noted, in the twenties that style was the hallmark of successful Broadway nightlife. Like the Cotton Club, which trumpeted its presentation of genuine "black savagery" while closing its doors to black patrons, successful nightlife enterprises offered sanitized underworld fantasy lands that catered to the tastes of middle-class patrons, all of them loud in their rejection of "prudery" but often less adventurous than they liked to admit.[7]

So in truth, *Diamond Lil* was not nearly the shocker its Broadway publicists claimed. All the same, like the nightlife milieu it sprang from, West's play made the Hays Office nervous. Since the 1920s Broadway had occupied a cultural niche from which the film industry was anxious to distance itself. It styled itself as a site of rebellion, of adventurous flouting of Victorian norms.

Though that rebellion was obviously tempered in practice, on the surface Broadway endorsed it wholeheartedly, spotlighting jazz, racial exotics, and the thrills of the underworld, all the while enticing consumers with the chance to let loose.[8]

As a potential source of actors, writers, and screenplays, that entertainment culture posed no end of problems for the Hays Office, always attentive to the fears of the provinces and their middle-class cultural guardians, who had long viewed the movies as an encroachment, and who had grown even more hostile as sound technology threatened to bring Broadway's much-publicized "realism" directly to Main Street. In Hays's view the film industry, like it or not, had to take this hostility seriously. While Broadway could afford to revel in its reputation for serving up metropolitan wickedness, filmmakers could not: they had to sell their product in small towns as well as big cities, under the scrutiny of state and municipal censor boards. In response Hays developed a public relations strategy of selling movies as a quintessentially mainstream amusement, detached from the world of urban nightlife and in line with the values of the American heartland. As part of the industry's "special endeavor to prevent the prevalent type of play from becoming the prevalent type of picture," Hays heralded Hollywood's production of "pure entertainment," which left spectators as morally untainted on leaving the theater as when they went in.[9]

If that "special endeavor" were to retain credibility, *Diamond Lil* and Mae West would have to be censored. Most obviously, the film would have to sever all direct links to the play. To that end, acting on Hays Office suggestions, Paramount changed the title to *She Done Him Wrong*, West's character became "Lady Lou," and publicity stressed West's most famous (if misquoted) catch-phrase, "Come up and see me sometime," instead of the play's best-known line, "You can be had."[10] Beyond that, however, the task grew more complicated: eradicating all traces of the Broadway style that James Wingate described as "sordid realism," a style that seemed to promise spectators a glimpse of authentic underworld vice.[11]

To blot out that style, the Hays Office looked to the conventions it had developed to regulate "sex movies," the tales of ambitious women who used love affairs to move up the social and material ladder. In vetting such stories, the censors had a clear aim: to get them onscreen in a form that could turn a profit without causing trouble for the film industry. That did not mean deleting sexual material entirely. Instead, the censors sought to walk a fine line between offending the traditional and boring the adventurous. This goal demanded strategies of screen representation in which sexual content was suggested, not overt, "from which conclusions might be drawn by the sophisticated mind, but which would mean nothing to the unsophisticated and inexperienced," as James Wingate's precursor Jason Joy put it.[12]

In practice, this meant infusing sex films with a high degree of ambiguity. The SRC urged that wherever possible, the heroine's sexual encounters be shown indirectly, through vague verbal or visual allusions, leaving it an open question when (or whether) they took place. Just as important, the SRC insisted, the film should not seem to endorse her conduct. If only for the purpose of disarming critics, it had to condemn her, whether through scenes in which she is denounced by others, repents of her own sins, or (as the SRC urged in 1932 in the case of MGM's *Red-Headed Woman*) is made so farcical that it would be impossible to take her conduct seriously.[13]

From the beginning the SRC staff approached *Diamond Lil* with an eye to the latter strategy, aiming to mute all echoes of its Broadway reputation by veiling the story in nostalgia and comedy. As Wingate put it, the film would caricature "the manners and customs of the period" and "develop the comedy elements, so that the treatment will invest the picture with such exaggerated qualities as automatically to take care of possible offensiveness."[14] The Hays Office, in other words, would out-West Mae West by employing precisely the devices that made *Diamond Lil* such a departure from her other Broadway forays.

They started with the Bowery setting, conspicuously thickening its air of nostalgia. The transition to film facilitated this. The movie employed period music as background accompaniment, which echoed behind the opening credits and heralded the appearances of Lady Lou. Those jangling melodies and barbershop harmonies helped to lend both the Bowery and Lou's exploits an even quainter sentimentality than West had managed to inject into the stage version. The atmosphere was established in a lighthearted montage that followed the opening credits. Introducing the Bowery setting through an organ grinder and monkey, two elegant women on bicycles, and an aggravated street sweeper cleaning up after a horse, it stressed the sexual innocence of the picturesque Gay Nineties, a time, as an explanatory caption put it, "when there were handlebars on lip and wheel—and legs were confidential!"

The Hays Office's main worry, however, was Lady Lou herself. Wingate bemoaned her "low-toned" characteristics, her seeming rootedness in the underworld, and sought to downplay her realism and make her a creature of fantasy. At Wingate's request, Paramount made several script changes that muted Lou's past transgressions, "soft-pedalling the many references to the number of Lady Lou's previous affairs" and leaving the nature of the relationships "open to debate."[15] In practice, this meant channeling most mentions of Lou's history through comic repartee with her black maid, a wholly new character, who (in

191

the words of the first script draft, titled *Ruby Red*) "knows everything about Lou," and whose sly familiarity with her mistress allowed viewers to infer what the film could not directly state.[16] It also meant replacing blunt references to the heroine's predatory passions with allusive one-liners. Gone, for instance, was Lil's recital of her encounters with "burnin' lovers"; in its place was Lou's memorable description of herself as "the finest woman who ever walked the streets."[17]

In the end, Wingate's attempt to tame *Diamond Lil* resulted in a substantial number of changes, but on screen, hardly anyone noticed them. They fit with uncanny neatness into the trajectory of the original script. More fully than the SRC ever realized, its strategy of investing the narrative with ambiguity and replacing sexual aggression with comedy and nostalgia had been part of the original play. Ironically, then, the more Paramount worked to implement SRC suggestions, the more like the play the film became. Successive drafts of the script make clear that West was able to use the Hays Office's insistence on comedy to her advantage in her battle to overturn script revisions ordered by Paramount screenwriter John Bright. Bright, who had made a name for himself with the violent gang tale *The Public Enemy,* initially sought to recast the script into a darker, more solemn underworld drama, dropping wisecracks and inserting moments in which Lou sees the error of her ways. By the time the cameras rolled, West had cut the new emphasis on melodramatic repentance, which disrupted the desired tone of humor and fantasy, and reinstated many of her one-liners.[18]

As a consequence, the film Paramount released in early 1933 struck *Variety* and most other observers as a carbon copy of *Diamond Lil.* By all appearances it seemed to have a nearly identical impact on audiences. The film came across, like the play, as a trip to a genial urban underworld; and despite the Hays Office's eagerness to avoid Broadway "realism," reviewers brought up that word again and again. To Wingate's certain chagrin, nearly all noted the screenplay's stage origins—and how little it had changed in transition. Still exuding "that lusty quality which made the play indigenous to both its star and to Broadway," the film altered little except the names and the title, "to deceive Will Hays, who seems easy to deceive."[19] The script and the backgrounds may have been toned down, but juxtaposed against them were sensational elements that succeeded in evoking West's Broadway origins, making the completed film much less safely fantastical than its regulators had hoped.

Most sensational of all was Mae West herself. Neither Wingate nor Hays nor anyone else had anticipated the nature of her performance, how completely it would prove resistant to external control. One look at the completed film convinced Wingate that West's acting style had subverted all his efforts to veil Lou and her surroundings in comedy. He wrote to Will Hays with obvious dismay, "Miss West gives a performance of strong realism."[20]

What Wingate saw as "realism" was West's highly conventionalized performance style, the oozing walk, the hard-boiled speech that lent an unexpected saltiness to seemingly innocent lines. It was a familiar phenomenon on Broadway, but on film it shone forth as altogether novel, not least because the camera served it up as spectacle, West's body an eroticized feast for the eye. While a stage audience might have chosen to focus on West alone, the screen audience was given no choice. As *Variety* noted, supporting characters are "never permitted to be anything more than just background. Miss West gets all the lens gravy and full figure most of the time."[21]

In reading her sexual style as "realism," Wingate was most likely joined by much of the film's audience. Studio publicity for *She Done Him Wrong,* like stage publicity for *Diamond Lil,* touted its authenticity and sexual frankness, attributing them to West's real-life links to the urban underworld. Newspaper stories and fan-magazine interviews generated by Paramount lavished attention on her Broadway arrests ("Welfare Island Fails to Tame the Wild West!"); her friendship with Broadway racketeer Owney Madden, "the Killer of Tenth Avenue"; and even the fact that she "freely admits she has been the patron big sister of the afflicted of what Broadway calls Fairyland."[22] This was no ordinary actress, and certainly no purveyor of fantasy, but a convicted sex offender who used the screen to display her true self. "Mae West actually courts gossip," the studio emphasized, "and your worst innuendoes are music to her ears."[23]

Such blatant appeals to sensationalism appalled the Hays Office—not least because they proved so effective. By early March it was apparent that Paramount had produced a sensation. Released in February around the time of Roosevelt's Bank Holiday, *She Done Him Wrong* defied the trend of declining attendance, raking in huge box office receipts even in areas where West had been previously unknown. Evidently, good-natured slumming excursions appealed nationwide, in Mississippi no less than Manhattan. In Birmingham, Alabama, her film became the biggest draw in town, and in Lincoln, Nebraska, it played three week-long engagements, attracting larger and more boisterous audiences each time.[24]

Clearly, the Hays Office's tactics had backfired. Despite all the efforts to sever its ties, *She Done Him Wrong* continued to evoke Broadway, and, as Wingate realized, the jibes about West's triumph over the ineffectual Will Hays only added fuel to the reformist fire, lending new justification to the contention that the industry was unfit to control its own products. Wingate was

Mae West appears in all her glory in *She Done Him Wrong* (Paramount, 1933). Photo courtesy Margaret Herrick Library, Academy of Motion Picture Arts and Sciences.

not alone in his worries. Sidney Kent, the head of Fox Film Company, saw *She Done Him Wrong* shortly after its release and wrote an aggrieved letter to Will Hays in New York.

> In my opinion it is the worst picture I have seen. It was the real story of Diamond Lil and they got away with it. They promised that that story would not be made. I believe it is worse than *Red-Headed Woman* from the standpoint of the industry—it is far more suggestive in word and what is not said is suggested in action.
>
> I cannot understand how your people on the Coast could let this get by. There is very little that any of us can do now.[25]

Kent's letter was a sign of forces brewing that would compel Mae West to change, despite her box office success. *She Done Him Wrong* infuriated reform groups already distressed by the onslaught of sex films and now horrified to discover that a convicted pornographer was parading on screen for all the world to see. As their protests intensified in the spring of 1933, Will Hays became increasingly nervous. With Hollywood receiving so much bad press, and with government intervention in business an apparent trend, Washington might well decide to subject the film industry to heavy-handed federal controls. The only way to quash the threat was to tighten the self-regulatory process. By April Hays was in Hollywood haranguing filmmakers in person. More ribald productions, he warned, more Broadway sensationalism, and they could be certain of punitive government action, for they would have provided their critics with precisely the ammunition they needed.[26]

By late spring, as West prepared to begin filming a follow-up, she found her employers at Paramount under new pressure to proceed with care. In truth, they might well have acted more prudently even without the Hays Office. *She Done Him Wrong* may have made a mint, but it also caused the studio more than a few headaches: much bad feeling within the industry, a profusion of deletions by the state censors, and an expensive last-minute cut demanded by a panicky Hays Office. One week before the premiere, and after all the prints had been sent to exhibitors, MPPDA official Vincent Hart saw the film and was shocked by West's performance, particularly her rendition of "A Guy What Takes His Time" (or "Slow Motion Man"), on paper a mild love lyric, but in West's hands a graphic celebration of languorous sex. At the insistence of Hart and Hays, Paramount recalled the prints and deleted all but the song's first and last verses. Compounding the studio's embarrassment, James Wingate wrote to the heads of all the major film companies to inform them of the Hays Office's action.[27]

This time around Paramount was determined to avoid any such wrangles and keep West's creative influence within bounds. Though she received a full screenwriting credit for the feature that took shape over the summer and probably did contribute a skeletal narrative,[28] the final product was almost certainly fleshed out by Paramount scriptwriter Harlan Thompson. "Harlan *wrote* the script," his widow insisted, and it seems indisputable that hands other than West's were involved.[29] At least on the surface, the new vehicle, *I'm No Angel,* was more circumspect than anything she had ever created alone.

The most obvious change was in the film's setting. The tale of a circus dancer turned lion tamer who wins the heart of a society man, *I'm No Angel* extricated West from the New York City underworld on which she had built her Broadway career. Gone was even a romanticized trace of the Bowery milieu, whose unsavory associations had so dismayed the Hays Office. Instead, the new film was rooted more securely in fantasy, following Tira, the "dancing, singing marvel," from a carnival sideshow to a penthouse apartment and the unreal luxury of the movieland rich.

Tira, too, represented a bow to caution. No queen of the underworld, she is a wisecracking gold digger, shrewd and ambitious, less explicitly out for sex than for money. "Somewhere there's a guy with a million waitin' for a dame like me," Tira says, and her eagerness to find him impels the narrative, leading her from a circus tent to the lap of luxury and the seductions of orchids, diamonds, and furs.[30] At the same time, there is a conspicuous if formulaic display of atonement. Unlike Lady Lou, seemingly an unashamed carouser to the final credits, Tira is reformed by love. "I never knew I could go for anyone like I have for him," she announces of her wealthy suitor, Jack Clayton, and the film goes out of its way to show that she means it. When Clayton believes her unfaithful and breaks their engagement, she is genuinely shattered. "I ain't never seen nobody so broken-hearted as you was when you and Mr. Clayton done bust up," testifies her maid, Beulah. "He's made me feel like a different dame," Tira agrees. "I ain't just a Sister Honky Tonk no more."

Clearly, Will Hays's admonitions had had some effect. Even Paramount's publicists got into the act, as *Variety* reported shortly before *I'm No Angel*'s release.

> To offset any possible backfire from women's club groups and hinterland censors, Paramount executives have given orders to the studio publicity department to change its policy on the type of publicity going out on Mae West, . . . with a soft peddling on any attempt to present her as the spectacular and bizarre character she is on the screen.[31]

The results put an end to fan-magazine profiles of West as an authentic sexual outlaw. "The difference between her and her characterizations amazed me," one colleague asserted in a press release. "Despite the lurid publicity her sensational stage plays and jousts with the law have earned for her, she has never had her name blemished by any personal scandal."[32] Quiet, generous, deeply religious, this was a woman who cared for her craft and served her jail sentence as a "sacrifice to her principle that honest views of love, life, and sex were less harmful than dishonest and glossed-over implication."[33] Certainly, the prison officials were never misled.

> How seriously the authorities regarded the sentence may be gathered from the fact that she spent none of that time in a detention cell with the real offenders against public decency.
>
> The warden saw in her a superior woman of charm and intelligence. For that ten days she was the guest in his house. His children loved the beautiful lady who taught them songs and dances. He is still one of her staunchest admirers.
>
> And many of the less fortunate inmates are grateful to Mae West for acts of kindness and charity.[34]

But it would be wrong to give the impression that *I'm No Angel* set out to purify West entirely. After all, her ribald performance in *She Done Him Wrong* had made her Paramount's hottest commodity. The challenge was to repackage West more acceptably within a contentious mass medium, not by deleting all sexual references, but by burying them more subtly beneath the film's surface. This *I'm No Angel* accomplished, to the Hays Office's evident relief. "While many of the gags border on questionable dialogue . . . most of the suggestions are left to the imagination," Vincent Hart noted approvingly.[35]

The chief food for the imagination was Mae West's persona. On paper Tira was an ambitious dancer with a craving for money. On the screen she exuded earthier desires. West's swiveling hips, knowing laugh, and appraising gaze injected a bawdiness that the script had carefully eschewed. Her one-liners were vague but allusive, and her delivery conveyed a full-fledged sexual history that the film did not otherwise avow.

Fortune-teller: You are very wise.
Tira: Oh, I profit by my experiences. (chuckles) Now, listen, honey—uh—you just tell me about my future. You see, I know all about my past.

As Joseph Furnas of the *New York Herald-Tribune* observed, while the plot

> seems to be trying to lace Miss West's pungency into the stiffly-boned confines of the screen formula for heroines, however reckless, . . . Miss West bursts gloriously forth from these restraining influences, much the same overblown,

gaudy and zestful lady as before. The scenarist may insist that she is the cus-
tomary hard-boiled heroine with the heart of gold, but through means best
handled by herself, she keeps the audience profitably reminded that her hard
confidence and carnal humor are something new on the screen.[36]

With its circus narrative so patently absurd, *I'm No Angel*'s true subject matter
was West's performance. To that extent the film made a lasting change in what
she herself would come to call the Mae West character. On Broadway and in
She Done Him Wrong she had plugged herself into the lore of the urban underworld, offering herself up as a genial scandal. This Mae West was different.
Stripped of her New York associations, she became more iconic, a universal
figure larger than life. The only lore at work was Mae West's—her style, her
wisecracks, her famous spectacle. As one critic put it, "The show, this time, is
entirely the Mae West personality."[37] West became an enigmatic plot in
herself.

At the heart of the enigma lay the issue of the "real" Mae West. Who was
she? Why did she specialize in sexual roles? What did she *intend* by her enactments? *I'm No Angel* heightened the debate. At the same time that Paramount's publicity department, in an abrupt about-face, was claiming that the
off-screen West bore no relation to her film persona, the script subtly but per-
sistently hinted the opposite, encouraging viewers to conflate actress and character through suggestively autobiographical details. Tira's birth date, August
17, is the same as West's; her cootch dancing in the circus recalls West's
shimmy dancing in vaudeville; her appearance in court near the end of the
film, rebutting Jack Clayton's slurs on her character, evokes West's notorious
courtroom battles on Broadway.[38]

Throughout the film, viewers are encouraged to watch and wonder at West's
flamboyant style. Often they can do little else as the action comes to a halt, or
rather, hangs suspended, while the camera focuses on West simply strutting
her stuff. To musical accompaniment, she banters with her maids and her ad-
mirers, parrying their compliments with ironic comebacks to a chorus of appreciative laughter. At times her encounters with suitors seem almost surreal
in their scrupulous avoidance of physical contact. The one kiss in *I'm No Angel,*
between Tira and Jack Clayton (Cary Grant), is filmed from behind, with Clayton's head filling the screen, completely obscuring our view. Clearly, West's
much-vaunted sexual frankness, as presented by Paramount, had little to do
with fleshly passion. Instead the film offered her style as a treat in itself, the
arched eyebrows and pelvic gyrations accentuating wisecrack after quotable
wisecrack, many bandied about in press releases even before the premiere.

Clayton: Ah, you were wonderful tonight!

Tira: Ummm. I'm always wonderful at night. (laughs)

Clayton: (laughs) Yes, but tonight you were especially good.

Tira: Well, when I'm good I'm very good, but when I'm bad, I'm better. (laughs)

Clayton: (laughs) . . . Of course, if I could only trust you.

Tira: Oh, you can. Hundreds have. (laughs)

Clayton: (laughs) Don't you know I'm mad about you?

Tira: I could tell you'd be the first time I saw you. (laughs)

Clayton: (laughs) Say, I must be transparent.

Tira: Honey, you're just wrapped in cellophane. (laughs)

It is difficult to exaggerate the sheer peculiarity of such exchanges. Almost ostentatious in their physical reticence, they amuse, but they also bewilder. They push West's artifice and secret bemusement to the foreground while leaving their meaning entirely unclear. Consciously or not, West had achieved a similar effect with *Diamond Lil,* her irony suggesting some private joke that she seemed to be savoring but never revealed. Now, thanks to the censors, audiences had even more cause to wonder exactly what she was laughing at. On that score the film remained stubbornly open-ended, leaving the task of interpretation up to the viewer.

And one need only examine the critical raves showered on West from the most unlikely quarters to see how varied the interpretations could be. In the wake of *I'm No Angel,* she was praised by a diverse collection of writers who united in adoring her performance style while holding flatly contradictory opinions about what it actually meant. To the French novelist Colette, West's manipulation of her heavyset body (the "powerful" breast, the "well-fleshed thighs," "the short neck, the round cheek of a young blonde butcher") signaled her defiant and explicitly feminist rejection of the demure, compliant Hollywood heroine.[39] To acerbic critic George Jean Nathan she was the embodiment of old-fashioned womanliness, in stark contrast to the "endless succession of imported lesbians and flat-chested flappers" foisted upon filmgoers before.[40] Gilbert Seldes saw West's air of good-humored mockery as a joyous affirmation of healthy heterosexuality and a populist rejection of the "infertile . . . and moribund" inversion of high-culture artists like Marcel Proust,[41] while George Davis and Parker Tyler read her irony as a homosexual style directly inspired by the theatricality of the gay male subculture.[42]

That Mae West could sustain all these interpretations and more was the secret of her Hollywood success. *I'm No Angel* was West's biggest hit, with good reason: male traditionalists could delight in a full-figured sex bomb, feminists in an unabashedly autonomous heroine, homosexual men in seemingly intentional camp, and the Hays Office in seemingly intentional restraint. "On the whole much better than we expected," wrote a relieved James Wingate. "In fact, the film contained nothing which we considered basically questionable or liable to cause trouble, and though it contained the expected number of wisecracks and Mae Westisms, we believe it will meet with no real difficulty."[43] Even some of West's harshest critics within the Hays Office found the picture delightful—not least the official who had been most outraged by *She Done Him Wrong.* Paramount, declared Vincent Hart, "is to be congratulated. This picture will be box office to the nth degree. . . . It is a knockout all the way through, and . . . I'm for it, irrespective!"[44]

That *I'm No Angel* succeeded so brilliantly was due not just to Mae West, but to the Hays Office. On this occasion, conventional wisdom to the contrary, censorship actually enhanced her appeal. Not only West, but also her censors, sought to mediate sex so as to appeal to the widest range of viewers. And it is hard not to argue that, though West had done it well on Broadway, in Hollywood the Hays Office did it even better.

If the story of Mae West and the Hays Office is not as simple as it is often made out, it is also true that over time West's relation to the censors would change. The key year in that process was 1934, when after months of moralist protest the Hays Office was reconstituted in a blaze of publicity and the SRC replaced by the Production Code Administration, marking the moment, as legend has it, when the Production Code was at last fitted with teeth.

In truth, what the new arrangement marked was a change in the Hays Office's procedures for regulating sex films. The PCA put an end to strategies of "leaving [sexual suggestions] to the imagination," at least as far as Mae West was concerned. Those strategies provoked an uproar in the wake of *I'm No Angel,* the very film that James Wingate had predicted would meet with "no real difficulty." He could not have been more mistaken. The film stirred up a storm, and not just because of West herself, but because of who came to see her.

I'm No Angel made abundantly clear that West's most ardent fans were young women. That fact flew in the face of all predictions. Given her burlesquian curves and ribald reputation, most had assumed she would prove a limited stag draw. On the contrary, *I'm No Angel* drew such a large female audience that an Omaha theater owner held women-only screenings, complete with complimentary coffee and rolls, so that women could savor West amongst themselves.[45]

Since the turn of the century, perceptions of young women's vulnerability and irresponsibility as consumers of popular culture had spurred calls for the regulation of dance halls, amusement parks, and other entertainments noted for drawing a large female crowd. Behind those perceptions of vulnerability lay intense suspicion of urban "amusement exploiters" who foisted corrupt moral values upon "impressionable" (female and working-class) consumers. Cramming their productions with sensationalism and sex, they readily influenced a defenseless audience that was unschooled in more "demanding" art forms and ill-equipped to exercise moral discernment.[46]

Though that criticism targeted all forms of popular culture, it gained particular force when applied to the movies, particularly in the early thirties, when Hollywood embarked on its cycle of sex films. None of the Hays Office's strategies for defusing their content had put a halt to allegations that such movies tempted suggestible girls to experiment with vice. Proof of that allegation, for many, was supplied in early 1933, with the publication of Henry James Forman's *Our Movie-Made Children.* Summarizing a series of investigations carried out from 1929 to 1932 into the influence of movies on American youth, the book compiled evidence to support the assertion that sex films were agents of moral decay. Forman argued that young women could not be trusted as viewers: they lacked the cultural skills, the intellectual acumen, to distinguish an act of performance. Conflating the glamorous star with her feckless screen character, young women romanticized her illicit behavior and interpreted the stories as virtual lessons in using their bodies for material gain. Even simple imitation was dangerous. In mimicking the behavior of provocative actresses—"learning to handle a cigarette like Nazimova, to smile like Norma Shearer, to use [their] eyes like Joan Crawford"—girls aroused potent sexual impulses they were too weak to control.[47] Forman supported that contention with quotes from young female reformatory inmates who blamed their downfall squarely and solely on the movies. His solemn presentation gave their responses the weight of fact.

> [From a fourteen-year-old]: After I have seen a romantic love scene, I feel as though I couldn't have just one fellow to love me, but I would like about five.

> [From a sixteen-year-old]: When I was on the outside I went to the movies almost every night, but only about twice in two months to a dance. I don't like dances as well as I do movies. A movie would get me so passionate after it was over that I just had to have relief. You know what I mean.[48]

In the midst of the uproar following the publication of Forman's book, in the spring of 1933 came the release of *I'm No Angel,* with its high-profile promotion of West's "PERSONALITY—swinging hips—bedroom eyes—and the throaty growl of an amorous cat."[49] To educators and clerics the success of West's film provided solid evidence of Forman's contentions. To them it seemed undeniable that young women were taking West as a role model. "There must be tens of thousands of high school girls all over the United States reading, hearing and seeing all they can of this particular star and her wanton heroines, imitating them so far as they can," lamented Presbyterian educator Harmon Stephens in a 1934 pamphlet entitled *Moral Welfare*. "On a 'character day' in one high school, nine girls came in imitation of her. 'She,' according to the billboard, 'is the kind of girl who can lose her reputation and never miss it.' Virtue lies prostrate."[50]

To reformers, as Stephens's words indicate, imitating Mae West was no laughing matter. She embodied the threat of the whole cycle of sex films with their glamorous and all-too-enticing gold diggers. In a decade short on material luxuries, she showed girls that wealth was theirs for the taking if they only made use of their bodies to follow her character's lead.[51]

Yet West was more than a run-of-the-mill gold digger, more than an ordinary sexual object. To that extent, the upheaval she provoked was unique. While both women and men objected to West, male detractors found her peculiarly unsettling, an unease provoked less by her immorality than by her unabashed pleasure in calling the shots. That was what fueled the outrage of industry critic Martin Quigley, who damned *I'm No Angel* by thundering, "There is no more pretense here of romance than there is on a stud farm."[52] West was a singularly disturbing sex symbol because her agency was too apparent. She too obviously relished her sexual power and her independence from male control.

In an era when men's status as breadwinners was so precarious, male control was a sensitive issue. One has only to look at oral histories of the Great Depression to see how often families were broken by sexual tension and men's flagging sense of authority.[53] In that context, West's popularity with women endangered the industry by making it vulnerable to male resentment, even among men who enjoyed West themselves, as the Hays Office's Ray Norr cautioned Will Hays. "The very man who will guffaw at Mae West's performance as a reminder of the ribald days of his past will resent her effect upon the young, when his daughter imitates the Mae West wiggle before her boyfriends and mouths 'Come up and see me sometime.'"[54]

As historian Nancy Woloch reminds us, the depression was not a feminist era. However ambiguously, popular amusements of the twenties had celebrated female sexual expressiveness, which in the thirties may well have stirred growing unease. The evidence from social history is largely speculative, but it does seem probable, as some historians have suggested, that depression-inspired fears of family instability were accompanied by a reaction against sexual liberalism, even by a sense that past moral profligacy was to blame for the present crisis.[55] It made sense that those tensions would center on girls. The moral transformations of the 1920s had been most visibly embodied by aggressive young women, by the revealing fashions and risqué tastes of the flapper. Insofar as she reached precisely that audience and seemed likely to inspire emulation, Mae West could indeed be seen as a threat.

In carefully shaping *I'm No Angel*, the Hays Office had tried to avert that prospect, but not only did the effort fail. In some ways, ironically, it made matters worse. Though no longer billed as an outright sensationalist, West became a larger-than-life sexual puzzle, an endlessly debatable erotic enigma who was more intriguing to viewers than ever before. One hostile critic argued that while in *She Done Him Wrong* she had been "amusing in a flamboyant way and different," *I'm No Angel* turned her into a "goddess, . . . an example and a model for the girlhood of the world."[56] By encouraging speculation about her intentions and leaving conclusions "to the imagination," the film provided too much ammunition for imaginations that could not be trusted and, as one outraged reformer put it, "compelled [the audience] to do its own dirty thinking on inferences that it cannot escape."[57]

To a large extent, then, the 1934 crisis was provoked by the Hays Office's own censorship strategies. Not surprisingly, in the years that followed precisely those strategies would change. Under PCA scrutiny, West was subjected to a new brand of censorship that altered her style nearly out of recognition— although not as completely out of recognition as the PCA would have liked. Gone was the open-endedness of *I'm No Angel*, where suggestions were "left to the imagination." The aim of this censorship, in contrast, was to prevent the imagination from playing too much.

The new regulatory strategy, and West's problems with it, can be seen in the trouble-fraught production of her 1936 release *Klondike Annie*, which starred West as the Frisco Doll, a rough-edged San Francisco dance hall singer who is implicated in a murder and flees to Alaska. En route she meets an idealistic young woman who is traveling to the Klondike to save souls for the Salvation Army. When the woman dies, the Doll adopts her uniform as a disguise but finds herself drawn by the woman's calling and reformed by her example.

In its heavy-handed insistence on pointing a moral, on showing the West character learning a lesson, *Klondike Annie* illuminates how radically the PCA attempted to alter West's style. As PCA head Joseph Breen put it, the film "depend[ed] for entertainment less on her wisecracks and more on a legitimate

Mae West comforts the sick in *Klondike Annie* (Paramount, 1935). Photo courtesy Margaret Herrick Library, Academy of Motion Picture Arts and Sciences.

story and sincere characterizations."[58] In other words, it downplayed what *I'm No Angel* had spotlighted, the enigmatic Mae West spectacle, and where the earlier film had solicited audience interpretation, *Klondike Annie* sought to suppress it. It stressed an unambiguous story marked by what Breen called "compensating moral values," narrative signposts that took viewers by the hand to prevent them from reading West's performance in a sensational way.

After 1934 that formula guided all of West's films, but it never worked as well as the PCA hoped. Even *Klondike Annie* caused problems, though it seemed unimpeachable on the surface. As Paramount's John Hammell stressed to Will Hays, it depicted an unmistakable conversion experience, the Frisco Doll's moral regeneration through her friendship with the settlement worker.

> In their close contact on board ship, we have the contrast and clash of the two characters—the earnest devout mission worker and the flippant product of a hard, cruel upbringing—West.

During the voyage, we see the gradual impression the mission worker makes
on West. She tells stories of her work among the unfortunates in the slum
district of San Francisco and the good work she hopes to do in her new field.
She tells the story of her life of service and sacrifice. West becomes, little by
little, deeply impressed with it all. . . . We have many scenes connected with
this work in which West is shown as helping the unfortunates, lifting the
fallen, etc.[59]

That was the idea, anyway. But even with this narrative, the PCA had objections: just how sincere that conversion appeared to be had everything to do
with how Mae West played it. With her performance style so imbued with
irony and ambiguity, even the most heartfelt conversion experience could remain open to question. In this regard, Hammell anticipated Will Hays's worries and attempted to quell them in advance.

At no time in our picture will West play the religious character with her
tongue in her cheek. At no time will religious services be held by West which
will have any indication of levity or burlesque. We are endeavoring to cast her
in a role in which we will take full advantage of those qualities which have en-
deared Mae West to millions of theatergoers, but the laughs that come from
our picture will never be at the expense of religion, religious people, or earnest
workers in the missionary field.

The ending of our story will be a romance between West and one of the
characters in our picture, and it will indicate for the future a normal life and
nothing that will bring condemnation from the most scrupulous.[60]

The PCA, however, was not convinced. Breen and his colleagues poured over
the script in pursuit of troublesome double meanings, moments when West
might seem to be giving the audience "a suggestion that has a flavor of sex."[61]
What, they asked indignantly (and no doubt with some reason), would West's
audience make of a statement like the following, when the supposedly reformed Frisco Doll preaches her philosophy of salvation: "You can't save a
man's soul if you don't get close to him. It's the personal touch that counts.
That's my experience."[62]

The PCA did its best to expunge such moments, cutting out double enten-
dres wherever they found them and bombarding Paramount with suggestions
for additional episodes that might make the Doll's conversion even more convincing. How about, Breen suggested, a scene of West doing "settlement-type
activities" with the rough, debauched miners—cutting out paper dolls,
or playing charades? How about turning the Frisco Doll into a Carrie
Nation–style crusader and showing her clearing out the saloons? Or, even

better, how about endowing the Doll with a large sum of money that she's determined never to give up, and at the end of the picture showing her spending it on some good cause—"an airplane to pick up serum for a dying child, or steamship fare home for some poor devil anxious to start life anew"? Breen's enthusiasm for these changes fairly carried him away. He wrote to Hammell exuberantly:

> It seems to me that you might be able to get a lot of fun out of this kind of an incident. I can imagine how Mae would put on a thing like this.
> Yours for bigger and better films!
> Cordially yours,
> Joseph Breen[63]

Scrutinizing West's scripts with meticulous care, the PCA attempted to tame her performances and in the process to eliminate "irresponsible" interpretation by her female audience. As they soon realized, it was a futile endeavor. West's viewers could never be made entirely passive as long as they remained equipped with a memory—as long as they brought their own knowledge of West and her past into the movie theater and could bring it to bear on what they saw on screen. With West at the helm, even the most scrupulously sanitized story could be subverted by a well-placed wink. That was the lesson a frustrated Joseph Breen took from *Klondike Annie,* which, despite all his precautions, proved impossible to render thoroughly innocent. He noted in a private memo:

> Just so long as we have Mae West on our hands with the particular kind of a story which she goes in for, we are going to have trouble.
> Difficulty is inherent with a Mae West picture. Lines and pieces of business, which in the script seem to be thoroughly innocuous, turn out when shown on the screen to be questionable at best, when they are not definitely offensive.[64]

For that reason, the PCA was fighting a losing battle in attempting to create a remodeled Mae West. Her style could not be made to fit into what was becoming the new Hollywood mold. Her fate after 1934 expresses in miniature the PCA's effect on the motion picture industry. West would be gradually weeded out of Hollywood, and, in just that manner, the interpretive variety her films had allowed would be gradually weeded out too.

In some ways, it may be true that West's experience of censorship was atypical. She would often complain that her films were regulated more severely than anyone else's, and she was probably right. As the lightning rod for the dirty-film crisis, West's films necessitated particular caution if the industry were to persuade its critics that Hollywood had learned its lesson and renounced immoral pictures at last.

At the same time, it is also true that the PCA introduced strategies for dealing with sex films that affected not just Mae West but the whole genre. Those new forms of censorship, as Lea Jacobs observes, transformed the viewer's experience by eliminating "the double meanings, the calculated ambiguities, and the narrative disjunctures which gave the films of the early thirties their zest."[65] They eliminated, in short, precisely those features that catered to a range of viewpoints on questions of sex by presenting viewers with a deliberately enigmatic spectacle and leaving them to read it however they pleased. But by the late thirties those "calculcated ambiguities" were gone, replaced by far more straightforward narratives that stressed conservative sexual values —female passivity, premarital chastity—packaged as apolitical "harmless amusement."

In January 1938 Paramount released a new Mae West film, *Every Day's a Holiday.* It was not a happy occasion. The film received withering reviews: "Sex ain't what it used to be, or maybe Miss West isn't."[66] In addition, it inspired little enthusiasm among fans. Even a prerelease scandal—West's banning from NBC radio after trading ribald jokes with Charlie McCarthy—stirred up only minimal audience interest. Most theaters gave the film a single week's engagement, in sharp contrast to the month-long runs accorded *She Done Him Wrong.* By the end of its release, the film had lost money, West's first out-and-out box office failure. For Paramount, its fate confirmed that West, for too long a source of Hays Office difficulties, had now become an embarrassment and a liability. *Every Day's a Holiday* ended West's association with Paramount once and for all.

The film itself provides sad testimony to the effect of the constraints under which West operated. Though she attempted to recapture her early success by returning to 1890s New York City, the plot lacked the rowdy good humor and the sly double meanings she had been able to employ in the past. West played Peaches O'Day, a New York con woman, whose adventures are kept carefully within high society and whose criminality consists of nothing more inflammatory than convincing a small-town yokel to buy the Brooklyn Bridge.

Late in January the film had its world premiere at the Paramount Theater in New York. As it turned out, it was a thrilling evening. The police department turned out in force, and uniformed officers swarmed through the theater. They were not there, however, to control Mae West. In an effort to draw in additional patrons, the Paramount Theater had arranged for an intermission performance by a new local sensation: Benny Goodman. The *New York Times* reported:

> It was like old times yesterday, with a new Mae West show opening and a squad of patrolmen marching down the aisles. The joker is that the police weren't after Miss West, but had been called in to restore order when a personal appearance by Benny Goodman and his band threatened to turn the Paramount into a playground for the intellectually suspect (we hesitate to call them mentally retarded). What with the adolescent exhibitionists dancing in the aisles, clawing their way upon the stage or swaying animalistically in their seats, Miss West's *Every Day's a Holiday* just couldn't escape being the second feature on the bill. And if there had been a Popeye or a Betty Boop on the program, she would have run third.[67]

By the end of the 1930s, the "adolescent exhibitionists" had abandoned not just Mae West but movies as a whole. Young women's desire to be rebellious, to use leisure to forge a sexual identity, would be sought out, not in the theater, but in music—in swing, jazz, and eventually rock and roll. Such areas were no less stigmatized than movies as a "playground for the intellectually suspect." But, for the moment at least, they were free from the heavy hand of "protective" control.

NOTES

1. *Variety,* October 17, 1933, 19.

2. Robert Sklar, *Movie-Made America: A Social History of American Movies* (New York, 1975), 175, 184–87. The most comprehensive biography of West is George Eells and Stanley Musgrove, *Mae West: A Biography* (New York, 1984).

3. Lea Jacobs, *The Wages of Sin: Censorship and the Fallen Woman Film, 1928–1942* (Madison, Wis., 1991), 23.

4. Quoted in Ellis Nassour, "Mae West," *Club* (undated interview in Mae West clipping file, Billy Rose Theatre Collection of the Performing Arts Research Center, New York Public Library).

5. Advertisement for *Diamond Lil* at the Flatbush Theater, Brooklyn, September 1929, in *Diamond Lil* clipping file, Billy Rose Theatre Collection.

6. Quoted in Montrose J. Moses and John Mason Brown, *The American Theatre as Seen by Its Critics* (New York, 1934), 305–7. For a full discussion of West's Broadway plays, see my forthcoming book, *"When I'm Bad, I'm Better": Mae West, Sex, and American Entertainment* (New York, 1995).

7. Lewis Erenberg, *Steppin' Out: New York Nightlife and the Transformation of American Culture, 1890–1930* (Westport, Conn., 1981).

8. Lewis Erenberg, "Impresarios of Broadway Nightlife," in William R. Taylor,

ed., *Inventing Times Square: Commerce and Culture at the Crossroads of the World* (New York, 1991), 158–77.

9. MPPDA Resolution of June 19, 1924, reprinted in Garth Jowett, *Film, the Democratic Art: A Social History of American Film* (Boston, 1976), 466.

10. Memo from Maurice McKenzie, November 29, 1932, *She Done Him Wrong* file, Production Code Administration Collection, Margaret Herrick Library, Academy of Motion Picture Arts and Sciences (AMPAS), Beverly Hills, California (hereafter cited as PCA).

11. Wingate to Will Hays, December 2, 1932, *She Done Him Wrong* file, PCA.

12. Joy to Wingate, February 5, 1931, *Little Caesar* file, PCA, quoted in Richard Maltby, "The Production Code and the Hays Office," in Tino Balio, ed., *Grand Design: Hollywood as a Modern Business Enterprise* (New York, 1993), 40.

13. For an incisive analysis of these representational strategies, see Jacobs, *Wages,* 27–105.

14. Wingate to Harold Hurley, November 29, 1932; Wingate to Hays, December 2, 1932, *She Done Him Wrong* file, PCA.

15. Wingate to Hurley, November 29, 1932, *She Done Him Wrong* file, PCA.

16. For this draft, dated November 8, 1932, see *She Done Him Wrong* file, Paramount Pictures Collection, AMPAS.

17. See release dialogue script, January 17, 1933, R2, 1, *She Done Him Wrong* file, Paramount Pictures Collection, AMPAS. The script for the 1928 production of *Diamond Lil* is held in the Shubert Archives, New York.

18. Contrast, in particular, Bright's initial draft of November 8, 1932, with the release dialogue script, both in the Shubert Archives.

19. *New York Daily News,* February 11, 1933, 20.

20. Wingate to Hays, January 13, 1933, *She Done Him Wrong* file, PCA.

21. *Variety,* February 14, 1933, 12, 21.

22. *New York Daily News,* February 24, 1933.

23. Ben Maddox, "Don't Call Her Lady!" (clipping in possession of author from an unknown 1933 movie magazine).

24. *Variety,* February 28, 1933, 8.

25. Undated letter from Sidney Kent to Will Hays, *She Done Him Wrong* file, PCA.

26. Maltby, "Production Code," 57.

27. Telegram from Vincent Hart to Wingate, February 3, 1933; Hays to Wingate, February 27, 1933; Wingate to Harry Cohn, March 2, 1933 (all in *She Done Him Wrong* file, PCA).

28. The origins of *I'm No Angel* remain less than clear, as with all West's films after *She Done Him Wrong.* Its basic premise—a circus dancer turned lion tamer who invades and conquers high society—developed out of a short story or treatment called "The Lady and the Lions" written by writer-publisher Lowell Brentano. From there the process of revision becomes murkier. My speculation that West contributed a skeletal plot is based on the fact that the film's narrative, particularly its early sequences, bears strong similarities to West's first play, *Sex.* In both, West plays a notorious woman who is eager to escape her sleazy surroundings and has a series of comic encounters—with her male protector (who accuses her of "getting high hat"), with an ingenue (whom she urges to find a rich lover), and with a suitor (who tries to embrace

her and before whom she dances). In both, she is implicated in a jewel theft and flees into a job as an entertainer, succeeding in enchanting a rich man until her past returns to haunt her.

29. Eells and Musgrove, *Mae West,* 121.

30. All quoted dialogue was transcribed from *I'm No Angel* (MCA Universal Home Video).

31. *Variety,* October 3, 1933, 3.

32. "Making Love to Mae West," *Picturegoer* 3 (December 30, 1933): 13.

33. "Why Mae West Went to Prison," *Picturegoer* 3 (December 23, 1933): 13.

34. Ibid.

35. Memo from Vincent Hart, October 4, 1933, *I'm No Angel* file, PCA, AMPAS.

36. *New York Herald-Tribune,* October 22, 1933, 3.

37. *New York Evening Journal,* October 14, 1933, 8.

38. Carol Ward, *Mae West: A Bio-Bibliography* (Westport, Conn., 1989), 84–86.

39. Colette, *Colette at the Movies: Criticism and Screenplays* (New York, 1980), 62–64.

40. George Jean Nathan, *Passing Judgements* (New York, 1935), 266–68.

41. Gilbert Seldes, *Mainland* (New York, 1936), 119.

42. George Davis, "The Decline of the West," *Vanity Fair* (May 1934): 46, 82; Parker Tyler, *The Hollywood Hallucination* (New York, 1944), 95–99.

43. Wingate to Hart, September 16, 1933; Wingate to Hays, September 20, 1933 (both in *I'm No Angel* file, PCA).

44. Memo from Hart, October 4, 1933, *I'm No Angel* file, PCA.

45. *Variety,* October 24, 1933, 23.

46. Kathy Peiss, *Cheap Amusements: Working Women and Leisure in Turn-of-the-Century New York* (Philadelphia, 1986); Daniel Czitrom, "The Politics of Performance: Theater Licensing and the Origins of Movie Censorship in New York," in this anthology.

47. Henry James Forman, *Our Movie-Made Children* (New York, 1935), 147.

48. Ibid., 222–23.

49. *I'm No Angel* ad quoted in *Christian Century* 50 (October 25, 1933): 1327.

50. "Churches War against Obscenity," *Literary Digest* 117 (March 3, 1934): 21.

51. Jacobs, *Wages,* 16–17.

52. Martin Quigley, *Decency in Motion Pictures* (New York, 1937), 35–36.

53. See, for example, Studs Terkel, *Hard Times: An Oral History of the Great Depression* (New York, 1970).

54. Quoted in Richard Maltby, "*Baby Face,* or How Joe Breen Made Barbara Stanwyck Atone for Causing the Wall Street Crash," *Screen* 27 (March–April 1986): 44.

55. Nancy Woloch, *Women and the American Experience* (New York, 1984), 458.

56. Malcolm D. Phillips, "What Price Hollywood Now?" *Picturegoer* 3 (November 4, 1933): 12–13.

57. Alice Ames Winter to Will Hays, November 21, 1933, Hays Collection, Indiana State Library, quoted in Jacobs, *Wages,* 108.

58. Breen to Hays, December 31, 1935, *Klondike Annie* file, PCA.

59. John Hammell to Will Hays, June 29, 1935, *Klondike Annie* file, PCA.

60. Ibid.

61. Breen to Hammell, October 22, 1935, *Klondike Annie* file, PCA.
62. Noted in Breen to Hammell, September 4, 1935, *Klondike Annie* file, PCA.
63. Breen to Hammell, September 5, 1935, *Klondike Annie* file, PCA; see also ibid.
64. Memo of February 10, 1936, *Klondike Annie* file, PCA.
65. Jacobs, *Wages,* 153.
66. *New York Times,* January 27, 1938.
67. Ibid.

Foreign Parts

Hollywood's Global Distribution and the Representation of Ethnicity

RUTH VASEY

Ethnicity is always a slippery term, resistant to precise definition. It is especially elusive when used in relation to the American screen, since Hollywood studios have frequently treated indicators of ethnicity as if they were interchangeable with indicators of culture or nationality. Recent critical work on movie ethnicity has maintained this level of ambiguity by subsuming the representation of the "foreign" within a notion of ethnicity defined almost exclusively in relation to American audiences. In explaining the origins of representations of ethnic difference, critical commentary has also favored an auteurist approach, which assumes that the prejudices of particular directors (or producers) provide the key to the ethnic complexion of their films. However, these approaches ignore both the global dimensions of Hollywood's audience and the mediating influence of the institution of Hollywood itself in the construction of motion picture representations.[1]

Concentrating on the representations of foreign nationals during the studio period, this article will argue that it is not enough to say that Hollywood's ethnic characterizations have resulted from "several generations of moviemakers responding to the world around them"[2] unless "moviemakers" is defined in the broadest possible sense to include the bureaucratic hierarchies of what has long been, after all, a complex international industry. Indeed, "ethnic" characterization reveals, perhaps more graphically than any other subject, the significance of Hollywood's global market as an active and systematic influence upon the treatment of motion picture material. It also demonstrates particularly clearly the connection between the American film industry's representational strategies and its wider political, diplomatic, and economic agendas.

From the time that the American film industry first moved into wide-scale international distribution during World War I, the health of its foreign relations could be measured in strictly economic terms. Between the world wars the industry consistently derived about 35 percent of its gross revenue from export earnings, and income from abroad formed an essential part of Hollywood's highly capitalized economic structure.[3] As company directors soon learned, offense to any substantial section of its foreign market could result in lost profits through the "mutilation" or banning of films. The Mexican market provided an example of the consequences that could attend deteriorating foreign relations. In 1922 its government, incensed by successive Hollywood westerns featuring Mexican villains, placed an embargo on the entire output of the offending companies.[4] This ban came at a time when the major studios were learning to act cooperatively with respect to matters in which they had a mutual and noncompetitive interest. In the same year they formed a new trade association, the Motion Picture Producers and Distributors of America, Inc. (MPPDA), which was designed to find ways of regulating, standardizing, and defending business practices within the "organized" (read oligopolistic) industry. One of the first official acts of the MPPDA, which provided its membership with a unified front in their negotiations with government agencies both at home and abroad, was to send a representative, Bernon T. Woodle, to Mexico to negotiate market access with the Mexican government. His mission resulted in the formulation of the Mexican Resolution, in which the members of the MPPDA resolved to "do everything possible to prevent the production of any new motion picture films which present the Mexican character in derogatory or objectionable manner."[5] The resolution by no means provided a final solution to the Mexican problem. In 1923 the products of First National (originally, First National Exhibitors' Circuit) were again banned because *Girl of the Golden West* had "hurt the sentiments of the Mexican public."[6] Insulting characterizations were followed by bannings, or threatened bannings, on a fairly regular basis. Nevertheless, the MPPDA's handling of the affair formed a milestone in Hollywood's foreign policy by creating a precedent for the negotiation of trade agreements through concessions in representation. This strategy was to become increasingly influential as studios, plagued by complaints about immoral and otherwise offensive products, acquiesced to the general need for industrywide regulation of themes and treatments.

In the early twenties European countries began to use legislative measures to resist Hollywood's domination of their screens, marking a new phase of the industry's relationship with its foreign customers. Germany led the way with a "contingent" plan, which stipulated that imported films should not outnumber those produced in Germany. When Britain, France, Austria, Hungary, and others initiated similar measures, comprising a wide range of quotas and tariffs, the MPPDA decided that action was in order. The association dispatched an emissary (this time Edward G. Lowry) to assess the situation. He reported:

> Broadly speaking, this is the condition our industry faces in Europe: virtually everywhere there is being made an effort to overcome the predominance of the American picture. These efforts spring from a variety of causes. One of them is the intense spirit of nationalism that now pervades all Europe. For patriotic and political reasons, governments of the several countries now seeking to restrict the importation of American pictures desire the establishment of a national picture industry in their own country that will serve as propaganda and that will reflect the life, the customs, and the habits of its own people.[7]

Although foreign producers usually spearheaded such agitation, they found allies in governmental circles and the press when they characterized Hollywood as a threat to their national identities. Pressure from European exhibitors, who depended upon Hollywood movies for a large proportion of their profits, ensured that Hollywood's access to most markets was not seriously affected; but the imposition of restrictive legislation committed Frederick Herron, of the MPPDA's Foreign Department, to a delicate round of negotiation over the precise nature and extent of import controls. One of his principal tactics was to insist that American products were culturally and ideologically neutral, if not benign.[8] As he constantly tried to impress upon producers, this argument could best be made in the movies themselves, most simply by the avoidance of blatant causes of offense. Gradually the MPPDA assumed responsibility for identifying sensitive material and warning studios of the need for caution in particular instances.

In some cases, foreign censorship and public protest reinforced the opinion of censors and civic groups in the United States. Sex and crime were sometimes censored more stringently abroad.[9] Several countries also imposed bans on themes involving revolutionary activity, a factor which strengthened the conservative political agenda of the Hollywood product.[10] But the most strongly voiced foreign protests targeted racial and cultural slurs and stereotypes: "square-headed" Germans, "silly ass" Englishmen, effeminate Frenchmen, excitable Italians, lazy Hispanics, and so on.

In the early years of the MPPDA, its president, Will Hays, attempted to head off each international crisis as it arose. An example is the MPPDA's intervention in the screen adaptation of the Denison Clift stage play *A Woman Disputed*.[11] The play was set before and during World War I and had the French heroine submitting to the advances of a German officer to secure the freedom of her five companions, one of whom was a French agent disguised as a priest. When Joseph Schenck, of United Artists, announced plans for a screen version, the acting German consul general informed Hays that such a production would jeopardize the industry's commercial prospects in Germany: "Alone the fact that the proposed action would become known in Germany might easily spoil all your and our efforts to bring about peace and cooperation on the field of film production and film presentation."[12] In 1918 the American industry had turned out such virulently anti-German productions as *The Claws of the Hun* (Famous Players–Lasky) and *Hearts of the World* (Artcraft), but in 1926 Germany's 5-percent contribution to foreign income could not be dismissed lightly. Moreover, their contingent arrangements were weighing on the minds of MPPDA officials. Hays sent the acting consul's letter to Schenck spelling out the problem:

> The negotiations to which [the acting consul] refers have been extending over a period of some months and touch the whole matter of developing better relations with the German Government, their nationals and the press. It is one of the most important activities which we now have on. It has to do, of course, with . . . the whole matter of the treatment of the industry in Germany.[13]

Schenck's solution to the problem was elegant testimony to Hollywood's essentially pragmatic attitude towards details of ethnic representation: "The girl will be an Austrian girl, the hero an Austrian and the villain a Russian. It will be laid at the time when the Russian army marched into Austria and there will be nothing in the picture that either Austria or Germany could have any objection to."[14] From an economic point of view, Schenck's choice of a Russian nationality for his villain was a logical one. Russians usefully combined minority market status with recognizable national characteristics. At the same time, they did not impose contingent arrangements on their importation of

American movies. Either American movies were allowed into the country for the sake of the revenue they generated at the box office, which was the case in the early twenties, or they were systematically excluded.[15] Consequently, American producers could perpetuate negative Russian stereotypes without having to worry about the possibility of boycotts and bans.

By the late twenties the MPPDA was managing to address recurrent public relations problems, including its relations with the foreign market, in a relatively systematic way. In 1927 it organized the Studio Relations Committee in Hollywood to communicate directly with production personnel. In the same year, it supplied its member companies with a list of "Don'ts and Be Carefuls," which summarized the themes and subjects most commonly resulting in censorship and urged its members to correct their movies before release. Most of the eleven subjects that they decided should "not appear in pictures" and the twenty-six subjects that required "special care" in their treatment dealt with sex and crime, but cultural and ethnic representation found a place on the "Be Careful" list in a warning to producers to "avoid picturizing in an unfavorable light another country's religion, history, institutions, prominent people, and citizenry."[16] Companies were not strictly obliged to comply with the advice they received from the committee, but, as their financial executives in New York realized, they disregarded it at the risk of censorship intervention and truncated distribution. In a wider sense, it was important for the industry to maintain an image of relative social conservatism and responsibility to counteract calls for government regulation of the movie business as a whole. If a studio was tempted to look for short-term profits through the production of sensational, provocative, or transgressive products, the MPPDA was charged by its member companies to negotiate representational strategies that would not damage the long-term interests of the industry. In effect, it was the role of the Studio Relations Committee to determine what constituted the allowable limits of representation and to scrutinize the output of each studio on behalf of all the others.

The introduction of sound considerably hastened industry self-regulation by making it much more difficult to modify prints during distribution to satisfy the demands of specific markets. It became imperative to satisfy as many sections of the global audience as possible at the point of production, as recognized by the industry's adoption of the Production Code, largely an expansion and restatement of the Don'ts and Be Carefuls, in 1930. The code addressed issues of cultural and ethnic representation in terms similar to those contained in the Don'ts and Be Carefuls, requiring that "the history, institutions and prominent citizenry of other nations shall be represented fairly."[17] In practice, the treatment of matters sensitive to sections of the foreign market was guided from within the MPPDA by the adoption of an encyclopedic casebook approach, in which a catalogue of previous censorship and diplomatic problems provided the basis for advice on future productions.

Not all American movies received distribution around the world. According to Warner Bros. executive Sam Morris, the only countries to be sent all of Warners' output in the late thirties were Great Britain and Australia. The rest of the world received, on average, two-fifths of Warners' regular output each year—about twenty pictures—and Morris thought this to be typical of the foreign business conducted by the major studios.[18] Many factors affected patterns of distribution. For example, some markets were receptive to action pictures but resistant to those characterized by dialogue.[19] However, the most consistent criterion for the extent of a movie's distribution was its cost. Expensive "prestige" films had to find global acceptance to go into profit, whereas routine program pictures did not have to be shown everywhere to make their money back and consequently had to make fewer concessions to foreign sensibilities. Nevertheless, even if a movie was not destined to be widely seen abroad, foreign sensibilities still had to be taken into account during its production. As Herron insisted to Jason Joy, head of the Studio Relations Committee, in a letter regarding insulting characterizations of the French in Fox's *Plastered in Paris* (1928):

> I have taken this matter up with the Fox office here and they assure me that
> the film won't be sent to France, but of course, that is not the question. I know
> it won't be sent to France because it would be impossible to release it there. It
> is the trouble that will result from its being distributed in this country or any
> other place in the world that I'm worried about.[20]

Because of the economic and diplomatic damage that could result from inadvertent offense, *every* movie produced within the industry was scrutinized for a "foreign angle" during the course of the MPPDA's standard reviewing procedures of synopses, scripts, and finished films, regardless of its intended range of distribution.

In some cases strong representation of national groups within the United States blurred the line between domestic and foreign public relations issues. The dignity of the Irish was vigorously defended by the Catholic Church, particularly the National Catholic Welfare Conference (see Francis G. Couvares's essay in this collection). Italians, on the other hand, formed a powerful and vocal domestic constituency even without the support of the church. The Italian ambassador was apt to protest to the industry at the behest of both Italian

217

Americans and the Italian government, as occurred, for example, during the production season of 1930–31, when several movies, inspired by the exploits of Al Capone, featured Italian American gangsters. The most notorious of these films was *Scarface* (Caddo). Despite the late addition of a speech by an (apparently) Italian American character condemning the activities of the gangsters, the movie still provoked protests from community groups and the Italian embassy. Hays wrote to the ambassador explaining that the movie was an anachronism, having been held up in production for more than two years, and that current practice was "to eliminate any reference in crime pictures to individuals with names that could be connected with any foreign country."[21]

The MPPDA's policy of clouding the origins of screen characters is clearly evident in the case files of the Studio Relations Committee. For example, in 1932 Jason Joy advised that excitable characters in both *As You Desire Me* (MGM) and *So This Is Africa* (Columbia) be rendered as "not too obviously Italian."[22] Joy's successor, James Wingate, issued the same suggestion in 1933 in relation to a criminal in *The Headline Shooter* (RKO);[23] and when advising on *Our Betters* (RKO) he recommended that since the character of Pepi was likely to cause objection in South American countries, "it would be wise to avoid difficulties in this regard by omitting any references in the dialogue that label him as anything more definite than a 'foreigner.'"[24] Even characters like Frankenstein and Dracula were considered in relation to possible ethnic offense, although, as a Studio Relations Committee reviewer commented, "Dracula is not really a human being so he cannot conceivably cause any trouble."[25] By 1934 Cline M. Koon could write, "The foreign villain—even the naturalized villain—is disappearing from the motion picture."[26]

A logical outcome of this policy was the restriction of villainy to all-American characters. Ironically, therefore, the ethnic heterogeneity of Hollywood's audience, both at home and abroad, encouraged the increasing homogeneity of the screen's cast of characters. Ethnically conspicuous extras were foregone as unnecessarily risky, and ethnic villains were displaced by all-American bad guys. As early as 1930 Frederick Herron worried that the MPPDA's efforts in this direction had been perhaps *too* successful. Writing in relation to the Richard Barthelmess vehicle, *The Lash* (Warner Bros., 1930), he commented:

> I was so mad after I saw it that I saw red for days. If the picture had been made abroad it would never have been allowed distribution in this country and would probably have been objected to in every place in the world where it was shown by American representatives, and I hate to think of the loss of prestige we will experience in Washington if the picture is shown there and seen by some of our friends in the State Department. I feel I am a lot to blame on pic-

tures of this type because of the continual harping I have been going through in telling people to lay off the foreign villains and make the villains American, but I didn't know they would go quite as far as this.[27]

However, at the same time that market considerations encouraged the ethnic effacement of minor foreign characters and villains, other economic factors encouraged the recruitment of foreign leading players. Indeed, between the world wars, Hollywood's most overt concession to foreign sensibilities was its employment and promotion of clearly recognizable international stars. Foreign audiences often responded particularly warmly to the appearance of their own compatriots in Hollywood's limelight, so when the American industry "poached" acting talent from other national industries it not only weakened its competitors, it also recruited the affections and loyalties of foreign populations. Gabriel L. Hess, an attorney for the MPPDA, spelled this out in a statement he made before the Naturalization Committee in the House of Representatives in 1937:

Some of the world-wide character and appeal of American motion pictures must be credited to the employment of foreign actors in American studios.

It is reasonable to assume that to a certain extent foreign markets have been created and held by the pride and interest of the people of a country in actors of their nationality who in pictures made in America become outstanding international screen personalities.[28]

Greta Garbo constituted the most conspicuous example of a Hollywood career designed to satisfy the international marketplace. While MGM could not have predicted her phenomenal appeal around the world, it is probable that their recruitment of a Swede represented a calculated overture to Scandinavian audiences. As the United States commercial attaché in Stockholm observed in 1930, Sweden had one of the highest per-capita expenditures on motion pictures in Europe and an exceptionally large number of cinemas for a country its size. It was therefore logical for American producers to use every effort to adapt their sound pictures to local tastes to maintain their dominant position in that market.[29] Today Garbo is remembered as the quintessential screen goddess of the late twenties and thirties, but she was never overwhelmingly popular in North America, and the profitability of her films was largely due to her status in foreign territories.[30] The extent of her standing overseas is indicated by United Artists' foreign records for 1936, in which she is listed as the most popular actress in twenty-six out of thirty countries surveyed.[31] Hess cited the example of Garbo to the Naturalization Committee, along with Charles

Laughton and Maurice Chevalier; one could immediately add Marlene Dietrich, Charles Boyer, Sonja Henie, David Niven, and many others.

In 1934 the Studio Relations Committee was reorganized as the Production Code Administration (PCA), directed by Joseph Breen. By this time influential lobby groups, including some customer nations, were practiced at influencing Hollywood's policies through the agencies of the MPPDA. For example, in 1937 the Italians took exception to the comic Italian musician in *Top Hat* and the ineffective professional co-respondent in *The Gay Divorcee,* and not only banned both films, but also informed Frederick Herron that no films featuring Italians or characters bearing Italian names would be given distribution in Italy unless those characters were wholly and utterly sympathetic. Breen protested to Hays:

> I take it, from the correspondence with Ted Herron, that we are not to use Italian names, even in comedy situations. If this be true, then it establishes a further step in the general mass of restrictions, which are rapidly crowding in on us.
>
> Heretofore, we have had to be careful not to identify the race or nationality of criminals or heavies; now we shall have to go a step farther and not identify comedy characters with any specific nation, or race, of people.
>
> This is all very much to be regretted. It suggests enormous difficulty for our producers, because, once we establish this kind of rule for the Italians, it is only a mere matter of a few months before we shall have to do the same thing for the Chinese, Japs, Spaniards, Russians, Germans, French, Czechs and Poles.[32]

By the late thirties the difficulties associated with overt ethnic characterizations had led to the development of cryptic representations that relied upon the practiced interpretive skill of audiences for their comprehension. For example, *The Roaring Twenties* (Warner Bros., 1939) contains a character called Nick Brown who both is, and is not, an Italian. Clearly, Brown is not an Italian name, and he does not have an Italian accent; nothing about his appearance suggests an Italian connection (he is played by Paul Kelly); and nobody mentions the Mafia, although we learn that Brown is part of a "syndicate that's running all the high-class [bootleg] merchandise that's being sold in this country." However, the audience is introduced to him in a sequence placed in a Chicago café that begins with a close-up of a plate of spaghetti, which Brown proceeds to eat throughout the sequence. The movie's protagonist, Eddie Bartlett (James Cagney), also makes reference to Brown's fondness for spaghetti in the only other sequence in which Brown appears. In terms of Brown's ethnicity, the result is subliminally contradictory, but presumably not especially problematic for audiences accustomed to receiving their screen entertainment filtered through the MPPDA's complex regulatory mechanisms. As this example suggests, while the institutional mediation of foreign market influences could result in the obfuscation of ethnic stereotypes, it rarely managed to dislodge them from the screen altogether, as will be discussed further below.

Most customer nations relied chiefly upon external, rather than domestic, channels to bring pressure upon the MPPDA. The responsiveness of the studios to specific demands depended upon the direct economic importance of the market in question and upon the extent to which those demands were supported by diplomatic action. The industry's most influential customer, excluding the United States itself, was Britain. Despite its relatively stringent quota restrictions, it provided 30 percent of the American industry's foreign gross and was indispensable to every producer.[33] Furthermore, Britain provided a lead in motion picture standards that was followed by its possessions and colonies. The British Empire constituted the overwhelming proportion of the foreign "English version" territories, which contributed approximately 50 percent of Hollywood's foreign income. For bookkeeping purposes, some companies classified this area as a single unit, as opposed to the "foreign language version territory," which comprised all markets supplied with subtitled or dubbed prints.[34]

The British Board of Film Censors had a range of idiosyncratic requirements. For example, they would not brook cruelty to animals on the screen (actual or suggested), and they always eliminated any discussion, or even suggestion, of insanity. They also had an inflexible list of standards relating to the representation of Christian ceremonies and would not allow the material representation of Christ. This last stricture severely limited the exhibition of Cecil B. deMille's prestige production of *King of Kings* in 1928, and in 1935 caused all manner of production contortions for RKO's epic *The Last Days of Pompeii,* in which the studio contrived to keep Christ off screen solely to guarantee the movie's British distribution.[35] A more pervasive effect of the British market's influence, however, was manifested in Hollywood's depiction of colonial relations. The British were concerned about the potential influence of motion pictures upon their prestige in their colonial possessions, an anxiety reflected in the censorship provisions they imposed throughout their empire. In 1928 the Hong Kong censor told the United States consul general that upholding British prestige was central to his activity in "a small settlement of white men on the fringe of a huge Empire of Asiatics." According to a report from a United Artists agent in Hong Kong, subjects banned by the censor included armed conflict between Chinese and whites, and depictions of "white women in indecorous garb or positions or situations which would tend to discredit our womenfolk with the Chinese."[36] Restrictions of this kind prevailed throughout Britain's colonies, sometimes phrased even more pointedly in support of the ruling regime. Although the Trinidad government's "Principles of Censorship" included a local ban upon scenes dealing with obeah and witchcraft, they also included "improper use of the names or descriptions of British institutions" and "scenes intended to ridicule or criticize unfairly British social life," in addition to the following:

> Propaganda against the Monarchy, Royal dynasties or any other method or form of constitutional government.
>
> White men in a state of degradation amidst native surroundings, or using violence towards natives, especially Chinese, negroes and Indians.
>
> Equivocal situations between men of one race and girls of another race.
>
> Any picture likely to be provocative to British sentiment.[37]

Within Britain itself the Board of Film Censors banned pictures depicting the degradation of white men in Far Eastern and native surroundings.[38]

A corollary to such provisions was that the colonized, whether they were Asian or black, could not be afforded roles which endowed them with sufficient sophistication, competence, or intelligence to call into question the politics of colonial domination. These requirements inevitably filtered back to the American producers via box office receipts and reports compiled by the MPPDA. In 1928, for example, Jason Joy warned production personnel that the British would not permit "the portrayal of the white man and woman (the conqueror and governing race) in a way that might degrade him or her in the eyes of the native, nor will they permit anything in films tending to incite the natives against the governing race or to commit crime."[39]

The expensive Warner Bros. production of *The Green Goddess* (1930) exemplified the kind of product to which the imperial authorities objected. The movie depicted the fate of a small group of British travelers marooned by a plane crash in a remote mountainous area of southern Asia. George Arliss played a turbaned rajah, highly educated but essentially barbaric, who was determined to make the party atone for centuries of subjugation and exaction (see photo). "Asia has a long score against you swaggering lords of creation," he told them, "and by all the gods I mean to see some of it paid tomorrow." Worse, he had undisguised sexual designs upon the heroine. Although the movie was widely acclaimed in the United States, especially for Arliss's performance, it was considered by the British to be so dangerous that they banned it

Neither the incongruous casting of George Arliss as an Asiatic despot nor the movie's fantastical location prevented *The Green Goddess* (Warner Bros., 1930) from provoking anxiety in Britain about the representation of colonial and interracial politics. Photo courtesy Margaret Herrick Library, Academy of Motion Picture Arts and Sciences.

in their territories in the Near and Far East. *The Bitter Tea of General Yen* (Columbia, 1932) was also banned in the British territories for its depiction of an attempted seduction of a white woman, this time by a Chinese general.

In view of American film's preoccupation with heterosexual relations, it is not surprising that colonial attitudes most commonly found expression in the movies through the politics of sexual dominance. The inevitable response, which came into force under the PCA, was the banning of interracial affairs in every context except that of the politically innocuous Pacific Ocean. Olga Martin, Joseph Breen's secretary, stressed the inadmissability of miscegenation but explained, "The union of a member of the Polynesians and allied races of the Island groups with a member of the white race is not ordinarily considered a miscegenetic relationship."[40]

The British influence in general, and its impact in the area of colonial relations in particular, had far-reaching implications for Hollywood's depiction of ethnic difference. Just as the depiction of race relations within the United States could only take place within limits determined by the southern states, the industry was bound to tacit, if not active, compliance with British notions of global white supremacy. Details of representation that were contrary to British requirements could be covered by protection shots (special shots that could be inserted in the relevant prints), but the central themes of the movies needed to be consonant with an imperialistic outlook. The fact that British Empire versions did not undergo subtitling or dubbing after the introduction of sound put extra pressure on American filmmakers to produce acceptable versions in the studio.

Although the British Empire achieved its clout in Hollywood through its overwhelming economic importance, size was not everything when it came to attracting the attention of producers. Creatively applied diplomatic pressure could be as persuasive as economic muscle, and even minor foreign markets discovered that they could take advantage of Hollywood's susceptibility to international pressures by cultivating a network of diplomatic channels. Virtually all censorship charters around the world contained clauses prohibiting the exhibition of motion pictures likely to give offense to friendly countries, but the French were the first to realize that they could exercise this to their advantage by using their own diplomatic channels to insist that other nations ban movies that were offensive to French sensibilities. French diplomatic intervention stopped the circulation of *Beau Geste* in Italy in 1928, following complaints in France that the movie insulted the Foreign Legion and the French character in general. The French ambassador in Romania also demanded that the film be taken off, and the Romanian government, "anxious not to disturb the good relations between the two countries," eventually agreed to confiscate the film.[41] As a result, when *Du Barry, Woman of Passion* was made with a historical French setting in 1930, it was the subject of intense scrutiny by the Studio Relations Committee. Herron and Joy were afraid that French diplomatic intervention would prevent the exhibition of the picture throughout the foreign field and "greatly embarrass the exhibition of it in this country."[42] The French already wielded power in Hollywood that was disproportionate to their 8.5-percent contribution to foreign income because of the sensitivity of their quota negotiations. They also had their own colonial possessions, so they, like the British, the Portuguese, and the Dutch, influenced markets beyond their own borders. Their enlistment of other foreign nations to bring pressure on their behalf further enhanced their importance in the minds of executives within the MPPDA.

China was one of several countries to follow the lead of the French in recruiting the influence of its allies and trading partners. Like the Mexicans, the Chinese were especially sensitive about their treatment by Hollywood because they had been subjected to racist stereotyping since the earliest days of the industry. In 1930 the Chinese government banned Harold Lloyd's first talkie, *Welcome Danger,* after its portrayal of the residents of San Francisco's Chinatown as kidnappers, gamblers, and opium smugglers led to a riot at the Grand Theatre of Shanghai.[43] This action was followed by vigorous campaigning by Chinese diplomatic officers in other countries, resulting in several more cases of the film's rejection. As a result, the Studio Relations Committee was especially vigilant during the preparation of Universal's *East Is West* (1930). Nevertheless, even though Joy was satisfied that "the Chinese point of view has been so carefully considered that we cannot conceive of any objection from that direction," the movie was banned in British Columbia, where the censors cited business and political connections with China as the reasons for their action.[44] Cuba also ordered its withdrawal after protests from the Chinese consul general in Havana. The Chinese objections arose mainly from a slave market sequence, and Herron urged Joy to take action over such sequences while the movies were still in production:

> As I have said many times before, it's not a question of whether we should or shouldn't do these things, but it's a question of box office receipts. Universal is losing a lot of money because this film is being banned in different places of the world. It would have been much to their advantage to have given a little more time and thought to this scene before the picture was made.
>
> These diplomatic and consular representatives in a good many places of the world have very direct contacts with the foreign offices, and are able to stop the showing of pictures that they object to. Even if we can go over their heads and have these pictures passed, which sometimes happens, it requires a tremendous lot of hard work and labor.[45]

Although many countries were involved in this kind of diplomatic networking, the Chinese probably developed this approach to its most sophisticated form, managing to keep a fairly high profile at the MPPDA despite the fact that China's contribution to total foreign revenue was less than 1 percent. In 1937 Frederick Herron could assert, "It is a deep dent in the box office receipts for world circulation of any picture that runs counter to the ideas of the Chinese."[46]

By the late 1930s ethnic characterization had become such a recognized factor in negotiating American access to international markets that in 1938 the American industry was able to turn the tables on Japan when that country threatened to cut its intake of films. The American negotiators warned the Japanese that if they did not constitute a reasonably lucrative market they might find themselves singled out to wear the black hats in American movies. According to the American consulate:

> In these interviews with the Japanese authorities and representatives of the American Motion Picture Association, the former were permitted to sense a certain danger which might accompany the exclusion of American films. Almost every plot must have a villain, and the American producers find it difficult to discover a suitable nationality for such villains, encountering violent opposition from any country of which the villain happens to be a national—an opposition which sometimes results in the exclusion or boycott of films with consequent financial losses—so that for the present a disproportionately large percentage of movie villains and characters arousing feelings of resentment are American. The same attitude of opposition is shown by foreign nations toward uncomplimentary news reels. Should the producing companies decide that some one country is determined to rule them out entirely so that resentment as to villains from that particular country would not diminish the financial returns of their films, they might consider it an opportunity.[47]

Similar considerations influenced the studios' willingness to make "preparedness" and anti-Nazi films prior to World War II. In 1937 all aspects of the German film industry were placed under government control, and quota restrictions applied throughout the German territories in 1938 were so severe that they "virtually shut out" American films. Similarly, on January 1, 1939, Italy placed film distribution under a government monopoly, and American firms virtually ceased doing business there.[48] Consequently, producers ceased to be inhibited about making movies that impugned the motives and characters of their formerly cosseted customers. In working on the script for the Warner Bros. picture *Juarez* in 1938, Wolfgang Reinhardt frankly intended that "every child must be able to realize that Napoleon, in his Mexican adventure, is none other than Mussolini plus Hitler in their Spanish adventure."[49] When Jack Warner wrote to producer Bryan Foy in 1939 to warn him about the dangers inherent in offending the Chinese, the Mexicans, and especially the French, he added, "If we don't do business in Italy and Germany, that is another story, as they can't very well blackball us."[50]

Meanwhile, as nations increasingly adopted diplomatic agreements to restrict offensive films, a series of permanent and formalized agreements began to emerge. Spain and Latin America had made moves in this direction in 1930 with the convening of the Hispano-American Motion Picture Congress in Madrid. The congress was primarily intended to promote Spanish American production and distribution, but one of its resolutions was to mutually prohibit films which misinterpreted local or national customs.[51] In 1935 Spain and San Salvador were the first countries to agree formally to prevent exhibition of movies disparaging to either party or to any other of the Hispano-American countries. Production companies guilty of repeated offenses would be mutually banned. This treaty formed a precedent, and before the military coup that initiated the hostilities of the Spanish Civil War in September 1936, Spain had struck similar agreements with Nicaragua, Peru, and Chile.[52] In 1937 the Italians arranged agreements with the Germans, the Chinese, and the Turks,[53] while Chile signed an agreement with Costa Rica.[54] By 1938 these agreements had become such a common factor in the international movie trade that the chief of the Motion Picture Division of the U.S. Department of Commerce considered it a matter for comment that Australia had not entered into any such formal arrangement.[55]

The routine nature of the MPPDA's accommodation of foreign pressures in the 1930s can best be demonstrated by the case of the vexed Mexican market. In contrast to the worst excesses of the 1920s, First National's 1930 adaptation of Porter Browne's play *The Bad Man* was heavily revised to avoid causing Mexican offense before it went into production.[56] By 1931 the threat to ban had become something of a formality on Mexico's part, not necessarily denoting serious offense. In the case of MGM's *Strangers May Kiss,* the Mexican foreign office took the position that scenes set in Mexico were insulting, and "unless the picture were withdrawn immediately or the objectionable scenes deleted the Mexican government would be forced to impose an embargo on the producing company." However, when John Wilson of the PCA looked at the picture with the Mexican consul, it became apparent that the movie could be corrected to everybody's satisfaction with the excision of three simple shots.[57] By 1934 consultations and modifications took place as a matter of course. For instance, in relation to the preparation of Paramount's *The Trumpet Blows,* Maurice McKenzie reported, "Botsford tells me that before they went into production they sent the script to the Mexican government, some changes were suggested, these changes were made, and they do not anticipate any trouble on that score."[58] When the PCA pronounced the Warner Bros. property *The Where To Go Man* to be inherently insulting to Mexico in 1935, plans for its production were dropped.[59]

Yet the stereotypes adhering to locations and characters perceived as "exotic" in the United States, including Mexico, continued to prove irresistibly attractive to producers. As United Artists executive M. C. Levee commented, "There is a difference between using the name Tia Juana and some other name that is not known, because it has certain connotations—it has a meaning to the audience and brings a reaction in them that an unknown name cannot."[60] Mexico offered filmmakers Spanish names, dusty streets, donkeys, haciendas, sombreros, and erotic Spanish women. Most of all it offered them the Mexican Bad Man—a large, raucous bandit who spoke semicomic pigeon English, exhibited varying degrees of barbarous behavior, and was understandably anathema to the Mexican government.

The conflicting impulses of the producers—to avoid condemnation while retaining a place on the screen for the Bad Man—typifies the central dilemma that the industry faced in relation to ethnic characterization. The dilemma is embodied in Paramount's 1935 production, *Woman Trap,* a routine program picture about a spoilt young heiress and a city reporter who become mixed up with a gang of jewel thieves and go through a series of dangerous exploits before being rescued. In the manner of *It Happened One Night* (Columbia, 1934), they fall in love along the way. The variation on the theme in this case is that most of the action takes place in Mexico, where the jewel thieves go to hide out. The criminals are sheltered by Ramirez, described in the movie's advertising as a "self-styled Mexican bad man," played by Akim Tamiroff. They need the local knowledge of this amiable but apparently unscrupulous character to survive in the desert but plan to shoot him before they go. Ramirez becomes involved in the kidnap of the hero and heroine (Keat and Buff), and he and his servant Pancho lead them on a hot and thirsty march across the desert. It finally transpires that Ramirez is actually a Mexican G-man who has been working under cover on the case of the missing jewels. Hence the film is able to deliver a classic Bad Man up to the very last minute, while ultimately managing to praise the Mexican government for its efficiency in the field of law enforcement.

Despite such attempts to minimize offense, *Woman Trap* manages to play to the worst of its audience's prejudices toward Mexico, portraying it as a hopeless, if picturesque, Third World country. The tone of the depiction can be gauged from the Paramount Publicity Department's suggestions for lobby exploitation:

> Sombrero Still Display: A huge sombrero can be cut out of compo board and covered with stills from the picture. This can be either a flat outline of the hat or a real three-dimensional affair, several feet in height.

> Hacienda in Lobby: An attractive lobby display can be built easily by erect-
> ing the front end porch of a typical Spanish hacienda. Only the front of the
> building, painted to resemble adobe is necessary, plus the tilted lean-to roof
> and a few posts and railings. The doorway leads to a small room—made from
> the junction of the hacienda with the lobby corner. The interior can be covered
> with stills from the picture, appropriately lighted. The outside of the hut
> should be hung with serapes, sombreros on pegs, blankets and other Mexican
> knick-knacks . . . gourds, lariats, a saddle, etc. Cactus, sand and a hitching
> post will add to the display. It can be completed by dressing an usher in typi-
> cal Mexican caballero costume, standing him at the entrance to the hacienda,
> giving out programs.[61]

Although Ramirez turns out to be Señor del Valle of the Mexican Secret Police, he has lines such as "Here ees a pretty tough hombre, myself, you know!"
and worse, "Oh, yes—I am the best G's man in Mejico." The evolution of the
Mexican male from a sadistic bandit to a genial but cunning clown was no
great improvement. MPPDA president Will Hays remarked in his memoirs
that the Mexicans "preferred that we use American locales in our films, feeling
that we were liable to make mistakes in using theirs, even with the best of intentions."[62] While the industry could accommodate complaints about specific
aspects of representation, it could offer little response to general objections to
its power to fictionalize and stereotype the objects of its gaze (see, for example,
the assortment of overdetermined "foreign" extras from *Morocco* on p. 230).

In view of the problems that often adhered to foreign locations, it is not surprising that the action of many films was displaced into wholly fictional
realms. Russia may have been comparatively safe in terms of the economic consequences of offense, but fictional states such as Freedonia or Ruritania had the
additional advantage of being culturally and historically more versatile. In trying to remove *The Command to Love* (1930) from the dangerous territories of
France and Spain, Universal Studios considered either option tenable and discussed placing it in "a mythical kingdom or Russia or some kingdom where it
will do no harm."[63] Theoretically, the "mythical kingdom" option could render movies politically safe for exhibition, without modification, virtually any-
where in the world. However, since most motion pictures were not located in
purely fantastic settings, many "mythical" settings suggested actual locations,
by the choice of landscape, dress, customs, or accent.[64]

A late-thirties example of this kind of pseudofantasy location in operation is
the port of Barranca in Columbia's 1939 production *Only Angels Have Wings.*
Barranca is a South American diplomat's nightmare. It is literally rendered as
a banana republic, its fullest geographical and political description occurring
in a title declaring it a "port of call for the South American banana boats." The

Exotic "foreign" stereotypes crowd the decks of a steamer in *Morocco* (Paramount, 1930). Photo courtesy Margaret Herrick Library, Academy of Motion Picture Arts and Sciences.

establishing shots show a night scene of a crowded wharf bustling with peasants, children, dogs, donkeys, ducks, and loads of bananas. Bonnie Lee (Jean Arthur) descends from a boat to experience the local color and discovers the natives, who for some reason are holding an impromptu song and dance in the middle of an operating port, to be charming and musical. Nevertheless, she is outraged when approached by two young men (Allyn Joslyn and Noah Beery, Jr.), until she discovers that they are Americans. She exclaims, "Why, I thought you were a couple of — !" (Perhaps "Barrancans" would have sounded too ridiculous). "It sure sounds good to hear something that doesn't sound like pig Latin," she tells them. The party is nearly mown down by a quaint-looking vehicle mounted on rails, driven by hat-waving locals, blasting its horn, and pursued by cheering children. "What was that?" asks Bonnie. "Fifth Avenue bus line," reply her companions. They take her through more throngs of banana-toting natives to meet Dutchy, the "postmaster and leading banker of Barranca."

There is clearly an element of self-parody and conscious artifice in all this.[65] Barranca is therefore identified as a wholly fictional location—or is it? When Edgar Dale analyzed the content of motion pictures in 1935, he distinguished those set in "foreign locales" from those set in "imaginary" settings. In the "foreign" category he included "Orambo, a little, hot, dreary town some place on the coast of South America."[66] To this extent, *Only Angels Have Wings* is South American too. Robin Wood does not hesitate to claim, "The opening shots vividly create Barranca, the South American town in which the film is set."[67] There is a level at which the movie's denials fail and Barranca proclaims the ethnic, cultural, and economic superiority of the United States. Although the movie displays no overt interest in these issues, the narrative hook which motivates much of the action is the securing of South American airline contracts, reflecting the contemporary corporate colonialism of American carriers such as TWA. More generally, cultural offense persists on the level of performance and decor—as is it did in *Woman Trap*—in the characterizations of the natives, the easy sexuality of the local girls, and the ubiquitous bananas. One of the most insistent claims of *Only Angels Have Wings* is the quintessentially picturesque nature of the foreign. The mythical kingdom is not an empty signifier but contains a quaint exoticism of its own which can be equally brought to bear upon regional representations as diverse as medieval Europe and contemporary South America. This condition was encouraged in the thirties by the fact that most foreign subjects were shot on the same studio lots. Although "foreign" locations were dressed differently, they were elaborated with similar qualities of the exotic and picturesque. At the same time, since foreigners' national origins were deliberately obscured, the population of Hollywood's universe came to be broadly comprised of "Americans" and "others" except where overriding stereotypes existed, as in such cases as the English aristocrat and the Mexican Bad Man.

The specific requirements of foreign markets, mediated by the regulatory agencies of the MPPDA, helped define the parameters of Hollywood's representational universe. Logically, the influence of the foreign market was most perfectly absorbed when it was invisible. For example, words known to be vulnerable to foreign censorship, such as "lousy," "bum," and "bloody," simply fell out of usage. More frequently, however, the MPPDA's ploys to remove "rejectionable" subjects from the screen, whether they involved sex, crime, or foreign characterizations, tended to render tendentious subjects invulnerable to objection without necessarily making them go away. The harder the industry worked officially to defuse problematic material by making it less explicit, the less control it exercised over the activity and experience of its consumers. It is arguable, for example, that the elimination of explicit sexuality from the screen invited an erotic response from audiences, whose imaginative elaboration of the action on the screen was only limited by their experience, imagination, and desire. Equally, it is arguable that the "mythical kingdom" option, with its indeterminate "foreign" population, exaggerated the problem of cultural offense rather than alleviating it by licensing both filmmakers and audiences to exercise their most extreme prejudices with little fear of effective protest. If these results of industry regulation were unlooked-for, they were also not inconsistent with the objectives of the MPPDA. As long as the Jason Joy and Joseph Breen found ways to allow the studios to draw profits without offering up tangible hostages to public or institutional disapprobation, they were successfully fulfilling the job for which the industry paid them.

The onset of war in Europe in 1939 inevitably threw Hollywood's foreign trade into chaos, closing off many markets and making international financial transactions uncertain. The Department of Commerce remained optimistic that the industry would retain its global dimension through the application of "sound business principles, with a shrewd, judicious appraisal of world psychology and world-outlook," as indeed it had through the depression and the introduction of sound, but the studios prepared to reorganize their business practices in the face of expected foreign losses.[68] In any event, in 1939 the war transformed the foreign situation in ways that nobody could have foretold. The industry forged conspicuous new links with the State Department; and as revenues from Latin America increased, offsetting losses in Europe, Hollywood cooperated closely with the Office of Inter-American Affairs, adopting a high-profile role in ideological promotion.[69] Yet in terms of the industry's construction of ethnic characterizations, the war was rivaled in significance by the effect of the federal antitrust suit filed against the major companies in 1938. The evolution of a consistent mode of treatment had depended upon the relatively stable framework provided by the cooperative operation of large, vertically integrated companies. If war-related developments brought powerful new factors into play in the industry's balancing act of social, diplomatic, and economic factors, then postwar conditions rendered the system unworkable. In 1945 "classical" Hollywood's industrial dismemberment by a Supreme Court ruling lay only three years away.

In the period of the studio system, then, Hollywood incorporated its strategies for depicting ethnic/national/cultural differences into the broader institutional mechanisms that regulated presentation on the screen. The studios responded to the expressed sensitivities of foreign markets by making increasingly sophisticated accommodations in themes and treatments, and customer nations became ever more adept at applying economic and diplomatic influences to production through the agencies of the MPPDA. Although Hollywood did not escape from the stereotypes of the foreign that were abroad in American popular culture, its representation of ethnic and national difference underwent a complex series of transformations, displacements, obfuscations, and ameliorations on the screens of the world. The movies' deployment and modulation of these stereotypes was informed not by the personal psychologies of individual production personnel, but by the economic imperatives of global distribution. As Frederick Herron told Jason Joy in correspondence concerning *The Cuban Love Song,* "It is not a question . . . of the sensibility of these things, but it is a question of dollars and cents."[70]

NOTES

1. Several examples of this approach occur in the collection of essays edited by Lester Friedman, *Unspeakable Images: Ethnicity and the American Cinema* (Chicago, 1991). See, for example, Paul Giles, "The Cinema of Catholicism: John Ford and Robert Altman," 140–66. Ian C. Jarvie's contribution, "Stars and Ethnicity: Hollywood and the United States, 1932–51" (82–111), offers a variation on the theme by suggesting that the predilections of *screenwriters* might explain the ethnic content of Hollywood's products. On the other hand, Neal Gabler's *An Empire of their Own: How the Jews Invented Hollywood* (New York, 1988) maintains that it was Jewish *producers* who structured Hollywood's representations, including those of ethnicity. Essentially the same argument structures Mark Winokur's discussion in "Improbable Ethnic Hero: William Powell and the Transformation of Ethnic Hollywood," *Cinema Journal* 27 (fall 1987): 5–22.

2. Lester D. Friedman, "Celluloid Palimpsests: An Overview of Ethnicity and the American Film," in Friedman, *Unspeakable Images,* 32.

3. Kristin Thompson, *Exporting Entertainment: America in the World Film Market, 1907–1934* (London, 1985), 103. Thompson provides a meticulous study of the process through which American motion picture companies expanded their field of distribution into foreign territories.

4. See Arthur G. Pettit, *Images of the Mexican American in Fiction and Film* (College Station, Tex., 1980); and Peter Stanfield, "The Western, 1909–14: A Cast of Villains," *Film History* 1 (1987): 97–112.

5. "Memo Commenting upon Document Entitled 'Code, Extra-Code and Industry Regulation in Motion Pictures,'" June 22, 1938, Industry file, reel 12, MPPDA Archive, Motion Picture Association, New York (hereafter cited as MPPDA).

6. J. G. Mullen to Karl G. Macdonald, June 11, 1938, *Juarez* file, Warner Bros. Archive, Special Collections, University of Southern California, Los Angeles (hereafter cited as Warner Bros.).

7. MPPDA internal memo, "Certain Factors and Conditions Affecting the European Market," November 20, 1928, p. 19, Foreign Relations file, reel 5, MPPDA.

8. This was a parallel to the situation in the American domestic sphere, where the industry used the promise of movies free of sex and violence to hold at bay the threat of government intervention in its business practices.

9. For example, Australia, New Zealand, and Canada were particularly zealous in upholding sexual propriety and "the sanctity of the institution of marriage," while several countries in Southeast Asia rigorously excluded displays of criminal activity.

10. For example, revolutionary themes were judged to be objectionable in Spain, Sweden, and parts of China in the late twenties, and in Japan, Italy, Iran, and Poland in the late thirties. Greece banned revolutionary subjects, including the French Revolution, throughout both decades.

11. See Ruth Vasey, "Beyond Sex and Violence: 'Industry Policy' and the Regulation of Hollywood Movies, 1922–1939," *Quarterly Review of Film and Video* 15 (1995): 74–75.

12. G. Heuser (acting German consul general) to Will Hays, December 20, 1926, Titles file, reel 5, MPPDA.

13. Will Hays to Joe Schenck, December 21, 1926, Titles file, reel 5, MPPDA.

14. Schenck to Hays, December 29, 1926, Titles file, reel 5, MPPDA.

15. See Vance Kepley, Jr., and Betty Kepley, "Foreign Films on Soviet Screens, 1922–1931," *Quarterly Review of Film Studies* 4 (fall 1979): 429–42.

16. "List of 'Don'ts and Be Carefuls' Adopted by California Association for Guidance of Producers, June 8, 1927," in appendix to Raymond Moley, *The Hays Office* (Indianapolis, 1945), 240–41.

17. "A Code to Maintain Social and Community Values in the Production of Silent, Synchronized and Talking Motion Pictures," 1930, MPPDA.

18. Sam Morris to Jack Warner, July 12, 1937, Jack L. Warner correspondence, box 59, folder 8, Warner Bros.

19. See Sam Morris to Jack Warner, November 12, 1937, Jack L. Warner correspondence, box 59, folder 8, Warner Bros.

20. Frederick Herron to Jason Joy, September 14, 1928, *Plastered in Paris* file, Production Code Administration Archive, Margaret Herrick Library, Academy of Motion Picture Arts and Sciences, Los Angeles (hereafter cited as PCA).

21. Will Hays to Giacomo de Martino, June 13, 1932, Scarface-Caddo file, reel 9, MPPDA.

22. Joy to Irving Thalberg, May 12, 1932, *As You Desire Me* file, PCA; Joy to Harry Cohn, October 12, 1932, *So This Is Africa* file, PCA.

23. James Wingate to Merian C. Cooper, May 19, 1933, *The Headline Shooter* file, PCA.

24. Wingate to David O. Selznick, December 22, 1932, *Our Betters* file, PCA.

25. James Fisher, review, January 14, 1931, *Dracula* file, PCA.

26. Cline M. Koon, *Motion Pictures in Education in the United States: A Report* (Chicago, 1934), 45.

27. Herron to Joy, March 21, 1931, *The Lash* file, PCA.

28. Gabriel L. Hess, statement before the House Immigration and Naturalization Committee, February 18, 1937, in opposition to H.R. 30 (the Dickstein Bill), O'Brien legal file, box 101, folder 1, United Artists Collection, Wisconsin Center

for Film and Theater Research, Madison, Wis. (hereafter cited as United Artists Collection).

29. T. O. Klath (American commercial attaché, Stockholm), "European Motion-Picture Industry in 1929," *Trade Information Bulletin* (U.S. Department of Commerce, Bureau of Foreign and Domestic Commerce) 694 (1930): 37.

30. See Gary Carey, "Greta Garbo," in *Cinema: A Critical Dictionary,* ed. Richard Roud (New York, 1980), 415–19.

31. Garbo is recorded as being most popular in Algeria, Argentina, Austria, the Baltic states, Belgium, Bulgaria, Chile, Cuba, Czechoslovakia, Denmark, Germany, Greece, Holland, Hungary, Italy, Netherlands East Indies, Norway, Philippine Islands, Poland, Portugal, Romania, Spain, Sweden, Switzerland, Turkey, and Yugoslavia. She failed to reach the top of the list in Cristobal (where they preferred Shirley Temple), France, Puerto Rico, and the Straits Settlements.

32. Joseph Breen to Hays, February 12, 1937, *The Gay Divorcee* file, PCA.

33. See, for example, Beddington Behrens to Murray Silverstone, August 13, 1936, Giannini file, box 1, folder 2, United Artists Collection.

34. See for example, Silverstone to Hubert T. Marsh (British and Dominion Films Corp.), April 13, 1934, W. P. Philips file, box 2, folder 3, United Artists Collection.

35. See Ruth Vasey, "Diplomatic Representations: Mediations between Hollywood and Its Global Audiences, 1922–1939" (Ph.D. diss., University of Exeter, 1991), 228–33.

36. Krisel and Krisel to United Artists, March 8, 1928, Censor-Foreign file, reel 5, MPPDA.

37. "Trinidad Government Principles of Censorship Applied to Cinematographic Films," internal circular, December 31, 1929, O'Brien legal file, box 97, folder 2, United Artists Collection.

38. See *Report of the Colonial Films Committee, Presented by the Secretary of State for the Colonies to Parliament by Command of His Majesty* (London, 1930).

39. Jason Joy, "Resume of Dinner-Meeting of the Studio Relations Committee," May 17, 1928, 6, Department of Public and Industry Relations file, reel 4, MPPDA.

40. Olga Martin, *Hollywood's Movie Commandments: A Handbook for Motion Picture Writers and Reviewers* (New York, 1937), 209.

41. James H. Smiley (U.S. Dept of Commerce) to Joy, April 17, 1928, *Beau Geste* file, PCA.

42. Joy to Joe Schenck, March 21, 1930, *Du Barry, Woman of Passion* file, PCA.

43. Paul K. Whang, "The Boycotting of Harold Lloyd's *Welcome Danger,*" *China Weekly Review,* March 8, 1930, 51.

44. T. B. Fithian to John Wilson, report of British Columbian Censors, December 4, 1930, *East Is West* file, PCA.

45. Herron to Joy, January 15, 1931, *East Is West* file, PCA.

46. Herron to Breen, April 16, 1937, *The General Died at Dawn* file, PCA.

47. American consul general, Tokyo, "The Japanese Motion Picture Market in 1938," *Motion Pictures Abroad* (U.S. Department of Commerce, Bureau of Foreign and Domestic Commerce), December 1, 1938, 20.

48. Nathan D. Golden, "Review of Film Markets during 1938," *Motion Pictures Abroad* (March 3, 1939): 2.

49. Wolfgang Reinhardt, "Explanatory Note," February 15, 1938, *Juarez* file, PCA.

50. Jack Warner to Bryan Foy, March 8, 1939, Jack L. Warner correspondence, box 57, Warner Bros.

51. See "The Motion-Picture Industry in Europe in 1931," *Trade Information Bulletin* 797 (1932): 63.

52. John Harley, *World-Wide Influences of the Cinema* (Los Angeles, 1940), 264. The Spanish Civil War, which Nathan Golden described as causing American distributors "considerable concern" and resulting in "substantial losses of revenue" may have rendered these treaties irrelevant and/or unenforceable (see Nathan D. Golden, "Affect of Trade Barriers Felt in Foreign Film Markets," *Motion Pictures Abroad*, February 15, 1938, 1).

53. *World Wide Motion Picture Developments* (U.S. Department of Commerce, Bureau of Foreign and Domestic Commerce), March 15, 1937, 2.

54. Harley, *World-Wide Influences*, 262.

55. Nathan D. Golden, *Review of Foreign Film Markets during 1938* (Washington, D.C., 1939), 252.

56. Chester Bahn, quoted in *Harrison's Reports*, October 4, 1930, 160.

57. John Wilson to Herron, December 1, 1931, *Strangers May Kiss* file, PCA.

58. McKenzie, memo, April 2, 1934, *The Trumpet Blows* file, PCA.

59. Breen to Hays, December 31, 1935, *Klondike Annie* file, PCA.

60. M. C. Levee, "Commercial Requirements," in *Introduction to the Photoplay*, ed. John C. Tibbetts (1929; reprint, Shawnee Mission, Kans., 1977), 250.

61. Bill Pine and staff, undated memo, *Woman Trap* file, New York Public Library.

62. Will H. Hays, *The Memoirs of Will H. Hays* (Garden City, N.Y., 1955), 556.

63. Hays, memo, July 23, 1929, *The Boudoir Diplomat* file, PCA.

64. See Vasey, "Beyond Sex," 79–81.

65. This sits strangely with Robin Wood's claim that the movie has a "total lack of self-consciousness" (see Robin Wood, *Howard Hawks* [London, 1983], 17).

66. Edgar Dale, *The Content of Motion Pictures* (New York, 1935), 30.

67. Wood, *Howard Hanks,* 17.

68. See, for example, Murray Silverstone, United Artists internal circular, October 2, 1939, O'Brien legal file, box 10, folder 2, United Artists Collection: "Some of our foreign markets have been cut in half and others have been wiped out entirely. Serious money restrictions in many countries throughout the world, together with falling rates of exchange, make it extremely difficult for the producers of important pictures to rely on receiving the kind of revenue it is necessary for them to procure in order to recover their big investments. . . . From now on, the American distributing company has to stand on its own."

69. See Ana M. Lopez, "Are All Latins from Manhattan? Hollywood, Ethnography, and Cultural Colonialism," in Friedman, *Unspeakable Images,* 404–21.

70. Herron to Joy, December 22, 1931, *Cuban Love Song* file, PCA.

Political Censorship During the Cold War

The Hollywood Ten

STEPHEN VAUGHN

The significance of the 1947 House Committee on Un-American Activities (HUAC) investigation of Hollywood extended far beyond the film industry and involved issues—communism, treatment of labor, racism, American expansion, the interpretation of history, freedom of expression—that would divide Americans in the post-World War II era. Censors had dealt with similar issues during the 1930s, but their major worries then focused on sex and crime. With the 1947 HUAC hearings, the primary concerns of censors turned for the first time to predominantly political themes.

The hearings became a media event of international proportions. They focused attention on movie stars and other celebrities, and sensationalized the question of communist infiltration. Two of America's most ardent anticommunist post-World War II presidents, who between them would win four United States presidential elections, participated in the hearings. Richard Nixon, then a young congressman from California, was a committee member (although he was more active in other phases of HUAC work such as the Alger

Hiss case). Ronald Reagan, then an actor and still a New Deal liberal, testified before HUAC as a friendly witness in his capacity as Screen Actors Guild president.

The targets of the investigation were Hollywood leftists, mostly writers. As the October 1947 hearings approached, HUAC assembled a list of witnesses and handed out subpoenas. Those who supported the purposes of the committee became known as "friendly" witnesses. Nineteen people, mostly writers and a few directors, were "unfriendly" witnesses, and eleven of them testified: John Howard Lawson, Dalton Trumbo, Herbert Biberman, Albert Maltz, Alvah Bessie, Samuel Ornitz, Adrian Scott, Ring Lardner, Jr., Lester Cole, Edward Dmytryk, and Bertolt Brecht. Brecht left the country after his testimony, and those who remained became known as the Hollywood Ten.[1]

Behind the drama of the HUAC hearings stood fundamentally different views of cinema. One view saw film as a potent ideological medium. Since the beginning of the movies, few commentators or critics on either the right or left doubted the screen's power to transform opinion. Indeed, for many of them, nothing less than the fate of the United States and the world seemed to hang in the balance. Father Daniel Lord, the Jesuit priest who helped write the 1930 Production Code, believed that cinema could undermine Christianity and "change our whole attitude toward life, civilization, and established customs." In the years immediately following World War II, this fear of Hollywood's role in an epic struggle "to capture the minds of men"—now defined as one between Communist Tyranny and Capitalist Democracy—intensified. "The film is ideology," wrote John Howard Lawson, in many ways the intellectual leader of the Hollywood Ten, and critical in the "battle of ideas." Eric A. Johnston, who became president of the Motion Picture Association of America (MPAA) in 1945, agreed with Lawson about cinema's importance, although he held drastically different opinions about what its purpose should be. Johnston saw the world "in terms of an expanding world market." He called movies "global showcases for American techniques, products and merchandise." Ronald Reagan agreed with both Lawson and Johnston that Hollywood was a "grand, world-wide propaganda base" in the struggle with communism. Reagan, whose views were moving increasingly toward those held by Johnston, warned that whoever controlled American films had a "weekly audience of about 500,000,000 souls."[2]

Where conservatives, revolutionaries, and would-be censors imagined cinema's potential to bring about dramatic change, studio executives saw mainly a virtually unlimited possibility to make money. This is to say neither that such Hollywood moguls as Jack and Harry Warner, Louis B. Mayer, and

Y. Frank Freeman lacked political opinions, nor that they failed to argue on occasion that movies enlightened viewers. But they were reluctant to take stands on controversial issues that risked alienating the moviegoing public, and they were extraordinarily sensitive to pressure groups that threatened the box office. They may have worried in the fall of 1947 about their industry being infiltrated, and a few of them may have been genuinely appalled at HUAC's roughshod tactics, but they were primarily distressed by the bad publicity the hearings brought to Hollywood.

The HUAC hearings were confrontational, and deliberately so. The Hollywood Ten based their defense on the First Amendment and challenged the constitutionality of HUAC.[3] The committee's chair, Congressman J. Parnell Thomas, had little sympathy for the Ten's First Amendment rights. Not until the sixth day was the first of them, Lawson, called to testify. "I am not on trial here, Mr. Chairman," Lawson declared. "This committee is on trial here before the American people." Before Lawson could go much further, Thomas ordered him from the stand, and officers removed him from the room to a mixture of applause and boos from the gallery. An investigator took the stand and gave the committee evidence on Lawson's affiliation with the Communist Party, and a nine-page memorandum on Lawson was read into the record. The committee then unanimously judged him in contempt of Congress. A similar pattern emerged when the other unfriendly witnesses appeared. The committee allowed only two of the unfriendly witnesses—Maltz and Bessie—to read from statements they had prepared.[4]

Lawson and the others refused to affirm or deny their Communist Party membership on the grounds that the question violated the Bill of Rights. They also realized that to admit membership was tantamount to professional suicide. But such technicalities mattered little. The House of Representatives later overwhelmingly upheld the committee's contempt citations. Then, after court convictions, the Ten served jail sentences ranging from six months to one year.

More damaging to free expression in Hollywood was the blacklisting of the Ten. It came in the so-called Waldorf Declaration, announced in late November 1947 not by HUAC but by producers, led by MPAA president Johnston. At first Johnston considered the hearings un-American, but he was most troubled by the bad publicity that had been brought to Hollywood. He proposed, and the producers agreed, that the movie companies either dismiss or suspend the Ten without pay until they resolved the contempt charges and took an oath that they were not Communists. When the producers met a short time later in early December, they made it clear that they had blacklisted the Ten not because of moral reservations about communism but because of the public's reaction. Louis B. Mayer, for example, admitted that his first priority was to protect his business, and he would take the Ten back if they would take a loyalty oath and avoid further offense to American opinion.[5]

The HUAC hearings left Hollywood under a cloud of suspicion. FBI director J. Edgar Hoover thought it "outrageous" that the committee had gotten "cold feet" and adjourned too soon. The movie industry launched a major public relations campaign to improve Hollywood's image by creating the Motion Picture Industry Council (MPIC) early in 1948. There, such anticommunist liberals as Reagan, Walter Wanger, Dore Schary, and Allen Rivkin joined forces with such conservative producers as Cecil B. deMille and Y. Frank Freeman. The MPIC further attempted to discredit the ideas of the Hollywood Ten as it tried to convince the public that the industry had been successfully purged of Communists.[6]

Given its power to generate negative publicity, the HUAC investigation proved as damaging to Hollywood as it was controversial. It destroyed careers and reputations, devastated the movie colony's left wing, and influenced the direction of Hollywood filmmaking for a generation and more as the film industry launched a major campaign to convince Americans that it was not a refuge for subversives. The Hollywood Ten were only the first of many who would become outcasts. HUAC revisited Hollywood in the early 1950s, and a more severe period of repression and blacklisting followed.

Because of its sensationalist focus on communist infiltration, HUAC obscured important aspects of the lives and careers of the Hollywood Ten. Communism was at issue, to be sure, because the Hollywood Ten were, or had been, pro-Soviet and Marxist-Leninist in ideological orientation. But what they represented was more complex. All of them saw cinema as a means to change society. Their efforts to enhance social awareness, though, went beyond screen stories and involved novels, books, short stories, speechwriting, stage plays, and more. In many ways the Ten were ahead of their time and supported social and political causes that became part of mainstream American culture during the 1960s, 1970s, and 1980s. They wanted to improve the plight of the poor and working people, especially minorities, and to end racism and discrimination. Some of them opposed the United States' expanding global presence and denounced American foreign policy as imperialistic. Some turned to history to support their purposes. Lawson even called for a full-scale reinterpretation of American history, one that anticipated the new social history of the last several decades in downplaying the role of Anglo-Saxon elites and gave much greater play to the accomplishments of minorities and others who had been outside traditional American historical writing.

At stake in 1947, therefore, was not only the question of Communist Party affiliation but also other issues that would influence the future of American society and culture. And at stake, too, was a question of power. Who would have access to, and control of, the modern communications technology that was transforming American culture?

The Production Code of 1930 had attempted to bind motion picture entertainment to an independent Judeo-Christian standard of morality. The executives reluctantly went along with the code, believing it would avoid costly government censorship and appease such pressure groups as the Legion of Decency. But most people who made movies believed the code limited creativity, and they preferred a system that allowed them to adjust film content to public taste.[7]

Unfortunately, public taste was mercurial and could also be quite repressive. As Hollywood became more politicized, movie censors, ever sensitive to changes in the winds of opinion, became more alert to the danger of subversive themes. Political activism thrived in Hollywood throughout Franklin Roosevelt's administration, and the movie colony often divided sharply over such issues as the Spanish Civil War. During the Great Depression, the Motion Picture Producers and Distributors of America (MPPDA), under president Will H. Hays, worked to eliminate radical ideas from the screen. Hays and his lieutenant Joseph I. Breen, who headed the MPPDA's Production Code Administration (PCA), were by nature conservatives, and they instituted an "industry policy" that often went beyond the letter of the 1930 code. Hays and Breen were especially alert to anything that hinted of communist propaganda or cast American business and industry in an unfavorable light.[8]

Hollywood's extraordinary sensitivity to public opinion meant that studios were also susceptible to outside coercion. Beyond Hays and Breen lay a formidable array of forces that worked to limit liberal themes on the screen. They included pressure groups, powerful publishing magnates, and the continued threat of government intervention. The Roman Catholic Legion of Decency, for example, exerted influence over Hollywood during the 1930s by threatening to lead its several million followers in a boycott against any movie it deemed immoral—not an insignificant threat during the early years of the depression, when studios were having difficulty breaking even financially.[9]

The reactionary publishing tycoon William Randolph Hearst demonstrated that he could bring a studio to its knees. In spring 1937 Warner Bros.' leading male star, Errol Flynn, traveled to Spain to see firsthand the Civil War because of the "confusing news and the fact that all the American press [was] in the hands of powerful 'trusts.'" Hearst threatened to brand Flynn a communist and launch a campaign against the actor that would destroy his career. "There have been altogether too many pictures made by . . . Reds, Pinks, and Punks in which the communist doctrine was surreptitiously spread," Hearst warned Jack Warner in April 1937. Warner quickly fell into line and muzzled Flynn when he returned to the United States. Even Warner Bros., a studio with a reputation for social consciousness, was unwilling to push reform very far in its films before World War II.[10]

As war approached, moreover, elements of the federal government showed themselves willing to bring pressure on the studios over movie content. In September 1941 the United States Senate held public hearings on whether Hollywood films were guilty of warmongering. The investigation petered out when committee members admitted they had not seen many of the pictures under consideration and, more importantly, as the international situation worsened. After Pearl Harbor, the political winds shifted. Now the national emergency legitimated both prowar propaganda and censorship on grounds of national security. Government interest in promoting patriotism and fighting subversion became, if anything, even more salient with the onset of the cold war. By the late 1940s, therefore, the movie industry had become more implicated in American politics and yet less likely to serve as fertile ground for social experimentation or attacks on national policy than it had ever been.

The Hollywood Ten had always experienced problems with censors. Many of their controversial ideas had been smothered at the studio level, and, of course, Breen and his staff in the PCA went over each script carefully. But in 1947 a far more drastic form of suppression, directed from Washington, D.C., was applied to the Hollywood Ten. The public hearings of October turned the spotlight of national publicity on them, and, once publicly associated with the Communist Party, they became box office poison for the studios.

HUAC chief investigator Robert E. Stripling claimed that the movie industry was part of a plan to "communize the country." The writers, he believed, were trying to subvert Americans' faith in their leaders and institutions by portraying capitalists, politicians, and other authority figures as "exploitative, brutal, and corrupt."[11] Although Stripling and the members of HUAC oversimplified matters, it was true that the Hollywood Ten had a history of activism that made them controversial. Most important in this regard were their ties to the Communist Party. Of course, during the Great Depression, many people in Hollywood flirted with Marxism and then abandoned it. Several of the Hollywood Ten, though, retained a commitment throughout their lives.

Lawson, the Ten's ideological leader, had achieved a reputation as a left-wing playwright, screenwriter, historian, and political and dramatic theorist. He joined the New York Communist Party in 1934, talked with Earl Browder about establishing a party unit in Hollywood, and led a group there that studied Marxism with party theoretician V. J. Jerome. Lawson headed the Communist Party in Hollywood from 1937 until he went to jail in 1950.[12] He also helped found the Screen Writers Guild and became its first president. During the war and after, meanwhile, he became a force in the Hollywood Democratic Committee, later called the Hollywood Independent Citizens Committee of the Arts, Sciences and Professions (HICCASP). In 1946 Lawson, together with Maltz, Trumbo, and Bessie, started the Marxist literary journal, *Mainstream.*[13]

Lawson exercised considerable influence over left-wing writers in Hollywood. It was "expected that you would show your work to Jack," Albert Maltz recalled, and it became "a widespread . . . malign thing, and . . . Jack just got a bigger and bigger ego, all of which was hidden by an outward show of modesty." Maltz further believed that by being too generous with his time, both the quality of Lawson's own work as well as the criticism he offered declined. Other Hollywood insiders agreed that his commitment to ideology destroyed his "vitality and creativity."[14]

One of Lawson's grandest goals was to change the economic organization of Hollywood. The studio executives, he said, were little more than "'cultural' servants of Wall Street . . . monopolists," whose movies were imperialistic propaganda for a "cult of war, racism and the 'superiority' of an elite class." "The ideological struggle must be waged nationally," he declared a few weeks before the 1947 HUAC hearings, "in the whole field of culture."[15]

Lawson's sympathy for the Soviet Union sometimes appeared in the scripts for such films as *Blockade* (1938) and *Action in the North Atlantic* (1943). The latter, which appeared while the USSR and the United States were allied against Nazi Germany, clearly had a pro-Soviet tone. At the film's end, as planes emblazoned with the Red star fly overhead, the Americans on board ship say, "They're on our side." Later, as a crippled ship enters port, the English-speaking sailors are greeted by Russians as "comrades."[16]

Dalton Trumbo was perhaps the most talented writer among the Hollywood Ten. His 1939 novel, *Johnny Got His Gun,* won the National Book Award, and another novel, *The Remarkable Andrew* (1941), was turned into a movie of the same name by Paramount in 1942. His screenwriting credits included *Kitty Foyle* (RKO, 1940), nominated for an Academy Award; *Thirty Seconds over Tokyo*

(MGM, 1944), which won a *Boxoffice Magazine* Award; and *Our Vines Have Grapes* (MGM, 1945), a *Parents Magazine* Medal picture. After being black-listed he continued to write under various pseudonyms while self-exiled in Mexico. Writing under the name Robert Rich, Trumbo won an Academy Award in 1957 for the screenplay for *The Brave One*. In 1960 he worked on screenplays for *Exodus* and *Spartacus*.

Possessed of a quick mind and keen wit, if Trumbo had a "fatal flaw," ac-cording to Maltz, it was that "he loved to live on a very grand scale." He owned a $100,000 Beverly Hills home and a ranch in the Tehachapi Moun-tains, all made possible by a lucrative contract with Metro-Goldwyn-Mayer. Maltz remembered him as "completely intolerant of dullness."[17] How he tol-erated the dullness of Communist Party meetings is a mystery, as is the date of his membership. He claimed to have entered the party in 1943 and severed ties with it in 1948. But screenwriter Paul Jarrico said he recruited Trumbo during the time of the 1939 Soviet-Nazi pact, and the Communist press seri-alized Trumbo's novels during this period.[18] Like Lawson, Trumbo saw capi-talism at the root of society's troubles. He also linked studio executives to Wall Street greed and wanted to change Hollywood's economic structure. "The fight for freer use of the screen as a weapon for human decency" depended, he claimed, "fundamentally upon an organizational basis." In addition to his screen work, Trumbo served as a speechwriter for several Hollywood stars in-cluding Edward G. Robinson, Katharine Hepburn, and Olivia de Havilland. Indeed, the speeches he prepared for de Havilland to deliver in June 1946 helped precipitate a crisis in HICCASP that led several anticommunist liber-als to resign over the issue of disassociating liberalism from communism.[19]

Other members of the Hollywood Ten held ideological views similar to those of Lawson and Trumbo. The director Herbert Biberman, who was mar-ried to the actress Gale Sondergaard (who herself would later be blacklisted af-ter appearing before HUAC in 1951), spoke with such "contagious enthusi-asm" and "with such authority and conviction that it was impossible not to believe him."[20] Lester Cole, who joined the party in 1934, recalled that Maxim Gorky's novel *Mother* had led him to communism.[21] Ring Lardner, Jr., the son of the well-known humorist and the youngest of the Hollywood Ten, consid-ered himself "a socialist, with the conviction that for Russia at least, the Com-munist variety of that doctrine was the most appropriate."[22]

Some of the Ten were occasionally at odds with one another over ideology. Alvah Bessie was a self-taught Marxist, who, like Lawson and Cole, was doc-trinaire. When, in early 1946, Albert Maltz attacked the Communist Party's dogma that art should be a weapon in the class conflict, Bessie denounced him as "un-Marxist." "We need more than 'free' artists," he declared. "We need *Party* artists."[23] After being attacked, Maltz retracted his criticism, although he continued to assert that a writer was obligated to be the "conscience of the people." In his first novel, *The Underground Stream* (1940), he wrote, "Intellectuals ally themselves to the revolutionary movements of their time out of a vision of a new society, or from indignation at injustice, or from an embittered idealism." He told about a party member who chose to die rather than compromise his beliefs. "A man must hold to his purpose. This—nothing less—is the underground stream of his life. Without it he is nothing." But in life, Maltz seemed to have trouble ascertaining where the stream led. When director Edward Dmytryk, with whom Maltz served in prison, broke with the Ten and left the party in 1951, Maltz tried to discredit him. In the end, Maltz, too, left the party in 1956 after Nikita Khrushchev disclosed Stalin's atrocities.[24]

Even had the Hollywood Ten not been associated with the Communist Party, it is likely that their outspoken left-wing views would have made them the center of controversy and the target of censors after the war. But the turmoil over communism served to discredit their ideas and those of many others who promoted causes, some of which a few years earlier had been part of the New Deal agenda, others of which a few years later became a part of mainstream American politics. "Over the years," Lester Cole would write in 1981, "yesterday's 'subversion'" became "accepted reality."[25]

Although unfashionable in the conservative postwar climate, the concern among the Hollywood Ten for workers was long-standing. One of Lawson's early works, *Processional* (1925), depicted labor strife in the coal fields of West Virginia. He participated in the effort to save Sacco and Vanzetti. In 1934 he had been part of a delegation that had visited and reported on the Scottsboro Boys, seven black boys falsely accused of raping two white girls on a freight train. Soon thereafter he returned to Alabama to investigate a steel strike and its impact on African Americans. On both occasions he was jailed by local authorities.[26] During the studio strikes that began in 1945, Lawson, Trumbo, Maltz, and Adrian Scott honored picket lines when workers struck Warner Bros. in the fall of that year. Lawson was especially visible on the picket lines and in organizational meetings. He so infuriated Jack Warner by his participation in the walkout at the studio in 1945, that in May 1947, when Warner testified before a closed session of HUAC, he gave the committee a picture of the writer with the strikers.[27]

Like Lawson, Maltz had been radicalized by the Great Depression. It was an "age of social change," he wrote in 1940, when history had taken the task of creating a new vision for society away from "philosophers, . . . thinkers and priests" and turned it over to the "humble and anonymous." In conducting research for his proletarian novel *The Underground Stream,* he went to Detroit in late 1936 to learn firsthand about the sit-down strikes in the automobile industry organized by the Congress of Industrial Organizations (CIO).[28] Trumbo, too, had been a longtime supporter of labor causes. In early 1941 Trumbo denounced the deportation hearings for the California director of the CIO, Harry Bridges, as contrary to the "principles of the Constitution and to the traditions of the American people."[29]

Although committed to radical causes, those who were to become known as the Hollywood Ten understood the virtual impossibility of bringing an openly anticapitalist picture to the screen. Lawson expressed pessimism about the possibility of producing prolabor films. He believed the economic realities inherent in the studio system prevented Marxist writers from accomplishing much.[30] Cole was more optimistic. He tried to "inject . . . reality" as he saw it into such pictures as *The President's Mystery* (1936). His prosocialist and prounion views, he believed, were "often . . . represented in attitudes of the characters" he created. In 1940 Cole undertook the screenplay for Universal's adaptation of *The House of the Seven Gables.* He changed one of Nathaniel Hawthorne's main characters, Holgrave, from "a 'radical' with only abstract philosophical tendencies, to an active abolitionist." Cole, who "showed Northern capitalists of 1850 engaged in illegal slave trade," hoped the movie would be a "radical bombshell." But he also realized that in this and other films his success was limited. He was particularly upset that the script for one of his projects, *Blood on the Sun* (1945), was altered to muffle its message. "It was worse than going to jail," he said; "the evisceration of a politically meaningful script cut right into my soul."[31]

Another one of the Ten, Herbert Biberman, directed one of the most accurate representations of working-class life ever to appear in an American film, but it was not completed until after he left prison. *Salt of the Earth* (1954), a film about striking New Mexico miners, employed real mine workers and their families in the leading parts. The movie received acclaim in Europe, especially in France and in Czechoslovakia, where it won awards. But in the United States, the Motion Picture Industry Council mounted a campaign to discredit it, and Roy Brewer's International Alliance of Theatrical and Stage Employees projectionists refused to show it. Not until 1965 was the movie shown widely.[32]

The Hollywood Ten united on yet another cause. They opposed racial and ethnic discrimination. That six of them were Jewish helps to account for their sensitivity to this issue and to explain opposition to their work by those who

Herbert Biberman and a Mexican American boy actor on the set of *The Salt of the Earth* (1954). Courtesy of the Biberman-Sondergaard Collection, State Historical Society of Wisconsin, Madison, Wisconsin.

were anti-Semitic. Lawson's grandparents came to the United States from Poland during a wave of German-Jewish immigration in the mid-nineteenth century. Sensitive about his heritage, he denied being Jewish while an undergraduate at Williams College but later understood that he "could not be American without also being Jewish."[33] Biberman's parents were Russian Jews. Cole (né Lester Cohn) was the son of Polish-Jewish immigrants. Bessie came from an upper-middle-class Jewish family. Maltz was the son of a Jewish Lithuanian immigrant who became a successful building contractor in the United States. When another of the Ten, Samuel Ornitz, testified before HUAC, he emphasized his Jewishness and denounced the bigoted Mississippian John E. Rankin, who was on the committee.[34]

During the 1930s several of the Ten had found the struggle for black civil rights to be a catalyst for their emerging activism. Probably none of them was more energized by the struggle than Lawson. After his visit to the South in 1934 to report on the Scottsboro Boys, he concluded that in both Alabama and Georgia, fascism was on the rise and "powerful groups of politicians . . . were proceeding to Hitlerize those states in defiance of the majority of white and Negro citizens."[35] During the war and afterward, as an influential member of the Hollywood Democratic Committee (later known as HICCASP), Lawson played a part in issuing a policy statement that called for "stamping out the sources of native fascism," that is, racism. Later he asserted that racism was "not a natural tendency of human beings" but "something which is developed artificially in the interest of certain powerful groups because it benefits them and returns a profit for them."[36]

In their linking of discrimination, capitalist oppression of labor, and imperialism, the Ten used history as a weapon. Sometimes they used it to justify the Soviet Union's interventionist foreign policy. Sometimes, though, they provided a solid critique of prevailing historical opinions, and at their best, they sought through their work to create a collective memory sympathetic to the causes of the poor and minorities. In this respect, Lawson made the most comprehensive reinterpretation of the past. He began to study history seriously in 1934, and by 1941 his ideas about American culture had taken form. He believed that contemporary writers faced "literally—the task of *making history.*" If at times Lawson sounded the standard Marxist line—for example, in 1947 criticizing historian Vernon Parrington, the author of *Main Currents in American Thought,* for failing "to grasp the essential fact that class struggle is the driving force of history"—at other times he engaged issues that also absorbed many professional historians of his own time and afterward. In 1941, focusing on the founding era, he argued that there was "no important development of social or economic theory in the early life of the Republic" and criticized Thomas Jefferson for a lack of "systematic thinking on social problems." He also called for a reinterpretation of Reconstruction, which he called the "proudest part of our Democratic heritage." Through such works as *The Hidden Heritage* (1950), Lawson encouraged a full-scale reexamination of the American past.[37]

Convinced of the "greatness and nobility" of African Americans, Lawson sought especially to recover their heritage. He criticized the historical profession in general and specifically condemned such prominent historians as Claude Bowers, who treated Reconstruction as a misguided attempt to elevate blacks and a cruel injustice to southern whites. "The monstrous myth of racism is rejected by social science," Lawson wrote in 1947, "but it is propagated shamelessly by every American official historian."[38]

In *Hidden Heritage,* a book Lawson started several years before the HUAC hearings and finished as he awaited prison, he condemned the entire structure of Anglo-Saxon superiority. The roots of racism lay in capitalist culture, whose "Protestant pirates" brought slaves to the New World and whose "Puritan conscience" had "accepted the servitude of the underprivileged as proof of God's grace." Sounding not unlike Stanley Elkins, whose *Slavery* (1959) would influence American views of "the peculiar institution" in the postwar era, Lawson condemned the white man who, having stolen the "fruit of the Negro's labor," now had "to accept the psychological disabilities and irrational prejudices that accompanied the gift."[39] Ranging beyond the United States, Lawson attacked white supremacy in South Africa. While in prison he prepared anonymously a screenplay based on Alan Paton's acclaimed novel, *Cry, the Beloved Country* (1948). Four years later, a film based on Lawson's screenplay was produced in South Africa.[40]

Like Lawson, virtually all of the Hollywood Ten tried to eradicate stereotypes of African Americans. Trumbo, who like Lawson believed capitalism encouraged racism, accused Hollywood movies of making "tarts of the Negro's daughters, crapshooters of his sons, obsequious Uncle Toms of his fathers, and . . . strutting peacocks of his successful men." In *The Underground Stream* (1940), Maltz had written that the "Party set up the standard of absolute equality between Negro and white." Biberman's production of *New Orleans* (1947) won praise from the black press as a perceptive treatment of African Americans.[41]

As they explored the history of African Americans, members of the Hollywood Ten also tried to rediscover the traditions and repudiate the mistreatment of southern and eastern European immigrants and other minorities. Lawson insisted, "One could not ignore the native culture of Indians, or the influences emanating from Spanish America or the significance of the more recent influx of people, with their distinctive beliefs, customs and skills, from Asia and the Pacific Islands."[42]

Anti-Semitism was one of the major targets of the Hollywood Ten. Cole tried to unmask Nazi cruelty toward Jews in *None Shall Escape* (1944), while Maltz attacked anti-Semitism in *The Pride of the Marines* (1945).[43] *Crossfire* (1947), the inspiration of Adrian Scott and championed by Edward Dmytryk (neither of whom were Jewish), was the first full-scale postwar assault on anti-Semitism in a Hollywood film. Most likely the content of this movie led to Scott and Dmytryk's being called before HUAC.[44]

The Hollywood Ten's Marxism inevitably set them at odds with the movie industry's leaders and made them outspoken critics of American expansionism.

Even before the Waldorf Declaration, according to Biberman, they had been warned that the new MPAA president, Eric A. Johnston, had been made president of the movie industry by financial interests that wanted "to turn Hollywood into a blurb factory for the political era based on the bomb." Biberman believed that business leaders had long wanted "to create an American world" and had turned to Hollywood to promote "tough-minded Americanism."[45]

It is difficult to imagine a person more ideologically different from the Ten than Johnston. The four-time president of the United States Chamber of Commerce, he replaced Will Hays as president of the motion picture industry in 1945. Hays, of course, had insisted that film endorse American business, but Johnston was even more enthusiastic about using motion pictures to advance capitalism and criticize the Soviet Union. During a visit to the USSR in 1944 he told his hosts that in "economic ideology and practice my country is not only different from yours," but "it is *more* different from yours than is any other country in the world." And, he continued, *"we are determined to remain so*—and even to become more so."[46]

In particular, he argued, one could not minimize how much American exports "profited through the demand for American merchandise initially observed by foreign moviegoers in American films." Johnson believed that film, which knew no international boundaries, was the "greatest conveyor of ideas—the most revolutionary force in the world today." Hollywood, he suggested, could become a part of a "partnership capitalism" with other countries that would ensure the "never-ending expansion" of "dynamic Capitalism" in the United States and worldwide.[47]

Given Johnston's strong opinions and the views of such like-minded men as Reagan, Cecil B. deMille, and Y. Frank Freeman, who dominated the Motion Picture Industry Council, it is little wonder than the Hollywood Ten became outcasts. Moreover, their actions came back to haunt them. As champions of a foreign power whose line they had faithfully espoused for years, many of the Ten not only indicted the American class and racial order, but they also attacked the American foreign policy as a manifestation of Western imperialism.

As far back as 1939, after the signing of the Soviet-Nazi nonaggression pact, some of the Ten became apologists for the USSR, arguing that imperialism threatened world peace more than did Hitler and trying to prevent American entry into the war. In their efforts, they blatantly misused history. Cole ransacked Finnish history to rationalize the Soviet invasion of that country. Maltz argued in 1940 that the French and British governments were helping Hitler dismember Europe. Biberman tried to convince American Jews in early 1941 that their real enemy was not so much Hitler as British imperialism. At a conference of the Jewish People's Committee held in Los Angeles, Biberman said, "There is no peace to be made with the bloody, avaricious, greedy imperialists the world over." The conference was "an outgrowth of a national movement to combat those groups and forces" which were using "the Jewish people's anti-Nazi sentiments to make of them pawns for British imperialism and line them up for American entrance into the war."[48]

Trumbo allowed those who wanted to keep the United States out of the war to exploit his novels, *Johnny Got His Gun* (1939) and *The Remarkable Andrew* (1941). *Johnny Got His Gun* was an antiwar story told through the thoughts of a World War I veteran who had lost his sight, hearing, face, and limbs, a person "without a single ray of hope to lighten his sufferings." *The Daily Worker* serialized the novel in early 1940, calling it a "passionate indictment of imperialist war" while describing Johnny as "one of many courageous young Americans out of whose bodies Wall Street built a barricade behind which they guarded their profits." (Interestingly, during the Vietnam War, *Johnny Got His Gun* was revived and in 1971 made into a film which Trumbo directed.) The *People's World* published excerpts from *The Remarkable Andrew* in April 1941. In that novel, Trumbo used the ghost of Andrew Jackson to criticize the British for being undemocratic and to question whether the United States should attempt to stop German aggression.[49]

When Hitler turned against the Soviet Union in 1941, the Ten suddenly embraced the Allied struggle and remained exuberant patriots throughout the war. In 1945 they just as abruptly abandoned their Popular Front enthusiasm for America's worldwide mission. As the Soviet-American alliance deteriorated, they resumed their sharp criticism of what Lawson called "imperial democracy."[50] At a HICCASP meeting Lawson condemned the United States for its belligerence and praised the USSR for its "peaceful" approach to other countries. Following his speech HICCASP members adopted a resolution that opposed American intervention in China's internal affairs.[51] Cole stated his belief that Stalin's paranoia sprang from the fact that "for decades, the Soviet Union was surrounded by military forces which had vowed to destroy the first socialist revolution." After World War II Trumbo accused American corporate interests of seeking war against the Soviet Union and protested nuclear testing on Bikini Island and military exercises in the Arctic. A few years later several of the Hollywood Ten opposed United States involvement in the Korean War. While incarcerated, Bessie sympathized with prisoners who contested the war. During their stays in prison, Cole and Lardner (who, in 1971, two decades later, would win an Academy Award for the screenplay of the antiwar film *M*A*S*H,* which was set in Korea) condemned the Korean War.[52]

Whatever the value of their views, the Hollywood Ten became easy targets for those out to settle scores or find scapegoats in the new political order that emerged with the cold war. Abandoned by former colleagues and employers, vilified in the press, and denounced by members of Congress, the Ten sought public support to little avail after the Waldorf Declaration in late 1947. Years of litigation followed as, collectively and individually, the Ten initiated eight civil suits against the studios, claiming conspiracy to blacklist and breach of contract. But they met with only limited success. For a while they held out hope that the U.S. Supreme Court might reverse their convictions for contempt, but the Court's makeup changed in 1949, when Justices Wiley Rutledge and Frank Murphy died, and more conservative judges replaced them. Prison was unavoidable.[53]

After prison one of the Ten, Edward Dmytryk, managed to regain employment in Hollywood by going through a rehabilitation process led by Reagan, Roy Brewer, and the Motion Picture Industry Council. It involved confessing past Communist Party affiliation, recanting all ties to the party, and naming other party members.[54]

Most of the others remained unbowed, however. "The fight for the conscience, for the soul, of the American film, is not ended," Lawson proclaimed in 1949. He remained an apologist for Stalin and the Soviet Union after his release from prison. In *Film in the Battle of Ideas* (1953), he offered a Marxist-Leninist critique of American civilization, quoted Stalin, and wrote approvingly of the USSR and communist China. The Soviet Union "emerged from the war [World War II] steeled and strengthened in the anti-fascist struggle, dedicating its vast resources to peaceful reconstruction and the cultural enrichment of its people," Lawson asserted. During the early 1960s he traveled and lived in the Soviet Union, dedicating his 1964 book, *Film: The Creative Process,* to the Association of Film Makers of the USSR.[55] Like Lawson, Lardner still considered, as late as 1976, the "basic tenets of socialist doctrine . . . as plausible" as they had been when he was younger—although he did acknowledge that he had deluded himself about communism "on a number of points."[56] Cole remained faithful to the Communist Party until the 1980s (although Maltz, as noted, left the Party in 1956).[57]

But in late 1947 the immediate future remained bleak for those members of the Hollywood Ten who did not recant. The House Committee on Un-American Activities hearings of that year and the blacklist that followed were only precursors of what was to come. In the midst of the Korean War, HUAC opened new investigations of communism in Hollywood in the spring of 1951. Such groups as the American Legion and Veterans of Foreign Wars exerted enormous pressure on the movie industry to purge itself of the disloyal. The studio heads quickly caved in, and blacklists greatly expanded.[58]

But important developments would also occur that helped open the screen to new ideas. In 1952 the United States Supreme Court in the so-called *Miracle* case (*Joseph Burstyn, Inc. v. Wilson*) gave motion pictures for the first time the same protection under the First Amendment as other forms of expression. The high court further extended that protection in such cases as *Roth v. United States* (1957) and *Ginzburg v. United States* (1966). The American public, ever changeable, became more permissive in what it would tolerate. Even the Legion of Decency liberalized the way it evaluated movies as its power declined in the new era. In 1968 the industry abandoned the Production Code and adopted a new rating system, which gave the public the final say in determining what could be seen (albeit not in determining what was produced or distributed). As a result of such developments, and in conjunction with the changes brought by the Great Society, the civil rights movement, and the protests against the Vietnam War, the Ten's critique of American society found much greater acceptance when a new generation came of age during the 1960s and 1970s. Then, as the filming of Trumbo's *Johnny Got His Gun* and the enormous success of Lardner's *M*A*S*H* indicates, some of the Hollywood Ten's message—now less associated with the party line and the cold war—reached a much larger, and more receptive, audience.

NOTES

1. This chapter is based on research in the following archival collections: the John Howard Lawson Papers, Southern Illinois University, Carbondale (hereafter cited as JHL-SIU); the papers of Alvah Bessie, Herbert Biberman and Gale Sondergaard, Melvin Douglas, the Hollywood Democratic Committee Papers (cited as HICCASP), Ring Lardner, Jr., Albert Maltz, Dalton Trumbo, and Walter Wanger, State Historical Society of Wisconsin, Madison (cited as SHSWM); the Jack L. Warner Papers, University of Southern California, Los Angeles (cited as JLW-USC); the files of Dallas C. Halverstadt, Harry S Truman Library, Independence, Mo. (cited as HSTLI); and the Oral History Research Office, Popular Arts Project, Butler Library, Columbia University, N.Y. (cited as BLCU-NY).

Among the best studies that place the Ten in the context of Hollywood politics are Larry Ceplair and Steven Englund, *The Inquisition in Hollywood: Politics in the Film Community, 1930–1960* (Garden City, N.Y., 1980); Nancy Lynn Schwartz (completed by Sheila Schwartz), *The Hollywood Writers' Wars* (New York, 1982); and Thom Andersen, "Red Hollywood," in Suzanne Ferguson and Barbara Groseclose, eds., *Literature and the Visual Arts in Contemporary Society* (Columbus, Ohio, 1985), 141–96.

2. See Daniel A. Lord, *Played by Ear: The Autobiography of Daniel A. Lord, S.J.* (Chicago, 1955), 273; Walter Wanger, "Tulsa Speech," April 12, 1949, folder 4, box 37, Wanger Papers, SHSWM; John Howard Lawson, *Film in the Battle of Ideas* (New York, 1953), 10, 11, 17, 22; and Ronald Reagan, with Richard G. Hubler, *Where's the Rest of Me?* (New York, 1965), 162. Eric Johnston quoted in Stephen Vaughn, *Ronald Reagan in Hollywood: Movies and Politics* (New York, 1994), 197.

3. On the Ten's legal strategy at the hearings, see Ceplair and Englund, *Inquisition,* 263–71.

4. The statements of the Hollywood Ten can be found in Gordon Kahn, *Hollywood on Trial: The Story of the Ten Who Were Indicted* (New York, 1948), 72–77, 82–84, 87–90, 92–94, 98–100, 101–4, 106–9, 111–12, 115–17, 118–20, 124–26. Testimony of John Howard Lawson, October 27, 1947, "Hearings regarding the Communist Infiltration of the Motion Picture Industry," in *Hearings before the Committee on Un-American Activities, House of Representatives* (Washington, D.C., 1947), 291, 294, 295–304.

5. See Vaughn, *Ronald Reagan,* 153.

6. For Hoover quotations, see D. M. Ladd to director, August 6, 1948, Ronald Reagan FBI file, SHSWM. On the MPIC, see Vaughn, *Ronald Reagan,* 182–93.

7. I have tried to provide a more detailed account of the code's creation and adoption in "Morality and Entertainment: The Origins of the Motion Picture Production Code," *Journal of American History* 77 (June 1990): 39–65.

8. For a discussion of industry policy, see Gregory D. Black, *Hollywood Censored: Morality Codes, Catholics, and the Movies* (New York, 1994), 244–91.

9. See the essays by Couvares, Parker, and Vasey in this collection.

10. *Hollywood Reporter,* April 15, 1937, 7; William Randolph Hearst to Jack Warner, April 22, 1937, folder 1, box 59, JLW-USC.

11. Robert Stripling, *The Red Plot against America* (Drexel Hill, Pa., 1949), 70–71.

12. On Lawson's leadership of the Communist Party in Hollywood, see Schwartz, *Hollywood Writers' Wars,* 88. See also Ceplair and Englund, *Inquisition,* 60–65.

13. For the publication's allegiance to Marxism, see "Statement of Purpose," *Daily People's World* (San Francisco), October 1, 1946, 5.

14. Albert Maltz, "The Citizen Writer in Retrospect," typescript interview by Joel Gardner, 2 vols., University of California Oral History Program, 1983, 1:515; and Margaret Brenman-Gibson, *Clifford Odets: American Playwright, the Years from 1906–1940* (New York, 1981), 285. See also Schwartz, *Hollywood Writers' Wars,* 153.

15. See Lawson, *Film in the Battle of Ideas,* 10, 17 (also 11, 22); and John Howard Lawson, "Introduction to Panel Discussion," August 3, 1947, 2, box 12, JHL-SIU).

16. The quotations are from film dialogue.

17. Maltz, "Citizen Writer," 1:329, 2:692.

18. See Helen Manfull, ed., *Additional Dialogue: Letters of Dalton Trumbo, 1942–1962* (New York, 1970), 435 n. 16; and Schwartz, *Hollywood Writers' Wars,* 185.

19. Dalton Trumbo to Sam Sillen, 1946, "Trumbo Correspondence (January 1–

December 1946)," box 1, Dalton Trumbo Papers, SHSWM. See also Vaughn, *Ronald Reagan,* 127–32.

20. Stephen Fritchman, quoted in Maltz, "Citizen Writer," 2:703. See also Lester Cole, *Hollywood Red: The Autobiography of Lester Cole* (Palo Alto, Calif., 1981), 266; and Alvah Bessie, *Inquisition in Eden* (New York, 1965), 44, 115.

21. Cole believed that Western industrial capitalism was "not just *in*human but *pre*human" (Cole, *Hollywood Red,* 9). See also Schwartz, *Hollywood Writers' Wars,* 152; Victor S. Navasky, *Naming Names* (New York, 1980), 80; Ceplair and Englund, *Inquisition,* 292–93; and Andersen, "Red Hollywood," 180.

22. Ring Lardner, Jr., *The Lardners: My Family Remembered* (New York, 1976), 254.

23. Alvah Bessie, "What Is Freedom for Writers?" *New Masses* 58 (March 12, 1946): 8, 10. On the "Maltz affair," see Albert Maltz, "What Shall We Ask of Artists?" *New Masses* 58 (February 12, 1946): 22; Maltz, "Citizen Writer," 2:570–85; Ceplair and Englund, *Inquisition,* 233–36; and Navasky, *Naming Names,* 287–302. See also Bessie, *Inquisition,* 12.

24. Albert Maltz, "The Writers as the Conscience of the People," address delivered July 11, 1947, reprinted in Maltz, *The Citizen Writer* (New York, 1950), 11; and Albert Maltz, *The Underground Stream: An Historical Novel of a Moment in the American Winter* (Boston, 1940), 103, 341. See also Maltz, "Citizen Writer," 1:375–77; and Ceplair and Englund, *Inquisition,* 236.

25. Cole, *Hollywood Red,* 153.

26. See John Howard Lawson, "Biographical Notes," *Zeitschrift für Anglistik und Amerikanistik* 4, no. 1 (1956): 73; and "A Southern Welcome (in Georgia and Alabama): A Report by John Howard Lawson," Report 7, 1934, New York Public Library Annex, New York.

27. Reagan, *Where's the Rest of Me?* 161. See also testimony of Jack L. Warner, May 15, 1947, reprinted in Warner's testimony, October 20, 1947, "Hearings," 50.

28. Maltz, *Underground Stream,* 103. See also Andersen, "Red Hollywood," 182; and Maltz, "Citizen Writer," 1:380–84.

29. Dalton Trumbo, *Harry Bridges: A Discussion of the Latest Effort to Deport Civil Liberties and the Right of American Labor* (Hollywood and New York, 1941), 2.

30. See Ceplair and Englund, *Inquisition,* 307.

31. Cole, *Hollywood Red,* 159, 172; Cole quoted in Ceplair and Englund, *Inquisition,* 303. See also Ceplair and Englund, *Inquisition,* 307; and John Howard Lawson, *Film: The Creative Process: The Search for an Audio-Visual Language and Structure* (New York, 1964), 120.

32. See *New York Times,* July 1, 1971, 50; Herbert Biberman, *Salt of the Earth: The Story of a Film* (Boston, 1965), 41–42, 245; and Andersen, "Red Hollywood," 180.

33. Robert Merritt Gardner, "International Rag: The Theatrical Career of John Howard Lawson" (Ph.D. diss., University of California, Berkeley, 1978), 9 (see also 30–31); and Lawson quoted in Brenman-Gibson, *Clifford Odets,* (New York, 1981), 223.

34. On Biberman, see address by Gale Sondergaard, April 21, 1950, in Gale Sondergaard and Albert Maltz, *On the Eve of Prison: Two Addresses* (Hollywood, ca. 1950), 6. See also Cole, *Hollywood Red,* 56–57; Bessie, *Inquisition,* 10; Maltz, "Citizen Writer," 1:2–4; and Ornitz's 1947 statement to HUAC, reprinted in Kahn,

Hollywood, 98–99. See also Ceplair and Englund, *Inquisition,* 424; and Navasky, *Naming Names,* 81.

35. Lawson, "Southern Welcome," 14.

36. John Howard Lawson, "Statement of Policy," August 18, 1944, box 1, HICCASP, SHSWM; meeting of the science and education division of HICCASP, June 17, 1946, box 2, HICCASP, SHSWM. See also minutes, Executive Board meeting, HICCASP, May 14 and 26, 1946; and minutes, Executive Council meeting, HICCASP, June 11, 1946, box 2, HICCASP, SHSWM.

37. John Howard Lawson, "The Heritage of American Culture," *Clipper* 2 (July 1941): 7, 11, 13; and Lawson, "Parrington and the Search for Tradition," *Mainstream: A Literary Quarterly* 1 (winter 1947): 34 (see also 24, 25). See also Lawson, "Biographical Notes," 74; and Lawson, *The Hidden Heritage: A Rediscovery of the Ideas and Forces that Link the Thought of Our Time with the Culture of the Past* (New York, 1950).

38. Lawson, "Biographical Notes," 74; and Lawson, "Parrington," 42.

39. Capitalism, argued Lawson, brought the devastation of indigenous cultures and a slave market. "The discovery of gold and silver in America, the destruction of native populations, the commercial exploitation of the African slave depots and the unpaid labor of the Negroes, signalized, as Marx observes, 'the rosy dawn of capitalist production.'" Modern thinking, still captivated by "white supremacy myths," remained blinded to slavery's social effects (Lawson, *Hidden Heritage,* 215, 216, 217, and 231–32; see also 527).

40. See box 40, JHL-SIU.

41. Dalton Trumbo, "Minorities and the Screen," in *Writers' Congress: The Proceedings of the Conference held in October 1943* (Berkeley, 1944), 497; and Maltz, *Underground Stream,* 150.

42. Lawson, *Hidden Heritage,* vii (see also 215–17, 231–42); Lawson, "Biographical Notes," 74; and Lawson (also known as Howard Jennings), "Revisionism and American History," *Political Affairs: A Magazine Devoted to the Theory and Practice of Marxism-Leninism* 25 (August 1946): 743, 747.

43. While in prison, Cole and Lardner tried to undermine the institution's Jim Crow practices in the cafeteria (see Cole, *Hollywood Red,* 318, 321). See also Adrian Scott's 1947 statement to HUAC, reprinted in Kahn, *Hollywood,* 106–9; and K. R. M. Short, "Hollywood Fights Anti-Semitism, 1945–1947," in K. R. M. Short, ed., *Feature Film as History* (London, 1981), 160–63. Maltz repudiated not only racial and ethnic intolerance, but also the validity of racial and ethnic identities of almost any sort. Thus his second novel, *The Cross and the Arrow* (Berlin, 1944), repudiated the notion that racial characteristics made the Germans inherently warmongers, that the "morality of [the] German soul" was "to conquer the world." (The United States government, through its Armed Services Edition, helped issue 140,000 copies of this novel for American servicemen abroad.) Maltz also sought to expose bigotry in *The House I Live In* (1945) (Maltz, *Cross,* 436). See also Maltz, "Citizen Writer," 2:523–24; and Maltz's 1947 statement to HUAC, reprinted in Kahn, *Hollywood,* 88.

44. See Edward Dmytryk, Oral History, 1328–29, BLCU-NY; Maltz, "Citizen Writer," 2:598; Schwartz, *Hollywood Writers' Wars,* 269; Navasky, *Naming Names,* 81; and Andersen, "Red Hollywood," 181.

45. Biberman, *Salt,* 10.

46. Eric A. Johnston, "A Talk to Russia," in *International Conciliation: Documents for the Year 1944* (New York, 1944), no. 404, 638. See also Johnston, "Talk," 639; Johnston, "After the Marshall Plan—What?" *Collier's* 123 (May 21, 1949): 69; Johnston, "The Modern Tool for Teaching," radio broadcast, American Broadcasting Company, September 1, 1946, 6, HSTLI; Johnston interview, 1959, 893–94, BLCU-NY; and Johnston, *We're All in It* (New York, 1948), 13, 31, 50–51, 75–121 (especially 89), 203, 207, 211.

47. Quoted in Vaughn, *Ronald Reagan,* 197 (see also 197–99).

48. See Cole, *Hollywood Red,* 171–72; on Maltz, Ceplair and Englund, *Inquisition,* 165, 168–71. *People's World* (San Francisco), March 14, 1941, 2. See also *People's World,* March 13, 1941, 1.

49. Advertisement, *Daily Worker* (New York), March 16, 1940, 4. For serialization of *Johnny,* see *Daily Worker,* March 17, 1940–April 29, 1940. See also Vaughn, *Ronald Reagan,* 152.

50. Lawson, "Heritage," 11 (also 7); see also Lawson, "Revisionism," 742 (also 759, 761); Lawson, "On Censorship," speech, October 30, 1947, 3, box 27, JHL-SIU; and Lawson, *Hidden Heritage,* 530–31.

51. Lawson to HICCASP membership, minutes, membership meeting, November 30, 1945, box 10, HICCASP, SHSWM.

52. Cole's family had also opposed American participation in World War I (Cole, *Hollywood Red,* 9). See also Vaughn, *Ronald Reagan,* 128, 152, 288 n. 38.

53. Only Lawson and Trumbo stood trial. The other eight, who had only limited financial resources, agreed that they would accept the verdicts given these two. Most were sentenced to prison in 1950 for one year. Dmytryk and Biberman, who appeared before a different judge, received six-month terms (see Ceplair and Englund, *Inquisition,* 350–54).

54. Dmytryk maintained that his disillusionment with the party began after a disagreement with Lawson and writer John Wexley over the script for *Cornered* (1945). Others noted, though, that Dmytryk attended party meetings regularly throughout the late 1940s and renounced the party only after he got out of prison to regain employment (Edward Dmytryk, *It's a Hell of a Life but Not a Bad Living* [New York, 1978], 71–72; Ceplair and Englund, *Inquisition,* 358; and Maltz, "Citizen Writer," 2:570–85, 798–99).

55. Lawson, *Film in the Battle of Ideas,* 9–10. See also Lawson, *Film in the Battle of Ideas,* 16; and Lawson, *Film: The Creative Process* (New York, 1964), v.

56. Lardner, *Lardners,* 256.

57. On Cole's continued allegiance to communism, see *San Diego Union,* January 12, 1982, D–1.

58. John Howard Lawson, "The Cold War and the American Film," speech, March 26, ca. 1949, 4, box 12, JHL-SIU.

"A Significant Medium for the Communication of Ideas"

The *Miracle* Decision and the Decline of Motion Picture Censorship, 1952–1968

GARTH JOWETT

I n 1952, for the first time since 1915, the Supreme Court of the United States agreed to hear a case involving motion picture censorship. This was the celebrated *Miracle* decision *(Burstyn v. Wilson),* which on May 26, 1952, reversed the 1915 *Mutual Film* ruling.[1] After ignoring the issue for thirty-seven years, the Supreme Court had at long last recognized the motion picture as an important medium for the communication of ideas and therefore entitled to the same protection under the First Amendment as speech and press.

On February 23, 1915, the Supreme Court had handed down a unanimous decision in *Mutual Film Corporation v. Industrial Commission of Ohio,* which denied the motion picture the constitutional guarantees of freedom of speech and press.[2] Concerns about the nature and role of the motion picture in American society, originating from a wide variety of sources, came to an early climax with this important ruling. Reformers, concerned especially with the enormous appeal that motion pictures seemed to have for children, as well as for the more "persuadable" elements in society, had attacked the content of movies from their first public showings.[3] The nickelodeons, those highly visible icons of change in turn-of-the-century American culture, represented for some a potential threat to the Progressive ideal then just beginning to take root.[4] The movies were attacked for being the source of every conceivable social ill, from sexual license to demonstrating the arts of pickpocketing to fomenting social revolution. By 1915 there were already several formal censorship boards in states and cities created specifically to deal with the "problem of the movies."

It is only against this background that the rather strange ruling of the Supreme Court in the *Mutual* case can be understood and explained. The case involved no specific film but was a challenge by the Mutual Film Corporation against an Ohio statute which provided for the creation of a motion picture censorship board whose duty it was to examine, in advance, all film that was to be shown publicly for profit in that state. Mutual claimed that this law was unconstitutional because it was an unfair burden on interstate commerce, failed to set up precise standards, and violated the free speech guarantees of the Ohio Constitution and the First Amendment in the Bill of Rights.

Speaking for a unanimous Court, Justice Joseph McKenna rejected all of Mutual's complaints. In regard to the free speech argument, the justice was clearly not prepared to accept the argument that the motion picture and the press were parallel. Despite their potential educational or entertainment value, explained McKenna, motion pictures were to be treated differently because

they may be used for evil, and against that possibility the statute was enacted. The power of amusement and, it may be, education, the audiences they assemble, not of women alone nor of men alone, but together, not of adults only, but of children, make them insidious in corruption by pretense of worthy purpose or if they should degenerate from worthy purpose. . . . They take their attraction from the general interest, however eager and wholesome it may be, in their subjects, but prurient interest may be excited and appealed to.[5]

In trying to gauge what was on the minds of the justices as they considered what to do with this new medium of information, there is little doubt that they were unwilling to leave the general public unprotected from what they saw as a powerful, unregulated social force. It is here that we see the clear articulation of the problem that the motion picture symbolized. In a telling passage, Justice McKenna declared,

It cannot be put out of view that the exhibition of moving pictures is a business pure and simple, originated and conducted for profit, like other spectacles, not to be regarded, nor intended to be regarded by the Ohio constitution, we think, as part of the press of the country or as organs of public opinion. They are mere representations of events, of ideas and sentiments published and known, vivid, useful and entertaining no doubt, but, as we have said, capable of evil, having power for it, the greater because of the attractiveness and manner of exhibition.[6]

Thus the movies were capable of disseminating ideas, but the fear of the Court was that they *could* be used for "evil" purposes by those seeking merely to make a profit, and that this danger was only increased by the enormous inherent attraction the medium held for the public, especially those classes who were more susceptible to outside influences. Clearly there were three fallacies in the Court's argument. First, other media such as newspapers and magazines had been operated for profit and were not subjected to censorship. Second, the classification of the movies in the same category as circuses and other sideshow spectacles belied their true function in 1915, by which time several important films had already been exhibited. Third, the assertion that the motion picture possessed a greater "capacity for evil" than other forms of mass communication was unwarranted and based to a large extent on the perceived nature of the primary audience for the movies—largely the immigrant working class.

The *Mutual* decision was a blow to the motion picture industry, but surprisingly, there was little formal protest, and for the next thirty-seven years it formed the legal basis for the existence of various agencies of prior censorship operating on the municipal, county, and state level. Despite such censorship, however, and despite the motion picture industry's self-regulatory system— the Production Code—which formed the basis of an elaborate public relations gesture symbolizing the industry's social conscience, there were always groups ready and willing to attack the movies for a variety of reasons. But for the thirty-seven years that the *Mutual* decision stood, there were no serious legal challenges to its basic ruling: movies were not the same as speech and therefore not to be accorded the protection of the First Amendment. Thus the motion picture represents a significant anomaly in American legal history. It has the distinction of being the only medium of communication ever subjected to systematic legal prior restraint in the history of the United States. So great was the perceived power of the motion picture, and so persistent were the reformers in their zeal, that this growing industry and important information medium was denied the same rights accorded other forms of communication. How much the *Mutual* decision stifled the creative development of the motion picture industry is a matter of interesting historical speculation.

It was ironic that the first intimation that the Court would entertain the idea of a challenge to *Mutual* came in 1948, in the *Paramount Antitrust* case. The antitrust suit against Paramount Studios had been filed originally in July 1938, and in the following ten years the entire industry operated under a series of consent decrees, all designed to break down the vertical integration under which it operated. In 1948 the Supreme Court ordered divestiture of all of Paramount's theater holdings.[7] It was in the process of deliberating these economic issues that Justice William O. Douglas asserted for the Court, "We have no doubt that moving pictures, like newspapers and radio, are included in the press whose freedom is guaranteed by the First Amendment."[8] Ira Carmen notes: "It is an ironic twist indeed that the movie industry should come of age before the 'bar of justice' in a manner so anticlimactic. Though Justice Douglas' statement was only a dictum of the most obvious sort, it was apparent that the death knell had been sounded for the *Mutual Film Corporation* precedent."[9] At the same time that the Supreme Court was essentially destroying the well-established practices of the motion picture industry by ordering the divestiture of its distribution and exhibition facilities, it was also granting filmmakers the protection of the First Amendment. Nevertheless, the Court waited four years before agreeing to listen to *Burstyn v. Wilson.*

The Supreme Court could have taken up other potential film censorship cases prior to the *Miracle* case, but for a variety of reasons they were not considered suitable for a frontal attack on *Mutual*'s basic finding that motion pictures were not parallel to the press in their ability to communicate information and ideas. In light of the significant role that motion pictures had played in World War II, Hollywood underwent a short-lived renaissance which saw the studios turning out a number of films dealing with subjects of social significance. A few of these films dealt specifically with issues such as racism or sexuality that were bound to create censorship problems. In the case of *United Artists Corporation v. Board of Censors,* the studio challenged a ruling by the notorious Memphis Censor Board, headed by the colorful Lloyd T. Binford, whose rulings were the subject of countless newspaper stories for more than twenty years. The Memphis Board had banned the 1949 film *Curley* because it dealt with "Negro children visiting at a school with white youngsters." According to Binford's philosophy, this provided more than enough reason for suppressing the production because "the South does not permit Negroes in white schools nor recognize social equality between the races even in children."[10] Because the lower court found that the transaction between the distributor and the exhibitor was not interstate commerce, it ruled that the plaintiff (United Artists) did not qualify to use the federal courts to advance his intended purpose. The United States Supreme Court evidently agreed that the decision in this case was on sound enough grounds not to interfere. In another case, *RD-DR Corp. v. Smith,* the motion picture *Lost Boundaries*—the story of a black doctor and his family who pass for white—was banned by the chief censor of Atlanta, Georgia, Christina Smith, on the grounds that it was "likely to have an adverse effect upon the peace, morals and good order of the city." Why the Supreme Court refused certiorari to this case (Justice Douglas was the lone dissenter) is unclear. Possibly in 1953 the Court was not eager to cloud the First Amendment issue with the social and political issue of racial discrimination, which had been the subject of several important recent cases, and so passed on this particular opportunity.[11]

In 1949 a case involving director Elia Kazan's film *Pinky* (Twentieth-Century Fox) became a prime candidate for the Supreme Court's breakthrough test case. The film dealt with a young nurse with white skin and black blood who returns to her home in Mississippi after having been raised in the North. A theater manager in Texas, W. L. Gelling, was fined after he showed the film in the town of Marshall, where a hastily formed censorship board had banned it. The case worked its way through the Texas Supreme Court, which upheld the conviction, and then on to the United States Supreme Court, where it was decided just one week after the *Miracle* ruling.

But the honor of breaking the hold that the *Mutual* ruling had on the American film industry went to *The Miracle,* a fairly obscure Italian film starring Anna Magnani, written by Federico Fellini, and directed by Roberto Rossellini. The story concerns a demented peasant woman who is seduced by a bearded stranger (Fellini) whom she thinks is Saint Joseph. The woman becomes pregnant, and after being tormented by the people of her village, she is forced to flee into the hills, where she delivers her child in an isolated church as the film ends. The film had been granted a license for exhibition in New York by the state censors and opened at the Paris Theater on December 12, 1950, as part of a trilogy consisting of Jean Renoir's *A Day in the Country,* Marcel Pagnol's *Jofroi,* and *The Miracle* under the collective title *Ways of Love.* Critical response to *The Miracle* was mixed. Some newspaper critics found it "sacrilegious" and "distasteful," while others found it imbued with compassion and "basic faith."[12]

Twelve days after *The Miracle* opened, New York's license commissioner, Edward T. McCaffrey, informed the management of the Paris Theater that he found the film "officially and personally blasphemous" and ordered it removed from the screen on penalty of having the license of the theater revoked. The theater complied the next day, which was the day before Christmas. McCaffrey, a prominent Democrat and former state commander of the Catholic War Veterans, claimed he had acted personally because he "felt that there were hundreds of thousands of citizens whose religious beliefs were assailed by the picture."[13] Joseph Burstyn, the film's distributor, took action to secure a temporary injunction against the commissioner, and on December 29 it was granted by Justice Henry Clay Greenberg of the Supreme Court of New York. On January 5, 1951, Justice Aaron Steuer of the Supreme Court of New York ruled that neither McCaffrey nor any other municipal official could interfere with the exhibition of a motion picture that had already received an official license from the New York State censors. When the Paris Theater resumed its showings of The Miracle, large crowds turned out to see what the fuss was all about. The Legion of Decency had already condemned the film as "a sacrilegious and blasphemous mockery of Christian and religious truth," when, on January 7, a letter from Cardinal Francis Joseph Spellman was read at all masses in Saint Patrick's Cathedral calling upon Catholics throughout the United States to remember their pledges to stay away from indecent and immoral films. The cardinal specifically urged Catholics not to see The Miracle and to avoid patronizing theaters where the film was scheduled to be shown. He further noted that the film tended to divide Americans, a technique used by "atheistic Communism."[14] On the afternoon that Spellman called for the boycott, a delegation of over two hundred pickets representing the Catholic War Veterans and other organizations of Catholic men began to march in front of the Paris Theater, announcing their intention to do so every evening for as long as the film continued to be screened. According to New York Times film critic and ardent opponent of film censorship, Bosley Crowther, "An ugly and fanatic spirit was often apparent among the marching men as they shouted in the faces of people lined up to buy tickets, 'Don't enter that cesspool!' and 'Don't look at that filth!' A grim sort of jingoism was also confused in their cries. 'This is a Communist picture!' and 'Buy American!'"[15]

On January 20, a busy Saturday night, the theater received a bomb threat, which caused a temporary disruption. No sooner had the audience been reseated than the fire commissioner, Edward Coughlan, served a summons on the house manager for allowing thirty-five people to stand in the rear of the theater.[16] The following Saturday night the police emptied the theater again because "two men were overheard talking in a bar" about throwing a bomb into the theater.

Perhaps the most reprehensible aspect of this affair was engineered by Martin Quigley, a prominent Catholic layman and coauthor of the 1930 Production Code, who was responsible for having the New York Film Critics' Awards ceremony moved from Radio City Music Hall because the critics had voted *Ways of Love* the best foreign film of 1950. Quigley suggested to the management of the Music Hall that their theater might be subject to boycott if they permitted their stage to be used for the presentation of an award to *Ways of Love*.[17] Quigley's warning was reiterated by Monsignor Walter Kellenberg, chancellor of the New York Archdiocese, in a letter to the Radio City management in which he suggested that holding the ceremony there would offend Cardinal Spellman. As a result of this pressure, the critics voluntarily withdrew, and the awards ceremony was moved to the Rainbow Room of the RCA Building.

Despite the pickets and the pulpit, attendance at the Paris did not decline; instead, the excitement seemed to draw crowds of customers who might otherwise never have seen a film of this type. After three weeks the picketing was voluntarily ended.

On the legal front, the New York Board of Regents made it known that they had received "hundreds" of complaints against the film, and on January 19, in an unprecedented move, Burstyn was called before the board to show cause why the film's license should not be revoked. In the meantime, a three-man team formed by the Board of Regents had found the film to be "sacrilegious." Burstyn's lawyers took the position that the board lacked jurisdiction to revoke a license once it had been granted. On February 15 the full board viewed *The Miracle,* unanimously agreed that it was "sacrilegious," and revoked its license. The film was subsequently withdrawn from exhibition at the Paris Theater. Burstyn immediately filed an appeal to the New York Supreme Court to review the board's decision.

On March 12 the Appellate Division of the New York Supreme Court heard the argument in the case known as *Burstyn v. Wilson* (Wilson, the commissioner of education for the state of New York, had actually rescinded the film's license). Burstyn's brief claimed that the statute violated the First and Fourteenth Amendments because it was a prior restraint upon the rights of freedom of speech and press and impinged upon the right of a free exercise of religion. It further argued that the term "sacrilegious" violated due process because it was vague and provided no guidelines for the scope of administrative authority. In each instance the New York court found in favor of the board's ruling, voting five to two to uphold "sacrilegious" as a valid censorship standard.[18]

Burstyn's last chance lay with the United States Supreme Court, and he duly filed yet another appeal. Throughout this lengthy, and costly, process, Burstyn had received no real support from the American film industry. Instead, the industry threw its weight behind the *Gelling* case, a similar censorship appeal which involved a movie produced in Hollywood—*Pinky.* On May 26, 1952, the Supreme Court unanimously reversed the New York Court of Appeals and struck down the ban on *The Miracle.* Speaking for the Court, Justice Tom Clark found that it was necessary to consider only the contention that the New York law was an unconstitutional abridgment of free speech and free press. Addressing that issue squarely, he declared, "It cannot be doubted that motion pictures are a significant medium for the communication of ideas. They may affect public attitudes and behavior in a variety of ways, ranging from direct espousal of a political or social doctrine to the subtle shaping of thought which characterizes all artistic expression."[19]

Thus the motion picture was, at long last, brought within the free speech and free press guarantees of the Constitution. Justice Clark noted that it was of no consequence that many motion pictures were designed to entertain or to be exhibited for private profit, nor that they might possess a greater capacity for evil than other forms of expression. The last "hypothesis," he noted, might be "relevant in determining the permissible scope of community control, but it does not authorize substantially unbridled censorship."[20] Clark was, however, careful to point out that movies were still not to be afforded the same full constitutional protection as books, newspapers, and other forms of publication, which were subject to the restraints of subsequent punishment, rather than prior restraint. He observed: "It does not follow that the Constitution requires absolute freedom to exhibit every motion picture of every kind at all times and all places. Nor does it follow that motion pictures are necessarily subject to the precise rules governing any other particular method of expression. Each tends to present its own peculiar problems."[21]

Prior restraint would be recognized by the Court only in "exceptional cases," and even then the state would have a "heavy burden" to clearly demonstrate that the particular restraint in question was justified. In the case of *Burstyn v. Wilson* the state had clearly not demonstrated the necessity for prior restraint, and the standard of "sacrilegious" was unconstitutional.

Justice Clark went out of his way to issue a warning to those anxiously awaiting this landmark decision. The Court, he noted, was not deciding such questions as whether or not a city or a state could censor motion pictures under a "clearly drawn statute designed and applied to prevent the showing of obscene films."[22] Thus the Court chose not to deal with the issue of the constitutionality of the institution of prior restraint. Therefore the Court did not entire rule out the censorship of motion pictures. Justice Stanley Reed added a concurring paragraph, which made this very clear:

> Assuming that a state may establish a system for the licensing of motion pictures, an issue not foreclosed by the Court's opinion, our duty requires us to examine the facts of the refusal of a license in each case to determine whether

the principles of the First Amendment have been honored. This film does not seem to me to be of a character that the First Amendment permits a state to exclude from public views.[23]

What, in fact, was the legal position of the movies at this point? Richard Randall, in his history of movie censorship, pointed out that the *Miracle* decision

left unanswered the question of how the theory of free speech—essentially elitist in terms of the tolerance it assumes and requires—would he reconciled with a mass medium which, except for a relatively brief period in its history, was neither distinguished for its self-restraint, nor subject to any collaborative restraint by advertisers. Would the theory of free speech undergo a kind of mutation that would allow the limited prior censorship of motion pictures? Or, on the other hand, would *The Miracle* decision be, in effect, only the first stage of a complete transition of status for motion pictures that eventually would see them entirely freed of official prior censorship?[24]

The decision had no immediate effect on the Catholic campaign against *The Miracle,* and the National Council of Catholic Men pointed out that now "the only effective bulwark against pictures which are immoral, short of being obscene, is public opinion manifested through such organizations as the Legion of Decency."[25] An editorial in the *Evangelist,* the weekly of the Albany diocese, claimed that the Court decision was a victory "for the forces of paganistic secularism" and "tragic in its implications."[26]

Richard Corliss, in his study of the Legion of Decency, suggested that the *Miracle* decision was the first great defeat for Catholic motion picture pressure and perhaps the beginning of a "new" legion. He noted: "For once the Legion had realized that a simple massing of the laity in front of a theater might not be enough to force an independent-minded exhibitor or distributor to knuckle under to the kind of pressure that had succeeded in Hollywood."[27]

One of the more interesting sidebars to the *Miracle* controversy was the editorial battle between the *New York Times* film critic Bosley Crowther on the East Coast, and the *Motion Picture Herald,* owned and edited by Martin Quigley, in Hollywood. These two polar positions on the issue of motion picture censorship encapsulated decades of frustration by those who wished to see the motion picture industry free to explore its full artistic potential, and those who wished to see it restrained to continue providing "wholesome family entertainment." Crowther had from the beginning championed *The Miracle,* both as a film and as a cause, and had written the first stories detailing the methods used by the Legion of Decency and the Knights of Columbus in their attempt to intimidate patrons entering the Paris Theater. Quigley, on the other hand, considered the film sacrilegious and had editorialized against it in the strongest terms.

In an editorial on March 3, 1951, Quigley attacked the *New York Times* for its "curious devotion" to *The Miracle* and questioned Crowther's objectivity and his role in promoting the film with his fellow New York critics who had voted *Ways of Love* the year's best foreign film. Quigley went on to say:

> The *Times* and Mr. Crowther insist on ignoring the fact that the organized motion picture industry in the United States asserts no right to exhibit obscene, salacious, sacrilegious and otherwise socially and morally harmful films. It has a Code which specifically forbids such things. . . . The *Times* seems to have developed an intemperate rush to abandon its own and America's traditional respect for the religious beliefs, sensibilities and practices of one's fellow citizens.[28]

When the Supreme Court issued its ruling in May a year later, Quigley again editorialized:

> In this decision it is apparent that the Supreme Court has once again left an important public question in a status which inevitably will lead to inter- minable controversy and litigation. . . . Happily, however, for the purposes of a decent society there are but few persons who wish to produce, exhibit or even patronize a film which is offensive to any man's religious sensibilities. . . .
> In the face of the confusion precipitated by the court's decision the American industry may well find cause for renewed rejoicing in its commitment to its own Production Code. With this self-regulatory plan the industry has a well- charted course to follow in protection of the public interest and its own, irre- spective of how winds blow in the troubled area of political censorship and judicial pronouncement.[29]

What Quigley was avoiding, as one of the principal architects of its creation, was the fact that the Production Code was also under scrutiny and attack. In the next decade the code would undergo major changes as the legal freedom of- fered by the *Miracle* decision and those that followed made many of the tenets of the code obsolete.[30]

This historic ruling made it clear that the achievement of free speech in the motion picture would take more than court decisions and restrictions on cen- sors. It would also require a desire on the part of the film industry to make the most of its newfound freedom to create the "mature and responsible" cinema it had promised for so long. It was not an accident that *The Miracle* was a foreign film, for the American audience for such films had not yet developed in suffi- cient numbers to support domestic production of a similar genre of mature motion pictures. When the Supreme Court made its decision in 1952, there were slightly more than one hundred first-run art theaters in the United States, most of which were fairly small and in the New York area.[31]

In the nine-year period after *Burstyn,* the Supreme Court heard six licensing cases, and in each one the powers of the censors were further reduced. In a series of per curiam decisions (usually one-sentence, anonymous opinions), the Court continued to strike down statutes authorizing censorship. Thus in *Gelling v. Texas* (1952), the Court reversed the conviction of a Texas exhibitor who had shown *Pinky* without censorial approval. The Supreme Court merely cited *Burstyn v. Wilson* in its per curiam opinion.[32]

In its next censorship case, the Supreme Court reversed the decision in *Superior Films, Inc. v. Dept. of Education of Ohio,* which removed "harmful" as a standard for censorship[33] and at the same time struck down "immoral" in *Commercial Pictures Corp. v. Board of Regents of New York.*[34] In 1955, in *Holmby Productions, Inc. v. Vaughn,* the Court reversed the Kansas Censor Board's decision that *The Moon Is Blue* was "obscene, indecent and immoral, and such as tend to debase or corrupt morals."[35] On the state level as well, courts were beginning to cite *Burstyn v. Wilson* as they reversed censorship ordinances. Thus in 1956 the Maryland Supreme Court reversed a state censorship board's ruling on *The Man with the Golden Arm* but refused to pass on the constitutionality of the censorship statute.[36]

After 1956 almost the only grounds for movie censorship that remained appeared to be "obscenity," and more and more, the state and municipal censors used this as the reason for ordering deletions.[37] Thus in the case of *Kingsley Pictures v. Regents* in 1959,[38] involving *Lady Chatterley's Lover,* Justice Potter Stewart, speaking for the Court as a whole (in the first non–per curiam motion picture ruling since *The Miracle*), noted that the film was clearly not obscene, nor would it incite to illegal action. The film had been banned because New York law required that no film could be granted a license if it approved of adultery. He also made the point that the Constitution guaranteed the freedom to advocate ideas even if they were not popular or were held by only a minority: "It protects advocacy of the opinion that adultery may sometimes be proper, no less than advocacy of socialism or the single tax. And in the realm of ideas it protects expression which is eloquent no less than that which is unconvincing."[39] But the Court still stubbornly refused to definitively rule on the issue of the constitutionality of prior censorship.

It was not until 1961 that the fundamental constitutional question of the permissibility of local censorship of motion pictures finally reached the

Supreme Court in the case of *Times Film Corp. v. Chicago.*[40] This involved *Don Juan,* a film version of Mozart's opera *Don Giovanni,* which was specially selected by the distributor to create a "test" case. After paying the permit fee, the distributor refused to submit the film to the police commissioner of Chicago for examination as required by the municipal code. The city refused to grant a license for exhibition, and the distributor sued on the grounds that the city's police power was limited to punishment after the fact and that a movie licensing system was unconstitutional. Both the district court and the court of appeals dismissed the complaint on the grounds that the case presented merely an abstract question of law, since neither the film itself nor evidence of its content had been involved in the proceedings.[41]

On January 23, 1961, the Supreme Court handed down a five-to-four decision which upheld the city's power to license films. Justice Clark, speaking for the majority, saw the distributor's complaint as a claim that constitutional protection "includes complete and absolute freedom to exhibit, at least once, any and every kind of motion picture." Such protection would automatically void the city ordinance requiring prior submission. Obscenity was clearly not protected by the Constitution, and to accept this argument against prior censorship would be to strip a state of "all constitutional power to prevent, in the most effective fashion, the utterance of this class of speech."[42] He also noted that the movies' "capacity for evil may be relevant in determining the permissible scope of community control" and that movies were not "necessarily subject to the precise rules governing any other particular method of expression."[43] However, the justice was careful to point out that the Court was not holding that censors should be granted the power to prevent exhibition of any film they found distasteful.

Chief Justice Earl Warren submitted a long, rambling dissent on behalf of the minority opinion, in which he agreed that First Amendment protection did not include unlimited freedom from prior restraint, but he claimed that licensing or censorship was never considered to be within the concept of "exceptional cases" as defined earlier. He specifically noted that the Chicago ordinance also offered no procedural safeguards, and there was no trial on the issue before restraint became effective. Finally, Warren noted that the Court had not even attempted to justify why motion pictures should be treated any differently from other media, to the extent that they should be denied protection from prior restraint or censorship. Even if they had greater impact than other media, this was not a sufficient basis for subjecting them to greater suppression. Justice William O. Douglas filed a separate dissenting opinion, together with Justice Hugo Black, in which he reiterated his steadfast position that censorship of films by governmental licensing was unconstitutional because it was a prior restraint on free speech.[44]

The immediate reaction to the Court's decision in the *Times* case was mostly critical. The *New York Times* favored the opinion of the minority judges, who "took the sounder view and the one that in the long run will prevail."[45] Bosley Crowther, long the champion of freedom for the movies, commented, "The effect is to continue the ancient stigma of motion pictures as a second-class, subordinate art."[46] Even the liberal Catholic publication *Commonweal* found the Court's ruling unacceptable and reprinted an anticensorship editorial from the *Catholic Register* in Peoria:

> If a government, city or otherwise, can prevent the showing of "undesirable" movies, what is to stop them moving into the fields of magazines and newspapers, and deciding that certain publications are "undesirable" on political or even personal grounds[?].
>
> Obscenity is evil. But for a free society, there is something a whole lot more evil—giving a government the right to silence ideas that are "undesirable" before they even have a chance to reach the public.[47]

In spite of the *Times* ruling, the expected flood of new censorship regulation did not occur, and no new state or municipal regulations emerged. City censorship, in fact, went into rapid decline all through the fifties and sixties.[48] More important, the *Times* decision did not result in lower courts upholding the censors. Richard Randall notes that in eleven appellate decisions between 1961 and 1965, not once were the censors upheld on the merits, and the highest courts of three states—Pennsylvania, Oregon, and Georgia—all found that motion picture prior censorship violated the free speech provisions of their respective state constitutions.[49]

The last of the cases following the *Miracle* breakthrough was *Freedman v. Maryland* in 1965. While it did not come to a definite ruling on the constitutionality of prior censorship, the Court did find a middle ground between the two positions in the *Times* case. In this case the distributor, Freedman, challenged the licensing procedures of the Maryland Board of Censors, and no question of obscenity was involved in the "test" film, *Revenge at Daybreak*. The right claimed by the distributor was freedom from criminal prosecution for showing a constitutionally protected film—one free from obscenity. The Supreme Court unanimously decided for Freedman yet did not find licensing procedures unconstitutional; rather, the justices were more concerned with the licensing procedure itself and what it required.[50] Essentially, the Court required the entire licensing procedure to be speeded up and judicial participation to be built into it. However, the decision still recognized the exercise of licensing power and noted that motion pictures "differ from other forms of expression."

The *Freedman* decision was immediately used to launch an attack upon licensing boards in the several states and many cities that still continued to censor films and also to challenge the Bureau of Customs inspection of imported films.[51] The result of these efforts was a wholesale reformation of movie licensing procedures and a complete collapse of censorial legislation where such reformation proved to be impossible. The *Freedman* case was most significant because it forced censors to adhere to unusually high standards of procedural fairness, although the whole issue of the constitutionality of prior censorship was still not settled.

By the mid-1960s the American motion picture industry had effectively been freed from the strictures it had operated under since 1915. It had taken fifty years, but at long last the movies were now accorded the protection of the freedom-of-speech articles of the Constitution. However, this newfound freedom placed the industry in a difficult position. No longer could the Hollywood studios rely upon the potent combination of its own self-regulatory mechanism (the Production Code) and the threat of legal censorship based on the *Mutual* decision to maintain control of the entire film industry. The organized self-regulatory system created and enforced by the major studios was a highly effective method of limiting the distribution of independent productions. The five major theater-owning studios were in firm agreement not to exhibit films that failed to obtain a Production Code Administration seal of approval. Because they controlled 70 percent of the first-run theaters in the major cities and 45 percent of all film rentals, this agreement effectively shut out any independent film producer trying to make a profit by exhibiting a film which had not received a code seal.[52] With the threat of legal censorship removed, and the Production Code under attack for being outmoded, the major studios were left without clear guidelines on what was permissible or what might be profitable.

The question of whether or not the motion picture industry welcomed censorship has always provoked controversy. Will Hays's position, for as long as he headed the Motion Picture Association of America (MPAA), had consistently been that official censorship was un-American, but that Hollywood welcomed self-regulation as the "American way." Nonetheless, the industry was slow to force the issue of government censorship in the courts. It is, however, incorrect to suggest that Hollywood was not interested in removing this legal barrier.

Rather, it was typical of the industry to avoid "rocking the boat" on contro-versial issues involving public morality. Past history had consistently shown that Hollywood was a very popular target for politicians and reformers wish-ing to demonstrate their concern for the moral welfare of the American people.

Nevertheless, after Will Hays's retirement in 1945, the MPAA under Eric Johnston's leadership began to fight back, albeit in a very quiet way, support-ing cases that it felt were legally sound and, importantly, when censorship was a threat to the success or failure of a major film. Thus in the *Gelling* case, in-volving the movie *Pinky,* the MPAA threw its full weight into fighting the Texas courts' rulings all the way to the Supreme Court. When the Court ruled on *Gelling* in 1952, Johnston said that it's action "had driven another nail into the coffin of motion picture censorship by Government." (He had said no such thing about the *Miracle* case a week earlier.) Johnston went on to say that the MPAA was "movie-starting to prepare" a number of legal actions to "require censor boards to carry out the mandate of the court."[53] The next target was a little-known but constitutionally interesting case involving the censorship of newsreels in Ohio. This case was swiftly decided in a municipal court in Toledo, where Judge Frank W. Wiley, citing both the *Miracle* and *Pinky* deci-sions, ruled that the Ohio statutes on the censorship of films were unconstitu-tional.[54] Following on these cases, the MPAA took a much more activist role in pursuing the total eradication of motion picture censorship.

In 1955 the MPAA, concerned with the Supreme Court's failure to issue a definitive ruling, went before Congress and warned that the refusal to outlaw all motion picture censorship "raises a grave threat" to all of the media. "If the freedom of the motion picture, which the court has made part of the press, can be limited," it reasoned, "then it clearly and inescapably follows that the free-dom of all media of expression may be limited. This means censorship."[55] The MPAA brief also raised the issue of censorship on television and pointed out, "It's an ironic footnote to the absurdities of censorship that motion pictures—even the same pictures cut or banned from theatrical exhibition—can be shown fully and free from censorship on television."[56]

The very threat of television was, in fact, a major impetus in the drive to "modernize" the Production Code. Faced on all sides with impending eco-nomic disaster as a result of shifts in the demographic patterns of moviegoers, the effects of the antitrust divestiture rulings, and the dramatic growth of tele-vision after 1952, the motion picture industry somewhat nervously welcomed a greater degree of freedom in what it could now show on the screen. Thus, by the mid-1960s the American motion picture industry had achieved a degree of judicial freedom that would allow it to move down many previously forbidden pathways. The Production Code was dead by 1966, replaced with a "ratings system" on November 1, 1968. The ratings system was designed to allow the filmmaker "unprecedented creative freedom, while at the same time maintaining a system of 'self-regulation' that would ease the pressures for some form of government classification."[57]

By the late 1960s it appeared to filmmakers and audiences alike that the screen was, at long last, free to explore with relative impunity (if not without criticism) controversial subject matter in a "mature" fashion in the hopes of attracting "the lost audience." The way was open for greater specialization of movies for people of all ages, but in a desperate bid to recover some of the tremendous financial losses the movie studios had sustained, much of this freedom was squandered on cheap sexual exploitation and gratuitous violence. Even today, as witness the recent attacks on the film industry from a variety of interest groups, congressional leaders, and even President Clinton, these freedoms have not always been used judiciously.[58] While there is no threat of the return of official censorship, the pressure on the American film industry to show social and cultural responsibility is as great now as it was fifty years ago.

NOTES

1. 343 U.S. 495 (1952). The best accounts of the importance of this case are found in Ira H. Carmen, *Movies, Censorship and the Law* (Ann Arbor, 1966); Ernest David Giglio, "The Decade of the Miracle, 1952–1962: A Study in the Censorship of the American Motion Picture" (D.S.S. diss., Syracuse University, 1964); and Richard S. Randall, *Censorship of the Movies* (Madison, Wis., 1968). See also Alan F. Westin, *The Miracle Case: The Supreme Court and the Movies,* Inter-university Case Program, no. 64 (Tuscaloosa, Ala., 1961).

2. 236 U.S. 230 (1915). For a detailed account of the *Mutual* case, see Garth Jowett, "'A Capacity for Evil': The 1915 Supreme Court *Mutual* Decision," *Historical Journal of Film, Radio and Television* 9, no. 1 (1989): 59–78.

3. For an account of these early concerns and their origins, see Garth Jowett, *Film: The Democratic Art* (Boston, 1976); and Robert Sklar, *Movie-Made America* (New York, 1975).

4. For the role of the movies in the Progressive era, see Lary May, *Screening out the Past: The Birth of Mass Culture and the Motion Picture Industry* (New York, 1980).

5. *Mutual Film Corporation v. Industrial Commission of Ohio,* 236 U.S. 242 (1915).

6. Ibid., 244.

7. For details of the history of this decision, see Michael Conant, *Antitrust in the Motion Picture Industry: Economic and Legal Analysis* (Berkeley, 1960).

8. 334 U.S. 131 (1948), quoted in Carmen, *Movies,* 45. A few months after *Paramount,* dissenting in *Kovacs v. Cooper,* Justice Hugo Black made the following

statement: "Ideas and beliefs are today chiefly disseminated to the masses of people through the press, radio, *moving pictures,* and public address systems. . . . The result of today's opinion in upholding the statutory prohibition of amplifiers would surely not be reached by the Court if such channels of communication as the press, radio, or *moving pictures* were similarly attacked" (336 U.S. 77 [1949], 102, emphasis added).

9. Carmen, *Movies,* 45.

10. Ibid., 208.

11. For an excellent account of the *Miracle* case and the background to its acceptance by the United States Supreme Court, see Ellen Draper, "'Controversy Has Probably Destroyed Forever the Context': *The Miracle* and Movie Censorship in America in the Fifties," *Velvet Light Trap* 25 (spring 1990): 69–79. On the reason for refusing certiorari in this case, Draper is quoting Theodore Kupferman and Philip O'Brien, Jr., "Motion Picture Censorship: The Memphis Blues," *Cornell Law Quarterly* 36 (1994): 276.

12. For a more detailed account of the motion picture and responses to it, see Bosley Crowther, "The Strange Case of 'The Miracle,'" *Atlantic* 187 (April 1951): 35–39.

13. Ibid., 37.

14. *New York Times,* January 8, 1951, 14.

15. Crowther, "Strange Case," 37.

16. *New York Times,* January 21, 1951, 53.

17. Crowther, "Strange Case," 38.

18. 303 N.Y. 142 (1951).

19. 343 U.S. 501 (1952).

20. Randall, *Censorship,* 29.

21. 343 U.S. 502–3 (1952).

22. Ibid., 506.

23. Ibid., 506–7.

24. Randall, *Censorship,* 31.

25. Ibid., 32.

26. Giglio, "Decade," 245.

27. Richard Corliss, "The Legency of Decency," *Film Comment* 4 (summer 1969): 44.

28. Martin Quigley, "The 'Objective' N.Y. Times," *Motion Picture Herald* 182 (March 3, 1951): 7.

29. Martin Quigley, "The Court Rules—Yes and No!" *Motion Picture Herald* 187 (May 31, 1952): 7.

30. See Jowett, *Film,* 413–27, for an analysis and summary of the major changes in the code during this period.

31. Douglas Ayer, Roy E. Bates, and Peter J. Herman, "Self-Censorship in the Movie Industry: An Historical Perspective on Law and Social Change," *Wisconsin Law Review* 3 (1970): 807.

32. *Gelling v. Texas,* 343 U.S. 960 (1952).

33. *Superior Films, Inc. v. Department of Education of Ohio,* 346 U.S. 587 (1954).

34. 305 N.Y. 336 (1953).

35. 350 U.S. 870 (1955).

36. *United Artists Corp. v. Maryland State Board of Censors,* 210 Md. 586, 124 A.2d 292 (1956).

37. In late 1957 the Supreme Court ruled that *The Game of Love* was not obscene (354 U.S. 476 [1957]) based upon the definition of obscenity it had previously given in two cases involving printed material earlier in the year: *Roth v. United States* and *Alberts v. California.* These two cases, decided together, created the famous "utterly without redeeming social importance" test for obscenity, and the Court also made clear that "sex and obscenity are not synonymous." To determine the obscenity of an utterance, the test would be "whether to the average person, applying contemporary community standards, the dominant theme of the material taken as a whole appeals to the prurient interest" (Randall, *Censorship,* 56.)

38. 360 U.S. 684 (1959).

39. 360 U.S. 684 (1959) at 689.

40. 365 U.S. 43 (1961).

41. In the court of appeals, Judge Schnackenberg dismissed the constitutional claims as a "theoretical remedy of prevention" and noted that the possible damage done by a film's exhibition could never be repaired. He continued: "A film which incites a riot produces that result almost immediately after it is shown publicly. Likewise, the effect upon the prurient mind of an obscene film may result harmfully to some third person within hours after the film has been shown" (Giglio, "Decade," 97).

42. Randall, *Censorship,* 35.

43. Carmen, *Movies,* 101–2.

44. For more details, see Randall, *Censorship,* 36–39; and Carmen, *Movies,* 102–5.

45. *New York Times,* January 25, 1961, P-32.

46. Ibid., January 29, 1961, sec. 4, 1.

47. "Censoring Movies," *Commonweal* 74 (March 31, 1961): 17.

48. For more explicit details on censorship at the municipal level, see Giglio, "Decade," 112–51, an excellent background treatment. For a more formal legal approach, see Thomas B. Lear and J. Roger Noall, "Entertainment: Public Pressures and the Law," *Harvard Law Review* 71 (1957): 344–53.

49. Randall, *Censorship,* 39–41.

50. Speaking for the Court, Justice William Brennan noted, "We hold that a noncriminal process which requires the prior submission of a film to a censor avoids constitutional infirmity only if it takes place under procedural safeguards designed to obviate the dangers of a censorship system" (380 U.S. 51 [1965] at 57–58).

51. For more details on the decision as it affected the Bureau of Customs, see Randall, *Censorship,* 45–50.

52. See details of the role of self-regulation in maintaining an economic monopoly in Conant, *Antitrust,* 40–43.

53. "Supreme Court Gives 'Pinky' Texas Freedom," *Motion Picture Herald,* June 7, 1951, 13.

54. "Newsreel Censoring in Ohio Unconstitutional," *Motion Picture Herald,* September 13, 1952, 15.

55. "MPA [*sic*] Scores Court on Censorship Refusal," *Motion Picture Herald,* November 26, 1955, 21.

56. Ibid. Of course, this reasoning was fallacious, because the television industry had by then adopted its own self-regulatory code, based largely upon the Production

Code of the MPAA, and it was also regulated by the Federal Communications Commission.

57. Stephen Farber, *The Movie Rating Game* (Washington, D.C., 1972), 15. This is an excellent examination of the history and early (mis)functioning of the ratings system.

58. "Hollywood: Tough Talk on Entertainment," *Time,* June 12, 1995, 32–35. See also the essay by Charles Lyons in this volume.

The Paradox of Protest

American Film,
1980–1992

CHARLES LYONS

Censorship would neither be created nor sustained without pressure groups. Today these groups are on the increase and one of their prime targets is the American movie. They constitute a form of censorship that is, in some ways, more dangerous than a code, because it can operate in secrecy with rules of its own making.

Murray Schumach, *The Face on the Cutting Room Floor: The Story of Movie and Television Censorship*

The paradox of protest is simply this: take away our right to protest against something, especially a piece of art that may offend our sensibilities, and you radically limit one of our most cherished and democratic freedoms—the right to dissent. But permit protest and you give life to the possibility of censorship by political pressure. How is this paradox resolved? Is the risk of permitting protest worth the possibility that censorship might occur? Or is it better to put some limits on protests? These questions energize the present study.

Over roughly the past decade in the United States, the word *censorship* has been bandied about with great frequency. While commonly associated with repressive acts performed by public officials with conservative agendas, in recent years the word has come to mean *any* kind of cultural repression that results from official or tacit pressure from either the political left or right. In the context of film production, distribution, and exhibition, the word *censorship* is certainly not monolithic. It refers to a set of practices by institutions or groups, either prior to or following a film's release, the result of which is the removal of a word, a scene, or an entire film from the marketplace. The most obvious forms of film censorship are actions by federal, state, and municipal govern-ments and the mechanisms of self-regulation established by the motion picture industry itself. A third kind of censorship occurs as a result of group protests. Not all protests lead to censorship; many are primarily a means of publicizing a group's complaint. But when, as a result of street protests, a movie is reed-ited or pulled from theaters, such protests can be said to result in censorship.

From 1980 to 1992, protests over cinematic imagery came to reflect the tense, larger cultural debates over a wide variety of art. But the battles over movies—many played out on street corners—deserve separate attention for at least two reasons: because left and right groups so visibly and aggressively par-ticipated in them; and because they demonstrate how direct-action campaigns have come to overshadow the only remaining formal means of movie regula-tion, the rating system.

Since the Supreme Court held censorship of films unconstitutional in 1952, and especially since the motion picture industry abolished the Hays Produc-tion Code in 1961, special-interest pressure groups have emerged as the pri-mary protagonists in an ongoing drama about how movie content should be controlled. For groups on the right, the movies were too "free" in their depic-tion of such subjects as sex and religion; for left groups, the abuse of freedom in the depiction of women, ethnic groups, and gays and lesbians made movies objectionable. Although their methods of protest often appeared the same, the results of protests on the right were strikingly different from those on the left. This difference raises essential questions about the nature of movie protests. For example, what do the successes of some groups and the failures of others in achieving censorship tell us about relations of power and about the operations of corporate capitalism in the United States? Most important here, what does the relationship of protest to censorship tell us about contemporary American democracy?

Years from now, cultural historians and statisticians may argue over whether the 1980s and early 1990s actually produced more censorship than did, say, the 1930s or 1950s. What is clear is that the years 1980 to 1992—twelve years of Republican control of the White House—comprise a period during which movie censorship controversies were inexorably linked to political struggles. Protests by historically marginalized groups such as women, Asian Americans, gays and lesbians, and, simultaneously, conservative groups from the new Christian right distinguish these years as a time when movies were battlegrounds in the ongoing "culture wars"[1]—wars that included skirmishes over works ranging from art funded by the National Endowment for the Arts, to library books, to rap albums and music videos. While some of these skir-mishes erupted late in the decade, the year 1980 signaled a sudden increase in the lengths to which conservatives and leftists—or as Steven Vineberg divides the opposing forces, "the conservative and politically correct camps"[2]—were willing to go to combat images in movies. For groups on the left, protests provided ways of testing the extent to which the empowerment they had fought for during the previous two decades had been realized and could be defended. For conservatives, the election of Ronald Reagan to the presidency seemed the beginning of a new era, during which what they saw as baneful cultural change might be halted or reversed and "traditional" or "family" values reasserted. The year of Reagan's election, 1980, was also marked by controversy over a large number of films either released or in production: *Dressed to Kill, Fort Apache, the Bronx, Charlie Chan and the Curse of the Dragon Queen, Monty Python's Life of Brian, American Gigolo, Windows,* and *Cruising.* Why so many protests in 1980 alone? How did it happen that traditionally left groups—responsible for all but the actions against *Life of Brian*—had grown so sensitive to the way in which Hollywood depicted them? Did defeat in the political arena breed a sense of powerlessness among minority groups and inspire them to combat negative images with a renewed energy? Such questions may never be answered satisfactorily, yet an empirical study of each group's actions against a single representative movie during these years will help explain what was at stake for each group of protestors and why they believed that the stakes were so high.

Because left groups—the feminists who protested against *Dressed to Kill,* the Asian Americans against *Year of the Dragon* (1985), and the gays and lesbians against *Basic Instinct* (1992)—shared reasons for resisting cinematic treatments, their protests are considered consecutively and, where possible, collectively in the first three sections that follow. Conservative groups who protested against *The Last Temptation of Christ* (1988) are treated subsequently and their efforts compared with the methods and results of other protest groups.

MURDER IS NOT EROTIC!

From the insidious combination of violence and sexuality in its promotional material, to scene after scene of women raped, killed, or nearly killed, [Brian De Palma's] *Dressed to Kill* is a master work of misogyny. If this film succeeds, killing women may become the greatest turn-on of the Eighties! Join our protest!

Protest leaflet for *Dressed to Kill*

Recent studies have tended to conceive of film censorship as an act performed by official institutions or dominant social groups.[3] Even reformulations of film censorship—such as that of Annette Kuhn, who defends censorship as a "web of force relations" rather than a prohibitive act by a single institution[4]—continue to associate censorship with cultural dominance. Such works overlook the attempts and successes of "minority" pressure groups to force the film industry to censor rigorously its product or to allow protestors to do it for the industry. Censorship can be a form of empowerment, a means through which historically marginalized groups can gain a measure of control over the way they are represented in dominant media.

Throughout the history of the American film industry, sexual words and images have provoked more censorship and group protest than any other subject. Charges of "obscenity" and "pornography" have repeatedly thrown religious leaders, industry regulators, studio and independent producers, and state and local officials into heated disputes over what the limits of cinematic treatment of sexual subjects ought to be. In the 1950s and 1960s studio and independent producers, encouraged by a flurry of "liberal" court decisions that freed from censorship a wide range of sexually explicit films, challenged and ultimately diffused the matrix of control over sexual imagery exercised primarily by the industry's Production Code Administration (PCA) and the Catholic Legion of Decency, both of which disbanded by the late 1960s. The legal climate that had made it possible for sexual imagery to be more explicitly used in films quickly changed in the early 1970s when President Nixon appointed four conservative judges to the Supreme Court. Moreover, in the mid- to late 1970s women made pornography a major feminist concern. While conservative groups were also opposed to pornography, feminists for and against pornography quickly dominated the public debate. The year 1980 marked both a high point of and an end to a brief period during which feminists against pornography staged protests in front of movie theaters.

Feminists viewed pornography as part of the wider system of male hegemony and focused their critique on its perceived denigration of women. Unlike other protest groups, women believed that the way they were depicted on screen extended beyond the issue of stereotyping, distortion, and silencing. By arguing that pornography was "conduct," not "speech"—not only a matter of representation but a system of oppression in itself—some feminists claimed that it violated women's civil rights and was a primary cause of sexual discrimination in the United States.[5] While feminists had begun publishing critiques of pornography in the early 1970s, they did not launch serious street protests until 1976. In that year a billboard depicting a bruised woman in chains and the caption, "I'm black and blue from the Rolling Stones and I love it," became a catalyst for a group of California feminists to demonstrate and organize a national press conference that ultimately forced Warner Brothers to remove the offending billboard. Women against Violence in Pornography and Media (WAVPM) formed shortly after this success.[6]

In New York and San Francisco, women with similar agendas formed Women against Pornography (WAP) and Women against Violence against Women (WAVAW) following the release of a film called *Snuff*. According to Laura Lederer, this film, which purported to show the actual murder or "snuff" of a young woman, was "the powder keg that moved women seriously to confront the issue of pornography."[7] Feminists in San Diego, Buffalo, Los Angeles, San Jose, Denver, Philadelphia, and Monticello and Rochester, New York, among other cities, protested in front of theaters showing the movie. Protests in front of New York–area theaters were the largest and best organized in the country. In addition to picketing, protesters lodged complaints with the FBI, the police, the district attorney's office, the mayor's office, and the United Nations delegates from Argentina, the country where the film was allegedly produced.

Protests against *Snuff* included the distribution of leaflets that posed and answered the question, "Why are we here?":

> We are opposed to the filming, distribution and mass marketing of the film "Snuff." . . .

> Whether or not the death depicted in the current film "Snuff" is real or simulated is not the issue. That sexual violence is presented as entertainment, that the murder and dismemberment of a woman's body is commercial film material is an outrage to our sense of justice as women, as human beings.

> We—and all are welcomed to join in our efforts—will leaflet, picket, write letters, to do what is necessary to prevent the showing of the film "Snuff" in New York City. We can not allow murder for profit.[8]

The language in this leaflet suggests that the protesters aimed at censorship. Other voices of protest were more ambivalent. Brenda Feigen Fasteau, a feminist lawyer, stated: "I want to emphasize that the First Amendment guarantees the right to view this stuff, but as feminists we have to look at the kind of society that is titillated by the idea of women being murdered. And we have to deal with the possibility that this film is going to create a demand for real snuff films and that real women are going to be murdered."[9] Whatever protesters said, some of the results of their protests did indeed amount to censorship. In Baltimore, Maryland, a judge banned *Snuff* because of the film's so-called psychotic violence.[10] Responding to feminist protests in Santa Clara, California; and Philadelphia, city officials forced theaters to close down *Snuff.* After a lengthy trial that followed protests in front of a Monticello theater, local authorities summoned to court on obscenity charges the theater owner responsible for exhibiting *Snuff.*[11] In most other places, protests failed to prevent exhibition of the movie.[12]

When *Snuff* premiered in Rochester in October 1977, antipornography feminists responded more militantly than in earlier instances. Feminists were especially angered by an advertisement that heralded *Snuff* as "the bloodiest thing that ever happened in front of a camera," depicting a women being cut into pieces by a pair of bloodied scissors. As a result, Rochester-area feminists vandalized theaters exhibiting the film and were arrested.

Actions against *Snuff* continued after 1977,[13] but feminist antipornography campaigns did not reach so intense a pitch again until the release of Brian De Palma's *Dressed to Kill* in 1980.[14] While feminist groups in San Francisco, Los Angeles, and Boston demonstrated against the film when it premiered early in August, the New York protests were the largest and best organized. On August 28 in front of the 57th Street Playhouse, several New York antipornography feminist groups, spearheaded by WAP, banded together to picket *Dressed to Kill.* An estimated 100 to 150 protesters carried such placards as, "Murder of women is not erotic," "*Dressed to Kill* is a racist and sexist lie," and "Women slaughter is not entertainment but terrorism."[15] They chanted, "Murder isn't sexy, murder isn't funny, but that's how Hollywood makes its money" and "No more profits off our bodies, no more pleasure off our pain."[16] The protesters also called on supporters to convey their anger by writing to Brian De Palma, care of Filmways, the film's distributor, and to boycott the film.

A WAVPM protest leaflet distributed in San Francisco coupled with statements made by activists Dorchen Leidholdt and Stephanie Rones suggests that antipornography feminists' actions against *Dressed to Kill,* though often bitter, were not intended to remove the film from the theaters.[17] WAVPM's leaflet details the group's objections to the film:

> From the insidious combination of violence and sexuality in its promotional material to scene after scene of women raped, killed, or nearly killed, *Dressed to Kill* is a master work of misogyny. . . . Though Kate Miller [Angie Dickinson] dies and Liz Blake bleeds time and again, three scenes—the rape, the necrophilia, and a slashing scene—were to have happened in women's minds. As if the eroticization of violence were not enough, *Dressed to Kill* asserts that women crave physical abuse; that humiliation, pain, and brutality are essential

to our sexuality. . . . If this film succeeds, killing women may become the greatest turn-on of the Eighties! Join our protest![18]

Nowhere in this leaflet does WAVPM state any intention other than to picket. Countering charges made by Andrew Sarris in the *Village Voice,* Dorchen Leidholdt of WAP insisted that none of the three national organizations protesting against *Dressed* had "anti-libertarian overtones":

> All are opposed to censorship; all respect First Amendment strictures against the imposition of prior restraints on any form of speech; all are opposed to general prohibitions of the production, distribution, and display of pornographic materials. . . . The demonstrations against De Palma's exercise in misogyny and bigotry were intended only to present an opposing voice in the din of critical acclaim that has helped make *Dressed to Kill* a major box office success.[19]

Stephanie Rones similarly defended feminists' protests while deriding film critics' reviews:

> A movie like "Dressed to Kill" encourages and perpetuates violence and pairs it with sexuality by having vicious acts instead of loving and caring. Film critics have enormous responsibility and often write about what they see in a very narrow sense, reviewing only the artistic relevance and ignoring the social relevance. . . . Is a woman being slashed in an elevator funny or erotic or entertaining? Critics should look at these films on a broader level.[20]

Rones also denied that WAVAW intended to censor *Dressed to Kill:* "We're only asking for responsibility from film critics," she told a *Los Angeles Times* reviewer. "What people see on the movie screen is more than art: its messages influence society."[21]

Rather than causing theater managers to close *Dressed to Kill* or dissuading producers from making similar films, protests against the movie seemed only to increase its box office profits. During the week when the protests against *Dressed* were largest, the movie rose from third to first place on *Variety*'s weekly listing of top-grossing films, placing it ahead of *Airplane* and *The Empire Strikes Back.*[22] Leidholdt lamented the fact that feminists' protests had assisted *Dressed* in becoming a commercial success:

> After *Dressed to Kill,* we realized that protesting the eroticizing of violence in Hollywood films was not effective. We had been especially scared about *Dressed to Kill* and wanted to educate the public that these movies were doing exactly

what so much of violent pornography is doing. We thought Hollywood might listen. But they didn't. They just kept producing one film after another.[23]

Leidholdt claims that after the protests against *Dressed* had backfired, WAP changed its view of protest campaigns in general. From 1980 on, her organization would no longer protest in the streets in front of theaters. The fact that there were hardly any feminist protests against the sexual imagery in specific movies during the 1980s confirms Leidholdt's claim.[24]

In the ensuing years, written debates over sexual imagery in mainstream movies such as *Body Double* (1985) and *Fatal Attraction* (1987),[25] and over pornography in general, came to replace street protests. While feminists who protested against pornography failed to overturn the system of male hegemony they perceived in mainstream as well as pornographic films, their direct-action campaigns during the late 1970s and in 1980 brought cohesion, recognition, and focus to a constituency. The shift of antipornography feminists from direct action to legal campaigns reflected a general change in methods of political activism in the United States. Feminists against pornography had learned that protests do not pay and as a group they were better off trying to change sexism through legal means.

STOP STEREOTYPING US!

The movie will have a negative effect, especially on people who have been in the Vietnam war and still hate Asians, and for people in areas where they have little contact with Chinese—like in the midwest, the South . . . The movie provides an excuse to hate.

Irvin Lai

Although it was not the first film to draw protest on account of ethnic and racial stereotyping, D. W. Griffith's *The Birth of a Nation,* released in 1915, created the widest controversy both at the time of its release and for many years afterward. Despite President Wilson's endorsement of the film, *Birth* aroused criticism from the National Association for the Advancement of Colored People (NAACP), which attacked the movie as a racist recreation of the reconstruction South. In succeeding years, African Americans, acting through the NAACP and other organizations, also attempted to remove stereotypes from such films as *Gone with the Wind* (1939) and *Song of the South* (1942), and succeeded in preventing *Uncle Tom's Cabin* (1946) from being made. Other ethnic groups protested against movies containing cinematic stereotypes with greater regularity and rigor than African Americans.[26] Coalitions of Italian Americans, Puerto Ricans, and Cuban Americans, among other groups, launched angry campaigns against the producers of *The Godfather* (1976), *Fort Apache, the Bronx* (1979–80), *Midnight Express* (1981), and *Scarface* (1983). Several of these coalitions convinced filmmakers to insert disclaimers qualifying the portrayal of a particular ethnic group, yet rarely did the protests produce censorious effects. In 1980, the interracial Committee against *Fort Apache* (CAFA), consisting primarily of African Americans and Puerto Ricans, staged protests before and after the release of *Fort Apache*. While CAFA achieved at least one victory for censorship when the Philadelphia City Council prevented all civic venues from showing the movie, Puerto Ricans' participation in protests against racist film imagery practically disappeared during the decade following the release of *Fort Apache*.[27]

On the other hand, Asian American groups emerged in the 1980s as the most active antagonists to Hollywood's practice of racial stereotyping. Asian American critics of Hollywood asserted that the civil rights movement had only influenced mainstream directors to develop "an essentially biracial consciousness (whites and blacks)."[28] By repeatedly casting white actors in Asian roles and depicting male Asian characters as villainous and females as sexually demure, critics charged, filmmakers perpetuated stereotypes and assisted in Asian Americans' marginalization and oppression. Unlike other racial and ethnic groups during the same period, Asian Americans challenged a series of films rather than just one or two and began to develop a general strategy for resisting the anti-Asiatic imagery produced by Hollywood.

During the late 1970s and 1980s the ability of specific groups to influence filmmakers' depiction of them corresponded to how important the film industry perceived each group to be, the persistence of the protest group, and the mechanism of protest employed. Of all the groups that staged protests during 1970s and 1980s, Asian Americans had been perceived by the film industry as one of the least threatening. Asian actors, directors, and producers did not wield great power in the movie industry, and prior to 1970 Asian Americas had shown little interest in challenging cinematic stereotypes. The release of *Charlie Varrick* (1973) and a remake of *Lost Horizons* (1973) elicited the most overt criticism of films by Asian Americans to that date. A group of Asian American artists was especially angered that a white actor, John Gielgud, was cast and cosmeticized to play the role of Chang in *Lost Horizons*. In 1977 the Association of Asian/Pacific Artists staged protests against the filming of a Dodge-Aspen commercial that featured another use of "racist cosmetology."[29]

Three years later these incidents were followed by protests against *Charlie Chan and the Curse of the Dragon Queen* (1980–81) and a revival of the Fu Manchu figure in *The Fiendish Plot of Fu Manchu* (1980). The simple fact that these films recreated two much-despised stereotypes alarmed Asian Americans.

By 1985 Asian Americans had established a network of political and cultural groups determined to fight discrimination and violence not simply by protest but also by using to advantage some of the apparatus of mainstream cultural production. Asian American groups planned to protest *Year of the Dragon* far in advance of its scheduled release date of August 16, 1985. In New York a coalition against the movie included nearly a dozen groups,[30] many of which associated Michael Cimino's movie with other racist and sexist television and film images of Asian Americans and with the increase in anti-Asian violence in America.[31] Upon learning of Dino DeLaurentis's plan to produce a film based on Robert Daly's novel *Year of the Dragon,* Asian Americans took notice. Several months before the film went into production, Janice Sakamoto and Forrest Gok, members of the National Asian American Telecommunications Association (NAATA), warned the Asian American community about any movie based on Daly's racist, "graphically sensationalistic" portrait of Chinatown and Chinese Americans.[32]

Cimino began filming *Year of the Dragon* on location in New York's Chinatown in early October 1984. During the ensuing weeks the Chinese Consolidated Benevolent Association (CCBA), the oldest and most powerful association of Chinese in the United States, staged protests at the movie set and criticized the making of the film in its weekly newsletters. The CCBA objected to what it viewed as unfair portrayals of Chinese Americans in the Daly novel. One of its letters reached City Hall, which responded with a note stating that in no circumstances would it "act as a censor."[33] On-location protests continued, but the *Dragon* producers made no concessions to the protesters.

Nearly one year later, on August 13, 1985, Asian Americans attended the previews for *Year of the Dragon* in Los Angeles and New York and were outraged. The following day, thirty-six groups formed the Coalition against *Year of the Dragon* and held organizational meetings in San Francisco and New York. The New York coalition, which spearheaded the national protest, issued a press release on August 14 explaining their organization's objections to the film and their reasons for protesting:

> Why protest? . . . We believe that the film grossly distorts the public's perceptions of Chinese Americans during a time of great misunderstanding and anti-Asian sentiment. Chinatown is portrayed as "an exotic foreign world deep

Demonstrators protest *The Year of the Dragon* (MGM/UA 1985). Photo by Kevin Cohen, courtesy *New York Post*.

within the city" that is dominated by criminals and youth groups. . . . Due to the scarcity of accurate and meaningful portrayals of Asian Americans in the mass media, there are few realistic images to counter balance the damage done by "Year of the Dragon." Asian Americans across the country have called for a national boycott of the MGM/UA release, demanding that the company withdraw "Year of the Dragon" from distribution.[34]

Another press release issued by the coalition similarly referred to *Dragon* as "an irresponsible, hostile film that must be stopped."[35] Renee Tajima, a New York–based writer and filmmaker, told *Variety:* "We know we're going to protest, we know we're going to outreach to other organizations, and we know we're going to demonstrate."[36] It remained to be seen how prerelease picketing, censorious threats, and outreaching would influence the distribution and exhibition of the movie.

Year of the Dragon opened on Friday, August 16, in New York, San Francisco, Los Angeles, Washington, Boston, Detroit, and other cities. An estimated three hundred protesters picketed in front of Loew's Astor Plaza on Broadway. Smaller protests were staged in front of other New York–area theaters. Protesters carried signs reading, "No More Racism and Sexism!" "Cimino Exploits Asian Youths!" "No More Suzie Wong's!" and "End the *Year of the Dragon!*" and chanted, "Drive this movie out of town—shut it down! Shut it down!"[37] The protest rally included a press conference attended by local and national newspaper, television, and radio journalists. Invited speakers included Manhattan borough president David Dinkins and other politicians, along with spokespeople from many Asian American groups.

On August 24 nearly one thousand protesters rallied against *Dragon* in San Francisco, several hundred in New York and Los Angeles, and about thirty in Boston. Janice Sakamoto, a spokesperson for NAATA in San Francisco, summarized the Bay Area's protest goals, some of which coincided with those of the New York coalition:[38] to educate people about Hollywood stereotyping; to suspend video rights and distribution of *Dragon;* to encourage MGM/UA and Hollywood to create an independent Asian American advisory board; to succeed in having a portion of the film's proceeds go to an Asian community project; to encourage Hollywood to hire more Asian Americans.[39] In Los Angeles picketers were organized by an ad hoc alliance, the Asian Pacific American Media Watch. They marched down Sunset Boulevard bearing "a symbolic coffin which they burned in front of Grauman's Chinese Theater,"[40] where *Dragon* was showing. One of the protesters, Irvin Lai, the national grand president of the Chinese American Citizens, told the *Los Angeles Times,* "We're afraid this film will poison minds. We want people to see our side. We don't like to demonstrate but we must let the people know we are outraged. The racism and sexism are just too prominent to ignore."[41] In Boston Julian Low, administrative director of the Asian American Resource Workshop, similarly told the *Boston Globe:* "I think it was the most racist [film] I've seen."[42] Marilyn Lee, Mayor Raymond Flynn's liaison to Boston's Asian American community, read a statement condemning "negative stereotyping of any community, regardless of the color of their skin or the cut of their coat."[43] Mayor Flynn, who had met with members of the Asian American community to listen to complaints about increased anti-Asian violence in the Boston area, supported the Asian Americans' protests. "I find films [like *Dragon*] offensive and insulting," the mayor said. "Diversity of our city should be our strength, not our weakness. For some movie to exploit a certain proud segment of our community is just not helpful—whether it be anti-Asian, anti-Catholic, anti-minority, anti-gay."[44]

Despite a score of negative reviews and Asian Americans' protests against the film, *Dragon* initially proved to be a box office success. Four days after its national release, *Variety* called *Dragon* "luke warm"[45] in one article, but "healthy" in another.[46] The word "healthy" referred specifically to *Dragon's* Washington, D.C., opening, where the film—which opened in thirty area theaters—earned $220,000 in a weekend, thereby placing it ahead of such other new releases as *Return of the Living Dead, Volunteers, Kiss of the Spider Woman, The Bride,* and *Pee-Wee's Big Adventure. Variety* labeled *Dragon* "delightful" in Detroit and "brisk" in Pittsburgh but only "sleepy" in Saint Louis. After three weeks, however, *Dragon* was a "disappointing" third place on *Variety's* "Top Grossing Films" list, having earned only four million dollars, an amount well below MGM/UA's expectations. On September 5, a full three weeks after the film had opened, the Coalition against *Year of the Dragon* reported in a press release, "*{Dragon}* has closed down in 36 theaters across the country and box office sales dropped 30% in its second week and 9% in its 3rd," although it is difficult to measure the precise influence of the Asian American protests on *Dragon's* national box office profits.

On August 29, five days after the national protest, the CCBA in conjunction with the Federation of Chinese Organizations of America filed a one-hundred-million-dollar class-action suit against MGM/UA.[47] On the same day, Frank Rothman, CEO and chairman of MGM/UA, announced at a meeting of the Los Angeles City Council his decision to attach disclaimers immediately to the nearly two hundred prints of *Dragon* in circulation in Los Angeles– and New York–area theaters. Rothman also promised to add disclaimers to all prints of the film in the near future. The disclaimer read, "This film does not intend to demean or to ignore the many positive features of Asian Americans and specifically Chinese American communities. Any similarity between the depiction in this film and any association, organization, individual or Chinatown that exists in real life is accidental."[48] Rothman told *Variety* that MGM/UA had decided to insert a disclaimer "because we have no desire to offend any group of people."

Rothman's inclusion of a disclaimer brought credit to Michael Woo, a newly elected Los Angeles city councilman and Los Angeles's first and only Asian American representative, who had been active in the protests against *Dragon.* Rothman stood side by side with Woo at the City Council meeting while Woo—whom *Variety* described as "beaming with satisfaction"[49]—said, "We are here today to announce an historical event. [Rothman and MGM/UA have] made it clear that 'we will not tolerate people telling them [*sic*] what films to make, but when we have offended groups we will listen.'"[50] Rothman promised that MGM/UA would issue a public apology to the Asian American community, and he agreed to consider Woo's and the coalition's requests to establish an industry advisory committee composed of Asian Americans assigned to examine scripts relevant to Asian Americans. Rothman also said that he was willing to discuss donating a portion of profits from *Dragon* or a future MGM/UA movie toward an Asian American community project and to hire more Asian Americans at all levels of the film industry.[51]

The insertion of a disclaimer into *Dragon* appeared to have appeased Woo and other protesters. The media heralded the studio's concession to the protesters as a rare instance when community-based pressure actually had succeeded. In a September 6 "update," the Coalition against Year of the Dragon stated that MGM/UA's agreement to add a disclaimer indicated that Asian Americans' protests "were working."[52] Some Asian Americans, however, remained skeptical. Writing in the *Asian American Network*, Antonio DeCastro reminded his readers that the roots of their protests against *Dragon* went deeper than opposing a single movie: "The issues that were raised around the movie cannot, as easily as the movie, disappear in the background. . . . The racism underlying [*Dragon* and other films] is a problem that pervades the foundation of American society. And until this problem and its root causes are overcome, the struggle continues."[53] It is clear that by the time the Coalition against *Year of the Dragon* had organized a national day of protest, censorious language had practically vanished from its slogans and press releases. The disclaimer itself, a "victory" that boosted Asian Americans' morale, did not constitute censorship, for the film was not removed from the marketplace, and no theaters canceled screenings because of subsequent legislative or civil actions.[54]

Educational and informational actions had become the campaign's primary goal. Nevertheless, subsequent demands, such as a plan to disrupt MGM/UA's distribution of *Dragon* in subsidiary markets as well as Woo's and others' call for Rothman to establish an Asian American committee to screen scripts, reveal that the censorious impulse was still alive.

Michael Cimino's *Year of the Dragon* angered and galvanized the Asian American community as no previous movie had. But what had Asian Americans really accomplished through their protests? Was the Coalition against *Year of the Dragon* successful in, as Gina Marchetti writes, "resisting . . . dominant culture's ability to label, limit, and define the racial other?"[55] Did Asian Americans who protested against *Dragon* in fact produce a counterhegemonic effect? On the surface, MGM/UA's decision to issue an apology to Asian Americans and insert disclaimers, an action that Rothman said was undertaken at "great expense" to the studio, revealed that the film industry had acknowledged Asian Americans' political power. The fact that Rothman chose to insert disclaimers but not to address any of the issues on the coalition's platform, however, undermined the latter's claim of empowerment. Noting that none of the coalition's significant demands—the suspension of subsidiary rights, the establishment of an Asian American community advisory board, the donation of production profits to an Asian American project—had been granted, NATA spokesperson Janice Sakamoto lamented:

> With the studios, we always feel we are at point zero. But this is also part of the process of the continued effort of empowering our community. . . . There are many battles in the war. . . . As you know, Hollywood is really about making money. Anything they can exploit to do that, I think they will do. Hopefully, there will be more enlightened directors who will challenge that.[56]

Sakamoto located the power over ethnic representation in the studio and the director and implied that, despite occasional responses to protest, Hollywood would remain indifferent to the real issues facing Asian Americans. MGM/UA's response, however, whether a sign of sensitivity or political chicanery, arguably made moviemakers and Americans more aware of the "model minority's" rising determination to combat racial stereotypes. And the widespread protests themselves showed that a diverse community had been galvanized. It also proved that, unlike antipornography feminists, Asian Americans had decided that, however much they desired to censor demeaning stereotypes, their gradual empowerment depended upon structuring demands in noncensorious ways so that Hollywood, which was acknowledged to have the final power over representation, might use that power in ways friendlier to their interests.

WE ARE NOT INVISIBLE!

We are not about censorship here, we're talking about balance. We had 2,000 years of one message. We want to have parity.
Tom Amaniano

Hollywood came, over the years, to expect protests against its products from a number of sources, but gay and lesbian groups' attempts to censor films were totally unexpected. Unlike women and ethnic groups, homosexuals were not only marginalized in society at large but almost completely ignored in films. During the 1950s and early 1960s the Motion Picture Producers and Distributors of America (MPPDA) rigorously forbade nearly all references to homosexuality. But such films as *Cat on a Hot Tin Roof* (1958), *Pit of Loneliness*

291

(1959), *Suddenly Last Summer* (1959), *Devil's Advocate* (1961), *Advise and Consent* (1961), and *The Children's Hour* (1962), each of which contained homosexual characters or themes, presented a strong challenge to the code. Under pressure from Hollywood directors and producers in the post–World War II years, the PCA gradually changed its policies toward films containing homosexual themes. In 1961 MPPDA president Eric Johnston announced that it would be "permissible [*sic*] under the Code for the PCA to consider approving references in motion pictures to the subject of sex aberrations, provided any references are treated with care, discretion and restraint, and in all other aspects conform to the Code."[57]

The Motion Picture Association of America's decision to permit producers to make "visible" homosexuality was no doubt a change welcomed by homosexuals who, during the 1960s, had begun to develop a politics of "coming out." Gays and lesbians, however, soon learned that screen visibility had its drawbacks: as depicted by mainstream filmmakers, homosexuals were, they believed, frequently stereotyped as psychotic and lonely individuals who could only be "cured" by the "normalcy" of the heterosexual world. In 1969 the Stonewall riots, in which patrons of a gay bar fought back against a police raid, helped to galvanize homosexuals and focus their anger. The release of *The Boys in the Band* (1970), *Fortune and Men's Eyes* (1971), *Death in Venice* (1971), and *The Perfect Couple* (1979), each of which contained stereotypes, elicited a wave of angry written criticism and caused gay and lesbian groups to demand change. *Windows, American Gigolo,* and *Cruising,* all either produced or released in 1980, galvanized a second wave of activism that included protests in front of theaters. Protests against mainstream movies became one highly visible way of challenging heterosexuals' cultural authority to construct homosexual identity.

Cruising provoked the largest protests among homosexuals to that date. "*Cruising* was the last straw in a long stream of Hollywood horrors," according to film historian Vito Russo. "Coming as it did in company with *Windows* and *American Gigolo,* it acted as a catalyst for a massive nationwide protest of the Hollywood treatment of gays."[58] The homosexuals who protested against *Cruising* were not unified in their desire to censor the film but were unquestionably angry about its stereotypes, especially in light of an increase in real-life violence against gays. Over the ensuing years, films such as *Making Love* (1980), *Personal Best* (1982), *Deathtrap* (1982), *Partners* (1982), *Victor/ Victoria* (1982), *La Cage aux Folles* (1984), *The Color Purple* (1986), *My Beautiful Laundrette* (1986), and *Kiss of the Spiderwoman* (1986) revealed a pattern of greater sensitivity and fewer negative stereotypes. The mass protests against *Cruising* appeared to have produced positive results. *New York Times* critic Leslie

Bennetts proclaimed there was a "new realism in portraying homosexuals" and seemed to imply that this development was both daring and desirable.[59] But many gays and lesbians felt that most of the above films did not represent real progress at all, but rather a continuation of the treatment of homosexuality as seen through heterosexual eyes.[60]

In the early 1990s a sense of exasperation with Hollywood underlay gays' and lesbians' protests against *Basic Instinct* before and after its release. While the 1980s had brought a series of AIDS television dramas and a handful of "positive" portrayals of homosexuality into mainstream movies, homosexuals believed that the Hollywood heterosexual hegemony, whether unconsciously or not, continued to depict them as villains. When the press reported that Joe Eszterhas had been paid three million dollars for a screenplay featuring a bisexual psychopathic killer,[61] gays and lesbians realized that their earlier protests had fallen on deaf ears. "The fury that has been called up by 'Basic Instinct,'" Michael Bronski wrote in *NYQ* just before the film premiered, "is due as much to the realization of our relative powerlessness as it is to the film itself. Twenty-five years after the Stonewall Riots, we are still at war with Hollywood. Only now we are not only smarter and savvier, but closer to our rage than ever before."[62]

Homosexuals who mobilized against *Basic Instinct* combined confrontational tactics with a carefully planned educational campaign. In February 1991, immediately after Carolco Pictures announced its plans to film *Basic Instinct* in the heart of San Francisco's gay community, the Gay and Lesbian Alliance against Defamation (GLAAD) and Queer Nation—members of which had read a widely circulated early version of Eszterhas's script—began to plan ways of protesting against the film. Letter writing was the first approach. Carolco Pictures reported that they had received hundreds of requests for the studio to cancel its production of *Basic Instinct* or to at least film the movie outside of San Francisco. A week before the crew was scheduled to begin shooting at their first San Francisco location—a country-and-western gay dance bar called Rawhide II—Hollie Conley, a member of the local GLAAD chapter, met with a Carolco representative to persuade the studio to make script changes. Carolco refused Conley's request. Carolco, however, anticipated trouble on the set.[63]

On April 10, 1991, Carolco began filming in San Francisco amidst protests. After two weeks of continual protests, Alan Marshall, the film's producer, agreed to meet with the activists on April 24. Representatives from GLAAD, Queer Nation, ACT UP, and Supervisor Harvey Britt's office sat across from screenwriter Joe Eszterhas, director Paul Verhoeven, and producer Alan Marshall and listed their demands. The activists, as Lynn Hirshberg recounted in *Vanity Fair,* "wanted Michael Douglas's character to be transformed into a lesbian, and further suggested that Kathleen Turner should be his replacement. They also wanted [the characters] Catherine and Roxy—both of whom murder men in *Basic Instinct*—to murder women as well; that way, they explained, lesbian and bisexual women would not be perceived as man-haters."[64] Eszterhas was the only person connected to the film who appeared receptive to these suggested script changes. A week after the meeting, he proposed thirteen pages of script changes to "reflect a sensitivity to many of the opinions expressed by gay community leaders."[65] One script change had Michael Douglas —who plays the police detective investigating the lesbian murderer—saying, "A lot of the best people I've met in this town are gay."[66] That Eszterhas had suggested script changes pleased the protesters, but Carolco executives were perturbed and flatly rejected them. "I consider his changes patronizing drivel," Peter Hoffman, president and CEO of Carolco, said. "Joe Eszterhas is a sniveling hypocrite and I have no use for him. Besides, we would never change a script in response to political pressure."[67]

On April 29, after a week of continued pickets, Marshall obtained a restraining order from the city of San Francisco that forbade demonstrators to come closer than 100 yards from the filming, protest in a "loud or boisterous" manner, or use lights or "glitter" to distract the filmmakers.[68] Three nights later, the protesters "unleashed their most extreme protest of the shoot."[69] In a deliberate violation of the San Francisco restraining order, members of Queer Nation came within 100 feet of the set, blew whistles, and chanted. The production crew was forced to stop filming. Before resuming, producer Alan Marshall successfully demanded that police arrest some thirty demonstrators. The following night, five more Queer Nationals were arrested.[70]

Gays and lesbians trailed the *Basic Instinct* crew to locations around San Francisco on every evening of filming until May 8, when the production returned to Los Angeles. During this period, protesters were relatively subdued, yet an angry debate erupted in the press. The written controversy centered on the question, "Were the mainstream media presenting homosexuals' protests accurately or revealing their own heterosexual and anti-censorship biases?" The *San Francisco Examiner* inveighed against "storm-trooper tactics" and asserted, "The thought police are at it again. This time it's the thought police of the left. The effort to shoot down the movie is wrong, and it is dangerous to boot. People of minority views—gay activists among them—should be especially careful to protect the freedom of speech and thought."[71] GLAAD found homophobia implicit in such reports: "[They] are trying to fit this issue into a slot they've created about 'political correctness' and 'censorship of the left,'" Hollie

Conley told the *Bay Area Reporter.* "I think they're trying to fit it into that mold as a way of creating this ogre of left-wing thought control which doesn't really exist."[72] A Queer Nation press release stated, "We will not let up until the censorship of our lives ends, and we finally see our richness and complexity as a community reflected back to us on the silver screen."[73]

The charge of "censorship from the left" in *Time* magazine and elsewhere may have had an effect on some protesters. In the months leading up to the *Basic Instinct* release date early in 1992, GLAAD San Francisco and the Gay and Lesbian Alliance advanced a less belligerent protest strategy. They coordinated a letter-writing campaign to exhibitors that read:

> We are writing to you and other film exhibitors to express our concern about the movie "Basic Instinct." . . . Our concerns arise from the fact that "Basic Instinct" is the latest example of a long Hollywood tradition of stereotyping lesbians and gays as evil, violent and psychopathic. This movie's villains are three killers, all of whom are lesbian or bisexual women. The hero is a homophobic, heterosexual man who forces himself sexually on a woman. . . . We at GLAAD . . . feel we must exercise our First Amendment right to challenge the current consensus, oppose Hollywood's censorship and bigotry, and seek more diverse and accurate representation of lesbians, gays and bisexuals in film.[74]

This letter reveals how determined GLAAD was to distinguish its resistance to *Basic Instinct* from a call for censorship.

As the March 20, 1992, premiere date approached, the militant and educational groups appeared to be growing more unified. "Our effort [will be] to give away crucial information about the film," said Alain Klein, a founder of Queer Nation, "to discourage people from seeing it."[75] Rich Wilson, the group's media coordinator, stated an additional goal: "to destroy the first weekend's box-office grosses."[76] In February a group consisting primarily of lesbians formed "Catherine Did It!" an organization named after the film's bisexual character, who becomes a serial murder suspect. "Our major focus is to keep people from going to the film," Annette Gaudino, a spokeswoman for the group told the *Los Angeles Times.* "We want to tell everyone as much about the movie as possible."[77] Gaudino explained that her group was resorting to protest because many of its proposed script changes had been ignored. "We know that they went ahead without doing what we asked for," she said. "So now we're going to do what we have to do to keep the public away from this film."[78] In an interview with the *Washington Post,* Phyllis Burke, the organizer of "Catherine Did It!" explained her group's decision to reveal the movie's ending: "If the viewer knows what the ending is, the manipulation of the viewer

Protesters gather outside a San Francisco theater showing *Basic Instinct* (Carolco, 1991). Photo by Marc Geller.

is eliminated. We hope the viewer will see more easily what we're talking about. Our problem is not that we want to see all perfect images of gays and lesbians. We just want to see a balance. Unfortunately, there hasn't been one."[79]

More than other groups, GLAAD continued to emphasize that its approach was educational. In New York, GLAAD organizer Donald Suggs asserted: "The thrust of our effort is educational. . . . We're not telling people, 'we don't think you should be able to see this film.' We think people can make those kinds of decisions themselves. We're just making them aware of the information out there . . . about the way Hollywood has dealt with gay and lesbian issues."[80] On the day before *Basic Instinct* opened, Ellen Carten of GLAAD New York declared:

[Our campaign] has been a great success already—there's been more media coverage and the media has been more fair. It has also been a success because we have gotten the word out. . . . We are changing the consciousness around issues—and I don't think anyone could go out and make a movie like this again or spend three million dollars in optioning a script like this. . . . The film hasn't opened publicly yet, and we have been successful in that, with the exception of a few bad pieces, we've been able to get our point across in print, radio, TV—and I'd say that that in and of itself spells success for this campaign.[81]

This statement suggested that the groups against *Basic Instinct* were ultimately content to spread their message against movie stereotypes, rather than attempt to suppress the film.

On March 19, the day before *Basic Instinct* opened, Tri-Star released a statement to the news media: "Freedom of expression covers filmmakers and movie goers as well as protesters. . . . We hope people will come see 'Basic Instinct' and make up their own minds. We feel it is a terrific film, and we expect that most people will agree with us."[82] This statement, similar to the one Carolco had issued during the prerelease period, showed that homosexual groups had succeeded in putting Tri-Star on the defensive. Exhibitors, however, were not perceptibly intimidated. In spite of the prerelease protests, the letters they had received from protesters, and the impending postrelease headaches, theater chains across the country zealously scheduled *Basic Instinct,* just as they would have any blockbuster.

On the evening of the premiere of *Basic Instinct,* in anticipation of massive street protests, many theater managers positioned extra security guards in front of their theaters. For the most part, however, this extra precaution proved unnecessary. Protests across the country were smaller and more orderly than expected. Homosexual groups and members of the National Organization of Women (NOW) demonstrated in front of theaters in Los Angeles, San Francisco, New York, Seattle, Washington, and other cities. The largest protests were staged in San Francisco, where, according to the *San Francisco Chronicle,* one hundred activists "swarmed in front of the Metro Theater on Union Street, badgering patrons who stood in line and entered the theater."[83] Demonstrators blew whistles, passed out leaflets, and carried placards reading, "Kiss My Ice Pick," "Hollywood Promotes Anti-Gay Violence," and "Save Your Money— The Bisexual Did It." For the most part, little attempt was made to dissuade moviegoers from entering the theater. Los Angeles protests were similar. The film opened in approximately one hundred theaters in the Los Angeles area, but the coalition of protesting groups focused their actions in front of one theater— the Westwood Coronet—where some thirty protesters handed out flyers and did not, by and large, attempt to prevent moviegoers from entering.[84]

In New York protesters from gay and lesbian groups and NOW staged their largest actions in front of Loew's Theater at 19th Street and Broadway. The Loew's protests involved leafleting, placard-waving, chanting, and lively debate between moviegoers and activists. Some of the people entering the theater proclaimed their First Amendment rights to see whatever they wanted and chastised the protesters for attempting to dissuade them from entering the theater. The protesters, however, were not unified in what they were telling moviegoers. "What we really want to do is tell [people entering the theater] not to go tonight," William Meyerhafer of Queer Nation said,[85] while Jill Frasca of NOW, standing nearby, said, "I'm not telling you not to see this film. I'm telling you that this movie is misogynist and it says queer people are sick. . . . We're both here [homosexuals and women] because if one of us is oppressed, we're all going to be oppressed. If society feels that it's okay to beat up women, then it's going to be okay to beat up queers."[86] In print, activists carefully avoided appearing censorious. A flyer jointly issued by Queer Nation, GLAAD New York, NOW New York, Women's Health Action and Mobilization, and the Bisexual Public Action Committee stated in bold letters: "Basic Instinct = Basic Hatred / Entertainment or Defamation / You Decide."

Everyone who protested against *Basic Instinct* agreed that the film stereotyped a minority group long victimized by the heterosexual majority culture, but GLAAD's educational protests contrasted sharply with Queer Nation's militant actions. During the prerelease period, both groups demanded that Eszterhas change the script according to very specific guidelines. When Carolco rejected these demands and continued to film in the heart of the gay community in San Francisco, GLAAD responded by issuing press releases and asking exhibitors to think twice about the film, but not to cancel it. Members of Queer Nation, on the other hand, took their anger to the streets and, on at least one occasion, prevented moviemakers from filming.

Upon the release of *Basic Instinct,* some members of Queer Nation once again revealed their censorious impulses, yet theirs and other groups' actions failed to result in censorship. Theater exhibitors did not refuse to show the film prior to its release, and on no occasion was the movie withdrawn on account of protest or governmental action. The most certain result of gays' and lesbians' protests was that they drew more customers to the film than might otherwise have been inclined to watch it. Tri-Star flatly denied that the demonstrators had raised the public's consciousness about homophobia, while expressing their gratitude for the free publicity the protesters had given to the movie. Many gay activists, however, proclaimed that their actions were successful. Although *Basic Instinct* earned close to fifteen million dollars during its opening weekend—a solid release by practically any movie's standards—Judy Sisneros of Queer Nation told the *Los Angeles Times,* "The success of the movie wasn't unexpected—All this publicity about the movie's ratings and the queer community's issues helped to generate interest. But that was a trade-off we had to accept in order to make our point."[87] This statement contrasts sharply with Queer Nation's prerelease goal of "killing" the movie's opening-week profits. Nevertheless, activists were in relative agreement that resistance to *Basic Instinct* had increased public awareness of degrading homosexual stereotypes in movies. And no one contested Amy Taubin's claim that one "upside" of the protests was that "homophobia ha[d] gotten a lot of ink in the straight media."[88]

But the larger question of how the entire controversy had affected homosexuals' status in respect to the film industry, and within society at large, elicited contrasting responses. On the militant side, Michelangelo Signorile claimed that the protests against *Basic Instinct,* combined with other actions such as demonstrations at the 1991 and 1992 Academy Awards, had proven that activism paid off:

> The entire two-year period beginning in 1990 seemed like an Academy
> Awards production in and of itself, a fantasy epic in which an industry begins
> to deal with an oppressed minority it has continually mistreated. Though they
> are just a start, the changes are many in comparison to the conditions prevail-
> ing only two years before. These events proved what could be done when the
> system was taken on full force.[89]

Michael Bronski, writing in *NYQ,* expressed a contrasting view: "'Basic Instinct' is a symbol of how deep is popular culture's hatred of queers and women," he wrote, "and its director's and producer's refusal to take seriously our criticism testifies to how little power we wield in this society."[90] Bronski ended his article by asserting, "Direct action works," but then qualified this statement with, "but we still have little actual influence." Taken together, both Signorile's and Bronski's opinions demonstrate the difficulty of assessing the extent to which any protest can have an influence on the film industry. Not long after *Basic Instinct* was released, however, the industry formed Hollywood Supports, an organization promoting the development of projects with positive images of homosexuals. This move suggested at least the possibility that a new era of sensitivity rather than censorship lay ahead.

THIS FILM IS BLASPHEMY!

The issue is not whether "Last Temptation" can be shown, but whether such a film should be shown. . . . With "Last Temptation," Hollywood is assailing the Christian community in a way it would never dare assault the black community, the Jewish community, or the gay community.

Pat Buchanan

Little critical attention has been paid to the ways in which censors have approached cinematic treatments of religion. While less controversial than sexual, ethnic, and gay images, representations of religion have provoked censorship challenges of varying degrees of intensity throughout the history of American film. The most frequent instances of censorship of religious content have involved Hollywood films made in the biblical spectacular tradition, including two Cecil B. deMille films, *King of Kings* (1926) and *Sign of the Cross* (1932), and, more recently, Norman Jewison's *Jesus Christ Superstar* (1973) and Martin Scorsese's *The Last Temptation of Christ* (1988). A second set of films that led to censorship challenges from religious groups is comprised of films either produced in Europe or directed by a European, including Roberto Rossellini's *The Miracle* (1951), Franco Zeffirelli's made-for-television drama *Jesus of Nazareth* (1977), *Monty Python's Life of Brian* (1979-80), and Jean-Luc Godard's *Hail Mary* (1985). A third, far smaller category of films that provoked censorship efforts by religious groups includes neither biblical spectacles nor religious fantasies. Indeed, films such as *The Callahans and the Murphys* (1927) and *Gone with the Wind* (1938) did not treat religious subjects at all, but their incidental use of religious imagery and "profane" language provoked protest from religious groups.

Whereas the protests over sexist, racist, and homophobic imagery treated above were launched by historically marginalized minority groups, attempts to censor cinematic treatments of religion came from traditionally dominant groups. Between 1980 and 1992 such religious groups sought to reestablish their influence over the film industry—an influence that was especially powerful during the formative years of the film industry, when many religious leaders were also reformers who helped to establish and operate censorship boards. During the 1950s and 1960s the number of films with religious themes increased, but few movies were censored on account of their treatment of religion. Attempts to censor rose after Jerry Falwell's moral majority emerged as a significant political force in 1979. In that year and the next, conservative religious groups protested against the comic treatment of the Bible in *Monty Python's Life of Brian*, resulting in censorship in Boston, Cleveland, and other cities. In 1985 Catholic-led protests against Jean-Luc Godard's *Hail Mary* were censorious in intent although ultimately unsuccessful in preventing theaters from exhibiting the film. Three years later Martin Scorsese's *The Last Temptation of Christ* elicited widespread protest. Religious opposition to and industry defenses of *Last Temptation* demonstrated that the larger political struggles between conservatives and liberals over issues such as homosexuality, abortion, AIDS, and prayer in school were integrally related to skirmishes over cultural production. The cultural authority that such powerful groups as Rev. Donald Wildmon's American Family Association claimed over cinematic treatments of religion, among other imagery, was similar to that exercised by the Legion of Decency and other religious pressure groups during the interwar years. Suddenly in the 1980s, however, the stakes seemed higher to many evangelical Christians. With the embarrassing public exposure and subsequent convictions of tele-evangelists Jimmy Swaggart and Jim Bakker, conservative religious groups came to see their campaign against *Last Temptation* as more than a case of cinematic transgression. The religious right's actions against Universal Pictures suggest that for them, nothing less than the survival of their religious coalition and its members' "vision" for America was at stake.

While religious critics had protested against *Last Temptation* when the film was in preproduction in 1983, they had full cause for alarm only after Scorsese had secured a contract with Universal and Cineplex Odeon and the film went into production in October 1987. Anticipating religious pressure, Universal hired Tim Penland, a born-again Christian and head of a marketing company specializing in fundamentalist interests, to serve as a "religious" liaison between the studio and religious groups. On February 29 Penland coordinated an agreement with Universal, the American Family Association, Bill Bright's

Campus Crusade for Christ, and other groups, guaranteeing them a private prescreening of the film in June. By mid-spring, religious leaders, some of whom had read one of the early versions of the screenplay, charged the makers of *Last Temptation* with blasphemy. A newsletter published by Baptist minister John Probst's Media Focus urged other groups to express their concern over *Last Temptation* by writing or calling Tom Pollock, chairman of MCA, Universal's parent company.[91]

Scorsese completed shooting the film but reported that there would be post-production delays. When Universal announced that the film would not be ready for the scheduled screening, religious leaders exploded, and Penland quit his post. Rev. Donald Wildmon reportedly said, "I've waited six months and I am not waiting any longer."[92] The Campus Crusade urged Christians to increase their letter-writing and telephoning campaigns. Universal thereupon issued a statement emphasizing, "Delays in the post-production phase are not uncommon in the motion picture industry," and Scorsese offered to screen an unfinished version of the film for evangelists on July 12. Wildmon and other religious leaders, however, considered Universal's schedule change a deliberate breach of faith and declined Scorsese's invitation. They were already preparing for battle.

The prerelease furor over *Last Temptation* escalated on July 12, a day on which, simultaneously, several conservative leaders issued public condemnations of the film, an unfinished print was screened for mainline religious leaders in New York, and evangelical groups met in Los Angeles to begin coordinating their protests. Wildmon called on Universal Pictures to cancel plans to release *Last Temptation* and warned the company that it would be committing "financial suicide" if it did not obey. Basing his comments on a script which journalists speculated was still the 1983 Paul Schrader version, Wildmon told a United Press International reporter, "[The film] is absolutely the most perverted, distorted account of the historical and Biblical Jesus I have ever read."[93] One especially offensive line of the script that Wildmon read—a line that had already been deleted from the shooting script—occurs at the moment when Scorsese's Jesus is fantasizing that he is making love to Mary Magdalene. Jesus says to Mary, "God sleeps between your legs." Enraged at this and other lines in the script, Wildmon stepped up his campaign, distributing more than two hundred copies of the entire script to religious leaders around the country as well as a cover letter urging them to send signed petitions of protest to their local theaters.

Taking to the media, religious groups' actions against *Last Temptation* continued as a national campaign. In California over 1,200 Christian radio stations condemned the film. Larry Poland's Mastermedia group placed a full-page advertisement signed by Christian professionals in the film and television industry in the *Hollywood Reporter,* which concluded with the following pronouncement.

> This film maligns the character, blasphemes the deity, and distorts the message of Jesus.
>
> We, the undersigned, professional members of the film and television community, ask that this film not be released.
>
> Whether the gain is a hundred million dollars or thirty pieces of silver makes no difference. Our Lord was crucified once on a cross. He doesn't deserve to be crucified a second time on celluloid.[94]

Poland further urged Christians to boycott the products and services of Universal and MCA.

On July 15 Bill Bright, the prominent southern California evangelical leader, offered to reimburse Universal Pictures for all the money the studio had invested in the making of *Last Temptation* in exchange for all existing prints of the film, which he promised he would destroy. Universal Pictures responded to Bright's offer with an open letter published as a full-page ad in *Variety,* the *Hollywood Reporter,* the *Los Angeles Times,* the *New York Times,* the *Washington Post,* and the *Atlanta Constitution:*

> We, at Universal Pictures, have received your proposal in which you have offered to buy "The Last Temptation of Christ" which you would then destroy so that no one could ever see it. While we understand the deep feelings and convictions which have prompted this offer, we believe that to accept it would threaten the fundamental freedoms of religion and expression promised to all Americans under our Constitution. . . . You have expressed a concern that the content of the film be "true." But whose truth? If everyone in America agreed on religious, political and artistic truths, there would be no need to our constitutional guarantees. Only in totalitarian states are all people forced to accept one version of the truth. . . . In the United States, no one sect or constituency has the power to set boundaries around each person's freedom to explore religious and philosophical questions whether through speech, books or film. These freedoms protect all of us. They are precious. They are not for sale.[95]

A spokesman for Campus Crusade for Christ criticized Universal's letter as "disappointing" because Bright's offer was "sincere."[96] On the same day the ad appeared, an estimated six to seven hundred Christians sponsored by Los Angeles radio station KKLA-FM picketed the MCA headquarters. Universal Pictures' letter seemed only to antagonize Christians opposed to *Last Temptation.*

While several entertainment reporters such as Gary Franklin of KABC-TV opined that Universal should not release *Last Temptation,* the media, as Michael Medved correctly points out in an otherwise biased account of the protests, published editorials mostly supportive of Scorsese, Universal, and the film.[97] In Hollywood Jack Valenti, president of the Motion Picture Association of America (MPAA), issued a statement supported by all of the major Hollywood studios. He attacked protesters for committing the sin of prior censorship. "Protest whenever and whatever you choose? Of course," he stated. "But prevent a creative work from being judged by the public? No. Not now or anytime. No prior censorship, ever."[98] The statement continued:

> The key issue, the only issue, is whether or not self-appointed groups can prevent a film from being exhibited to the public, or a book from being published, or a piece of art from being shown. . . . The major companies of the MPAA support MCA/Universal in its absolute right to offer to the people whatever movie it chooses.[99]

Last Temptation was still scheduled for an August release, and neither Scorsese nor Universal had made any known concessions to the protesters.

Attacks against *Last Temptation* by conservative Christians continued on both local and national levels. Petitioning, phonecalling, street protests, written criticism, and anti-*Temptation* radio broadcasts increased on all Christian radio and television stations. Pat Buchanan, the nationally syndicated columnist and conservative spokesperson, condemned the film in a *Philadelphia Inquirer* op-ed piece entitled "Anything for a Buck: Hollywood's Sleazy Image of Christ." Buchanan challenged Valenti's and other industry leaders' sensitivity in supporting the film:

> Christians, America's unfashionable majority, may be mocked; their preachers may be parodied in book and on film; their faith may be portrayed as superstitious folly. And secular society, invoking the First Amendment, will rush to the defense of the defamers, not the defamed. The battle over "Last Temptation" is one more skirmish in the century's struggle over whose values, whose beliefs shall be exalted in American culture, and whose may be derided and disparaged.[100]

Buchanan's article was widely reprinted, admired, and quoted by groups opposed to *Last Temptation,* and it strengthened the quickening tide of protesters.

No matter what anyone on either side of the "Holy War," or "Culture

War"—as newspaper articles often referred to the controversy—wrote, said, or did, ultimate victory or defeat depended on what both sides achieved. For their part, Universal and Scorsese promised to release the film they had spent so much time and money to produce. By the end of July, however, it was unclear how successful religious leaders' efforts had actually been, where their threats and petitions would lead, and, most importantly, what the protesters would do when Universal released *Last Temptation.*

During the first few days of August the scale appeared to tilt in favor of the protesters. On August 1, several days after Universal released a statement affirming that it and Cineplex Odeon Films would "stand behind the principle of freedom of expression and hope that the American public will give the film and the filmmaker a fair chance,"[101] managers of several theater chains expressed their uneasiness about scheduling the film. Most notably, James Edwards, Jr., owner of 150 Edwards Theaters across the nation, warned that unless "certain changes" were made to *Last Temptation,* which he had heard was a film "demeaning to Christ," he would not show the film in any of his theaters.[102] This statement suggested that religious pressure was working and would in fact produce censorious results.

Three days later, on August 4, Universal took the offensive. Exhausted by the barrage of attacks and allegations, perhaps aware of the upcoming press conference at which Wildmon planned a new wave of actions, the studio issued the following statement:

> Few motion pictures in recent memory have generated such heated debate, especially when so few people have actually seen the film. Rumors have proliferated. Exaggerations, misconceptions and scenes taken out of context have added fuel to the fire. The best thing that can be done for "The Last Temptation of Christ" at this time is to make it available to the American people and allow them to draw their own conclusions based on fact, not fallacy.[103]

Universal announced that the film, originally scheduled for a September 23 release, would be shown on August 12 in nine selected cities in the United States and Canada. It is clear that this decision meant that the studio wished to capitalize on the publicity the protests were giving the movie. But releasing *Last Temptation* nearly six weeks ahead of schedule provoked religious groups to step up their attacks.

The events that occurred between August 6 and August 12, the day *Last Temptation* was released, suggest that while in several instances prior restraint was certainly a goal, religious groups were ultimately satisfied to demonstrate to the American people how consolidated and massive their opposition to

Demonstrators outside Universal Studios in Hollywood protest *The Last Temptation of Christ* (Universal, 1988). Photo by Michael Tweed, courtesy NYT Pictures.

Scorsese's "blasphemous" film was. Despite the fact that the radical Rev. R. L. Hymers had led one hundred fundamentalists in a protest outside of a synagogue where he believed MCA/Universal chairman Lew Wasserman worshipped, that some of the protesters carried placards with "Take Out the Sex" written on them, and that Hymers told *Variety* that Universal "can probably expect violence" and "we'll stop the showing of the movie,"[104] it appeared that the majority of religious groups continuing to protest against *Last Temptation* had ceased to believe that censorship was possible.

One week before the movie opened, however, religious protesters seemed in several instances to achieve censorious effects. In Orange County, California, James Edwards made a definitive announcement that his chain of theaters would not show the film.[105] The United Artists chain, which owned 2,000 screens across the country in 1988, and General Cinema Corporation, which owned 1,339 screens, also announced their refusal to show *Last Temptation*.[106] In Hazleton, Pennsylvania, the City Council voted unanimously to oppose the film on grounds that it was blasphemous.[107] During a heated argument among residents and the City Council, John Ford, the council president, insisted that his resolution did not actually bar the film from being shown locally, although it did "urge residents not to patronize [the film] and to write filmmakers opposing it."[108]

On August 11, the day before *Last Temptation*'s scheduled opening, Citizens for a Universal Appeal, an ad hoc coalition of religious groups and leaders from Orange County, organized a protest in front of Universal Studios in Los Angeles that attracted an estimated twenty-five thousand Protestants, Catholics, and some Jews. Carrying wooden crosses and bibles, many of those who gathered chanted "J–E–S–U–S" and "Boycott MCA." They waved placards reading, "Don't Crucify Christ Again," "Some Things Are Sacred," "Stop This Attack on Christianity," "Universal Is Anti-Christian," "Father Forgive Them for They Know Not What They Do," "Don't Distort History," "Don't Trash My Lord," "Jesus Is Not to Be Mocked," "Lead Us Not into Temptation," "Our Lord Jesus Christ Reigns," "Read the Bible; Know the True Story," and "Scripture Not Scripts." At a lunchtime rally, Donald Wildmon addressed the crowd. "We're unleashing a movement," he said. "Christian-bashing is over. . . . We demand that anti-Christian stereotypes come to an end."[109]

Universal released *Last Temptation* on August 12 in Los Angeles, New York, San Francisco, Washington, Chicago, Seattle, Minneapolis, Montreal, and Toronto, as planned. Protesters met the premiere at nearly every theater in the nine cities cited above, but in no instance did exhibitors cancel the movie. During the weeks that followed *Last Temptation*'s successful premiere,[110] the size of the audience and the number of protesters steadily decreased. When the film opened in an additional thirty-five cities over the next month, however, groups in several cities and towns attempted and achieved censorship. In New Orleans, Louisiana, and Santa Ana, California, city officials passed resolutions to ban *Last Temptation.* In New Orleans, a police jury in two city districts, Saint Bernard and Kenner, supported the ban on *Last Temptation,* even though no theater in those districts had planned on showing the film.[111] An insurance company in Montgomery, Alabama, threatened to cancel coverage at the Capri Theater, which had said it would show the movie if it could schedule it. Alabama governor Guy Hunt, the City Council, the city's mayor, and a publisher of a local newspaper went on record opposing the showing. Hunt said, "Our nation does not need films which persecute those who believe in the values upon which this nation was built."[112] In early September another official ban was attempted in Pensacola, Florida. In this instance a federal district judge blocked a county ordinance banning theaters from showing *Last Temptation.* While the film was allowed exhibition, the attempted censorship clearly affected the box office, for only fifty people reportedly attended the opening.[113]

Official bans in Savannah, Georgia, and in Oklahoma City, Oklahoma, were more successful than the attempts cited above. In Savannah, the Chatham County Commission passed a resolution encouraging citizens "not to participate in any showing of the movie."[114] When the film was due to open at Oklahoma State University (OSU) in late September, the school's regents demanded that, before exhibition, OSU administrators answer legal and ethical questions related to the separation of church and state and the First Amendment. OSU regents further expressed their concerns that showing the movie could cause "extensive damage to the public interest of the University" and "highly offend a major segment of the Oklahoma citizenry." Due to this controversial response, the university canceled its plans to show *Last Temptation*.[115]

Large, peaceful protests followed the southern and southwestern premieres of *Last Temptation* in Atlanta, Dallas, and Fort Worth with little incident.[116] Vandalism occurred in at least two cities. On August 27 a print of *Last Temptation,* due to be shown in the Salt Lake City Cineplex Odeon Center Theater, was stolen, and the theater screen was slashed.[117] On September 5 vandals at the Los Angeles Cineplex Odeon Showcase Theater, in which the film had not been scheduled to open, spray-painted threats against Universal Pictures executives and slashed seats. One message, written below the movie screen, read, "Lew Wasserman: If you release 'The Last Temptation of Christ,' we will wait years and decimate all Universal property. This message is for your insurance company."[118]

The release of *Last Temptation* proved that even in a year when theologically conservative Protestants had been publicly embarrassed by the Jimmy Swaggart and Jim Bakker sex scandals, religious groups such as Donald Wildmon's American Family Association and James Dobson's Focus on the Family still had an enormous influence on public opinion and could affect the distribution and exhibition of a film. The entire pre- and postrelease controversy over *Last Temptation* reveals how much economic power the religious right could wield. Universal Pictures' decision to open *Last Temptation* three weeks ahead of schedule and in only nine metropolitan cities suggests this power, while protesters' successes in several small cities around the country in 1988 and afterward confirm it.[119] Using a wide array of media resources, the religious right spread the word about the "blasphemy" in *Last Temptation* to every region of the country. Many communities and local theater managers were therefore predisposed to refuse the film long before it premiered. When Universal managed to schedule *Last Temptation* in such cities as Savannah and Omaha, the combination of protests and official actions caused censorious effects: in both cases, the film was canceled before it was screened. Prior censorship was also achieved in Montgomery and New Orleans, and attempted in Pensacola. These and other censorious intentions aside, the fact that a coalition of evangelical Protestants and orthodox Catholics had achieved censorship in a number of cities and towns demonstrated that the religious right was capable of winning significant victories in the ongoing culture wars.

CONCLUSION

Debates over film censorship from 1980 to 1992 reflected a culture in conflict over sex, race, family values, and homosexuality. They also demonstrated that political struggles were being fought in a cultural arena. Similar conflicts within society and art have existed throughout history, but during these years the "cultural divide"[120]—as Vice President Dan Quayle referred to the split between conservatives and liberals—widened. This widening occurred because Presidents Reagan and Bush led stridently ideological administrations, and, at the same time, groups on the left expressed growing frustration with a film industry and a majoritarian culture that stereotyped, silenced, and distorted their lives.

Among the groups that have protested against movies—antipornography feminists, Asian Americans, and gays and lesbians on the left, and religious groups on the right—the only ones to achieve censorship during these years were associated with the new Christian right. As stated above, religious groups achieved censorship of *Last Temptation* upon its release in several cities around the country. Antipornography feminists found protests an ineffective means of combatting the sexism in pornography as well as Hollywood films, and their actions against *Dressed to Kill* had little if any direct impact on Hollywood filmmakers. But protests were catalysts enabling women to organize politically, and some feminists carried their activism to legal arenas. Moreover, during the ensuing twelve years such movies as *Thelma and Louise* (1991) provided at least some small comfort to feminists anxious for change.

After Asian Americans and homosexual groups protested against *Year of the Dragon* and *Basic Instinct,* respectively, these constituencies found Hollywood more willing to listen to them. Asian Americans have since been portrayed favorably in *The Joy Luck Club* (1993), a movie based on the best-selling novel by Amy Tan and directed by Wayne Wang. This film, which lyrically recounts the lives of five Asian women and their daughters, was a critical and a commercial success. It represents for Asian Americans a welcome change from *Year of the Dragon* and *Falling Down* (1992). Similarly, Oliver Stone's *Heaven and Earth* (1993) centers sympathetically on a strong female Asian character. Set during the Vietnam War, it is told from the vantage point of a young Vietnamese woman who, after being brutally raped by a Vietcong soldier and treated like a whore by American GIs, learns to stand up to men—including the American she marries. Homosexuals have been sympathetically depicted in several recent movies. In the independently produced *The Crying Game*—a film nominated for a "Best Picture" Academy Award in 1992—a heterosexual Irish nationalist develops a love interest for a British, black, gay transvestite, whom he at first believes to be a woman. In Jonathan Demme's *Philadelphia* (1992), Tom Hanks plays a successful lawyer who loses his job at a prestigious law firm when the senior partners discover that he has AIDS. The film sides with Hanks, the victim of homosexual discrimination, in his struggle for legal vindication. But these isolated instances, for Asian Americans and homosexuals alike, do not mean Hollywood is committed to change. It is impossible to predict whether or for how long patterns of sensitivity will continue.

Despite more favorable images, left groups insist that Hollywood continues to produce negative stereotypes which themselves reflect patterns of social domination in the United States. Some conservatives, however, claim that left protests have produced a feeling of caution among Hollywood executives and producers faced with controversial depictions of nearly *any* minority. Invoking the "PC" (political correctness) debates, they speak of "self-censorship," "censorship from the left," and a "new McCarthyism," and they warn that the result will be ideologically correct imagery—an insidious form of censorship. But left groups ask conservatives to reflect on who really has power over imagery in the United States and claim, as this essay suggests, that the forces of corporate capitalism, patriarchy, and white supremacy have been and remain truly in the saddle.

The latest protests against and censorship of movies show that not having rules to govern screen imagery is—as Murray Schumach predicted in 1964— as dangerous as having them. During the 1950s and 1960s a liberal cultural climate assisted in the demise of the Hollywood Production Code, and a liberal Supreme Court led to the near-dissolution of legal censorship. But from the 1960s through the years dealt with here, interest groups with no connection to government or industry have sought to influence movie content and, as suggested above, have sometimes been successful. Reflection on group protests, which proceeded from both the left and right, finally teaches us the contradictory outcome of the First Amendment's democratic right to protest. While groups may wave placards and chant against any movie they choose, it

310

is evident that protests can produce unanticipated effects. Some protests, such as those from the religious right, result in recognizable acts of censorship; others, such as those from left groups, create an environment that legitimizes suppression and encourages self-censorship. Thus, protest of all kinds risks some form of censorship. But without protest, some of our democratic ideals are crippled: groups are denied the chance to play a participatory role in cultural production, and their views are themselves censored. Permitting protests from either side of the political spectrum, regardless of their effects, is therefore a risk worth taking.

NOTES

1. The expression "culture wars" has been popularized within such books as William J. Bennett, *The De-Valuing of America: The Fight for Our Culture and Our Children* (New York, 1992); Richard Bolton, ed., *Culture Wars: Documents from the Recent Controversies in the Arts* (New York, 1992); Steven C. Dubin, *Arresting Images: Impolitic Art and Uncivil Actions* (New York, 1992); Marilyn French, *The War against Women* (New York, 1992); Patrick M. Garry, *An American Paradox: Censorship in a Nation of Free Speech* (Westport, Conn., 1993); Henry Louis Gates, Jr., *Loose Canons: Culture Wars* (New York, 1993); Robert Hughes, *Culture of Complaint: The Fraying of America* (New York, 1993); and James Davison Hunter, *Culture Wars: The Struggle to Define America* (New York, 1991). The idea of a wide-ranging culture war also figures prominently in the "canon" or "PC" debates over great works on college campuses (see, for example, Paul Berman, *Debating P.C.: The Controversy over Political Correctness on College Campuses* [New York, 1992]).

2. Steven Vineberg, *No Surprises, Please: Movies in the Reagan Decade* (New York, 1993), 21.

3. In the field of film censorship studies, see, for example, Lea Jacobs, *The Wages of Sin: Censorship and the Fallen Woman Film, 1928–1942* (Madison, Wis., 1991); and Leonard J. Leff and Jerold L. Simmons, *The Dame in the Kimono: Hollywood, Censorship, and the Production Code from the 1920s to the 1960s* (New York, 1990).

4. See Annette Kuhn, *Cinema, Censorship, and Sexuality, 1909–1925* (London and New York, 1988), 7. Broader work on censorship outside of film studies that share this view include Richard O. Curry, ed., *Freedom at Risk: Secrecy, Censorship, and Repression in the 1980's* (Philadelphia, 1988); Sue Curry Jansen, *Censorship: The Knot that Binds Power and Knowledge* (New York, 1988); and Michael Parenti, *Make-Believe Media: The Politics of Entertainment* (New York, 1988).

5. This argument is prominent in the much of Catherine MacKinnon's writing (see, for example, *Feminism Unmodified: Discourses on Life and Law* [Cambridge, Mass., 1987]). Other feminists who share this view include Kathleen Barry, *Female Sexual Slavery* (Englewood Cliffs, N.J., 1978); Susan Brownmiller, *Against Our Will: Men, Women and Rape* (New York, 1975); Mary Daly, *Pure Lust: Elemental Feminist Philosophy* (Boston, 1984); Andrea Dworkin, *Pornography: Men Possessing Women* (New York,

1979); Susan Griffin, *Pornography and Silence: Culture's Revenge against Nature* (New York, 1981); Susanne Kappeler, *The Pornography of Representation* (Minneapolis, 1986); Laura Lederer, ed., *Take Back the Night: Women on Pornography* (New York, 1980); and Dorchen Leidholdt and Janice G. Raymond, eds., *Sexual Liberals and the Attack on Feminism* (New York, 1990).

6. See Lederer, *Take Back the Night,* 15.

7. Ibid., 272.

8. A copy of this leaflet appears in the Billy Rose Theatre Collection, Library of Performing Arts, in a vertical clipping file entitled "Snuff, c. 1976."

9. Quoted in "'Snuff' Film Stirs the Wrath of Feminists," *New York Post,* February 21, 1976.

10. For more information on the Maryland ban, see Lou Cedrone, "Maryland Bans 'Snuff' Based on Its 'Psychotic Violence,'" *Variety,* April 7, 1976; and "Snuff Ban Is Upheld by Baltimore Judge," *Box Office,* April 5, 1976.

11. See Beverly LaBelle, "Snuff—The Ultimate in Woman-Hating," in Lederer, *Take Back the Night,* 278.

12. One commentator suggests that distributors of *Snuff* organized their own protests in front of various theaters around the country as a means of stimulating box office profits (see "'Snuff' Biz Goes When Pickets Go," *Variety,* March 24, 1976; and Gerald Perry, "Women in Porn: How Young Roberta Findlay Grew up and Made 'Snuff,'" *Take One,* September 1978, 28–32).

13. When *Snuff* opened in August 1983 at Greenwich Village's Eighth Street Playhouse, for example, WAP and the National Organization of Women (NOW) protested, leafleted, and demanded that the theater owner, Steven Kirsh, close the film. NOW president Jennifer Brown called the film "especially insidious because its audience was made up primarily of adolescent boys and younger men." Kirsh agreed to close *Snuff* down, stating: "Some members of the community have found this film offensive, and we don't want to offend anybody" (see Laurie Johnston, "Snuff Is Snuffed," *New York Times,* September 6, 1983).

14. In a telephone interview on October 7, 1992, WAP founder Dorchen Leidholdt told me that her organization protested against *The Texas Chainsaw Massacre,* among other slasher movies and credited such protests with the decline of the slasher genre in the early 1980s—a bold claim, to say the least. WAP, WAVAW, and WAVPM, however, are no longer active organizations, and the history of their actions against slasher and other movies is largely unwritten.

15. See Peter Lester, "Redress or Undress? Feminists Fume While Angie Scores in a Sexy Chiller," *Camera 5,* fall 1980, 71–72, 81; Andrew Sarris, "Dreck to Kill," *Village Voice,* September 17–23, 1980; and Dorchen Leidholdt, "Women against De Palma," letter to the editor, *Village Voice,* October 1, 1980. I have yet to discover why the New York protests against *Dressed* were staged three weeks rather than immediately after the opening of the movie.

16. Quoted in Michael Musto, "Drag Stir," *Soho Weekly News,* September 3, 1980.

17. It is interesting to note that more militant protests against *Dressed to Kill* occurred outside of the United States in Leeds, England. "Several hundred Leeds women last month stormed movie houses showing 'The Beast' and 'Dressed to Kill,' horror films in which women are raped and killed. They pummeled men in the audi-

ences and hurled red paint at the screens before police dragged them out" (see *Boston Globe,* December 8, 1980).

18. From a protest leaflet reprinted in "Dressed to Kill Protested," *Jump Cut* 21 (September 1980).

19. Leidholdt, "Women against De Palma." For Andrew Sarris's criticism of WAP and other feminist protests against *Dressed to Kill,* see "Dreck to Kill."

20. Quoted in Lee Grant, "Women vs. 'Dressed to Kill': Is Film Admirable or Deplorable?" *Los Angeles Times,* September 12, 1980, 13.

21. Ibid., 13.

22. I draw this conclusion from studying the weekly *Variety* "Top Grossing Films" list on the following dates in 1980: August 6, August 13, and August 20.

23. Telephone interview, October 7, 1992.

24. One exception was feminists' protests against *Once upon a Time in America* in 1984; another, in the early 1990s, came when members of NOW joined gay and lesbian protesters against *Basic Instinct* (1992; see below).

25. The debates over *Body Double* are recorded in "Sex, Violence, and De Palma," *Film Comment* 20 (September–October 1984); and "Sex and Censorship," *Film Comment* 20 (November–December 1984). The first article features a dialogue between Marcia Pally and Brian De Palma; the second contains articles by legal scholars, antipornography and procensorship feminists, and other figures in the debates over pornography. Among the writers included are Alan Dershowitz, Edward Donnerstein, Dorchen Leidholdt, Marcia Pally, Janella Miller, Lois P. Sheinfeld, and Ann Snitow. For information on feminists' objections to *Fatal Attraction,* see Susan Faludi, "Fatal Distortion," *Mother Jones* 13 (February–March 1988): 27–30. Also see Susan Faludi, *Backlash: The Undeclared War against American Women* (New York, 1991), 126–39.

26. One notable pre-1970s censorship attempt by an ethnic minority occurred in 1951 when American Jewish groups protested against the stereotypes in the British film *Oliver Twist* (see Murray Schumach, *The Face on the Cutting Room Floor: The Story of Movie and Television Censorship* [New York, 1964], 103–4). Protests by other ethnic groups against stereotypes during the 1970s and 1980s occurred at a time when film historians began increasingly to focus their attention on ethnicity. The following are among the books published during this period: Donald Bogle, *Toms, Coons, Mulattoes, Mammies and Bucks: An Interpretive History of Blacks in American Films* (New York, 1991); Thomas Cripps, *Slow Fade to Black: The Negro in American Film, 1900–1942* (New York, 1977); Ralph and Natasha Friar, *The Only Good Indian: The Hollywood Gospel* (New York, 1972); Daniel Leab, *From Sambo to Superspade: The Black Experience in Motion Pictures* (Boston, 1975); and Eugene Wong, *On Visual Media Racism: Asians in the American Motion Picture* (New York, 1978). Studies of ethnicity in the cinema include Les and Barbara Keyser, *Hollywood and the Catholic Church: The Image of the Roman Catholicism in American Movies* (Chicago, 1984); and Lester D. Friedman, *Hollywood's Image of the Jew* (New York, 1982). For a more recent collection of essays on ethnicity in the cinema, see Lester D. Friedman, ed., *Unspeakable Images: Ethnicity and the American Cinema* (Chicago, 1991).

27. In *Chicanos and Film: Essays on Chicano Representation and Resistance* (New York, 1992), Chon Noriega claims that Hispanic groups have "resisted" filmic stereotypes since the earliest motion pictures were released and continue to resist such stereo-

types. Noreiga's term *resistance*, like Charles Musser and Robert Sklar's use of the term in *Resisting Images: Essays on Cinema and History* (Philadelphia, 1990), however, primarily refers to strategies of oppositional filmmaking rather than to activism by Hispanic groups against particular films. With the exception of the protests against *Fort Apache*, I have found little evidence that Hispanic groups staged protests against stereotypes from 1980 to 1992.

28. Wong, *On Visual Media Racism,* 183.

29. Ibid., 109.

30. Upon the release of *Dragon,* the protest actually included nearly fifty groups.

31. See Martha Gever, "Dragon Busters," *Independent* (October 1988): 8–9.

32. See Janice Sakamoto and Forrest Gok, "Michael Cimino and the Chinese Mafia," *Asian American Network* 2 (1984): 4.

33. Quoted in "Statement by the Chinese Consolidated Benevolent Association," August 16, 1985, copy in *Year of the Dragon* file, Asian CineVision, New York.

34. Press release, Coalition against *Year of the Dragon,* August 14, 1985, *Year of the Dragon* file, Asian CineVision, New York.

35. Quoted in Jim Robbins, "Asian-Americans Planning 'Dragon' Boycott Campaign," *Variety,* August 14, 1985, 26.

36. Ibid.

37. Gene Ruffini, "Big New Film in Reel-Life Drama," *New York Post,* August 17, 1985.

38. See minutes of Coalition against *Year of the Dragon,* August 19, 1985, *Year of the Dragon* file, Asian CineVision, New York.

39. Telephone interview with Janice Sakomoto, July 10, 1992.

40. Gever, "Dragon Busters," 8.

41. Quoted in John Horn, "Demonstrators Picket 'Year of the Dragon,'" *Los Angeles Times,* August 26, 1985.

42. Quoted in Thomas Palmer, "'Dragon' Protested as Racist Film," *Boston Globe,* August 25, 1985.

43. Quoted in Guy Livingston, "Mayor of Boston Blasts 'Dragon,' Pickets Converge on Sack House," *Variety,* August 28, 1985.

44. Ibid.

45. "'Volunteers,' 'Dragon,' Bow Well but 'Future' Still Tops Nat. B.O," *Variety,* August 21, 1985.

46. Dennis Wharton, "'Year' Healthy $220,000 in DC," *Variety,* August 21, 1985.

47. This suit, filed in the Los Angeles Superior Court, claimed that because MGM/UA's *Year of the Dragon* included a shot of Chinese pictographs that allegedly translating to "CCBA," the filmmakers had implied that members of the CCBA were "trafficking in drugs and otherwise engaged in organized crime" (quoted in "Chinese Defamed in Film, Suit Charges," *Atlanta Journal and Constitution,* August 31, 1985). See also John Horn, "The 'Dragon' Wars: Hard-Fought Month," *Los Angeles Times,* September 7, 1985.

48. Quoted in Ray Loynd, "MGM/UA Sending 'Year' Disclaimers out to Exhibitors," *Variety,* September 4, 1985.

49. Ibid.

50. Ibid.

51. See Gever, "Dragon Busters," 8–9; and Janice Sakomoto, "Communities Unite against 'Dragon,'" *Asian American Network* 3 (summer–fall 1985): 7.

52. See "Coalition Update," the Coalition against *Year of the Dragon,* September 5, 1985, *Year of the Dragon* file, Asian CineVision, New York.

53. Antonio DeCastro, "A Deeper Look into the 'Year of the Dragon' Furor," *Asian American Network* 3 (fall–winter, 1985): 4–5.

54. On September 5, 1985, New York councilwoman Miriam Friedman attempted but failed to pass legislation against *Dragon.*

55. Gina Marchetti, "Ethnicity, the Cinema, and Cultural Studies," in Friedman, *Unspeakable Images,* 112–39.

56. Telephone interview, July 10, 1992.

57. Quoted in Vito Russo, *The Celluloid Closet: Homosexuality in the Movies* (New York, 1985), 205.

58. Ibid., 239.

59. Leslie Bennetts, "The New Realism in Portraying Homosexuals," *New York Times,* February 21, 1983.

60. See Mary Richards, "The Gay Deception," *Film Comment,* January 1982, 15–18; and Andrea Weiss, "From the Margins: New Images of Gays in the Cinema," *Cineaste* 15 (1986): 4–8.

61. See Nina J. Easton, "Carolco Buys Joe Eszterhas Script for Record 3 Million," *Los Angeles Times,* June 26, 1990; and Nina J. Easton, "Eszterhas v. Verhoeven: The Screenwriter Has Left the 'Basic Instinct' Project in a Dispute with the Director over Sex Scene," *Los Angeles Times,* August 23, 1990.

62. Michael Bronski, "Homos v. Hollywood," *NYQ* 22 (March 29, 1992): 28.

63. See David Tuller, "Gay Protest at Movie Location: Filming of Joe Eszterhas' 'Basic Instinct' at South-of-Market Bar," *San Francisco Chronicle,* April 11, 1991. For a more thorough account of the *Basic Instinct* controversy, see Charles Lyons, "Don't Watch That Movie! Censorship and Protest of Films in America, 1980–1992," (Ph.D. diss., Columbia University, 1994), 313–35.

64. Quoted in Bronski, "Homos," 28.

65. Ibid., 70.

66. Ibid.

67. Quoted in Lynn Hirshberg, "Say It Ain't So, Joe," *Vanity Fair,* August 1991, 82.

68. See David J. Fox and Donna Rosenthal, "Gays Bashing 'Basic Instinct,'" *Los Angeles Times,* April 29, 1991; and Keith Clarke, "Film Producers Order Arrest of Protesters," *Bay Area Reporter,* May 2, 1991.

69. Hirshberg, "Say It Ain't So," 82.

70. See Clark, "Film Producers." See also Jim Harwood and Claudia Eller, "Citizen's Arrest on 'Basic Instinct' Set," *Variety,* May 6, 1991, 14; and Hirschberg, "Say It Ain't So," 82.

71. Quoted in Michael Dorgon, "'Instinct' Triggers Gay Reflexes," *Daily News,* May 13, 1991.

72. Quoted in Keith Clark, "Filming Concludes: 'Instinct' Producer Arrested; Protests Called Major Success," *Bay Area Reporter,* May 9, 1991.

73. Ibid.

74. Jesse Greenman, cochair, GLAAD-San Francisco, to theater exhibitors, GLAAD–San Francisco files.

75. Quoted in Andrew Kirtzman, "Gays Bare Film Plot," *New York Daily News,* March 10, 1992.

76. Ibid.

77. Quoted in Andy Marx, "Film Clips: A Look inside Hollywood and the Movies: Politically Correct File," *Los Angeles Times,* February 16, 1992.

78. Ibid.

79. Quoted in Carla Hall, "'Instinct' Battle Plan: Gay Groups Prepare Assault, Eye Oscars," *Washington Post,* March 19, 1992.

80. Quoted in Russel Smith, "Gays Outraged at New Film's Portrayal of Homosexuals," *Dallas Morning News,* March 10, 1992.

81. Telephone interview, March 19, 1992.

82. Quoted in "Protest Set for 'Basic Instinct' Opening," United Press International, March 20, 1992.

83. Dan Levy, "Gay Rights Protesters Greet 'Instinct' Opening: Demonstrators Assail Homophobic Portrayals," *San Francisco Chronicle,* March 21, 1992.

84. See Scott Harris, "Opposition to Film 'Basic Instinct' Rises," *Los Angeles Times,* March 21, 1992; and David J. Fox, "'Instinct' Sizzles at the Box Office," *Los Angeles Times,* March 23, 1992.

85. Street interview, March 20, 1992.

86. Street interview, March 20, 1992.

87. Quoted in Fox, "'Instinct' Sizzles."

88. Amy Taubin, "Ice Pick Envy: The Boys Who Cried Misogyny," *Village Voice,* April 28, 1992.

89. Michelangelo Signorile, *Queer in America: Sex, the Media, and the Closets of Power* (New York, 1993), 320.

90. Bronski, "Homos," 28.

91. Pat H. Broeske, "'Last Temptation': Is It Already Bearing Its Cross?" *Los Angeles Times,* April 17, 1988.

92. John Dart, "Church Leaders Upset at Delay in Film Screening," *Los Angeles Times,* June 18, 1988.

93. "Minister Blasts Universal Movie as 'Perverted,'" *United Press International,* July 12, 1988.

94. Quoted in "Evangelists Intensify Struggle to Stop Film," *Los Angeles Times,* July 12, 1988.

95. Universal Pictures, "A Letter to Bill Bright, Campus Crusade for Christ," *New York Times,* July 21, 1988.

96. Quoted in Nina J. Easton, "Studio Fires Back in Defense of 'Temptation,'" *Los Angeles Times,* July 22, 1988.

97. See Michael Medved, *Hollywood vs. America: Popular Culture and the War on Traditional Values* (New York, 1992), 46–48. While I agree with Medved's general assessment of the media's reporting of the *Last Temptation* controversy, his account is tendentious and suffers from a lack of substantive citations from the numerous news articles and television programs covering the events.

98. Quoted in "MPAA Supports Universal's 'Temptation,'" *Variety,* July 27, 1988.

99. Quoted in Aljean Harmetz, "Top Studios Support 'Christ' Film," *New York Times,* July 25, 1988.

100. Pat Buchanan, "Anything for a Buck: Hollywood's Sleazy Image of Christ," *Philadelphia Inquirer,* July 27, 1988.

101. Quoted in *Orange County Business Journal* 2 (August 1, 1988): 3.

102. Quoted in Tim Robbins et al., "'Last Temptation' War Rages On; Exhibs Pressured, Italy Quakes," *Variety,* August 3, 1988.

103. Ibid.

104. Quoted in Kim Masters, "The Careful Strategy of 'Temptation'; Limited Release, Avoidance of TV Ads Planned," *Washington Post,* August 10, 1988. For more information on the Hymers controversy, see John Dart, "Two Steps Back from Protest over Anti-Jewish Tone," *Los Angeles Times,* July 23, 1988.

105. See Aurelio Rojos, "Fundamentalists Demonstrate against Controversial Film," *United Press International,* August 6, 1988. See also "Edwards Cinema Chain Won't Run 'Last Temptation,'" *Los Angeles Times,* August 7, 1988.

106. See David Grogan et al., "In the Name of Jesus," *People,* August 8, 1988, 40.

107. See "Catholics Urged to Shun Film," *Philadelphia Inquirer,* August 19, 1988.

108. "Actress's Kin and Others Protest Council's Stand on Film," *Scranton Times,* August 10, 1988.

109. Quoted in ibid.

110. In *Hollywood vs. America,* Michael Medved argues that *Last Temptation* was not nearly as great a book office success as the press claimed it was. Box office figures contradict this. The film averaged $44,579 per screen and had a first-weekend gross of $401,211 nationwide. Considering the film's very limited release, this figure is in fact respectable (see *Philadelphia Inquirer,* August 17, 1988).

111. See Rebecca Theim and Chris Cooper, "St. Bernard, Kenner Officials: Don't Be Tempted by Movie," *Times-Picayune,* August 18, 1988.

112. Quoted in "Stolen Print Is Latest Chapter in the 'Last Temptation' Saga," *Variety,* August 31, 1988, 25.

113. "Judge Overturns Ban on Film," *New York Times,* September 10, 1988, pt. 1, 34.

114. Quoted in "Exhibs Digress on 'Temptation,'" *Variety,* August 24, 1988, 28.

115. Jim Killackey and Michael McNutt, "Regents Block Controversial Film at OSU," *Oklahoman & Times,* September 23, 1988.

116. An incident in Fort Worth exemplifies one result of attempted official censorship. The chairman of the Torrent County Republican Party resigned his post because the party's executive committee refused to join him in voting to condemn the film (see "The Last Temptation," *United Press International,* August 25, 1988). For more information on the Atlanta protest, see "Stolen Print Is Latest Chapter in 'The Last Temptation' Saga," *Variety,* August 31, 1988. For information on the Dallas protest, see "Peaceful Prayerful Protest Rally Opposes Opening of 'Last Temptation' in Dallas," *Southwest Newswire,* August 31, 1988.

117. See "Stolen Print."

118. Quoted in "Theatre Is Vandalized in 'Temptation' Protest," *New York Times,* September 6, 1988. See also Amy Daves, "'Tempt' Protests Continue; Vandals Damage H'wood House," *Variety,* September 7, 1988.

119. In addition to the censorship that resulted from protests cited above, *Last Temptation* suffered other censorships in the ensuing years. In 1989, Blockbuster Video, the nation's largest video chain, decided not to distribute the video version of *Last Temptation* in any of its stores (see "Chain Won't Stock 'Last Temptation,'" *Fayetteville Observer,* June 22, 1989). In January 1991, the Board of Trustees of Seminole Community College (Orlando, Florida) attempted to restrict the seating for a university screening of *Last Temptation.* Responding to pressure from local religious groups, the trustees ordered the film moved from the 370-seat Five Arts Concert Hall to a classroom that seated far fewer people. During the spring of 1992, the American Civil Liberties Union sued Seminole Community College, holding that the film should be reshown in the larger theater (see Sara Isaac, "ACLU Poised to Go to Court over Screening," *Orlando Sentinel,* January 29, 1991).

120. Vice President Dan Quayle, address to the Republican National Convention, August 20, 1992, quoted in *Facts on File* (New York, 1992), 608.

Contributors

FRANCIS G. COUVARES is professor of history and American studies at Amherst College. He is the author of *The Remaking of Pittsburgh: Class and Culture in an Industrializing City* (1984) and articles on the history of movie censorship, which will be the subject of a forthcoming book.

DANIEL CZITROM is professor of history at Mount Holyoke College. He is author of *Media and the American Mind: From Morse to McLuhan* (1982) and coauthor of *Out of Many: A History of the American People* (1994). He is currently completing *Mysteries of the City: Culture, Politics, and the Underworld in Turn of the Century New York.*

MARYBETH HAMILTON is a lecturer in American history at Birkbeck College, University of London. Her book *When I'm Bad, I'm Better: Mae West, Sex, and American Entertainment* was published by HarperCollins in 1995.

GARTH JOWETT is a professor in the school of communication, University of Houston. He is the author of *Film: The Democratic Art* (1976), *Movies as Mass Communication* (with James M. Linton, 1980), and the forthcoming *Children and the Movies: Media Influences and the Payne Fund Controversy* (with Ian Jarvie and Kathryn H. Fuller).

319

CHARLES LYONS received his Ph.D. in drama and film from Columbia University. His book *Don't Watch That Movie!* is being published by Temple University Press.

RICHARD MALTBY is research professor of film studies at Sheffield Hallam University and associate director of the Bill Douglas Centre for the History of Cinema and Popular Culture at the University of Exeter. The author of *Hollywood Cinema: An Introduction* (1995) and *Harmless Entertainment: Hollywood and the Ideology of Consensus* (1983), he is currently completing *Reforming the Movies: Politics, Censorship, and the Institutions of the American Cinema, 1908–1939.*

CHARLES MUSSER is associate professor of American studies and film studies at Yale University. His books include *The Emergence of Cinema: The American Screen to 1907* (1990) and (with Carol Nelson) *High-Class Moving Pictures: Lyman H. Howe and the Forgotten Era of Traveling Exhibition, 1880–1920* (1991).

ALISON M. PARKER is currently assistant professor of history at Goucher College. She is the author of *Purifying America: Women, Cultural Reform, and Pro-Censorship Activism, 1873–1933* (forthcoming, University of Illinois Press).

CHARLENE REGESTER teaches in the curriculum in African and Afro-American studies at the University of North Carolina–Chapel Hill and serves as coeditor of the *Oscar Micheaux Society Newsletter,* published by Duke University. She has published articles in the *Journal of Film History* and the *Journal of Film and Video.*

RUTH VASEY teaches in the School of Theatre and Film Studies, University of New South Wales, Sydney. Her book *The World according to Hollywood, 1918–1939* will be published by the University of Wisconsin Press in 1996.

STEPHEN VAUGHN teaches history of communication at the University of Wisconsin, Madison. His most recent book is *Ronald Reagan in Hollywood: Movies and Politics* (Cambridge University Press, 1994).

Index

Abbey, Henry E., 43, 49–52

Action in the North Atlantic, 243

adaptation: authenticity vs. commercial appeal and, 99–100; author's rights and, 106–12; censorship and, 101–2, 104–5; criticism of, 97–98; dominant cultural ideology and, 114–21; entertainment as a social function and, 119–20; the Formula and, 104–5, 106; of *The Hunchback of Notre Dame,* 114–15, 116; Production Code and, 105; public opinion vs. authors, 106; Roman Catholic prohibitions and, 115; of *Show Boat,* 115–16; sound and, 105, 106; source material for, 103–4

Advise and Consent, 292

African Americans, 159–62. *See also* ethnicity representation; Micheaux, Oscar; racism

ageism in movies, 74

alcohol: in New York City, 18; WCTU and, 73, 74, 75, 82, 87–88

Aldrich, Maude, 79–80, 84, 85, 86–89

Algonquin Round Table, 120

Allied States Association, 141

All Quiet on the Western Front, adaptation of, 103

Amaniano, Tom, 291

American Family Association, 301, 308

American Federation of Labor, 139

American Film Institute, 5

American Gigolo, 279, 292

American Tragedy, An (Dreiser), 98; adaptation of, 103, 107–13, 120–21; stage version of, 117; *Variety* review of, 101

Andrew, Dudley, 110

Andrews, George Reid, 135–36, 144

Ann Vickers (Lewis), 107